Questions of Controversy:
The Kennedy Brothers

Mel Ayton

**University of
Sunderland Press**

© University of Sunderland Press

ISBN 1 873 757 88 3

First published 2001

Cover Design Tim Murphy Creative Solutions

Published in Great Britain by
University of Sunderland Press
in association with Business Education Publishers Limited
The Solar Building
Doxford International
Sunderland
SR3 3XW

Tel: 0191 5252410
Fax: 0191 5201815

British Cataloguing-in-Publications Data
A catalogue record for this book is available from the British Library

Printed in Great Britain by Athenaeum Press Limited.

Dedication

I dedicate this book, first of all, to my wife Sheila and my children Laura and Tim, who provided me with love and support during its preparation. I am grateful to Professor Andrew McDonald of the University of Sunderland who has given me constant encouragement and who has spent many hours of labour to assist in the publication of this work. And I owe much to the University of Sunderland Press reviewer, Professor Tony Hepburn, who believed in my work from the beginning.

Contents

Introduction

An historical antidote

"Every journey into the past is complicated by delusions, false memories, false namings of real events..."

Adrienne Rich

"How can we know the dancer from the dance?"

W. B. Yeats

President Kennedy was assassinated nearly 40 years ago and since that tragic day in Dallas the Kennedy legend has become invulnerable despite a steady stream of "revelations" many of which are inaccurate, or implausible or simply malevolent. The fact that the Kennedy brothers have, for 25 years, been subject to intense scrutiny has not destroyed the effect they have had on the American body politic. Scandals concerning President Kennedy's private life have distorted the image but have not destroyed his central role as a leader who inspired a generation. Robert Kennedy's legacy as an inspiration for minorities and the underprivileged has remained in spite of attacks on his character by unscrupulous authors. And Edward Kennedy's reputation for committed liberal ideals, and his untiring efforts to see them enacted through Congressional legislation, is respected by both Republican and Democratic Senators despite the tabloid "demonisation" of his character.

Americans still see John Kennedy's three year presidency as the last in which the American century flourished. Even today polls have consistently shown that most Americans believe he was the greatest post-war president. Pierre Salinger, Kennedy's press secretary, has said he has not lived one single day without someone walking up to him, wherever he was in the world, to make a comment about John Kennedy.[1] In 1996 a CBS/New York Times poll asked which president Americans would pick to run the country today. Kennedy won conclusively with 28%, beating Ronald Reagan with just 13%. He scored three times higher than the next three presidents, FDR, Truman and Lincoln who equally rated 8% each. And in a 'greatness' poll taken in 1997 of 'knowledgeable' people in the United States (mostly teachers), John Kennedy stood 15th among the nation's 41 presidents. As a man of character he ranked 34th. As a leader he ranked 8th.[2]

John Kennedy's brothers were not alone in seeking to benefit from the martyred president's remarkable popularity. Every election since 1964 has produced a wealth of candidates seeking to emulate the charismatic president. In 1968 Robert Kennedy inherited the Kennedy legacy embarking on his three month 'Unfinished Odyssey' to secure the Democratic presidential nomination by challenging Lyndon Johnson and then Hubert Humphrey in State primary elections across America. His ambition to secure the presidency, however, was cut short by his tragic assassination in Los Angeles. Every election from 1968 to 1988 was dominated by the presence on the political stage of the last of the Kennedy brothers, Edward, although he ran only once in 1980. Even after this failure Edward Kennedy was still considered a threat by other leading contenders in 1984 and 1988.

In 1976 Americans saw many JFK similarities in leading presidential contenders. Both Jimmy Carter and Frank Church sought to benefit from the 'Kennedy style' in their campaigns for the presidency. In 1984 and 1988 Gary Hart benefited from his Kennedy-like image; some of his staff thought he deliberately copied JFK's gestures.[3] And in 1992 Bill Clinton successfully seized every opportunity to link himself to the Democrats' last successful president.

Bill Clinton's inauguration and two terms as President were fraught with references to John Kennedy. He maintained strong links to the Kennedy family, frequently visiting Kennedy playground, Martha's Vineyard, and sailing with the family off Cape Cod. His speeches made allusions to Kennedy rhetoric and he visited places made famous because Kennedy spoke there.

President Clinton attended the John F. Kennedy Library Dinner in 1998. Clinton spoke of his admiration for the 35th president and his brother Robert, "...I am here because President Kennedy and Robert Kennedy, their generation, made me admire and believe in public service...John Kennedy made us believe that in public service you could fight for the things that ought to be fought for, you could fight against things that ought to be fought against, and that the sole purpose of power, fleeting though it is, was to be applied to the best of your God-given ability to those worthy goals...President Kennedy helped me to believe that the political process leaves the ultimate power in the people and gives its elected representatives a precious chance just to bring out the good and stand against the bad...the least we can do is keep the torch burning."[4]

Clinton was only one of millions who were inspired by the 35th President. Shaking hands with JFK in 1963 made a deep impression on the 16 year old from Arkansas. Clinton considered President Kennedy to be one of his true heroes and his entry into state and then national politics was in no small measure accomplished because he wanted to emulate Kennedy.

The Kennedy legacy is destined to run well into the new millennium despite the tragic death of its 'Crown Prince', John F. Kennedy Jnr., in a plane crash off Martha's Vineyard in the summer of 1999. Although Joseph P. Kennedy II, son of Robert, has withdrawn from national politics many of his cousins, notably Bobby's daughter, Maryland Lieutenant-Governor Kathleen Kennedy Townsend and Ted's son, Rhode Island Congressman Patrick Kennedy, have a bright future ahead. Other cousins are active in public service including the arts, environmental concerns and helping inner city African-American and Hispanic youths. Notwithstanding the many scandals attached to a minority of the Kennedy second generation (drug abuse, alcoholism and reckless driving), their joint efforts will be remembered for the grace of JFK's presidency and for the moral passion of RFK's 'Impossible Dream'.

The Kennedy legacy has served the nation and the family well but the memories of tragic accidents and personal improprieties scar it. So which in the end will prove stronger? Will it be the high idealism which the Kennedys generated or the memories of tragedy and scandal which the family had to endure?

Beginning in the 1970s many authors have probed the 'Dark side of Camelot'. The tearing down of the Kennedy legacy was simple enough. It started with Watergate and has continued unabated ever since. The new climate in American society was generated by the desire for sensational revelations but climaxed in a lost sense of awe for public servants and institutions of government. The first shocks came with disclosures shortly after the Watergate scandal that President Kennedy countenanced some Nixon-style malpractices in his time. His Administration, it was revealed, was involved in wiretapping and in the political use of federal agencies. Kennedy himself carried on an affair with a mafia-linked woman by the name of Judith Campbell Exner. The media pounced and many liberal commentators have regretted that he was not treated as Nixon was. Destroying the Kennedy legend became fair game but in their desire to 'correct' the historical record many writers exceeded their remit. Joan and Clay Blair (1977), for example, in their book 'The search for JFK' wrote that Kennedy's heroism in the Second World War was bogus. They maintained that JFK's rescue efforts after a Japanese destroyer collided with his PT boat 'was not a major one'. He did not 'save his crew', as legend maintains, but 'he helped save one man'. Yet in the same excerpt they suggest he at least saved that man without help. 'To his credit Kennedy single-handedly saved the life of crewman Patrick (Pappy) McMahon, who had been badly burned...'.[5] The Blairs also criticise Kennedy for covering up his many ailments in order to serve in the U.S. Navy in time of war. Typically, for Kennedy detractors, the Blairs do not seem to be aware that by his actions Kennedy heroically put himself in harm's way.

The 'new biographies' of the Kennedy family have skewered reality and made serious debate about the Kennedys almost impossible. H. L. Mencken wrote about "the virulence of the national appetite for bogus revelation". Many authors have emphasised the salacious, producing a generation that knows everything about the negative aspects of Kennedy family but next to nothing of the role the Kennedy brothers played in American government. Serious analysis of their roles is thus elbowed out. And the misrepresentation of the Kennedy era is not confined to 'popular biographies'. Hollywood's interpretation of the Cuban missile crisis in the movie '13 days' grossly misrepresented the roles played by the Kennedy brothers, according to leading American academics. Jamie Beech, an expert on the crisis said: "This ('13 days') will add to a malaise of ignorance already engulfing the Kennedy era, it could cause great damage."[6] This matters because the way we think about the past - in this case the role the Kennedys played in American life - conditions how we act and shape the future.

There is much to admire in the way the media has become the watchdog on government institutions. But at what cost? Investigative reporters are a vital component in the democratic structures of a free society and they contribute to the checks and balances of American government. Their constant search to find corruption in the corridors of power has produced some remarkable results over the years. But there are many authors and journalists who have abused their new found virility to pursue stories without any of the constraints of the past - checking the veracity of sources, interpreting evidence free from the constraints of bias, and publicly acknowledging any mistakes they have made in the process. The reading public thus becomes confused as to what is truth and what is fiction.

This lack of integrity has been developing for many years in the fields of journalism and publishing. And it reveals itself in recent works about the Kennedy family. Each decade a new crop of Kennedy revisionist history adds to the unprecedented attack on a family whose lives have been grossly misinterpreted. The debate climaxed in the 1990s with the publication of three books about John, Robert and Edward Kennedy; Seymour Hersh's (1997) 'The dark side of Camelot', C. David Heymann's (1998) 'RFK - a candid biography' and Joe McGinniss' (1993) 'The last brother'. These books quickly and decisively shaped a new public image of the Kennedy brothers.

Most 'popular' biographies of the Kennedy brothers contain kernels of truth but on the whole they are inaccurate and misleading. Many repeat false stories which have never been researched fully or accurately but they have, nonetheless, entered the national consciousness and are accepted as true. Many authors have written about the so-called relationship between Marilyn Monroe and Bobby Kennedy, relying as they do on original research carried out in the 1980s which has never been closely scrutinised. For example, many authors cite Jeanne Carmen as a witness to 'Bobby and Marilyn's affair' yet Monroe biographer, Donald Spoto, has proven that she is unlikely to have even met the Hollywood actress. It is quite evident that scepticism about statements made by weak sources like Carmen is a methodological necessity. Yet it has not been practiced by numerous authors who have been willing to believe every anti-Kennedy source. Christopher Andersen's (1998) 'Jackie after Jack' and C. David Heymann's (1998) 'RFK: a candid biography of Robert F. Kennedy' have stated categorically that Robert Kennedy had an intimate and sexual relationship with his sister-in-law Jackie Kennedy. Andersen quotes Charles Spalding, a long-time friend of John Kennedy as saying: "Bobby and Jackie were definitely a unit, a twosome. She relied on him for everything and he adored her. There was definitely an intimacy."[7] However, on learning of the quotation in Andersen's book, Spalding stated that the relationship between Jackie and Bobby was innocent and there was nothing salacious about the contacts.[8]

Andersen cites Secret Service reports confirming that Jackie and Bobby were often in each other's company yet the actual documents, which can be read by anyone with access to the Internet, prove nothing. Furthermore, in the same book, Andersen alleges that Lyndon Johnson suffered an anxiety attack on Air Force One immediately after the assassination of President Kennedy.[9] Witness after witness, who were present for the whole journey from Dallas to Washington, say nothing of the kind occurred. Andersen also took a story straight from Jerry Oppenheimer's (1994) book 'The other Mrs. Kennedy' without verifying whether it was true or not. He said that at the funeral wake for the dead President someone snatched a blonde wig from Ethel Kennedy and began throwing it around the room finally landing on Secretary of Defense Robert McNamara's bald pate. McNamara says he was not consulted by the author and in any case the story was a total fabrication.[10]

In the same book Andersen states that Marlon Brando's account of the so-called affair between himself and Jackie was deleted by the actor's publishers. Brando's co-author, Robert Lindsay, maintains that this is not so. The story about the Jackie/Brando relationship was simply not true. Yet the media repeat the story as if it was.[11]

What is sad about these authors is that their books are bereft of empathy, balance or filtering intelligence. There is little of the John Kennedy who inspired a nation and successfully guided his country through the perils of nuclear confrontation and Civil Rights. In Heymann's book, I read little of the Robert Kennedy who hugged a black child in the poorest area of Mississippi without cameras present or of the Robert Kennedy who marched with Cesar Chavez and the farm workers, or of the Robert Kennedy who journeyed to Indian reservations to hear about the suicide rate with absolutely no benefit to his political career. Instead, he has written an unbalanced narrative of the most negative aspects of RFK's character, notably his alleged sexual transgressions which are based on numerous unreliable sources. I also read little of the Edward Kennedy who devoted his career to the problems of the ill-educated, the sick, the aged and the poor in American society, and who took on the role of father to his assassinated brothers' children.

The fault, however, cannot be laid solely at the feet of authors motivated primarily by financial gain. The publishing industry has changed over the past two decades. The demands of the market dictate that no publisher is now willing to publish an account of a celebrity's life unless the author or investigating journalist has something scandalous to report. The rush to find something new to write often obliterates any ethical considerations.

There is much in the history of the Kennedys that has proven to the antithesis of the legend. The majority of historians now accept that John Kennedy's personal life was less than exemplary and, in a number of incidents, downright reckless. The Kennedys did many things that were illegal - wiretapping, for example. In order to find Pentagon leaks Robert Kennedy approved wiretaps on two 'New York Times' and 'Newsweek' reporters. Other targets included steel executives, congressmen, lobbyists and others, including Martin Luther King, author Victor Lasky, military aide Godfrey McHugh and national security official Robert Amory. From July 1962 until November 1963 Kennedy secretly recorded 260 hours of White House meetings and telephone conversations. Former aides were appalled to learn that Kennedy had recorded them without their knowledge. The Justice Department searched George Lodge's and Eddie McCormack's military service records when Edward Kennedy ran against them for the Senate in 1962.[12] Although Kennedy provided level-headed and wise leadership during the Cuban Missile Crisis he did try and get Kruschev to consider a joint American/Soviet air strike at China to destroy their nuclear capability.[13] The 'dark' side of the story, therefore, will not be ignored. If the revelations, for example, about JFK's affair with Judith Campbell Exner had been made when he was president the climate of the times would not have allowed him to stay in office. A vote of impeachment by Congress would surely have followed. This is the view held by President Kennedy's friend, Ben Bradlee, then reporter and future editor of the Washington Post.[14] Had these revelations been published during President Kennedy's Administration it would have been more damaging to the American body politic than Watergate. The knowledge that the U.S. President had been placed on trial for questionable relationships with mafia-linked women would have torn the nation apart and left it with the kind of cynicism that did not develop until Watergate. Some commentators have even averred that it was better that JFK died a mythical if not actual hero and that the truth about his private life emerged gradually in order for the nation to come to terms with such startling revelations. Had the United States been forced to consider the dark side of Camelot all at once, they believe, the consequences may have been unbearable.

Other negative aspects of the Kennedy family have been established by authoritative historians. Patriarch Joseph Kennedy used questionable methods in acquiring his wealth and conducted numerous adulterous relationships. Edward Kennedy's private life, by his own admission, was less than adequate for a public servant. He agreed that the American people had a right to expect more from him. All of these facts serve to remind us, as does the impeachment of Bill Clinton, that we live in an imperfect world led by less than perfect leaders.

However, most 'popular' biographies about the Kennedy brothers concentrate only on the negative side of the Kennedy legend, real or imagined, and ignore or understate the Kennedys' real contributions to public service and American history. Many contain a mixture of truth, conjecture and distortion. Some do not realise there are limits to 'knowing'. In the absence of certitude they create sophisticated 'scenarios' and present them as fact. This skewers the historical record. Authentic history enriches our lives; distorted history impoverishes them. And, in the age of the Internet, when billions of words can be downloaded from around the world, it is necessary now more than ever to be able to rely on authoritative and authentic sources of information.

There have been many excellent books about the Kennedy brothers but their image is 'academic' and so they do not have the impact of the 'popular biographies'. These books are bereft of innuendo and speculation and are written by scholars and who have made a major contribution to this study. Most of these writers are not, contrary to the views of some critics, Kennedy hagiographers.

The central aim of this book is to examine the controversial parts of the Kennedy brothers' lives which have engendered controversy over the years and to assess the inaccuracies which exist in Kennedy books. During my research I was often struck by the fact that many stories about the Kennedy brothers have been based upon unverifiable evidence and upon sources who lacked veracity and credibility. Richard Reeves highlighted the weaknesses of many Kennedy writers and their choice of sources when he sought to explain his own methodology:

> "...basically...people who work for presidents or who deal with presidents are like athletes dying young; that is, the peak for most of them is so high that they write down everything and

remember everything so that in meeting after meeting or scene after scene, I was able to talk to 6 or 8 people who were in a room of 10, and the rest of them had either notes on what they did or had talked about the scene in their own oral histories at the Kennedy Library. The oral histories...were done mainly in 1964...many people in 1988 tell different stories...than what they were telling in 1964, so you've got a real reality check of what happened. "[15]

The following questions have been central to my research - do the witnesses to a particular event have 'authority'? Are we able to construct an understanding of events and actions consistent with the methods of true historical enquiry? In short, are the things we are reading in the 'new biographies' based upon verifiable and corroborated fact or are they the second hand accounts and musings of unreliable gossips?

I have found that many Kennedy authors' interpretations and use of sources confuses rather than clarifies key issues concerning the lives of the brothers. Evidently they have rarely engaged in analytical dialogue with the basic sources and with previous accounts and interpretations. Frequently these authors have ignored or have put their own interpretations upon some of the basic facts supplied by a source. It is intellectual dishonesty cloaked in the freedom of the press. Their work demands the most searching scrutiny. And, for the first time, I provide incontestable and verifiable evidence that President Kennedy's mistress, Judith Campbell Exner, has lied about her relationships with John and Robert Kennedy.

As a focal point for my study I have been influenced by the numerous questions which have been asked by friends and colleagues and which have been issues of contention for many years:

- Did Kennedy 'rig' the 1960 presidential election by buying votes and enlisting the help of the Mafia?

- Why did John Kennedy act recklessly and immorally in his private life?

- What is the truth about John and Jacqueline Kennedy's marriage?

- Did J. Edgar Hoover force Kennedy to accept Lyndon Johnson as his Vice-Presidential candidate? Did J. Edgar Hoover 'blackmail' the Kennedys?

- Was John Kennedy responsible for the Vietnam tragedy? What is the likelihood that Kennedy would have withdrawn American Armed forces from Vietnam had he lived?

- Did President Kennedy act irresponsibly in the 'Bay of Pigs' debacle?

- Did President Kennedy needlessly bring the world to the brink of nuclear war during the 1962 Cuban Missile Crisis?

- Was President Kennedy's involvement in the Civil Rights movement important or did he simply respond to events already in place?

- Did President Kennedy have an 'affair' with Marilyn Monroe?

- What is the truth about the relationship between Frank Sinatra and John Kennedy?

- Did the young John Kennedy have an intimate relationship with a Nazi spy?

- Did President Kennedy have an affair with a communist spy?

- What is the true story of President Kennedy's relationship with Judith Campbell Exner, girlfriend of Chicago mob boss Sam Giancana? Did she act as a courier, carrying messages about murder plots against Fidel Castro, between President Kennedy and Sam Giancana?

- Did Robert Kennedy have a romantic relationship with Marilyn Monroe? And does he bear some responsibility for her death?

- Did Robert Kennedy have an affair with Jacqueline Kennedy?

- Is there any truth in the allegations that Robert Kennedy had a string of affairs throughout his marriage to Ethel Kennedy?

- Did Robert Kennedy have any real chance of becoming President?

- Is there any truth in the speculation that Robert Kennedy would have swiftly ended the War in Vietnam?

- What is the truth about Robert Kennedy's assassination?

- Did Edward Kennedy act immorally and illegally during the 'Chappaquidick Incident'?

- What is the truth about Edward and Joan Kennedy's marriage?

- Did Edward Kennedy, by his reckless behaviour in his private life, destroy the Kennedy legacy?

All of these questions, and more, have become part of the Kennedy legend and have been speculated upon endlessly. Numerous answers to these questions have been provided by eminent historians and reputable biographers and I acknowledge the results of their excellent research. Other truths have been discovered whilst researching this book. I do not claim that I have found all the answers - my efforts have been directed towards sorting fantasy from verifiable fact insofar as the personal lives of the brothers are concerned. As to their involvement in public affairs - Cuba, Vietnam, Civil Rights etc. - I have given what I believe is a fair assessment of their roles using the historical evidence available. And I state at the outset that the evidence has persuaded me to take a favourable view of their contributions to American history whilst recognising that the Kennedys were never as good as the 1960s legend portrayed them nor as bad as Kennedy detractors allege. The reader is asked to assess whether my accounts of the controversial episodes in the lives of the Kennedy brothers have verisimilitude.

Notes

1. "20th anniversary of JFK's assassination", GMTV broadcast, 22 November 1983.

2. CNN Interactive Home News, 31 January 1998. (http://www.cnn.com). In a 1983 poll Robert K. Murray of Pennsylvania State University surveyed 1000 Ph-D historians.

Kennedy was rated 13th. (*Time Magazine*, 14 November 1983, p. 40).

3. Sabatoto, L. 'Many presidents had affairs', ABC News. (http://abcnews.go.com).

4. Remarks by President Clinton at the John F. Kennedy library dinner, JFK Library, 2 March 1998. (http://library.kennedy.nara.gov).

5. Blair, J. and Blair, C. (1977). *The search for JFK*, Berkeley Medallion Books. p. 615.

6. *Sunday Times*, 23 July 2000, p. 12.

7. Andersen, C. (1998). *Jackie after Jack*, William Morrow and Company Inc. p. 102.

8. 'In fact it's fiction', *New York Daily News*, 22 February 1998. (http://www.nydailynews.com).

9. *Ibid*.

10. *Ibid*.

11. *Ibid*.

12. Reeves, R. (1993). *President Kennedy - profile of power*, Simon and Schuster. p. 324.

13. *Ibid*, pp. 546-548.

14. Bradlee, B. C. (1995), *A good life - newspapering and other adventures*, Simon and Schuster. p. 484.

15. Lamb, B. 'An interview with Richard Reeves', *C-Span*, 12 December 1993. (http://www.c-span.org).

Prologue

"I came into politics in my brother Joe's place. If anything happens to me, Bobby will take my place, and if Bobby goes, we have Teddy coming along."

John F. Kennedy

In August 1989, at the Capitol Building in Washington D.C., I was introduced to Senator Edward Kennedy as a Fulbright Exchange teacher from England. I had thought about this impending meeting for some time and what I would eventually say to the Senator. Like many of my generation I was inspired by John and Robert Kennedy's leadership and I supported Robert's efforts to end the war in Vietnam. A generation later I had an opportunity to talk to Senator Kennedy about the contributions his brothers made to American history.

Kennedy looked down, lost in his thoughts and unable to respond to my comments about his brothers. He seemed one moment to be full of life, smiling and gregarious, but the next to be transported somewhere else and lost in his own thoughts. I instantly realised the impact of my words. I thought of the funerals he had attended these past 40 years and of the hundreds if not thousands of people, including my errant self, who had mentioned his brothers. Books, television documentaries, movies and magazines must have brought it all back, forcing him to relive the many tragedies in his life. It was quite evident that the suffering had not abated but had become a constant in his life. What could it possibly be like, I thought, to have suffered a life filled with tragedy?

I felt a sense of shame about resurrecting painful memories. He had been able to speak of his brothers in speeches across the country yet he was unable to talk privately of his inner scars. Of his four dead brothers and two sisters, Kathleen and Joe Jnr., died in their twenties; two, John and Robert, in their forties. It was Edward who had to tell his father, who two years previously had been felled by a stroke, that his son the President had been killed. It was Edward who helped escort the body of his murdered brother Robert from Los Angeles to New York. It was Edward who had to tell his son Teddy Jnr. that his leg would have to be amputated to stem the spread of a cancerous growth. Year by year the youngest Kennedy brother had to endure a curious mixture of life and death, and of success and misfortune.

Throughout the 1970s and well into the 1980s Edward Kennedy had to constantly reassure his children that their father would not suffer the same fate as their uncles; every day he would telephone his children from his Senate office just so they could hear his voice and know he was safe. In the most painful period, the 1970s, he kept a copy of Shakespeare's 'Julius Ceasar' on his Senate office desk between books by Thoreau. On page 36 he had underlined the following passage:

> *"Cowards die many times before their deaths;*
> *The valiant never taste of death but once.*
> *Of all the wonders that I yet have heard,*
> *It seems to me most strange that men should fear;*
> *Seeing that death a necessary end,*
> *Will come when it will come."*

Edward Kennedy's struggle to cope with unbearable loss was monumental but the pain of the tragedies had to take its toll. He found solace in liquor and lived life on the edge. But he could never show fear. He told his aide Dun Gifford: "I can't let go. We have a job to do. If I let go, Ethel (Robert's wife) will let go and my mother will let go, and all my sisters."

Throughout the 1950s and early 1960s John Kennedy had Robert and Edward to support and advise him. After Dallas Robert had Edward. After Robert's assassination Edward had no one. Every action he took was judged against their standards. He had a terrible burden and legacy to bear, constantly having to live up to the expectations of the 'best and the brightest' who had worked for his brothers. He also had to endure a news media 'death watch' on the campaign trails comprised of reporters who either believed Kennedy would self-destruct politically or suffer the same tragic fate as his brothers.

During his run for the presidency in 1980, Edward Kennedy was forced into demonstrating he was as good as his martyred brothers - an almost impossible feat. He tried to resurrect the lost 'Camelot' but the country was in a different mood. America had turned to the right in the intervening years. The country was tired of liberal solutions to social problems. And he faced an uphill struggle to defeat an incumbent president of his own party who cloaked himself in patriotism after American hostages were taken in Iran.

Edward Kennedy was viewed as the trustee of the Kennedy legacy and a future president throughout the period leading up to the 1988 Democratic Convention. After that period everyone knew Kennedy's presidential ambitions had evaporated. And the stories about his private life and the startling revelations about his brothers were beginning to chip away at the Kennedy legacy. It appeared the Kennedy torch had finally burnt out.

Edward Kennedy's sad farewell to presidential politics was in stark contrast to the bright prospects the Kennedy's held for America in the beautiful autumn days of 1963 - before Dallas, Los Angeles and Chappaquiddick. The three brothers were at the summit of political power and success - John was a young, charismatic President leading an Administration which had seen many successes over the previous thousand days; Robert was Attorney General, America's highest law enforcement official; Edward was a newly-elected senator who had taken over Jack's Massachusetts's senate seat at the beginning of the year. In the brief 10 months they were together in the nation's capital everything seemed possible for the Kennedy brothers.

In the autumn of 1963 the Kennedy Administration was enjoying the peak of its popularity and self-assurance. A near euphoria reigned in the White House after the Cuban Missile Crisis of the previous year. There was almost universal praise for the way it was handled. The Peace Corps had earned admiration around the world; it had become an American ideal of co-operation and partnership. There was a general acceptance that the United States was being led well by a youthful, charismatic, mature and scholarly leader. By this period in the lifetime of Kennedy's first Administration, several crises around the world had seemed to have been successfully resolved - Berlin, Laos, nuclear arms reduction and co-operation between the Soviet and American leaders using the newly installed 'hot-line'. The Kennedy Administration also seemed to be handling the Civil Rights question well - Kennedy's June 1963 speech to the nation had put the American Federal Government firmly behind the aspirations of African-Americans. Trade expansion, tax reduction and development of 'New Deal' and 'Fair Deal' programmes had been put high on the Administration's agenda as had the war on poverty and further legislation to ensure the human and voting rights of African-Americans. There was trouble ahead; Kennedy was having problems with Congress in enacting some of his programmes. But after the 1964 election, Administration officials thought that a strong mandate for Civil Rights and Poverty legislation should effectively negate the position of many congressmen and southern Senators.

This sense of power and success was symbolised by an event held on Sunday November 17th 1963. A large crowd had gathered in front of the Warner Cinerama on New York's Broadway near 47th Street to observe celebrities arriving for the movie premier of 'It's a mad, mad, mad, mad world'. Over 1,500 people had paid 50 dollars each for the screening which was a charity benefit instituted by the Kennedy family - the Kennedy Child Study Centre for Retarded Children in New York (established in honour of Joseph and Rose Kennedy's retarded daughter Rosemary) and the Lt. Joseph P. Kennedy Jnr. Institute in Washington (established to honour Joe Jnr. who was blown up over the southern skies of England on a high risk mission to bomb Nazi military installations in northern France). The crowd applauded Robert and Edward and their wives as they arrived at the entrance to the cinema. Rose Kennedy, Eunice and Sargent Shriver, Jean and Stephen Smith and Patricia Lawford also attended. Kennedy Administration officials, Ted Sorensen (President Kennedy's aide and speechwriter), Kenneth O' Donnell (Kennedy's 'Chief of Staff'), Arthur Schlesinger Jnr. (Kennedy's in-house historian and Special Assistant), Lawrence O' Brien (Advisor and 'political guru') and many more movie stars and officials of the 'New Frontier' arrived. Later, guests were taken to the New York Hilton hotel where a dance was held in the grand ballroom. Robert and Edward celebrated the family success.

Five days later events were to take a tragic and historically momentous change as the brief period of the three brothers' lives together in Washington D.C. came to an end. At 12.30 p.m. on November 22nd, as President Kennedy's limousine turned the corner from Main Street to Houston Street in Downtown Dallas, Robert and Edward Kennedy were hundreds of miles away in the capital. Robert was swimming in the pool of his mansion, Hickory Hill, a beautiful estate that once belonged to John and Jacqueline Kennedy and situated in a Washington suburb, McClean, Virginia, across the Potomac River. Edward was presiding over the Senate, a job often given over to newly-elected senators.

Painters at work on the Hickory Hill mansion were working on a new wing of the house. They were the first to hear the news on a portable radio. They ran down the hill shouting something which was incomprehensible to the guests. They approached Robert Kennedy's Justice Department colleagues, Robert Morgenthau and Sylvio Mollo, who had been invited to have lunch with the Attorney-General. Before the painters could say anything clear a maid ran out of the house to say that Director of the FBI, J. Edgar Hoover, was on the telephone. An extension telephone rang across the pool and Robert's wife Ethel picked it up and handed the phone to her husband. When Robert took the phone Hoover said, matter of factly: "I have news for you. The President's been shot. I think it's serious. I'll call you back... when I find out more". Robert turned away and clapped his hand to his mouth. He said "Jack's been shot. It may be fatal."

Robert Kennedy walked to the house and managed to make telephone contact with Secret Service agent, Clint Hill, the agent who had caught Jackie as she climbed on to the rear of the presidential limousine after rifle bullets had struck President Kennedy. Hill told Robert the wounds looked fatal. Robert turned his thoughts to Hoover and commented how Hoover seemed to savour the news he was passing on. After this Robert talked on the telephone to Kennedy people in Dallas. He came downstairs and told Morgenthau, "He's dead."

Inside the Senate chamber Edward was once again in the Vice-President's chair. Eight senators were in the chamber and Senator Winston Prouty of Vermont was on the floor speaking. At 1.42 p.m., as the Senate was considering bill S. 2265 amending the Library Service Act, a congressional worker, Richard L. Riedel, ran onto the Senate floor. This was an act certain to heighten awareness as the rules regulate against such breaches of protocol. Only moments earlier he had ran into the President's room near the Senate floor and saw on a news ticker machine a bulletin which said that President Kennedy had been shot. The first person he saw was Senator Spessard Holland and told him the news. Next he told Senate Minority leader Everett Dirksen. The Senators were shocked. Riedel then looked around to see Edward Kennedy presiding over the Senate. He approached Kennedy and said, "Senator Kennedy, your brother the President has been shot."

Edward Kennedy rushed to the lobby and tried to telephone the White House. Meanwhile the senators on the floor wandered around confused and stunned by the incredible news. They gathered around a radio and watched the news ticker until word came that President Kennedy had died.

Edward was unable to reach the White House as so many people were communicating the news by phone. The city's telephone system could not stand the strain and collapsed. Years later this simple explanation would be used by conspiracy theorists to suggest a concerted effort by conspirators to disable government communications. The young Senator went to his office and tried phoning but without success. Accompanied by two aides, he drove to his house in Georgetown in a borrowed car, listening to the radio. Finally he got through to his brother Robert who asked him to inform their parents and sisters what had happened. Eventually Edward got through to his parents' house in Hyannisport and spoke to his mother. For the following four days the surviving brothers were at one with the American people as the nation came to terms with the tragedy in Dallas.

The assassination inevitably transformed what was becoming a successful presidency into a legend. And the legend was carried throughout the 1960s and 1970s by the murdered President's brothers. Books and television documentaries highlighted the successes and promises of President Kennedy and the Kennedys were quickly becoming America's 'Royal' family.

Slowly and inexorably revisionists found the idealistic promise of the Kennedy myth too difficult to swallow. The American right-wing had always had an animus towards the liberal Kennedys. But now in the years following the Chappaquiddick tragedy even liberal commentators, wrapped in the cynicism of post-Watergate America, dug deep to reveal a less than pristine legend.

History will always re-interpret, eventually weighing and balancing in order to chronicle the good and bad of every period. This constant re-evaluation has targeted every famous American family and every president. Yet the Kennedy brothers, beginning in the mid-1970s and reaching its height in the late 1990s, received a different and much more negative and unbalanced form of writing. Consequently, the Kennedy legend has metamorphosed into a sordid and corrupt fantasy propagated by a new form of popular biography which is devoid of intellectual discourse relying, as it does, on presenting 'fact' through the questionable auspices of malevolent gossip and a reliance on second-hand accounts.

To revisionists John Kennedy became a self-indulgent fraud who risked his presidency by his associations with mobsters and his womanising. He recklessly took us to the brink of nuclear disaster and shamelessly attempted to murder heads of state. He led the American people down the quagmire of a disastrous war in South-east Asia. Robert Kennedy was painted as a ruthless opportunist who used the War in Vietnam as a stepping stone to the presidency. He metamorphosed from the brother who was faithful to his wife into a charlatan pursuing the most famous movie star in the world after she had been rejected by his older brother. A dark cloud now hung over his memory - did he have Marilyn Monroe murdered? Or did he push her to commit suicide? Edward Kennedy's image as an idealistic liberal politician changed accordingly. He became a shameless playboy devoted to his own selfish indulgences, turning his wife into an alcoholic and recklessly destroying what was left of the Kennedy legacy. New interpretations of the Chappaquiddick tragedy prompted accusations of manslaughter and murder.

Not even the Nixon Administration had received the level of adversarial reinterpretation to which the Kennedy brothers have been subjected. As a result the public became confused and many people have, therefore, asked the question, "What is the truth about this star-crossed family?"

Notes

1. Burns, J. M. (1976). *Edward Kennedy and the Camelot legacy*, WW Norton and Co. Inc. p. 328.

2. Collier, P. and Horowitz, D. (1984). *The Kennedys – an American drama*, Summit Books. p. 364.

Accounts of RFK's and EMK's reactions to the assassination of President Kennedy are taken from: Goldfarb, R. (1995). *Perfect villains, imperfect heroes*, Random House; Hersh, B. (1972). *The education of Edward Kennedy*, William Morrow and Co. 1972; Burns, J. M. (1976). *Edward Kennedy and the Camelot legacy*, WW Norton and Co. Inc.; Manchester, W. (1968). *The death of a president*, World Books London; and David, L. and David, I. (1986). *Bobby Kennedy - the making of a folk hero*, Sidgwick and Jackson.

The Author

Mel Ayton with Senator Edward Kennedy in the United States Capitol Building in 1989. His discussions with Senators Kennedy, Byrd, Glenn, Hatfield and Specter provided the author with many insights into the "Kennedy Legacy". This is Mel Ayton's second book. His first book, "Questions of conspiracy" (1999) was an investigation into the methodology of JFK conspiracy authors. Mel Ayton was formerly a teacher and lecturer in the UK. He has also taught in Zambia and the United States. He is presently writing and researching his third book, "A racial crime - James Earl Ray and the murder of Martin Luther King."

University of Sunderland Press

"We aim to produce books of high academic quality..."
Professor Jeff Brown
Deputy Vice Chancellor, University of Sunderland

The University of Sunderland Press (UoSP) is a joint venture between the University of Sunderland and Business Education Publishers Limited. UoSP was established in 1997 to enable the publication of refereed academic works in learning and teaching, literature, research, conference proceedings, and popular treatments of academic subjects.

The Press adopts a personal interest in each project it undertakes. It works closely with authors and editors to produce high quality publications. UoSP is committed to producing works of the highest standard and to maintaining those same standards throughout the entire publication process.

Chapter 1

JFK's Presidency

Was John F. Kennedy a 'Great President'?

"The fall of great personages from high places (casus virorum illustrium) gave to medieval politics their festive and brutal character."

George Steiner

What are we to believe about John Kennedy's presidency? Was he a president who used his charisma and idealism to inspire millions; a politician who, in the words of Arthur Schlesinger (1965) "gave his country back to its best self" and an activist president whose term in office was stamped by numerous domestic and international successes? Or was his presidency an illusion of success which held more promise than performance - a triumph of style over substance? Was he, as Kennedy detractors maintain, a Cold War belligerent defender of American interests around the world and a politician without any strong ideological or moral beliefs who reacted to the growing Civil Rights crisis but had no hand in furthering the equal rights of African-Americans?

An examination of John Kennedy's position in American history has gone through five different periods. The first period began after the assassination and the publication of two early biographies - Arthur M. Schlesinger Jnr.'s (1965) 'A thousand days' and Theodore Sorensen's (1965) 'Kennedy'. As self-confessed admirers of the President, these two accounts of President Kennedy gave a positive image that lasted until the 1970s.

By the 1970s a first revisionist period came along. The Watergate crisis had given investigative journalism a new boost and authors, with the assistance of Congressional investigations into the activities of the FBI and CIA, began to reveal aspects of Kennedy's life which were previously unknown. Other authors, concentrating on the work of the Kennedy Administration began to criticise Kennedy's Cold War policies and judged his domestic programme to be a failure.

There was a common theme in a number of books about JFK. They suggest that Kennedy had been a mediocre president with a few concrete results and achievements. His rhetoric overwhelmed accomplishment and his indiscretions greatly tarnished his presidency. These books include 'Promise and performance' by Lewis J. Paper (1975), 'Decade of disillusionment' by Jim F. Heath (1975), 'The Kennedy promise: the politics of expectation' by Henry Fairlie (1973), and 'JFK: the presidency of John F. Kennedy by Herbert S. Parmet (1983).

The second revisionist period, from the 1980s onwards, saw the publication of books which concentrated on Kennedy's personal life and his character. Gary Wills' (1981) 'The Kennedy imprisonment', Thomas C. Reeves' (1991) 'A question of character' and Nigel Hamilton's (1992) 'JFK: reckless youth' all examined Kennedy's lifestyle and concluded that he was a person who was immoral, reckless and corrupt. Any positive comments about him were subsumed by the barrage of details delineating his personal relationships and overweening arrogance in office. Other authors claimed that Kennedy should not have been accepted into the military during the Second World War because of his poor health (as opposed to the thousands who were trying to secure deferment). They belittled his heroism claiming that his boat was sliced in two by a Japanese destroyer because of his incompetence and that his bravery in seeking help in infested Japanese waters was not all that brave after all.

The 30th anniversary of the assassination in 1993 and the death of Jacqueline Kennedy the following year saw an overlapping period of 'Camelot' nostalgia. Whilst acknowledging Kennedy's womanising, some writers promoted the idea that the Kennedy years were indeed ones in which a new period of hope and idealism imbued the American spirit. These authors included Pierre Salinger (1997), President

Kennedy's Press Secretary, Jacques Lowe (1998), who photographed the president, and William Manchester (1968, 1975 and 1983), they looked back to a time of genuine revolution and excitement. Other authors, like Christopher Andersen, produced a contradictory assessment. On the one hand they acknowledged the romanticism of the Kennedy years whilst promoting their books as exposes of new salacious material. It was left up to Richard Reeves (1993) and his book "President Kennedy - profile of power" to provide an in-depth analysis of Kennedy's day-to-day activities as president, concentrating on the effect he had as a national leader. Reeves provided a contemporary view of a multi-dimensional personality and showed who John Kennedy was - a role model for a generation rather than a self-indulgent clown.

The late 1990s saw the height of Kennedy debunking with the publication of Seymour Hersh's (1997) 'The dark side of Camelot'. Hersh's Kennedy is a compulsive womaniser who often procured prostitutes; a corrupt president who plotted the murders of foreign leaders, walked hand in hand with the Mafia and fooled the press into believing his Administration was idealistic. Kennedy was a belligerent Cold War warrior responsible for the placement of nuclear missiles in Cuba through his reckless drive to topple Fidel Castro. His portrait of the president is one-dimensional and wholly negative. Many historians have agreed with Hersh, revelling in the excitement of destroying the Kennedy legend.

Every popular president inevitably faces the onslaught of revisionist history, but with Kennedy it has become nothing less than a vendetta, a political assassination in the truest sense of the phrase, or, as James DiEugenio called it a "posthumous assassination".

This wealth of material about the Kennedys and the Kennedy presidency has caused a lot of confusion as to the success or failure of the Kennedy Administration and whether or not the Kennedy legacy was a genuine force for good in the politics of a nation or a fraudulent construction designed to ensure the continuation of a Kennedy dynasty.

President Kennedy's reputation, according to some revisionist historians, rests on style not substance; that his legacy was in the promise not the performance. No doubt his ironic and self-deprecating wit, his style in office and his public personae caught the American imagination - but his rhetoric, they maintain, aroused expectations that politics could never realise. Revisionists maintain that Kennedy cared only about projecting his image and never worried about passing legislation.

Thomas C. Reeves is typical in his revisionist judgements of Kennedy's presidency. Reeves maintains that Kennedy's bad character played a major role in making him a poor president. He had little interest in domestic affairs, made a number of bad judicial appointments, demonstrated cautious optimism in dealing with pressing Civil Rights issues and was a disaster in dealing with the Bay of Pigs invasion and with the escalating American involvement in Vietnam. Kennedy was "pragmatic to the point of amorality, his sole standard seemed to be political expediency...Jack's character lacked a moral centre, a reference point that went beyond self-aggrandisement."[1]

In domestic policy, revisionists argue, history will remember John F. Kennedy as a minor president. JFK was a conservative who feared risking his popularity in exchange for radical reform of institutions in American society thus passing over an opportunity to tackle the problems of health, poverty, age and the inner cities. His liberalism was pragmatic, they say, designed to 'half-succeed' and his 'New Frontier' was nothing compared to his successor's 'Great Society' - Kennedy promised and Johnson delivered.

The revisionists find a bellicose and belligerent style when it comes to an examination of Kennedy's foreign policy. He was, allegedly, a rigid Cold War warrior, who was reckless when it came to dealing with the Soviet Union and the handling of international crises. He was a 'macho' leader who tried to fulfil his own psychological needs 'in action'. Instead of preventing crises he provoked them through his constant need to prove himself; he brought the world to the brink of nuclear disaster over Soviet missiles in Cuba and he started the Vietnam War.

Kennedy's handling of the Cuban Missile Crisis and Vietnam will be examined in later chapters. But how far is it true that President Kennedy is now the object of disillusionment and what level of judgement can we place on his presidency?

The whole idea of 'Camelot' is dismissed by some authors who maintain that Kennedy's presidency was nothing special. However, John Kennedy himself would have derided the idea that he led the American people in an American renaissance populated by heroic leaders and ushered in a new form of governing. It was Jacqueline Kennedy, speaking to author Theodore H. White, who first used the term 'Camelot' shortly after the death of her husband and it sparked the legend which has become part of American political consciousness. John Kennedy never alluded to the mythical king when he was President.

Kennedy was no King Arthur and his Administration no Camelot, but his role in American history is not necessarily diminished for that. Kennedy's position in American history cannot rest simply on whether or not his legislative programme was wholly or partly successful. The presidency is more than the sum of its legislative parts. Success rests also on whether or not a president can inspire, lead and direct a nation in times of conflict or adversity. It also rests on whether or not a president's ideas and policies have an impact beyond his years in office.

In his memoirs of the Kennedy Presidency, 'A thousand days', historian Arthur Schlesinger Jnr. (1965) recalls Kennedy's response to academics' rating of previous presidents. Kennedy was pleased that Truman ranked among the 'near great' and was amused that Eisenhower stood near the bottom of the list 'average'. He was also surprised at Woodrow Wilson's high rating - fourth on the list and 'great'. He remarked that although Wilson was a great speaker and writer, he failed to accomplish a number of his objectives. And he wondered about Theodore Roosevelt who "really got very little important legislation through Congress." It was evident to Kennedy that Teddy Roosevelt's standing rested upon his ability to inspire and lead a nation and not in carrying out his duties on the legislative front.[2]

If the prerequisites for success applied to Theodore Roosevelt were equally applied to Kennedy there is little doubt his administration and leadership had many successes. Legislation did not account for his mature handling of the Cuban Missile Crisis which became a model of how presidents should act in moments of crisis. Legislation did not account for the Nuclear Test Ban Treaty, the setting up of a 'hot-line' between Washington and Moscow, the Peace Corps, the programme to land a man on the moon before the end of the 1960s and Kennedy's response to the growing movement for equal rights for African-Americans. Many of his policies emerged in the last year of his life: to end the dangerous and antagonistic relationship between America and Russia; to open up relations with China and Cuba; and to provide health care for the poor and aged. These cannot be judged by the volume and quality of Acts of Congress. Kennedy's promises lived after him - an agenda for change in tax reduction, civil rights legislation, the moon landing programme, federal aid to education, executive action to improve life in the inner cities and Medicare. Many of these policies were eventually fulfilled during the presidencies of Lyndon Johnson and Richard Nixon. Johnson had promised 'to continue' JFK's policies after assuming office and Nixon's détente with China had its origins in the Kennedy years.

But these arguments did not dissuade most Kennedy critics. Henry Fairlie (1973) is typical in describing the New Frontier as depending too much on superficial calls to action rather than substantive programmes. Political scientist Richard Neustadt (1965), on the other hand, found Kennedy's lack of legislative success as entirely consistent with the nature of the office he held. Neustadt argued that because of the make-up of the American presidency and its relationship with other government institutions, Kennedy was only able to articulate his policies, stressing that the modern presidency has suggested a certain rhythm: intensive learning dominates the first two years; the fourth brings the test of re-election; and the seventh and eighth are years in which the president becomes a 'lame-duck'. The key years then are the 3rd, 5th, and 6th. Kennedy had only one of these and, as was suggested earlier, it was one of considerable achievement.[3]

The most important decisions a president makes concerns what range of issues he wants to promote. The job is to create a list and choose which issues are required for attention. Kennedy set his agenda to concentrate on a range of liberal and progressive measures for the nation and, after the terrifying experience of the Cuban crisis, a policy to find areas of agreement with the Soviet Union and Cuba. And at the time of Kennedy's death, the most intense re-examination of American foreign policy since the initiation of the Cold War was taking place in the inner sanctums of the executive branch. Kennedy went through a process of initial confusion to self-confidence as he approached the 1964 election. Long before Nixon's accommodation with China and the Soviet Union, Kennedy was considering the possibility of Soviet-American and Sino-American détente. The 'politics of confrontation' had given way to the 'politics of accommodation'. The great issues between America and Russia were being worked out to Kennedy's advantage. And contrary to the claims of some authors, Kennedy's modus operandi in foreign affairs was not marked by belligerency and recklessness. His presidency was testimony to his capacity to refuse escalation - at the Bay of Pigs, in Laos, in Berlin and especially in the Cuban Missile Crisis. Kennedy liked to quote Liddell Hart: "Never corner an opponent and always assist him to save face. Put yourself in his shoes - so as to see things through his eyes. Avoid self-righteousness like the devil - nothing is so self-blinding."[4]

By November 1963, Kennedy had defined for himself and his presidency a series of purposes or what Neustadt (1960) called "irreversible commitments to defined courses of action." Kennedy failed to accomplish many of his domestic goals, however, because of an intransigent Congress or, more likely, because of simple parliamentary arithmetic. He faced a House of Representatives controlled by a conservative coalition of Republicans and southern Democrats who stalled Kennedy's programme at every opportunity.

Though Kennedy insisted on 'moving the country forward', the Congress was determined to take a conservative approach to passing New Frontier legislation. Neustadt (1965) said Kennedy was "an innovative president confronting a reluctant Congress". Arthur Schlesinger (1987) described Kennedy as a 'beleaguered president' when it came to domestic affairs. Kennedy himself often quoted Jefferson, "Great innovations should not be forced on slender majorities."[5]

With his legislation bogged down in committee, Kennedy set about planning for its fulfilment in his second term. Kennedy was, by 1963, a much more self-confident president and far stronger than he had been in 1961. Kennedy's close 1960 victory had been eclipsed by two and a half years of popularity in the polls. His Congressional relations team were now effective and southern Democrats were coming around to his way of thinking, fearing that his popularity would have a negative effect on their own campaigns. According to James L. Sundquist (1968), Senior Fellow at the Brookings Institution, the polls in 1963 "showed a substantial readiness among Republicans and Democrats to embrace activist solutions to domestic problems".[6]

There is little doubt amongst pro-Kennedy historians like Arthur Schlesinger (1987) that Kennedy's entire domestic programme would have been enacted 'within 18 months'[7] as Kennedy predicted in a press conference shortly before he was killed. His major proposals - Civil Rights, tax reduction, aid for education, and proposals for dealing with health and poverty - were all controversial and according to some commentators, they were also flawed arising out of fundamental misconceptions about the nature of poverty. But by the time of his death they were on their way to enactment.

John Kennedy took office in January 1961 after the quietude of the Eisenhower years. His victory the previous November over the Republican Richard M. Nixon was due, in part, to his promise to 'get America moving again'. After John Kennedy's return from the Pacific theatre of war, he persuaded veterans to support his campaign for Congress in much the same way returning veterans supported a new generation of leaders in the 1945 British national election. After two wars it was time to consider new ways to govern America and a new generation of leaders was required. Youth, vigour and optimism were the keys to Kennedy's success and his Massachusetts constituency responded favourably. After his election as President, Kennedy applied the same principles of new leadership to his Administration. There was a feeling that government could be used for good things and government service was a noble purpose. Kennedy wanted to inspire the American people to solving the nation's problems and he tapped the intellectual resources of Harvard University. This group of committed intellectuals became a 'ministry of talent', as Ted Sorensen called it. There was a sense that the Administration should not be tied to the shibboleths of the past and as the first president born in the 20th century he exemplified an air of anticipation. John Kenneth Galbraith said: "I look back on the Kennedy period as a bright, shining light in my life. There was enormous pride in public service, and many things seemed possible. The Kennedy Administration had a sense of youth and purpose. Part of my pleasure was being with this younger generation."[8]

Kennedy brought with him to office not only a new style but also new ideas of activist politics and a new programme for national reconstruction. Thus the idea that the country needed to 'get going again' was also meant in an economic sense. The conservatism of the Eisenhower years had produced a nation whose economy was slowing down and whose population was overrunning its public services and facilities. The Eisenhower years had seen three recessions, the last of which resulted in seven percent unemployment. Expansionist policies were needed and Kennedy responded with the investment tax credit, the liberalisation of tax depreciation guidelines and with the containment of long-term interest rates through 'monetary twist'. Indeed, after his death, the Johnson Administration succeeded in enacting a general tax reduction.

It was inevitable that this new call to action could not have ignored the growing demand for equal rights for African-Americans. After a slow beginning, Kennedy eventually committed the moral authority of the presidency in handling the Civil rights problem. As historian Hugh

Brogan (1996) wrote: "It (the Civil Rights Movement) was one of the brightest moments in American history, and Kennedy's part in bringing it about is the brightest part of his record."[9] There was a telling clue as to Kennedy's likely response to the problem of equal rights at the beginning of his presidency when he ordered the immediate integration of the Coast Guard because no African-Americans marched in the service's inaugural parade detachment. It is true the protests of the Freedom Riders in the Deep South on the eve of his departure for the 1961 meeting with Kruschev irritated him as he was fearful they would embarrass the United States at a critical moment. However, although he was overcautious, he began to use the executive powers of the presidency broadly promoting an end to discrimination in voting, schools, the federal government, jobs, public facilities and housing. In Civil Rights, Kennedy had begun his presidency with a policy of executive action now and legislation later. His majority in the 1960 election had been slender and so he was cautious in asking Congress to enact legislation which did not have great support throughout the country.

At the start of Kennedy's term of office the South was a tinderbox about to ignite. There were riots at the all-white University of Mississippi when James Meredith tried to enrol. Kennedy called out federal troops to ensure he registered. In Birmingham Alabama, Public Safety Commissioner, 'Bull' Connor, did more for the Civil Rights movement than any demonstration when he set dogs and fire hoses on demonstrators. The news photographs of such brutality helped persuade many southerners that their's was a lost cause. Kennedy later told African-American leaders: "You shouldn't all be totally harsh on Bull Connor. After all, he has done more for Civil Rights than anybody else."[10]

The political risks were high yet he responded positively and directly to the demands of African-Americans. He was guided not only by the moral effect abroad but also by his own personal attitudes to discrimination. There were certainly minuses. He appointed segregationist judges to placate the South.[11] But this occurred because he needed the support of Southerners in Congress, especially as he wanted the Senate Judiciary Committee to appoint Thurgood Marshall to the federal circuit court. And 'bartering' was entirely consistent with political realities.

Unfortunately, Kennedy failed to appoint African-Americans to high positions in the federal government. He preferred a policy of 'gradualism'. But he did make major efforts to improve the conditions of African-Americans, without involving Congress, by desegregating federal facilities and directing federal agencies to hire more minorities.

Kennedy certainly failed to secure legislation. But the positive benefits were considerably larger. He had started with a policy of executive action now and legislation later. He knew that a Civil Rights Bill would have divided the country in 1961 and 1962 and besides it had no chance of being accepted by Congress. However, after the murder of Medgar Evers, Kennedy committed himself fully to the cause and embarked on a course of action which would have eventually led to the 1964 Civil Rights Act and the 1965 Voting Rights Act. Nicholas Katzenbach, who worked alongside Robert Kennedy at the Justice Department, and Mike Mansfield, the Senate Majority leader, believed a Civil Rights Bill would have been passed in 1964 and that Kennedy's assassination had made no difference.[12]

In a television speech broadcast in June 1963, President Kennedy did what no other president had ever done since Lincoln – he put the moral authority of the presidency behind the issue of Civil Rights. A Louis Harris poll taken in the summer of 1963 asked African-Americans who had done the most for Civil Rights: the National Association for the Advancement of Coloured People (NAACP), Martin Luther King or John F. Kennedy.[13] And as Medgar Evers' brother Charles said of Robert Kennedy's role in the Civil Rights movement: "He (Robert) has done more for us than any other public official. Had it not been for him, there would have been many more murders and many more beatings than we have ever had in Mississippi in the last four years. Mr Kennedy did more to help us get our rights as first-class citizens than all other U.S. Attorney-Generals put together."[14]

The overwhelming evidence to support the contention that the Kennedy brothers played an important role in the furtherance of Civil Rights has not prevented revisionist historians from suggesting that the Kennedys conspired to bring down Civil Rights leader Martin Luther King. Critics of John and Robert Kennedy often refer to the fact that Martin Luther King was 'wiretapped' on the authority of the Attorney General and was kept under surveillance during the Kennedy years. Unfortunately, many fail to put the story in the correct context. Opponents of Kennedy said that the Civil Rights movement was communist-led and King had been under communist control. Both brothers supported King but they acceded to J. Edgar Hoover's wishes that King be 'surveilled' hoping to prove Hoover and their critics wrong. John Kennedy took King for a walk outside the Oval Office to warn him that he was being watched by the FBI. Although King would not abandon his advisor, Stanley Levison, who was suspected of being a communist, he went along with Kennedy. And, although King laid down a principle of not supporting a presidential candidate, he changed course and was planning to endorse the president in the 1964 election.[15]

Kennedy was significant in the area of Civil Rights not only for what he did but also for what he started. His presidency marked a profound change from the inaction of the past decade. As Professor Carl M. Brauer (1977) described it: "Kennedy both encouraged and responded to black aspirations and led the nation to it's Second Reconstruction."[16] James David Barber (1972) in his book 'Presidential character' described his commitment as 'active-positive' and his "vigorous, open and optimistic personality...enabled him to overcome his earlier detachment toward the problem of Civil Rights and to plunge into the racial turmoil of 1963 with decisive and courageous action...Kennedy's commitment was complete."[17]

Kennedy's effectiveness in the area of Civil Rights does not depend upon the sometimes biased interpretations of Kennedy revisionists. Kennedy came to be loved in African-American communities across the United States and his picture is still displayed in villages throughout Africa. His legacy as a great leader for human rights, therefore, is validated by black communities throughout the world. Kennedy's greatest success was in the way he provided symbolic leadership, the effects of which cannot be quantified in terms of substantive legislation. The impact of Kennedy's death was felt around the world in places like India and Africa because Kennedy recognised their sense of nationhood to a far greater extent than had been shown before. He gave them a sense of expectation. He felt he could reach people in other countries by the power of his ideas and personality. There is little doubt in the minds of many that the image of the United States changed because he was its leader.

Moreover, few can argue that for a generation Kennedy's call to action was very effective. His sense of adventure was contagious when he announced that America would put a man on the moon by the end of the decade. Kennedy also had an infectious optimism which influenced the young to a selfless desire to help the poor and underprivileged and one of the ways in which this idealism was harnessed was the Peace Corps which was described by Robert B. Textor as: "... an ethical enterprise, a way for an excessively fortunate country to share its optimism and generosity with parts of the world that, at a moment in time, are in need of what the volunteers can best offer."[18] As one of the volunteers said, "I'd never done anything political, patriotic or unselfish because nobody ever asked me to. Kennedy asked."[19]

In the final analysis Kennedy's legacy as an inspirational and effective leader rests on his abstract accomplishments. As House Speaker Tip O'Neill (1987) wrote: "...it would be unfair to judge Jack Kennedy only in terms of legislation. Despite his lack of success in dealing with Congress, his leadership set the stage for so many important changes in America. What would we have achieved in Civil Rights without Jack Kennedy? Or in space exploration? Or arms control? When you consider the larger picture, it's clear that Jack Kennedy left a shining legacy. Perhaps his most important achievement was to draw a new generation of young Americans into politics and government."[20] O'Neill's perceptive comments about Kennedy's presidency are in keeping with received wisdom about the skills necessary to be a successful president. Speaking of the candidates in the 2000 presidential election, acclaimed presidential historian David McCullough said: "What we want most in a leader is the sense of the possibilities. It isn't just that we have a great country and we've demonstrated greatness but that 'you ain't seen nothing yet'. That's the spirit that this country has thrived on. Now, it's very easy to dismiss that as a myth, it isn't a myth at all. Adversity, overcoming difficulties, has been the story of our whole American civilisation. If we marshal all the intelligence and the ingenuity and the wealth of this country there is literally nothing we can't do. And the candidate who catches that reality is the candidate who could be a very strong and effective president."[21]

Revisionists have devalued Kennedy's successes as president and have reinterpreted his popularity with the American people as misguided nostalgia, as grief over his death and because of his eloquence unmatched since the days of Lincoln. However, those authors who belittle his accomplishments and dismiss his importance as an inspirational and charismatic leader, fail to comprehend the positive effects that his persona had on both the nation and the world, and that this enhanced America's international image. As David McCullough said: "Kennedy will be remembered for hundreds, perhaps thousands of years almost entirely on what he said."[22]

Notes

1. Reeves, T. C. (1991). A question of character - a life John F. Kennedy, Bloomsbury. p. 415.

2. Schlesinger, A. M. (1965). *A thousand days - John F. Kennedy in the White House*, Andre Deutsch. p. 585.

3. Neustadt, R. (1960). *Presidential power - the politics of leadership*, Wiley New York. p. 163.

4. Schlesinger, A. M. (1987). *The cycles of American history*, Andre Deutsch. p. 416.

5. Bernstein, I. (1996). *Guns or butter*, Oxford University Press. p. 298.

6. Sundquist, J. L. (1968) cited Bernstein, I. (1996). *Guns or butter*, Oxford University Press. p. 288.

7. Schlesinger, A. M. (1987). *The cycles of American history*, Andre Deutsch. p. 411.

8. "25 Years Later", U.S. News and World Report, 24 October 1988, p. 38.

9. Brogan, H. (1996). *Kennedy*, Longman. p. 151.

10. Reeves, R. (1993). *President Kennedy - profile of power*, Simon and Schuster. p. 531.

11. Brogan, H. (1996). *Kennedy*, Longman. p. 158.

12. Bernstein, I. (1996). *Guns or butter*, Oxford University Press. p. 297; Schlesinger, A. M. (1987). *The cycles of American history*, Andre Deutsch. p. 411.

13. Arthur M. Schlesinger, "U.S. liberalism: the Kennedys and civil rights", *The Times*, 17 March 1970, p. 21.

14. *Ibid.*

15. Schlesinger, A. M. Jnr. (1978). *Robert Kennedy and his times,* Houghton Mifflin Co, 1978. p. 388.

16. Brauer, C. M. (1977). *John F. Kennedy and the second reconstruction,* Columbia University Press. p. 320.

17. Barber, J. D. (1972). *The presidential character,* Prentice-Hall Inc. p. 342.

18. Bernstein, I. (1991). *Promises kept,* Oxford University Press. p. 277.

19. *Ibid,* p. 279; *see also* "Idealism's rebirth". U.S. News and World Report, 24 October 1988, p. 37.

20. O'Neill, T. (1987). *Man of the House,* St Martin's Press. p. 207.

21. "History's lessons", CNN/Time broadcast, 14 August 2000.

22. *Ibid.*

Chapter 2

The Bay of Pigs

Was President Kennedy irresponsible and reckless during the Bay of Pigs invasion?

"The necessity of procuring good Intelligence is apparent and need not be further urged - all that remains for me to add is, that you keep the whole matter as secret as possible. For upon Secrecy, success depends in Most Enterprizes of the kind, and for want of it, they are generally defeated..."

Letter from General George Washington to Colonel Elias Dayton, July 1777

"It fell upon him to endure that defeat and he was brave; he was brave when he said that 'victory has many fathers but defeat is an orphan'. He took on all responsibility but he didn't resign himself to those results."

Fidel Castro, CNN interview, October 1998

For nearly 40 years historians have disagreed about President Kennedy's decisions during the ill-fated invasion by Cuban exiles at the Bay of Pigs. Kennedy defenders maintain that the young and inexperienced President was misled by the military and intelligence community but showed maturity by admitting responsibility for the debacle. They also contend that his insistence on limiting the American role in the affair was wise and prevented international accusations of 'gunboat diplomacy'. Kennedy detractors describe a woefully inept commander-in-chief who recklessly allowed Cuban exiles to die on the invasion beach by refusing to order a second air strike which would have prevented Castro's forces from defeating the invasion group.

The origins of the debacle began with the Eisenhower Administration which formulated judgements about American interests in the Western Hemisphere. American policy in Latin America in the late 1950s and early 1960s centred around America's economic interests and its anti-communist policies in the region. George Kennan, who helped formulate American containment policy towards the Soviet Union in the late 1940s, spoke to the U.S. Chiefs of Mission in Rio De Janeiro in 1950:

> *"(American policy had several purposes in the region) to protect the vital supplies of raw materials which Latin American countries export to the USA; to prevent the 'military exploitation of Latin America by the enemy'; and to avert 'the psychological mobilisation of Latin America against us'. "*[1]

Guerrilla leader, Fidel Castro, overthrew Cuba's dictator, Fulcencio Batista, in 1959. At this time Castro was not a committed communist although his brother Raul and his comrade Che Guevara were. Shortly after coming to power, the new Cuban leader met with Vice-President Nixon hoping to secure American support for his regime. The meeting was arranged because Eisenhower refused to meet with the Cuban leader suspecting he held anti-American sentiments. During the meeting Nixon took an abrasive and arrogant attitude with Castro.[2] It was quite evident that the American government was not about to form any agreeable approach to the Cuban leader and enter into serious negotiations with him. The Eisenhower Administration had been displeased with Castro when he held a number of Americans hostage, including United States Marines, during his military campaign against Batista.[3] The Administration's suspicions about Castro's true ideological beliefs were also not without some foundation in truth - the Cuban leader had been accepting Soviet aide in the form of Czech military supplies since 1957.

Fearful of Castro's revolution, the Cuban middle class began to flee the island shortly after Castro came to power. The majority of them settled in the Miami and the New Orleans area of the United States. To prevent the loss of United States capital investments in Cuba, Castro nationalised leading businesses and in the process came into conflict with leading American corporations. The process of 'socialisation' began with little compensation. There were also fears that Cuban leaders would try to spread their revolution to Latin America.

Eisenhower refused to grant economic aide to Cuba. Rejected, Castro turned to the Soviet Union and secured a 100 million dollar loan. The Soviet Union also authorised the supply of weapons from Poland and Czechoslovakia. It was in this climate that the American intelligence community began to advocate the overthrow of Castro.

The CIA already had a 'blueprint' for his overthrow. It is likely the successful overthrow of Jacobo Arbenz as President of Guatemala in 1954 gave the intelligence community a sense of overconfidence.[4] The CIA led revolt had succeeded so why not use the same means to deal with a communist dictator only 90 miles from the shore of the United States? CIA Deputy Director for Plans, Richard Bissell, believed that the success of the operation was to stir up rebellion in Castro's forces rather than to defeat them. The CIA wanted Castro to act like Arbenz and flee the country in the belief that U.S. Marines were about to wade ashore. Bissell also remembered that Eisenhower had saved the faltering Guatemala coup by sending in more planes for air cover.

In the spring of 1960, President Eisenhower approved a plan called 'Operation Pluto', to send small groups of Cuban exiles to work in the underground as guerrillas, to overthrow Castro. By the autumn the plan had expanded to a full blown invasion with air support in planes supplied by the United States.

The CIA trained some 1,400 Cuban exiles for the invasion. Some were trained as ground forces and the remainder as pilots flying American B-26's made to look like Cuban Air Force planes. This would create the illusion that Castro's own men were rebelling against him. The CIA were convinced that once the invasion started, the Cuban people and armed forces would revolt and join the invading exiles.

On April 15th 1961, eight planes conducted air strikes against three Cuban air bases with the intention of destroying the Cuban Air Force on the ground. They were unsuccessful. After this failed mission the invasion went from bad to worse. When the invasion force landed at the Bay of Pigs, it met considerably more resistance than it had expected. Despite broadcasts by the CIA - run Radio Swan, there was no uprising. The Castro Air Force began to inflict severe damage on the invading forces. CIA planners had led the brigades to believe that in the event of such occurrences they would be able to flee to the Sierra

Madre mountains.[5] However, it was impossible and swampy marshes were the only routes to escape.

U.S. air cover, which was to provide assistance for one hour, never materialised as communications between the Cuban brigades and the U.S. Air Force broke down. The Cuban Brigade and their CIA 'handlers' called for a second air strike but Kennedy refused to countenance it. McGeorge Bundy, Kennedy's National Security Advisor, and Secretary of State, Dean Rusk, decided to recommend no more air strikes until the Cuban exiles had seized an airstrip on the Cuban mainland that could legitimately be used as a base. It was imperative, all along, that the United States must not be seen to be an accomplice in the invasion.[6] Consequently, the anti-Castro forces were defeated. The most important part of the effort to topple Castro was the uprising which the invasion was supposed to spark. However, popular support was not forthcoming and the mission was doomed to failure. What remained of the anti-Castro brigades were soon captured. The Castro forces took 1,189 prisoners and 26 were rescued.[7] The rest had been killed. Over 1,000 prisoners were later released in December 1962 in exchange for 53 million dollars worth of medicine and food.[8]

The Bay of Pigs was a personal disaster for President Kennedy and the new Administration was severely criticised. At a press conference after the debacle the President admitted failure, "...there's an old saying that victory has a hundred fathers and defeat is an orphan...I'm the responsible officer of the government and that is quite obvious."[9] In private he was furious with his military and CIA advisors. He told one aide, "You always assume that the military and intelligence people have some secret skill not available to ordinary mortals."[10]

Kennedy had gone along with the Eisenhower Administration plan to topple Castro for a number of reasons. The previous year Kennedy had campaigned for some form of action against Cuba and he would appear to be hypocritical if he cancelled any previously formed plans. CIA chief, Allen Dulles, later wrote about the President's inheritance of the plan: "It was a sort of orphan child JFK had adopted. He had no real love and affection for it...(he) proceeded uncertainly toward defeat unable to turn back, only half sold on the vital necessity of what he was doing."[11] Secondly, a cold war atmosphere mitigated against backing down from an exercise designed to show the Soviet Union that America would not allow a challenge to its hegemony in the area. Always at the back of Kennedy's mind was the idea that Kruschev was testing his mettle. Thirdly, Kennedy was in awe of the legendary CIA spymasters,

Allen Dulles, and his deputy, Richard Bissell and placed too much trust in their confidence that the plan was sound. And Bissell had taught several of Kennedy's staff at Yale and so they tended to defer to him. Fourthly, Kennedy felt that a cancellation of the military plan would reveal him as a weak leader especially as he succeeded a Second World War hero in the White House. Finally, the timing of the invasion was important. American intelligence indicated the arrival of Soviet MIGS with first class Cuban pilots who had been trained in Czechoslovakia.

Sargent Shriver, Kennedy's brother-in law and head of the Peace Corps, summed up Kennedy's position when he said: "He was the youngest president ever elected allegedly who didn't know enough, hadn't had the experience. That was one of the big things that Nixon was running on or Eisenhower was stating and others were saying, 'This guy's just a kid, he doesn't know.' For him to have stopped that (Bay of Pigs invasion) as soon as he became president I think would have immediately opened him up to second guessers. They would have said 'Well, it would have worked...He's soft on communism. He doesn't understand the threat of Castro. He doesn't understand world politics. He has aborted something that was just about to move."[12]

In his book 'The dark side of Camelot', Seymour Hersh (1997) criticises President Kennedy for his weakness and confusion in handling the CIA - led, anti-Castroite invasion. Hersh explained Kennedy's cancellation of the planned air strike to rescue the defeated invaders by claiming the President expected Castro to have been assassinated in the run up to the landing. He maintains that Kennedy pulled back and cut his losses when he learned the assassination of the Cuban leader had not been carried out and effectively abandoned the exile brigades to imprisonment or death.

Hersh has no solid evidence that Kennedy knew about the CIA plots against the Cuban leader or that he cancelled the second air strike when he supposedly found out that Castro had not been killed. It is true that the CIA plot was an integral part of the invasion plans but it is likely that Kennedy believed that Castro and his top men would be a target of the anti-Castro forces. After all, the object of any coup is to dispose of a regime's leaders, often in a violent manner.

As far as the Kennedy brothers involvement in the murder plots against Castro are concerned, this will be dealt with in a later chapter. But what were Kennedy's decisions and actions during the Bay of Pigs invasion?

Did he, for political reasons, allow Cuban exiles to die on the beaches of the Bay of Pigs?

The idea of a Soviet-oriented communist dictatorship 90 miles from the United States caused considerable concern for Eisenhower and his policy-makers. In the virulent Cold War context of the time, no president was willing to act against the anti-communist and anti-appeasement sentiments of the American people. Castro's regime was undemocratic and showed obvious signs of becoming 'socialist' if not 'communist' - anathema to even the most liberal leaning of Americans. Failure to act against Castro would have rendered any president open to severe criticism from all political factions, except the small left-wing elements within American society. At the time accommodation was unthinkable because Castro was unwilling to introduce more democratic methods of governing. Furthermore, the fires of anti-Castroism were stoked by the right-wing media who saw anti-Castro Cubans as the equivalent of 'Revolutionary America' patriots.

After taking office in January of 1961, John Kennedy had no real alternative but to support the anti-Castro Cubans and their efforts to rid the island of a revolutionary dictator. To do otherwise would have opened him up to charges of weakness and appeasement - powerful words especially in the decades following the Second World War. In short, it was politically impossible either to ignore Castro or reconcile the Cuban leader's political views with the American electorate's. After all a communist dominated state was about to become the vanguard of international communism in the Western Hemisphere and it was only an 8 minute flight from the United States.

Furthermore, Castro had anticipated an invasion and was receiving a heavy flow of Soviet arms. The CIA reported to the new President that a delay in invading Cuba would be fatal - if Kennedy cancelled the invasion then 1,400 embittered Cubans would be returned to the Cuban community in Miami, and many would speak of 'betrayal'. The Republicans would accuse Kennedy of being 'soft on communism'. The Guatemalans were annoyed at the presence on their soil of the Cuban Brigade and wanted them out of their country.

It is unlikely, given the political climate, that the other democratic hopefuls of 1960 (Symington, Humphrey, Johnson and Stevenson) and Kennedy's opponent, Richard Nixon, would have taken any other course of action which the Eisenhower Administration had set in place.

This is not to say that voices of caution were missing in the executive and Congressional branches of government. William Fulbright, Senate Foreign Relations Chairman, had been passed over as Secretary of State because of his anti-integrationist views. Upon learning of the plans for the invasion in early 1961, he sent a memo to the White House saying that if American Forces were drawn into the battle: "We would have undone the work of 30 years in trying to live down earlier interventions...To give this activity even covert support is of a piece with the hypocrisy and cynicism for which the United States is constantly denouncing the Soviet Union in the United nations and elsewhere. This point will not be lost on the rest of the world nor our own consciences. And remember always, the Castro regime is a thorn in the side but not a dagger in the heart".[13]

President Kennedy decided on a compromise position. He would allow the CIA and anti-Castro Cubans to proceed with their plans but under no circumstances were U.S. forces to give overt assistance. The stipulation was for air cover for a period of one hour only. He pressed for a lower 'noise level' for, as he told the CIA, he had greater political considerations to deal with, not least his imminent meeting with Soviet Premier, Nikita Kruschev, in June.

Hersh (1997) and others have criticised the actions of President Kennedy for not allowing U.S. military air strikes to accompany the invasion thus allowing the Cuban exiles to be defeated. It is evident, however, from recently released CIA and State Department documents, that the Bay of Pigs invasion would have failed with or without the air strikes. State Department documents reveal that Kennedy was badly advised and received conflicting reports as to the viability of the mission.[14] He was forced to limit overt U.S. involvement in the operation because of diplomatic considerations. He wrongly took the advice of CIA Deputy, Richard Bissell, as opposed to more knowledgeable and experienced advisors in the State and Defense Departments. He waited for his top military advisors to speak frankly but they did not and instead the advice was 'it may succeed, it may not succeed'. It was a horrendous decision made under intense pressure from CIA leaders who assured the President that the plan had a great chance of success. Kennedy thought his failure to ask enough questions was his worst mistake.

We can see from these documents that the instruments of failure were complex: a CIA eager to put the invasion plan into operation; a cautious State Department concerned that U.S. involvement might spoil relations with the rest of Latin America; a cautious military not directly involved in the planning; and a president torn between a desire to topple the Cuban dictator and a concern about the political debacle that would ensue if the world learned of direct U.S. involvement. Consequently, Kennedy delayed decisions, he shifted the landing site to a more remote area (from the Trinidad site to the Bay of Pigs), he cut back airstrikes, he limited the role of U.S. Navy ships and he revised the timetable. But then Richard Bissell, Robert McNamara and Lyman Lemnitzer, Chairman of the Joint Chiefs of Staff, never told him about the flaws in the alternative plan even though they knew what they were. Had Kennedy known about the objections to the plan made by men like Marines General Harkins, who trained the exile brigades, he would likely have stopped it.

Kennedy's Secretary of State, Dean Rusk, advised the President to make these changes to the plans but failed to pass on a memo written by Under-Secretary of State, Chester Bowles, two weeks before the invasion. In the memo Bowles clearly states that the plan was 'highly risky' and that the mission was a 'mistake'. Kennedy was always reluctant to go ahead with the plan and paid little attention to, or never saw, warnings from military heads in memos to Secretary of Defense, Robert McNamara. And Dean Rusk 'deeply regretted' not airing his views more clearly to the President.

In his autobiography Dean Rusk (1990) wrote: "The CIA told us all sorts of things about the situation in Cuba and what would happen once the brigade got ashore. President Kennedy received information which simply was not correct. For example, we were told that elements of the Cuban Armed forces would defect and join the brigade, that there would be popular uprisings throughout Cuba when the brigade hit the beach, and that if the exile force got into trouble its members would simply melt into the countryside and become guerrillas, just as Castro had done."[15] This was not the first time the CIA had got it wrong. In 1956, the intelligence agency had encouraged a rebellion against a communist government without the certitude of full support from a president and without a realistic assessment of the realities of the situation. 32,000 people had died in Hungary in an anti-communist uprising encouraged by CIA radio broadcasts.

Unfortunately, Kennedy chose to trust the overly optimistic CIA assessments many of which appeared to be heavily tilted towards assuring the President that, even with his changes, the plan would work. While the invading forces were small compared to Castro's

40,000 member army and 200,000 strong militia, the CIA persuaded Kennedy that a popular uprising would support the invaders. They chose to ignore a public opinion poll taken in Cuba showing that support for Fidel Castro at that time was widespread.[16] Even if the invasion had been successful, it would not have created the popular uprising on which the strategy depended. As Robert Kennedy wrote in a June 1961 memo: "We kept asking when the uprisings were going to take place...of course, no uprisings took place...(we were told that)...even if the force was not successful...the men could become guerrillas and, therefore, couldn't be wiped out...I think that the President might very well not have approved of the operation if he had known that the chances of these men becoming guerrillas was probably nil."[17]

There were other factors involved in the operation's failure. There existed a breakdown in communications between some of Kennedy's advisors. One advisor, for example, who influenced Kennedy's decision-making, claimed he would have given a negative reply had he known the air strikes were to be cancelled.[18]

Even though Kennedy would ultimately accept blame, he had always been reluctant to go ahead with the plan but was never directly advised to abandon it by his top military, Cabinet and CIA advisors. Kennedy waited for his military leaders to speak frankly but he mostly received neutral analysis. The CIA were the most aggressive and persuasive in making their case and the military, which harboured some reservations, rarely got a chance to make their case to the President - McNamara was always the 'go-between'.

Kennedy was also naively unaware that the CIA's Directorate of Plans (Operations) was separate from Intelligence and during the planning for the Bay of Pigs, Operations deliberately failed to consult Intelligence.

It was a recipe for disaster which Kennedy would never repeat. In the soul-searching he carried out after the debacle he promised never to put his trust in the CIA again and threatened to "splinter it into a thousand pieces".[19] He also learned a clear lesson never to put complete trust in crisis assessments made by military planners - a lesson that would benefit him 18 months later when Soviet missiles were discovered in Cuba.

The blame for the Bay of Pigs debacle lies fairly and squarely on the CIA's own institutional arrogance, ignorance and incompetence. And this is confirmed by CIA documents released in 1998 which include the CIA's own highly secret internal investigation of the failed invasion. The report on the Bay of Pigs debacle was written by the CIA's Inspector-General, Lyman Kirkpatrick.[20]

The first point the documents make is that the job of overthrowing governments belongs to the agency more suited to this - the United States Military. The CIA report goes on to paint a picture of the CIA as self-deceptive and whose secret operations were both tragic and ludicrous. The report states that the planning for the operation began in April 1960 and it was to be a classic covert operation "in which the hands of the United States would not appear". As the report tells it, the plan called for a group of exiled Cuban leaders, supported by a team of CIA officers, to build political momentum toward toppling Castro. It said that CIA officers became so involved in the operation, however, that "they lost sight of ultimate goals".

The report also stated that the budget for the operation grew out of all proportion to the nature of the mission - from 4.4 million to 46 million dollars. Within a year they had built an organisation which was unruly and ill-trained. It was also well-observed by Castro's intelligence agents, contrary to the statements made by CIA advisors who were unaware that Castro's intelligence had infiltrated the exile groups based in Miami.

'Plausible deniability', the concept that the U.S. needed to lie about its involvement, became a "pathetic illusion". The report went on to say that other reasons for disaster were the CIA's lack of knowledge of Latin American affairs and that most CIA officers assisting the exiles could not speak Spanish. The relationships between the CIA's agents and Cuban exiles were poor. The agency's 'puppets' - the Cuban Revolutionary Council - were stationed in a Miami 'safe house' and were unable to plan their own invasion although CIA 'bulletins' were written in their name.

Furthermore, the report confirms that the CIA did indeed delude itself - and consequently two presidents - that the invasion would mysteriously create a popular uprising when there was no evidence to assume this would happen. The CIA placed too much reliance on obviously biased views held by the Cuban exile groups whose own judgements were distorted by their virulent hatred of the Cuban leader.

The 150 page report exonerated Kennedy. It stated categorically that: "...the fundamental cause of the disaster was the CIA's incompetence, rather than President Kennedy's failure to follow through with the air raids in support of the commandos...(The CIA misled the President by not informing him) that success had become dubious and (by failing) to recommend that the operation be therefore cancelled."[21]

Lucien S. Vandenbrouke (1984) writing in the American 'Political Science Quarterly', analysed the Bay of Pigs affair and concluded that the mission's failure occurred because the CIA: "supplied President Kennedy and his advisors with chosen reports on the unreliability of Castro's forces and the extent of Cuban dissent." Of the CIA's behaviour, he concluded: "By resorting to the typical organisation strategy of defining the options and providing the information required to evaluate them, the CIA thus structured the problem in a way that maximised the likelihood the President would choose the Agency's preferred option."[22]

However, something good sometimes comes from something bad. The lessons learned from the Bay of Pigs failure contributed to the Kennedy brothers' successful handling of the Cuban Missile Crisis - a crisis in which the possible catastrophic consequences were much greater than any that resulted from the earlier Cuban disaster.

Notes

1. Ranelagh, J. (1987). *The agency – the rise and decline of the CIA*, Sceptre Books. p. 275.

2. Ambrose, S. (1987). *Nixon - the education of a politician, 1913-1962*, Simon and Schuster. p. 516; Breuer, W. B. (1997). *Vendetta - Castro and the Kennedy brothers*, John Wiley and Sons Inc. p. 54; Quirk, R. E. (1993). *Fidel Castro*, W W Norton and Co. p. 240.

3. Breuer, W. B. (1997). *Vendetta - Castro and the Kennedy brothers*, John Wiley and Sons Inc. p. 29.

4. Ranelagh, J. (1987). *The agency – the rise and decline of the CIA*, Sceptre Books. p. 365; Thomas, E. (1995). *The very best men - four who dared; the early years of the CIA*, Simon and Schuster. p. 204.

5. *Ibid*, p. 248.

6. *Ibid*, p. 258.

7. Fursenko, A. and Naftali, T. (1999). *One hell of a gamble*, Pimlico. p. 96.

8. Salinger, P. (1997). *John F. Kennedy - commander-in-chief*, Penguin Studio. p. 42.

9. Reeves, R. (1993). *President Kennedy - profile of power*, Simon and Schuster. p. 101; Salinger, P. (1997). *John F. Kennedy - commander-in-chief*, Penguin Studio. p. 42; Fursenko, A. and Naftali, T. (1999). *One hell of a gamble*, Pimlico. p. 97.

10. Thomas, E. (1995). *The very best men - four who dared; the early years of the CIA*, Simon and Schuster. p. 266.

11. Grose, P. (1995). *Gentleman spy - the life of Allen Dulles*, Andre Deutsch. p. 516.

12. Wheeler, C. "The Kennedy legacy". BBC Documentary, November 1983.

13. Reeves, R. (1993). *President Kennedy - profile of power*, Simon and Schuster. p.78.

14. Benedetto, R. "Kennedy played a big role in the Bay of Pigs", *USA Today*, 24 June 1997 p. 12; U.S. State Department. *Foreign relations of the United States, Cuba, 1961-1962*. Volume 10.

15. Rusk, D., Rusk, R. and Papp, D. (1990). *As I saw it*, Norton New York. p. 210.

16. Turner, R. L. "Putting the word out on secrecy", *The Boston Globe*, 29 September 1998. (http://www.boston.com).

17. Schlesinger, A. M. (1978). *Robert Kennedy and his times*, Houghton Mifflin Co. p. 477.

18. Benedetto, R. "Kennedy played a big role in the Bay of Pigs", *USA Today*, 24 June 1997 p. 12.

19. Freemantle, B. (1983). *CIA - the 'honourable' company*, Futura. p. 38.

20. Central Intelligence Agency, *Inspector General's Report*, 1961. (http://www.foia.ucia.gov/popdocs1/bayofpigs.htm).

21. *Ibid*.

22. Vandenbrouke, L. S. *Political Science Quarterly (U.S.)*, Spring, 1984. (http://www.psq.com).

Chapter 3

The Cuban Missile Crisis

Did President Kennedy needlessly risk nuclear war?

"He's the one playing God, not us."

John Kennedy

"Bullfight critics row on row
Crowd the enormous plaza full
But there's only one man who knows
And he's the man who fights the bull."

Robert Graves

In his searing attack on the presidency of John F. Kennedy, Seymour Hersh (1997) wrote:

> *"...Kennedy remained obsessed with Cuba, and so it became Kruschev's turn to be humiliated. Over the next 13 days, the President eschewed diplomacy and played a terrifying game of nuclear chicken, without knowing all of the facts. For the first time in his presidency, Kennedy publicly brought his personal recklessness, and his belief that the normal rules of conduct did not apply to him, to his foreign policy. On October 27, at the height of the crisis, when the downing of an American spy plane threatened to move events beyond his control, Kennedy was forced to seek a compromise and to rely on Kruschev's common*

sense and dread of nuclear war to keep the superpowers apart...Kennedy brought the world to the edge of nuclear war to gain a political victory: to humble an adversary who had humbled him before. "[1]

Hersh thus paints a portrait of a reckless, irresponsible warmongerer playing with the lives of millions in order to avenge his humiliation by Kruschev at the Vienna summit and by Castro at the Bay of Pigs. What began as payback at the Bay of Pigs evolved into a nuclear crisis with the Soviet Union. Descriptions of President Kennedy as magnanimous and statesmanlike are nowhere to be found in Hersh's account of the crisis. Instead Kruschev is described as having 'common sense' and Kennedy as 'reckless'. Yet two paragraphs after the above quote, Hersh writes: "In May 1962 Nikita Kruschev decided to make the boldest gamble of his career: he would station Soviet nuclear weapons in Cuba...and do it in secret." With this statement in mind the reader is asked to believe that Kruschev was a man of 'common sense' and Kennedy was 'reckless'.[2]

Kennedy's handling of the Cuban Missile Crisis thus becomes an issue of controversy: did Kennedy, as Hersh implies, precipitate the crisis and act recklessly? Indeed, Hersh was not the first writer or political scientist to make these claims and scholars have debated Kennedy's handling of the crisis ever since it came to a satisfactory and safe conclusion.

Nearly 40 years later we have a clearer understanding of how the crisis emerged and of how it was handled through the release of previously secret documents held in the Russian and American archives and through two conferences which included officials who participated directly in the crisis. Masses of written material and oral data declassified by the American, Cuban and Russian governments confirm that the situation was far more dangerous than anyone had imagined. They also reveal the real reasons for the origins of the crisis.

At the conferences, one held in the Soviet Union in 1989 and the other in Havana in 1992, the world learned for the first time since the crisis how dangerous the situation was.[3] The first conference was held at the invitation of President Mikhail Gorbachev and included 30 government officials who had participated in the decision making during the Cuban Missile Crisis - 10 Americans, 10 Cubans and 10 Russians. At the conference it was revealed that a particular document purloined from CIA files convinced Kruschev that an invasion of Cuba would occur in

October 1962 and that the strength of troops in Cuba, originally estimated at 10,000, was in fact 50,000.[4] Fidel Castro had tried early on in the crisis to convince Kruschev to launch the missiles against the United States. At a conference held in Havana in 1992, Kennedy Administration officials and members of the Cuban and Russian governments met. The world learned that, apart from the intermediate range nuclear missiles, the Soviets had deployed nine 'Luna' tactical nuclear missiles to be used against any U.S. invasion force. Furthermore the Soviet commanders in Cuba had been given strategic autonomy - they had been given permission to use their own judgement in the use of the tactical missiles. The implications became obvious especially with the knowledge that Kennedy knew nothing of this. Had Kennedy chosen an invasion of Cuba instead of a blockade (the term 'quarantine' was used since 'blockade' was internationally recognised as an act of war), then the tactical nuclear weapons would most likely have been used and an escalating full-scale nuclear war would have most likely ensued. The situation would have been further compounded given the mind-set of the Cuban leader who took an aggressive, dangerous and belligerent position during the crisis. At this conference further details emerged of how Castro had urged the Soviet leader to launch a pre-emptive nuclear strike on the U.S. mainland to forestall an invasion.

The crisis had its roots in a number of post-World War II realities: the growing nuclear arsenals of the United States and the Soviet Union; the efforts by successive Soviet and American governments to gain an edge in nuclear superiority; Cold War tensions in Europe, especially Berlin, and around the world; the misunderstanding and miscalculation of the two adversaries' intentions with regard to military and political strategies; and the inability of the United States to solve the Cuban problem - a communist state on its doorstep which became a thorn in the side of the Eisenhower and Kennedy Administrations.

Historians disagree as to the reasons why the Soviet leader, Nikita Kruschev, placed the missiles in Cuba in the first place. Reasons given generally fall into four categories:

- At a stroke Kruschev would double the amount of Russian nuclear missiles capable of reaching the United States.

- Kruschev had supported the Castro regime and he would prevent a U.S. invasion of Cuba through the installation of missiles. Castro himself fanned the flames - during the last year of the Eisenhower Administration, when U.S. Intelligence became alarmed that the U.S. Naval base at Guantanamo was threatened by Castro forces, Kruschev had boasted that he would "support Cuba with missiles".

• Kruschev had been angered at the stationing of U.S. Jupiter missiles on the periphery of the Soviet Union.

• In defending Cuba with nuclear missiles, Kruschev would eclipse the Chinese as the leaders of international communism.

The crisis itself began in the summer of 1962 when suspicions arose that the Soviet Union was installing a military base in Cuba. In September Kennedy had warned the Soviet Union that a military base in Cuba would be viewed by the United States as grave provocation. The Soviets denied that 'offensive' missiles were stationed in Cuba and said they had assisted the Cuban people with 'defensive' weaponry. It was not until American U-2 spy planes discovered the Soviets were constructing bases for Intermediate Range Nuclear Missiles (IRNM's) that the alarming nature of the situation became apparent. The Soviet effort had included 50,000 military personnel organised in five missile regiments, four motorised regiments, two tank battalions, one MIG-21 fighter wing, 42 IL-28 light bombers, 12 SA-2 anti-aircraft units with 144 launchers and a squadron of 11 submarines, (seven equipped with nuclear missiles). There were 36 SS-4 Medium-Range Ballistic Missiles (MRBM's) and 24 SS-5 Intermediate-Range Ballistic Missiles (IRBM's) together with their nuclear warheads. There was no question that the United States must act. As Under Secretary of State, George Ball, wrote many years later: "...America had fought two world wars without damage to its own territory. The American people had grown accustomed to thinking that the moat of two oceans was an effective barrier to external aggression, and their leaders had made it clear since the Monroe doctrine that they would not tolerate a European intrusion in the Western Hemisphere. If the American public had painfully adjusted to the thought of ICBM's capable of reaching our cities, it was largely because those missiles were still thousands of miles away and the danger seemed unreal. The prospect of Soviet missiles 90 miles off our borders was something altogether different; it would be an affront to our history."[5]

The missiles were first identified from U2 photos on Monday, October 15th 1962. Through information supplied by a CIA Kremlin spy, Colonel Oleg Penkovsky, the American government was able to gauge the precise range of the missiles and techniques for bringing the weapons into operational readiness. The President and his advisors discussed the options. Secretary of Defense, Robert McNamara, told the President he had three possible courses of action[6]:

- political - he could ask that all three leaders come together to resolve the issue diplomatically.

- a blockade against offensive weapons entering Cuba.

- military action starting with an air strike.

At first, the choices all appeared to be military - air strikes to destroy the missiles followed by a larger attack, or an air strike against airports and storage areas, or a large scale invasion of the island. Kennedy refused to act impulsively but he did believe that an air strike taking out the missiles would be inevitable. The idea of a blockade to give Kruschev breathing space was not considered initially and by Saturday October 20th it was only given half-hearted support.

On Tuesday October 23rd 1962, the eighth day of the crisis, President Kennedy and his advisors considered a nuclear attack from Cuba if the situation got out of hand. A civil defence expert told Kennedy that 92 million Americans were vulnerable to attack and shelters were available to only 40 million.[7] Agonising aloud Kennedy pondered the grave implications for his country and the world if the single most dangerous episode in the history of mankind spiralled out of control.

After Kennedy's television speech outlining the crisis to the American people the world understood they were facing the gravest confrontation of the Cold War. One in five Americans believed World War III was about to start. Had most Americans been aware of some of the courses of action Kennedy considered, the figures would have been much higher. None of the courses of action proposed by his political and military advisors were guaranteed to prevent a nuclear holocaust. One, however, the blockade of Soviet ships carrying the missiles to Cuba, succeeded. Had another course of action been chosen the history of the world may have looked very different.

However, many failed to understand that the course of action which was eventually decided upon was not without grave dangers. The risks were high even for this non-belligerent action. Any delay or advance notice of military action in taking out the missiles or invading the island, for example, would have allowed for the speeding up of the missile sites or enable them to be moved to more secure sites. Some argued that a blockade would have created an American-Soviet confrontation rather than one between the United States and Cuba.

There was no doubt amongst Kennedy's advisors that the missiles had to be removed. To allow them to remain would have severely harmed the security of the United States and its allies around the world. It was nearly universally recognised by Congress and the policy-making establishment that nuclear missiles in Cuba could not be accepted by the American people. Robert Kennedy also recognised that the status quo would have had grave implications for U.S./Latin relations: "The other problem is in South America a year from now. And the fact that you got these in the hands of the Cubans here and then say some problem arises in Venezuela. You've got Castro saying...'you move troops down into that part of Venezuela...we're going to fire these missiles."[8]

President Kennedy weighed the alternative courses of action but finally settled on a blockade as the least dangerous path to take. He was convinced, at this time, that the blockade would buy time for further diplomatic and political moves to reduce the tensions. Eventually, he thought, only two options would remain - an invasion of Cuba or massive air strikes against the missile sites and major Cuban installations. And if that had happened war would be inevitable.

Once the strategy had been decided upon it became a matter of implementing it - constant surveillance of the island and putting the Navy ships in place to begin the long wait to see if Soviet ships would respond to American orders to halt. The Russians continued to construct the bases whilst the decision-making in Washington continued.

On Friday October 26th, an opening to solving the problem appeared. Kruschev sent a secret telegram which seemed to offer a deal - the missiles would be removed from Cuba in return for an American promise not to invade Cuba. A resolution of the crisis seemed to be near.

It was not to be. A Russian ship, the Grozny, was fast approaching the blockade line, threatening the face-off that everyone feared. Later news arrived at the White House that a U2 spy plane which had been photographing the construction of the bases had gone missing - it had been shot down and the pilot killed. More importantly Kruschev appeared to have changed his mind about the offer he made the day before. Now he was becoming more intransigent and 'upped the ante' - the deal would now have to include the removal of the American nuclear missiles from Turkey.

However, this added condition caused grave problems for Kennedy. If the proposal to remove the missiles from Turkey had been accepted publicly it would appear that America had abandoned its allies in favour of self-interest. The implications for the NATO alliance (which had preserved the peace since the end of the Second World War) were profound.

Kennedy had been caught in another bind - why should a war start over obsolete American missiles? It became a dilemma for Kennedy and his advisors. Eventually a solution was found. RFK initiated 'back-channel' communications with Georgi Bolshakov, a GRU agent in the Russian embassy in Washington DC. It was through Bolshakov that the exchange of Jupiter missiles in Turkey was first broached. Kennedy promised that discussions about the U.S. missiles would eventually take place after consultation with Turkey and NATO, but this deal had to remain secret. Giving up the Jupiter missiles was not a defeat, as Dean Acheson, the former Secretary of State under Harry Truman, said. In fact it was a prudent move. If Kennedy had to lose face it was a small price to pay to prevent nuclear annihilation.

The plan succeeded. Kruschev announced that Soviet missiles would be returned to the Soviet Union. As Kruschev's son-in-law Alexsei Adzhubei said: "He (Kruschev) got scared because Kennedy was putting up such stiff resistance."[9]

Beginning in the 1970s, many writers began to adopt a revisionist position about Kennedy's role in the crisis. Up to this time it had generally been accepted that the President had acted wisely in his response to the placing of the missiles. Kennedy had been praised by most Americans for not invading Cuba and for not precipitating an escalation of the crisis. However, many critics now believed Kennedy should not have brought the world to the brink of a nuclear holocaust in the first place. Later, in the 1980s and 1990s, authors like Gary Wills (1981) and Seymour Hersh (1997) accused Kennedy of precipitating the crisis by pursuing a policy which included plans for invading Cuba and a reckless support for 'Operation Mongoose'. This plan, under the control of Robert Kennedy, was designed to topple the Castro regime by using the CIA and Cuban exile groups in a concerted effort to sabotage Cuban installations, destroy the Cuban economy and remove Castro from power. The CIA interpreted this last initiative to include the assassination of the Cuban leader. Wills wrote in his book 'The Kennedy imprisonment' (1981):

> "...Kennedy could have explained to Americans that Castro was the object of secret warfare on the part of the CIA. This was something that would have been hard, and no doubt seemed impossible, to do. But the course was 'unthinkable' only because Kennedy's search for 'options' imprisoned him in the lies told to cover those options; and refusal to admit that his own acts caused the missile crisis in the first place makes it impossible to claim that EVERY effort to make peace was explored and EVERY possible chance for manoeuvre allowed to the other side."[10]

Seymour Hersh told 'Atlantic Unbound' reporter Katie Bacon: "He (Kennedy) took us to the edge of World War Three. I think the one thing you have to remember about John F. Kennedy and the missile crisis is that Kennedy and his brother Robert understood more than anyone else, with the exception of Nikita Kruschev and Fidel Castro, how much Kennedy's reckless desire to have Castro assassinated led to the missile crisis."[11]

However, the reasons for the placement of the missiles in Cuba are much more complex than Hersh, Wills and others suggest.

For Moscow, Cuba was a means to an end - the defeat of 'American Imperialism'. Evidence that 'Operation Mongoose' and the Kennedy desire to get rid of Castro were not the real reasons for the placing of the missiles can be gleaned from statements made by Carlos Franqui, friend of Fidel Castro and editor of the Cuban newspaper 'Revoluçion' from 1956 to 1963. Franqui had been invited to interview Kruschev in Moscow in October 1960. Franqui maintains that Kruschev had been planning to make Cuba a Soviet base ever since relations were formed with the Caribbean nation and before the Kennedy Administration took office. Franqui's evidence thus disputes Wills' and Hersh's claims. He told BBC researchers: "Nikita Kruschev spoke about missiles in Cuba. I spent an entire evening discussing this with him in the Kremlin. The idea was to negotiate from a position of equal strength. He meant to propose a treaty whereby the United States would withdraw its bases from Turkey and elsewhere. He'd then withdraw from Cuba and the Americans would guarantee that Cuba wouldn't be invaded."[12]

Two years later Alexander Alekseev, the KGB agent who had been sent to Cuba to determine if the new Cuban leader was indeed a communist, was given the job of discussing the deployment of the nuclear missiles with Fidel Castro. Alekseev was told by Kruschev to emphasise that the missiles were not meant to serve Soviet ambitions but to defend Cuba. However, even Castro saw through this ploy. Alekseev told BBC researchers: "Fidel thought for a moment and said, 'Yes, it's a very interesting idea. If it will really help the socialist camp then we'll consider it.' (Alekseev said) 'No, Fidel, it's not a matter of it being needed by the socialist camp. It's a matter of saving the Cuban Revolution. There's no other way.' But Fidel understood that we were, of course, pursuing our own interests."[13]

It is true that Kruschev had received intelligence reports that the Pentagon had included in its planning an invasion of Cuba for late 1962.[14] Cuban intelligence had infiltrated the CIA and purloined a number of documents. One CIA document stated that if by October 1962 Castro had not been removed from power, "we will have to do something tougher". Another purloined document 'from a well-placed source in the U.S national security bureaucracy' claimed that America had decided to launch a pre-emptive strike on the Soviet Union in September 1961.[15] This information was interpreted as an invasion plan and Cuban intelligence passed it on to the KGB which in turn informed Kruschev. Kennedy had no intention of invading the island. He had told the press, in response to Republican calls to invade, "unilateral military intervention on the part of the United States cannot currently be either required or justified."[16] The Pentagon plans were a natural part of contingency planning and not a definite blueprint for invasion. The military had been advocating an invasion of Cuba prompted by an 'excuse' to go in. One such idea involved John Glenn's spaceflight. In the event something went wrong with the flight Castro could be blamed.[17] In the Spring of 1962 the practice invasion of a Caribbean island (code-named 'ORTSAC', Castro spelled backwards) was designed only to take Castro's attentions away from his plans to export his revolution to other Latin American countries. Again, the Soviets believed this was planning for the invasion of Cuba.

Cuban intelligence officers had also infiltrated the CIA-led exile groups and learned that the final success of 'Operation Mongoose' would require U.S. military intervention. But Kennedy had not authorised military intervention at any stage. Soviet Intelligence THOUGHT they knew of Pentagon plans to invade the island but the reality of the situation was that another invasion of Cuba to simply topple Castro would have destroyed America's relationship with the OAS (Organisation of American States) and Kennedy's 'Alliance for Progress'. And Kennedy had always maintained, even before and during the Bay of Pigs debacle, that an invasion would not be in the interests of the United States. As recently released classified documents testify, Kennedy had no plans for invasion - at least for the three month period after September 1962. This is why he vigorously supported 'Operation Mongoose', the CIA-led plan to support Cuban exile groups - it was these groups and not the American military which had to be responsible for ridding Cuba of Castro's regime.

Domingo Amuchastegui served with the Cuban general staff and later in the Ministry of Foreign Affairs and the intelligence department of the Cuban Ministry of the Interior. He has stated that he knew that Kruschev lied to Castro about the reasons why the missiles were deployed and that they were neither a response to America's plans to 'invade Cuba' nor a response to the assassination attempts against Castro. Amuchastegui said that from the Bay of Pigs invasion until the summer of 1962 the evidence "suggested precisely the opposite trend, that a U.S. invasion of Cuba was becoming less likely all the time." He wrote in 'Intelligence and National Security' magazine: "The Cuban intelligence community was initially inclined to credit the sincerity of Soviet assessments and to try and account for the differences between the Soviet and Cuban judgements (about invasion plans). However, the discrepancies were simply too great to explain. After Soviet nuclear forces began to arrive in Cuba, Cuban intelligence concluded that the Soviets had skewed their assessments in order to persuade Castro to agree to the deployment, which was intended primarily to serve Soviet geo-political objectives and not, as Kruschev professed, to deter an American invasion."[18]

Furthermore, if the sole purpose in placing the missiles was to prevent an invasion of Cuba, Kruschev could have deployed Soviet troops without the missiles, thus making a conflict between Soviet and American forces too dangerous if an invasion had indeed been planned. Kruschev could also have deployed only the short range tactical nuclear weapons that could have reached offensive U.S. ships offshore but held no threat to the American mainland. Hersh's (1997) and Wills' (1981) arguments that Kruschev's prime motivating factor in deploying the missiles was a response to Kennedy's Cuba policy, are thus made redundant.

Hersh and Wills were, in effect, relying too much on Kruschev's own explanations of why he placed the missiles. The Soviet leader's reasons do not stand up to careful scrutiny. Kruschev maintained that on the evidence presented by his intelligence that an invasion was being planned for October 1962, it became incumbent upon him to protect the Cuban Revolution. But installing missiles to simply prop up the Castro regime was simply too risky and the pay-off would have been minimal. A communist Cuba was not essential to Soviet security and the same ends could have been achieved by simply concluding a Soviet-Cuban Mutual Defence Treaty whereby any attack on Cuba would be treated as an attack on the Soviet Union. This was exactly the position taken by the United States in its relationship with West Germany and the NATO countries. Kruschev wanted to build a full-scale strategic base, not simply to prevent an invasion of Cuba, but to transform the Soviet Union's strategic power - why else would plans for a nuclear submarine base have been part of his plans?

The first cause of the crisis is to be found in the larger Cold War context. The crisis cannot be viewed in the context of Cuban/American relations alone but in the adversarial conflict between America and Russia. It had become apparent, after the U.S. 1960 presidential election, that the United States arsenal of nuclear weapons far outnumbered the Soviet's. Moreover, the Soviet arsenal consisted of primitive technology. Kruschev had a burning desire to 'catch up'. Kennedy had said to his advisors during the crisis: "What is the advantage? Must be that they're not satisfied with their IRBM's." Later he said: "It makes them look as if they're co-equal with us...this is a political struggle as much as military."[19] Kruschev (1971), writing in his memoirs said: "...now they would know just what it feels like to have enemy missiles pointing at you, we'd be doing nothing more than giving them a little taste of their own medicine. And it was high time...America has never had to fight a war on her own soil, at least not in the past fifty years. She's sent troops abroad to fight in two world wars - and made a fortune as a result. America has shed a few drops of her own blood while making billions by bleeding the rest of the world dry."[20]

The United States had surrounded the Soviet Union with medium-range missiles in Europe capable of reaching important targets in only a few minutes. Soviet ICBMs were thousands of miles from targets in the

United States and their guidance systems were primitive. In effect, Kruschev was concerned that the United States had the upper hand. America's deployment of Jupiter missiles in Turkey simply made it easier for Kruschev to rationalise his decision to place missiles in Cuba - a decision, as we have seen, which had been made a few years previously. If preventing an invasion of Cuba was indeed the motivating factor why did Kruschev later say: 'It was high time America learned what it feels like to have her own land and her own people threatened.'? Kruschev was willing to gamble that missiles in Cuba, 'putting a hedgehog under America's T-shirt', as he put it, would correct the imbalance.

Kruschev was also becoming frustrated with his inability to remove the Western powers from Berlin. This is the key to understanding why missiles were placed in Cuba. Kruschev had plans for Berlin in 1962. He would rid the city of the Western powers but he knew that the United States had irrevocably committed its nuclear might to protect the citizens of West Berlin. Kruschev could only accomplish his aims for Berlin if he held a trump card and, something to bargain with.

During this period Kruschev was also experiencing severe criticisms about his inability to address serious errors of judgement especially in agriculture, and he failed to take opportunities which arose in Africa and South-East Asia. He also mishandled the ideological battles with the Chinese and Albanians who accused the Soviet Government of being 'revisionist'. The military was upset because Kruschev had cut their budgets. Kruschev was therefore under extreme pressure to 'do something'. He desperately needed a quick victory. At this point a Soviet military movement in Berlin was out of the question - Kennedy had made his intentions clear and any change in the status quo would lead to war. In a televised address on July 25th 1961 he said: "we have given our word that an attack upon that city will be regarded as an attack upon us all...if war begins, it will have begun in Moscow, not Berlin."[21]

Kruschev decided that Cuba was to be the excuse for the placing of missiles but there is some evidence that he really believed he was also protecting the only 'socialist' state in the Western Hemisphere. He had genuine fears for Cuban security. Kruschev liked and admired Castro and was susceptible to the Cuban leader's demands for further assistance against the Cuban exiles' major threat. He also believed Castro when he said that a second U.S. invasion was imminent. There was also an element of pride in Kruschev's desire to aid Cuba. If he could not support the new and only communist regime in the Western hemisphere how would other 'revolutionary' nations around the world respond to the Soviet Union? He was obsessed with the question in his mind - 'What would happen if we lost Cuba?'[22] However, it is likely that Kruschev's sympathies for his socialist comrades in the Caribbean was a convenient mask to hide his real intentions. According to Anastas Mikoyan, the Soviet Foreign Minister at the time, Kruschev's prime motive was to bring about a "definite shift in the power relationship between the socialist and capitalist worlds".[23] Even Castro recognised Kruschev's underlying motives. He told a CNN reporter that if it had simply been a question of Cuba's defence, then the Cuban leaders would not have accepted the missiles.[24] The defence of Cuba was to be the umbrella under which all Kruschev's ambitions could be achieved. The deployment of the Jupiter missiles simply made it easier for Kruschev to rationalise his decision. In effect Kruschev was closing the gap 'on the cheap'.

Kennedy has come under criticism from revisionist writers and scholars for his recklessness in not immediately offering to exchange the Jupiter missiles in Turkey for the missiles in Cuba. He has also been criticised for not simply allowing the missiles to remain on Cuban soil. However, in 1962 and, in the context of Cold War power politics, these options would likely have been dangerous. And the danger would have emerged from Kruschev's perceptions of President Kennedy.

Kruschev knew that Kennedy had done nothing when the Berlin Wall was erected in August 1961. He had judged Kennedy as weak after the young and inexperienced President had backed off from supporting the Cuban exiles in their invasion of Cuba. When the Berlin Wall had been erected, Kennedy had accepted it. If Kennedy had done nothing and allowed the missiles to remain in Cuba, the outcry from the American people would likely have led to his impeachment by Congress, according to Arthur Schlesinger (1978).[25] The climate of the time mitigated against any American moves which smacked of 'appeasement'. The Cold War realities of the time prevented any response from an American president that would have indicated weakness. Munich and the folly of appeasement were uppermost in the minds of most politicians, both Democrat and Republican. If Kennedy had immediately responded by offering to dismantle the U.S. missile bases in Turkey, Kruschev would likely have taken this move as further evidence of Kennedy's weakness - it was Berlin that Kruschev was really concerned about and he would have 'upped the ante' to include Berlin in the negotiations - Kruschev's determination to force Western troops out of Berlin played a large part in his thinking. The consequences for Germany, NATO and American guarantees to allies around the world would have been catastrophic. And it was not only De Gaulle who mistrusted American promises. A settlement which did not show 'American resolve' would have led European leaders to believe that, in times of crisis, Americans would retreat. This option, then, would have made the world a less safe place, damaging international stability and virtually guaranteeing that the Soviets would use similar threats in the future. It should be remembered that Europe's freedom depended on American guarantees of support if the Soviet Union invaded. The Soviets had lied about the Cuban missiles - what would happen if they lied again? Kennedy's decision was both balanced and judicious - it was not safe to do nothing and it was not safe to overreact - his answer lay in a compromise of options.

Kennedy was only too aware of how Kruschev thought and acted, but this did not prevent him from being bullied by Kruschev. However, his lessons about 'realpolitik' were lessons learned well during his June 1961 meeting with Kruschev in Vienna. As British Prime Minister, Harold MacMillan, was to observe: "The President was completely overwhelmed by the ruthlessness and barbarity of the Russian Chairman. It reminded me in a way of Lord Halifax or Neville Chamberlain trying to hold a conversation with Herr Hitler".[26]

It is unlikely, therefore, that Kruschev would have responded in a meaningful way if Kennedy had presented photographic evidence of the missiles in secret negotiations. It is likely that Kruschev would have used private negotiations to his advantage. After all the Soviet premier, in the early stages of the crisis, was belligerent and stubborn. Two of his closest advisors called Kruschev "azartnyi" meaning "reckless" or "hotheaded". Kennedy was well aware that Kruschev could be domineering, arrogant and stubborn. In short Kennedy mistrusted his adversary. And he had good reason. The Soviet premier not only lied to his Ambassador in Washington, Anatoli Dobrynin, but also to Fidel Castro.

Former Cuban Intelligence officer, Domingo Amuchastegui, has revealed how, against the advice of his own espionage service, President Castro believed Kruschev's opinion that America planned to invade Cuba - thus justifying the deployment of the nuclear missiles and thousands of troops on the island. Kruschev had lied to Castro.

The most telling aspect of the whole affair is the way in which Kruschev lied to Kennedy. It reveals something about Kruschev's view of the American President. He knew Kennedy had shown weakness in the Bay of Pigs debacle and at his meeting in Vienna. Kruschev had concluded he was weak, ineffectual and spoilt. In lying to Kennedy about the missiles, he was again showing a lack of respect for the young and inexperienced President, no doubt believing Kennedy would freeze with indecision when U.S. intelligence presented him with evidence about the missiles.

'The Kennedy tapes', (May and Zelikow, 1997) reveal in stark detail that Kennedy's actions and demeanour during the crisis were not how Seymour Hersh and other revisionist authors characterised him. Barry Gewen of the 'New York Times' wrote: "(The Kennedy tapes show) the image of a Lincolnesque Kennedy, lonely, melancholy, grimly persevering...the aptly titled 'Kennedy tapes' stands as a lasting testament to one man's judgement and character."[27]

From these recordings of the decision-making processes within the White House, we can see that Kennedy's cool perseverance and determination were critical in resolving the crisis. He displayed a willingness and a capacity to listen, question, weigh and consider. There is little doubt that his own experiences in the Second World War informed his judgement. During that conflict he had written to his father: "When I read that we will fight the Japs for years if necessary and will sacrifice hundreds of thousands if we must - I always like to check from where he is talking - it's seldom out here. People get so used to talking about billions of dollars and millions of soldiers that thousands of dead sounds like drops in the bucket. But if those thousands want to live as much as the ten I saw - they should measure their words with great, great care."[28]

At each turn Kennedy chose the most moderate available option sometimes or often against the specialised advice of the military and State Department. He wisely rejected the advice of Senator Richard Russell, Chairman of the Senate Armed Services Committee, who told him that a war on which America's destiny was hinged was "coming someday, Mr President...Will it ever be under more auspicious circumstances?" He also rejected the advice of Senator Carl Vinson, Chairman of the House Armed Services Committee, who wanted to "strike with all the force and power (America possessed) and try to get it over with as quickly as possible."[29] And Kennedy's emotional response to the crisis and bearing exemplified Hemingway's definition of courage - "grace under pressure". As Isaiah Berlin told Arthur Schlesinger for the JFK Library: "He was very amiable. He was in a jolly mood which was remarkable considering that that was the morning on which he had been shown the photographs of the Soviet installations on Cuba. And I must say the sang-froid which he displayed and the extraordinary capacity for self-control, on a day on which he must have been intensely preoccupied was one of the most astonishing exhibitions of self-restraint and strength of will that I think I've ever seen."[30]

Throughout the two weeks of the crisis, Kennedy took cautious and wise decisions at every turn of the conflict:

- Instead of an invasion he preferred an air strike on military bases.

- Instead of a total air strike he preferred selective strikes only.

- He insisted that no strikes go ahead until a warning had been given.

- Kennedy opted for a naval blockade instead of immediate military action and a partial naval quarantine instead of a blanket blockade of all ships.

- Kennedy chose a non-Soviet ship (Panamanian) for the symbolic initiation of the quarantine, carefully choosing not to belligerently challenge a Soviet vessel.

- The quarantine was not undertaken until his staff made sure that all legal and possible international support had been obtained. Kennedy did not want to shake the Allies confidence and so his actions had to be prudent and legal. There were long memories of the Suez crisis when America had acted in its own self-interest.

- Kennedy rejected advice to seize the missile carrying ships in order to learn more about Soviet weaponry. Instead he ordered the ships be stopped and turned back.

- A contingency plan had been set up which planned for the immediate destruction of any SAM site if any of America's spy planes had been shot down. He rejected this aggressive response after Colonel Rudolf Anderson's U-2 was shot down over Cuba. Kennedy said he needed time to consult with Kruschev.

- Kennedy seized the opportunity to use the Jupiter missiles as an instrument of bargaining and indeed ordered the missiles defused during the crisis.

- Kennedy reduced the quarantine zone from 800 to 500 miles.

- In 1962 a CIA spy camera held within a satellite launched from Vandenburg airbase in California had changed the psychological position of nuclear, Cold War confrontation. It revealed detailed information that the Soviet Union did not have four or five hundred ICBM's but less than 25. Consequently, although the Soviet Union was at a disadvantage of 17-1 in intercontinental missiles, Kennedy wisely took no notice, believing as he did, that enough Soviet missiles would survive a U.S. attack to kill millions of Americans. He stated that: "No responsible political leader would expose his nation to such catastrophe."

- Repeatedly, Kennedy told his advisors that the object was to get the missiles out of Cuba but that the tactical goal was "to give Kruschev room." Kennedy said: "I don't want to put him in a corner."

- Seymour Hersh paints a picture of Kennedy gloating at the victory over Kruschev. On the contrary Kennedy prevented his government from issuing any statement which would have indicated this. When Kennedy watched CBS news and saw two correspondents reporting an American 'victory' he told his press secretary, Pierre Salinger, to tell them to stop.[31]

- It has emerged that Kennedy would never have pushed the crisis to insane levels. He had a secret 'reserve position'.[32] If everything else had failed to bring the situation to a satisfactory conclusion he would have authorised Secretary of State, Dean Rusk, to encourage UN Secretary General, U Thant, to propose a 'public' missile swap which the U.S. would then have accepted. This, in itself, is proof that Kennedy was willing to go to any length to avoid a nuclear war and, if necessary, back down to Kruschev's proposals even if, as stated above, this may have irreparably damaged the NATO alliance and encouraged future irresponsible moves by the Soviet leader. However, he knew that at least initially he must show resolve and strength. Republicans were issuing severe criticism during the summer of 1962 for Kennedy's irresolution over the issue of Cuba. And he was well aware of a recent Congressional resolution which sanctioned the use of force to protect the hemisphere against Cuban or Russian aggression. Leading statesmen and political scientists had continually advised Kennedy, correctly, that the only way to deal with the Soviets was from a position of strength and resolve, given the nature of the communist ideology and the Soviet leadership's acceptance of Lenin's adage: "if a man sticks out a bayonet and strikes mush, he keeps on pushing, but when he hits cold steel he pulls back."

All of the above actions and decisions were made in the face of severe criticism from some or all of his military advisors, many of whom were 'disgusted' at Kennedy.

Kennedy obtained the best possible results under the circumstances - he was not just lucky but used his skills of patience, moderation, independent judgement, a preference for negotiation above confrontation, wisely to bring the crisis to an end. In short, as the authors of 'The Kennedy tapes' (May and Zelikow, 1997) suggest: "It seems fortunate that, given the circumstances that he had helped to create, Kennedy was the president charged with managing the crisis."[33]

The consensus amongst historians and political scientists who have studied the newly declassified documents from the American and Russian archives is that both Kennedy and Kruschev overcame severe pressures from their 'hawks'. Kennedy held firm against insistence by the U.S. military on air strikes and invasion while Kruschev ignored Castro and Soviet military leaders in his decision to order the return of the missiles.

Kennedy had achieved victory but at a cost. Quite rightly he used a certain amount of compromise to settle the crisis - if he had done otherwise this would have given Seymour Hersh and other Kennedy critics reason to describe his behaviour as 'reckless'. His actions during the Cuban Missile Crisis were a model of presidential conduct - do not humiliate your adversary, give your advisors time to consider the issues, weigh all options, do not respond impulsively and consider the larger context. Above all, safeguard the vital interests of the United States through resolution and strength.

In addressing the controversy as to whether or not Kennedy was a 'hero' of the confrontation (as Kennedy supporters argue) or a man dishonestly playing electoral politics (as revisionists argue), it should be remembered that Kruschev's own advisors called the Soviet leader's actions as 'irresponsible'. Thirty years after the event, one of the Soviet officials in Washington at the time of the crisis, Soviet Foreign Ministry official, Georgy Kornienko, said: "There is no doubt it (Soviet acquiescence to U.S. demands to remove the missiles) was a humiliation, no doubt a well-deserved humiliation...because it was really a stupid thing."[34] And Kruschev himself, in his memoirs, predicted that history would judge Kennedy as "an outstanding statesman...I'll always remember the late President with deep respect because, in the final analysis, he showed himself to be sober-minded and determined to avoid war. He didn't let himself become frightened; nor did he become reckless."[35]

Kruschev had acted recklessly in trying to change the nuclear balance of power in one swift move. Kennedy had responded in the only sane way possible within the strictures of his leadership of a nation which could not accept any Soviet moves outside the accepted confines of Cold War realities. To do nothing would have led to further conflict; it was an impossible option. As Dean Rusk said 30 years after the crisis: "The political aspects of the problem would have been devastating not only in the Western hemisphere but also in NATO, had we not responded to these missiles 90 miles off the American coast."[36] To settle the conflict by immediately giving away the Jupiter missiles and promising not to invade Cuba, Kennedy would have proven once and for all that Kruschev had been correct - Kennedy was ineffectual and weak. The message would have been clear to Kruschev and NATO - the Soviet Empire could be confident enough that any belligerent moves on their behalf in the European arena would be met by irresolution and retreat. The implications for a stable world would have been disastrous and it would behove writers like Seymour Hersh to consider and weigh this stark fact.

Notes

1. Hersh, S. (1997). *The dark side of Camelot*, Little Brown and Co. p. 345.

2. *Ibid*, p. 345.

3. 'The Cuban missile crisis'. Narrated by Michael Jayston, executive producer Mick Csaky (for Antelope Films), producers Shinji Masuda and Hioshi Yasuda (for TV Asahi). BBC Television, 1992; 'Larry King live'. Interview with Robert McNamara. CNN, 1992.

4. Fursenko, A. and Naftali, T. (1999). *One hell of a gamble*, Pimlico. p. 188.

5. George Ball, "JFK's big moment", *New York Review of Books*, 13 February 1992, p. 40.

6. 'The Cuban missile crisis'. Narrated by Michael Jayston, executive producer Mick Csaky (for Antelope Films), produced by Shinji Masuda and Hioshi Yasuda (for TV Asahi). BBC Television, 1992.

7. May, E. R. and Zelikow, P. D. (1997), *The Kennedy tapes - inside the White House during the Cuban missile crisis*, The Belknap Press of the Harvard University Press. p. 339.

8. Beschloss, M. R. (1991). *Kennedy v. Kruschev - the crisis years 1960-1963*, Faber and Faber. p. 442.

9. 'The Cuban missile crisis'. Narrated by Michael Jayston, executive producer Mick Csaky (for Antelope Films), producers Shinji Masuda and Hioshi Yasuda (for TV Asahi). BBC Television, 1992.

10. Wills, G. (1981). *The Kennedy imprisonment*, Little Brown and Co. p. 265.

11. Bacon, K. "Darker than we want to know", *Atlantic Unbound*, 8 January 1998. (http: //www.the atlantic.com).

12. 'The Cuban missile crisis'. Narrated by Michael Jayston, executive producer Mick Csaky (for Antelope Films), produced by Shinji Masuda and Hioshi Yasuda (for TV Asahi). BBC Television, 1992.

13. *Ibid.*

14. Hershberg, J. G. 'New evidence on the Cuban missile crisis: more documents from the Russian archives', *Cold War International History Project*, Wodrow Wilson International Center for Scholars. (http://wwics.si.edu/internat.htm).

15. "The peasant premier", BBC Timewatch Documentary, 1995.

16. May, E. R. and Zelikow, P. D. (1997), *The Kennedy tapes - inside the White House during the Cuban missile crisis*, The Belknap Press of the Harvard University Press. p. 37; Hilty, J. W. (1997). *Robert Kennedy – brother protector*, Temple University Press. p. 443. Robert McNamara was "absolutely positive that President Kennedy never, at any time" between 20 January 1961 and 14 October 1962 "had any intention whatsoever to invade Cuba." Also, McNamara said: "There were public voices...who said...the next time...we would have to support it with U.S. military force...The Cubans and the Soviets looking at that concluded...there would be a next time." 'The Cuban missile crisis'. Narrated by Michael Jayston, executive producer Mick Csaky (for Antelope Films), produced by Shinji Masuda and Hioshi Yasuda (for TV Asahi). BBC Television, 1992.

17. Lardner, G. and Pincus, W. 'Military plan to blame Cuba if Glenn's space mission failed', *Washington Post*, 19 November 1997. (http://washingtonpost.com).

18. Eans, M. 'Kruschev lied to Castro to get missiles into Cuba', *The Times*, 5 October 1998, p. 12.

19. Reeves, R. (1993). *President Kennedy - profile of power*, Simon and Schuster. p. 373.

20. Kruschev, N. (1971). *Kruschev remembers*, London Book Club Ass. p. 494.

21. Beschloss, M. R. (1991). *Kennedy v. Kruschev - the crisis years 1960-1963*, Faber and Faber. p. 259.

22. May, E. R. and Zelikow, P. D. (1997), *The Kennedy tapes - inside the White House during the Cuban missile crisis*, The Belknap Press of the Harvard University Press. p. 671.

23. Schlesinger, A. M. (1978). *Robert Kennedy and his times*, Houghton Mifflin Co. p. 544.

24. 'Castro in his own words'. Fidel Castro interviewed by Pat Mitchell. CNN, 16 October, 1998.

25. Schlesinger, A. M. (1978). *Robert Kennedy and his times*, Houghton Mifflin Co. p. 552.

26. May, E. R. and Zelikow, P. D. (1997), *The Kennedy tapes - inside the White House during the Cuban missile crisis,* The Belknap Press of the Harvard University Press. p. 30.

27. Gewen, B. 'Profile in caution', *New York Times*, 19 October 1997. (http://www.nytimes.com).

28. Goodwin, D. K. (1988). *The Fitzgeralds and the Kennedys*, Pan Books. p. 659.

29. Sorensen, T. 'The leader who led', *New York Times*, 18 October 1997. (http://www.nytimes.com).

30. Schlesinger, A. M. 'An interview with Isaiah Berlin', JFK Library. (http://library.kennedy.nara.gov).

31. Reeves, R. (1993). *President Kennedy - profile of power*, Simon and Schuster. p. 424.

32. Rusk, D., Rusk, R. and Papp, D. (1990). *As I saw it*, Norton New York. p. 240.

33. May, E. R. and Zelikow, P. D. (1997), *The Kennedy tapes - inside the White House during the Cuban missile crisis*, The Belknap Press of the Harvard University Press. p. 696.

34. 'The Cuban missile crisis'. Narrated by Michael Jayston, executive producer Mick Csaky (for Antelope Films), produced by Shinji Masuda and Hioshi Yasuda (for TV Asahi). BBC Television, 1992.

35. Kruschev, N. (1971). *Kruschev remembers*, London Book Club Ass. p. 500.

36. 'The Cuban missile crisis'. Narrated by Michael Jayston, executive producer Mick Csaky (for Antelope Films), produced by Shinji Masuda and Hioshi Yasuda (for TV Asahi). BBC Television, 1992.

Chapter 4

The Castro Murder Plots

Did President Kennedy authorise the CIA to kill Castro?

"Who will rid me of this turbulent priest?"

King Henry II, December 29th 1170

One of the most famous statements made during the Watergate Hearings which led to the downfall of President Nixon came from Senator Howard Baker. "What did the President know and when did he know it?" he asked, referring to Nixon's knowledge of the burglary of Democratic Party headquarters in the Watergate Building and the subsequent cover-up.

The 'smoking gun' Oval Office audio tape recording eventually gave the unequivocal answer to Baker's questions. The same questions may be asked about President Kennedy's alleged involvement in the CIA plots to kill Cuban leader Fidel Castro - what did the President know about the plots and when did he find out?

Unfortunately we will never learn the answer from the recordings that President Kennedy made in the Oval Office. Kennedy Library archivists state that no recordings concerning the matter exist. Many authors have speculated that the recordings were destroyed in order to cover up the President's involvement, but they present no evidence to indicate that the tapes which were removed from the White House after the President's assassination included material pertinent to the Castro plots.[1]

President Kennedy's role in the CIA inspired plots against Castro first surfaced in the late 1960s when investigative reporters Drew Pearson and Jack Anderson intimated Kennedy's involvement in a series of newspaper articles. The 'revelations', incredible as they are, were not met with national attention. Many fellow reporters and newspapers dismissed Anderson's stories as 'not credible'. The story faded away. But it prompted President Johnson to call for a secret internal CIA report on the murder plots. It was released in 1997 and was entitled "The Inspector General's report of 1967 on CIA plots to Assassinate Fidel Castro". No blame was put on either John or Robert Kennedy for 'authorising' the plots to murder Castro.

It was not until 1975 that the American public learned of the details of the CIA plots when the United States Senate conducted an enquiry into the affairs of the Central Intelligence Agency. At the same time President Ford appointed a special commission to also investigate the Agency. The commission was headed by Ford's Vice-President, Nelson Rockefeller, and became known as the Rockefeller Commission. However, the Rockefeller Commission did not go too deeply into the CIA's foreign assassination plots but instead concentrated on the Agency's domestic transgressions.

The Senate's report (called the Church Committee Report after its Chairman, Senator Frank Church of Idaho) and the Rockefeller Commission Report concluded, after thorough investigations, that murder had been used as an instrument of foreign policy. The reports implied that, on balance, Presidents Eisenhower, Kennedy, Johnson and Nixon probably knew about the murder plots. They suggest it was more likely that they did than they did not. However, they produced no concrete evidence to prove any president authorised them. The matter has become an issue of controversy ever since stimulated by books which purport to 'prove' the Kennedy brothers knew and approved of the CIA murder plots against Castro.

The Senate Report spanned the post-war era of American foreign policy. It dealt with plans to kill the Congolese nationalist, Patrice Lumumba; the sending of vital aid to the assassins of Dominican Republic dictator, Rafael Trujillo; and eight attempts to kill Fidel Castro (it is likely there were many more but not necessarily CIA inspired. In 1999, Colonel Jose Ferez Fernandez of the Cuban Interior Ministry said there had been a total of 637 attempts) and connivance at some level in the assassination of South Vietnamese leader, Ngo Dinh Diem.[2]

Many Americans were shocked to discover that President Kennedy may have ordered an assassination attempt. The revelations about the murder plots against Castro threatened to destroy the reputations of many New Frontiersmen and alter the historical record of John Kennedy's presidency.

Understanding the context of the murder attempts and the Kennedy brothers' responses to them requires a knowledge of the contemporary international political climate. For many it is difficult to understand, 40 years later, that Cuba was tied in to the global struggle between the United States and the Soviet Union. In the post-war struggle around the world, forces seemed to be turning against the West. In Europe the Russians appeared determined to alter the status of Berlin unilaterally. The post-war revolutionary fervour that had begun in China and had moved to Korea, was about to influence Africa, Latin America and Asia. Ho Chi Minh, Patrice Lumumba and Fidel Castro were ready to tip the balance and there was a conviction that the Soviet Union had caught up with the West in the manufacture of Intercontinental Ballistic Missiles. The two superpowers were struggling to secure 'outposts' around the world in an ideological competition. Events in the Dominican Republic, the Congo and Cuba, amongst many others, appeared to offer the Soviet Union additional opportunities for communist expansion. Additionally, after the Bay of Pigs debacle, Castro felt secure enough to export his 'socialist revolution' to other countries in Latin America. The fear was so great that two Latin American Presidents (Guatemala and Venezuela) and a former president (Costa Rica) approved a 1961 plan, named 'Operation Condor', to assassinate Fidel Castro, his brother Raul Castro and Che Guevara. The operation was directed by Guatemala but the CIA made it possible. The plot collapsed.[3]

Covert action in fighting 'surrogate wars' was, during the 1950s and 1960s, an acceptable means to fight control and subversion by hostile forces committed to the Russian world view. From 1955 to 1970 the basic authority for covert operations was a directive of the National Security Council (NSC 5421/2). This directive instructed the CIA to counter, reduce and discredit 'international communism' throughout the world in a manner consistent with United States foreign and military policies. It also directed the CIA to undertake covert operations to achieve this end. Covert operations was defined as any covert activities related to propaganda, economic warfare and political action (including sabotage, demolition and assistance to resistance movements).

Beginning in 1955, the responsibility for authorising CIA covert action lay with the Special Group of the NSC composed of military and intelligence leaders with the support of presidential advisors. By the end of 1959, CIA Director, Allen Dulles, presented to President Eisenhower a CIA operational plan code-named the 'Cuban Project'. It was approved by the President and its goal was to 'eliminate' Fidel Castro. Shortly afterwards U.S. Government intelligence became alarmed about reports that Castro was planning to invade the U.S. Naval base at Guantanamo.

During the Eisenhower Administration, then, America's Central Intelligence Agency became engaged in subverting Third World regimes, supporting and supplying dissident groups for the purposes of supplanting the regimes in power. There was no question of whether or not these groups would attempt to kill government officials during these attempts. They surely would. This consequently raised the question - if deaths in these struggles were acceptable then why not the murder of leaders? After all, some reasoned, there was a good deal of evidence that the KGB were applying the same strategies.

After the election of John F. Kennedy and the subsequent failure of the Bay of Pigs invasion, the new President was determined to continue with the Eisenhower policy of ridding the Western Hemisphere of a communist regime. It was inevitable that the process would also include the 'toppling' of Cuban dictator, Fidel Castro, by Cuban exile groups stationed in the United States. By November 1961, another covert plan, 'Operation Mongoose', was taking off. This time the plan was to destabilise the Castro regime rather than topple it. Mongoose did not envision a U.S. military intervention until the internal revolt had succeeded. The idea was for the regime to be weakened by exiled terrorist groups who had illicitly entered Cuba in order to initiate an internal revolt or coup d'etat. Every possible tactic was used, including manipulating the price of sugar on international markets, paramilitary sabotage, psychological warfare and hostile diplomatic efforts. JFK installed his brother Robert to oversee the plan. It became the Administration's top priority and Robert was obsessed with seeing the project succeed. The younger brother pressured the CIA to 'get rid of Castro'. The first phase of 'Operation Mongoose' lasted from February until August 1962. The second phase, a more stepped up covert sabotage campaign, lasted from August until October or the end of the Missile Crisis. After this, the Kennedy Administration moved all such activities off the mainland of the USA and gradually began to cut any funding for them. By the summer of 1963, Kennedy was using the FBI to actually shut down certain exile training camps and activities in Louisiana and Florida.[4] However, it is likely JFK was pursuing a 'two-track' approach. Castro had been impressed with Kennedy's 'Peace' speech of June 1963 at the American University in Washington D.C. and was susceptible to 'talks'. But President Kennedy still involved himself with 'contingency plans' to topple the Castro regime.

The CIA believed that the assassination of Fidel Castro was within the brief they had received from Presidents Eisenhower and Kennedy. The serious nature of the lethal plots against Castro (as opposed to the non-lethal plots designed to make Castro's beard fall out and to make him appear crazy during his broadcasts to the Cuban people by spiking his drinks with LSD etc.) was highlighted during the Church Committee hearings when CIA Director, William Colby, handed a pistol to Chairman, Frank Church. Resembling a Colt .45 equipped with a telescopic sight, the gun was able to fire a toxin-tipped dart, almost silently and accurately up to 250 feet. The dart was tiny, the width of a human hair and a quarter of an inch long. The poison was undetectable and left no trace in the victim's body. Later CIA scientists came up with an array of similar tools, including a box of Castro's favourite brand of cigars made lethal with botulinum toxin. The cigars were delivered to an unknown person who was supposed to make them available to Castro. However, the box vanished. They also came up with a shellfish toxin. After receiving the toxin orally or by pinprick, the potential victim would first have felt a tingling sensation in the fingers and lips and would then have expired within 10 seconds of administration. U2 pilot, Gary Powers, carried the toxin as a suicide device hidden in a silver dollar at the time he was shot down over Russia in 1960.[5]

The plots to murder Castro really began on July 21st 1960 when a Cuban agent working for the CIA offered to kill Castro.[6] The agent was an Air Cuba pilot and was due to fly Castro, Che Guevara and Castro's brother, Raul, to Prague. The agent suggested 'an accident could occur'. However, Tracy Barnes, who was deputising for Deputy Director, Richard Bissell, at the time, was countermanded by CIA chief, Allen Dulles. Dulles rescinded the authority to go ahead with the plan. Unfortunately, the cable to the Cuban agent/pilot arrived too late. Luckily for Barnes the agent got cold feet and the 'accident' was averted.

This was quite a departure from normal CIA proceedings - it was the first time the assassination of a foreign leader had been authorised by CIA Headquarters. Assassination plots had been considered in the past, especially against Nassar and Stalin, but there was always the concern that these leaders would be replaced by men who were far worse.[7]

But the genie was now out of the bottle. Assassination to these World War II generation agents was not unthinkable and 'executive action' became a serious option. From 1959 onwards, beginning with a discussion about President Sukarno of Indonesia as a possible target, the idea that the CIA should use 'elimination with extreme prejudice' became institutionalised within the Agency.

Later, in 1960/61, the Mafia were called in through Robert Mahue, an ex-FBI man with close links to the CIA and who later became Howard Hughes' employee. Maheu made contact with mafia mob bosses Sam Giancana, Johnny Rosselli and Santos Trafficante who all had lost gambling interests in Cuba after Castro took power and had a natural grudge against the dictator. They accepted the assignment to kill Castro but turned down the 150,000 dollars which was offered. They, did however, accept 11,000 dollars in 'expenses'. Rosselli and Giancana were not told that the U.S. Government had put the contract out on Castro, but they 'guessed or assumed the CIA was behind the project', according to State Department documents released in 1997.[8]

The CIA suggested the gangsters carry out a 'gangland killing', but Giancana and Trafficante (both of them amongst the 10 most wanted criminals on Attorney-General Robert Kennedy's list) suggested something 'clean and quiet'. The CIA produced botulinum pills to be dropped in Castro's drink at a restaurant known to be frequented by the Cuban leader, but the Cuban agent lost his nerve.

The attempts against Castro, however, continued. In 1962 William Harvey was ordered by Deputy CIA Director, Richard Bissell, to establish a capability for disabling or eliminating foreign leaders, code-named ZR/RIFLE. One of its hired assassins was a former Luxembourg based smuggler named Jose Mankel who was given the code name QJ/WIN. He advised the CIA on the programme's first major task, the elimination of Castro. Under this programme William Harvey gave some poison pills and weapons to Rosselli, but the effort did not succeed.

The plotting continued. In 1963, a skin diver's suit was dusted with fungus calculated to cause a skin disease and its breathing apparatus was contaminated with tuberculae bacilli. James B. Donovan, the lawyer who negotiated the release of the Cuban exiles who were captured after the Bay of Pigs invasion, was to present it to Castro unwittingly, but the plan aborted in the laboratory. CIA officials never considered for a moment that, since the suit was a gift from the U.S. government, grave international embarrassment would surely follow Castro's death. Nor did they consider that the unwitting Donovan might try the suit on before he handed it over to the Cuban leader.

On the day President Kennedy was killed (November 22nd 1963), Rolando Cubela Secades, who was close to Castro, was meeting with CIA official Desmond Fitzgerald's envoy, Nestor Sanchez, in Paris.[9] Sanchez gave Cubela (code named AMLASH) a Papermate ball-point pen designed to inject poison. The poison suggested was Black Leaf 40. Cubela, a member of the Castro government, promised he would assassinate the Cuban leader as long as it was in conjunction with a coup d'etat and that he would have American support. Sanchez responded by calling attention to a speech President Kennedy had made four days earlier which the CIA official said Desmond Fitzgerald had helped to draft. He said the President had called the Castro government "a small band of conspirators" whose removal would assure Cuba of American support for progressive goals. That, he told Cubela, was the signal of the President's support for a coup. In testimony to the Church Committee, however, CIA Deputy Director for Plans, Richard Helms, insisted that the CIA was just 'temporising' and humouring Cubela to keep him working for the Agency. In any case the murder plot was called off.

The plots using AMLASH did not end, however, with JFK's assassination. In March and June of 1964 and early 1965 arms caches were provided for prospective Cuban assassination teams. AMLASH was provided with a silenced pistol through another group code-named B-1. These were low level schemes: Richard Helms had known of them; CIA director, John McCone, did not; and the evidence suggests that President Johnson was unaware. It was not until 1967 that Johnson angrily told one of a group of journalists: "We have been operating a damned Murder Inc. in the Caribbean."[10]

The Church Committee called the former CIA Deputy Director for Plans, Richard Helms (who succeeded Richard Bissell), to testify before the Senate body about plans to kill Castro. Helms became CIA Director in the late 1960s but was retired at the time of the Senate hearings. Helms said that when he was working under President Kennedy as head of the 'dirty tricks department', he came under 'intense pressure' from the Kennedy Administration which led him to believe that the assassination of Castro was not precluded. He told the Committee: "I believe it was the policy at the time to get rid of Castro and if killing him was one of the things...that was to be done in this connection, that was within what was expected."[11]

Others recalled that Bissell was 'chewed out' by John and Robert Kennedy for 'sitting on his ass...not doing anything about Castro'.[12] Therefore, according to Helms: "there were no limitations put on the means and we felt we were actually well within the guidelines...nobody wants to embarrass a president...by discussing the assassination of foreign leaders."[13]

It has been alleged by some writers that assassination as an instrument of foreign policy within a modern democratic system was first nurtured by John Kennedy. Seymour Hersh (1997) in his book 'The dark side of Camelot' relies heavily on Samuel Halpern, CIA executive assistant to three Directors for clandestine operations, who said that the Kennedys were obsessed about wanting Castro dead "for personal reasons - because the family name was besmirched by the Bay of Pigs."[14] Hersh maintains that Kennedy, unlike his predecessor Eisenhower, gave the orders to kill Castro. In an interview with journalist Katie Bacon, Hersh said that John and Robert Kennedy knew all about and approved the CIA's efforts to assassinate Castro.[15] Hersh (1997) notes that during the failed Bay of Pigs invasion, Kennedy was expecting Castro to have been eliminated before the invasion began thus paving the way for a jubilant Cuban people to join forces with the exile brigades. His fateful decision to abandon the exiles when they were trapped on the beachhead was, according to Hersh, taken when he learned the news that Castro was still alive. Hersh also presents, as part of his 'evidence', Judith Campbell Exner's story that she delivered 'documents' relating to the Castro plots to mob boss, Sam Giancana, and that JFK was briefed about the plots before the 1960 election by Richard Bissell or CIA Director Dulles. We will return to Exner's role in a later chapter.

Many writers have used testimony by ex-CIA agents who were angry at Kennedy for not fully backing the Cuban exiles during the Bay of Pigs invasion. Other agents and officials gave testimony to the Church Committee which was self-serving and was obviously designed either to rid themselves of culpability or constructed in a way which would protect their colleagues. From the evidence available, it is likely that. John and Robert Kennedy were aware of some form of 'elimination' - Castro would be naturally 'targeted' by anti-Castro Cubans during either an attempted coup by Castro's own military officers or a group which had been infiltrated into Cuba. But this is a far cry from suggesting knowledge of individual "CIA murder plots" or "presidential authorisation". It is the opinion of the present author that the 'knowledge' took the form of an 'expectation' that the Cuban exile groups, with the support of the CIA and the United States military, would most likely try to kill the Cuban leader in their efforts to topple the Castro regime.

Kennedy's CIA Director, John McCone, who had succeeded Allen Dulles, was unaware of the CIA murder plots and did not learn of them until they were supposedly cancelled. William Colby, who became Director of the CIA in the early 1970s, and who was responsible for releasing the information about the murder plots to a Congressional committee, called John McCone "the best director the CIA ever had. (He) was helped by Kennedy's style of open committee discussion of the issues before him, and by his own unerring instinct for pushing himself into the Oval Office to assert his position."[16] It is, therefore, unlikely that Kennedy kept his knowledge of the plots from this CIA Director. It would have been a bureaucratic nightmare had Kennedy known of the plans but his CIA Director did not. The CIA officers would have had to say to Kennedy: "By the way don't mention this to John McCone."

There is further evidence to support the contention that President Kennedy was unaware of the CIA plots to murder Fidel Castro. Three government investigations during the 1970s failed to find any evidence that JFK had ordered the assassination of Castro. Critics would argue that this is entirely consistent with the policy of 'plausible deniability', a concept which, as we will see later, lies at the heart of an understanding of the chain of command involving the attempts to eliminate the Cuban leader. However, Senator Frank Church asked Richard Bissell how he and Dulles could have briefed President-elect Kennedy about the Cuban project and not told him about the attempts to assassinate Castro. Bissell replied: "It is quite possible that Mr Dulles did say something about an attempt to, or the possibility of making use of, syndicate (mafia) characters for this purpose. My belief is that had he done so he probably would have done so in rather general terms and that neither of us was in a position to go into detail on the matter."[17]

The project to eliminate Castro originated in the Eisenhower Administration and continued two years into the Johnson Administration. The argument is made that because Kennedy was President, he must have known about the plots. But the same argument applies equally to Johnson and Eisenhower. However, no credible historian has accused these two Presidents. It should be recalled that Johnson did make the angry statement that "we had been running a damned Murder Inc in the Caribbean" - not the words of someone who had been directly involved. Similarly, it defies logic that the CIA would single out Kennedy alone to be informed of the CIA plots and not his successor. The plots ran two years into Johnson's presidency.

There are two important meetings which suggest that President Kennedy resisted the pressure from the CIA to authorise the murder plots. On November 9th 1961, President Kennedy met with 'New York Times' reporter, Tad Szulc. Kennedy asked Szulc, who had met with Castro on a number of occasions: "What would you think if I ordered Castro to be assassinated?" Szulc replied, "I don't think that's a good idea...that would not necessarily change things in Cuba. Personally, I don't think the United States should be a party to political assassinations."

President Kennedy agreed with Szulc and said he was just testing him and that he too thought it was morally wrong. Robert Kennedy agreed. But it did not stop with that simple remark. Kennedy continued for 'quite a while' about how wrong it would be to assassinate the Cuban leader, saying, during the conversation: "That's the kind of thing I'm never going to do. We can't get into that kind of thing, or we would all be targets." Szulc made contemporary notes of the meeting, writing: "JFK said he raised the question because he was under terrific pressure from advisors (think he said intelligence people, but not positive) to okay a Castro murder, said he was resisting pressures."[18] However, Seymour Hersh (1997) maintains that Kennedy's comments were disingenuous and that the President was laying down a disclaimer.

The Church Committee heard testimony from Senator George Smathers, a close friend of the President's. He told the Committee that when the subject was brought up, Kennedy got so mad that he smashed a dinner plate and told him he never wanted to hear of such things again. President Kennedy, he related, seemed 'horrified' at the idea of political assassination.[19]

And, in his March 31st 1964 oral history interview for the Kennedy Library, Smathers said: "We had further conversation of Fidel Castro, what would be the reaction, how would the people react, would the people be gratified? I'm sure he had his own ideas about it, but he was picking my brain...As I recollect, he was just throwing out a great barrage of questions - he was certain it could be accomplished...But the question was whether or not it would accomplish that which he wanted it to, whether or not the reaction throughout South America would be good or bad. And I talked with him about it, and frankly, at this particular time I felt and I later on learned that he did, that I wasn't so much for the idea of assassination, particularly when it could be pinned on the United States."

Yet Smathers told writer Michael Beschloss, for the historian's 1991 book, that Kennedy expected Castro would have been killed before the Bay of Pigs landings. And in 1994 Smathers said: "Jack would be all the time, 'If somebody knocks this guy off, that'd be fine...' But Kennedy obviously had to say he could not be party to that sort of thing with the damned Mafia."[20] We shall return to this conundrum later in the chapter.

The assassination attempts continued during 1963. In the Autumn of 1963, Kennedy changed his Cuban policy and sought an accommodation with Castro. Special Advisor to the U.S. Delegation at the UN, William Attwood, was set to make a secret visit to Cuba after having met with the Cuban United Nations ambassador. It is conceivable that at this time Kennedy had preferred some accommodation with the Cuban leader and, concurrently, pursued a 'two-track' approach - if anti-Castro Cubans killed Castro as part of a coup attempt that would have been acceptable - if not then Kennedy would try to improve relations. Many Kennedy advisors have testified to the fact that JFK was operating, at this time, a policy of 'détente' with Cuba.

Although the CIA was forced publicly to admit to the assassination plots in 1975, the Senators on the Church Committee were unable to resolve who authorised the CIA to attempt the murder of Castro. Kennedy and Eisenhower officials, when called to testify, strongly denied any involvement.

CIA Deputy Director for Plans, Richard Bissell was in charge of 'executive action' although the actual planning was led by William Harvey. He testified to the Senate Committee and later, in the early 1990s, and before his death in 1994, he expanded on his reasoning: "From time to time individuals would appear on the scene and it would be very important to have them disappear from the scene. I came to believe it would be desirable to have a very small office that developed the techniques and methods for executive action; action targeted to a particularly and dangerous individual in some other country- action designed to immobilise him."[21] Bissell was confident he acted with presidential authority. The implication here is authority from both Eisenhower and Kennedy.

Understanding Bissell's assumptions and a knowledge of the chain of command may give a clue to what exactly happened when the idea for the elimination of Castro was formulated. Allen Dulles stated that he never gave his deputy authorisation from President Kennedy, Bissell simply 'assumed' it. Furthermore, Bissell could not claim any support from the Eisenhower officials - Eisenhower's National Security Advisor, Gordon Gray, confirms that no authorisation had been forthcoming from President Eisenhower.[22]

When Bissell was questioned by the Church Committee, he volunteered that he had discussed 'executive action' with JFK's National Security Advisor, McGeorge Bundy, as "an untargeted capability rather than the plan or approval for an assassination operation."[23] However, it was only a 'standby' tool. Bissel said he might have mentioned Castro. McGeorge Bundy told the Rockefeller Commission: "I recall the words 'executive action capability'...I think it was something like...a plan to have some kind of standby capability for actions against individuals."[24]

Bundy told the Church Committee that Bissell had been "testing my reaction" and not "seeking authority" for assassinations. He said he took no action to stop it as it would not come into operation until a named individual had been targeted. He added that as far as he could recall he had not told the President. Furthermore Bissell had not told Bundy that the CIA had already tried to assassinate Castro. When Bissell told William Harvey to set up ZR/RIFLE, the executive action capability, he said he had been asked twice by the White House to do so. However, at that time he had not yet spoken to Bundy. The Church Committee concluded that Bissell had been looking for implied authority for the plots already up and running and that he did this in order to cover his tracks. Thus Bissell was being disingenuous.

Seymour Hersh quotes Samuel Halpern as saying that the person in charge of ZR/RIFLE, William Harvey, told him that JFK had personally authorised Bissell to set up the executive action capability.[25] Harvey's statements, however, should be treated with suspicion. Harvey hated the Kennedys with a vengeance.[26] He also had a personal grudge against Robert Kennedy who he especially disdained. Harvey was an alcoholic who had a loud and aggressive personality and frequently spoke out of turn at meetings with his superiors. During an inspection of the CIA station in Florida, Harvey had snatched a secret memo out of RFK's hands as he was about to leave the building. He frequently referred to the Kennedy brothers as 'fags'.[27]

One senior ex-CIA official, Chester Cooper, also supported the notion that Bissell acted precipitously in assuming Dulles had received presidential authority.[28] Many intelligence officials recognised that, in the culture of secrecy a different language was used - a language designed to infer rather than to announce. There are some who were close to Dulles who are not even sure if he had meant 'assassination' during the times he engaged Bissell in 'circumlocutious' conversations. Seen from this perspective it becomes clear that Bissell may have reasoned that, because Eisenhower and Kennedy did not say 'Don't do it', it was alright to go ahead with the plots. Thomas Parrot (CIA officer), and Lyman Kirkpatrick (CIA Inspector-General in the late 1950s and early 1960s), believed that Bissell authorised the assassination plots on his own initiative.[29]

As Evan Thomas (1995) wrote: "...Bissell had no explicit authority. He had 'assumed' that Dulles had received authorisation from President Kennedy, perhaps when Dulles first met with Kennedy on the Cuba operation in November 1960. But Dulles never told him so. A parade of former Kennedy Administration officials testified before the Church Committee in 1975 that Kennedy had never authorised any assassination attempts and would never have condoned such a terrible act."[30]

Peter Grose (1995), in his excellent biography of Allen Dulles, notes that by 1959, Dulles had "passed effective leadership of the CIA to Bissell".[31] It would seem likely, according to Bob King, Bissell's executive assistant, that Dulles simply wanted Bissell to get on with the job but not to tell the CIA Director of any 'horrible' matters. And, of course, the loyal Bissell believed that in not telling his superiors, he was carrying out the CIA's rationale of 'plausible deniability'. Peter Grose maintains that Dulles, nevertheless, knew of the plots.

Both Dulles and Bissell believed that assassination was a legitimate weapon in the fight for freedom. Bissell believed that the CIA should not be subject to ordinary legal restraints or moral precepts. The Agency, he said, owed allegiance to a higher law, a higher loyalty. This was the mind-set of most CIA officers in the harsh Cold War realities of the 1950s and 1960s. The two CIA leaders both agreed that the plot against Hitler was moral and, as former OSS operators, probably knew that Churchill had sanctioned acts of assassination. This would have acted as a powerful stimulant in their reasoning. Later Bissell came to believe that the CIA assassination plots were bad judgement but not bad morality. And there were real fears amongst CIA officers that the KGB, with the help of Castro's agents, were attempting to destabilise Central American countries by helping to instigate rebellions in Nicaragua, El Salvador and Guatemala. Indeed, the Cuban Government established a formal structure to aid armed revolutionary rebellion in Latin America. Robert Mahue summed up the general feeling of the times when he said in 1998: "We were at (ideological) war. Would it be folly to go after Saddam Hussein during the Gulf War or to go after Hitler during World War II? ...War will make you do certain things. Frankly people seem to forget that this madman was 90 miles off the shores of the United States constructing launching platforms directed at us...In World War II if we had known the exact bunker that Hitler was in we would have done a great disservice not to try to take care of him."[32]

CIA detractors also fail to see the Cuban leader for what he was. Even before his leadership of a guerrilla army he had attempted to murder one of his rivals for the presidency of his student body. Castro, with two others, ambushed Leonel Gomez outside Havana University Stadium. Although seriously wounded Gomez eventually recovered.[33]

Castro once offered a bounty of 50,000 dollars to anyone who assassinated Admiral Bulkeley, commander of the U.S. Naval base in Cuba.[34] Furthermore, the extent to which the Cuban leader went to keep his regime in power disturbed and angered many officials in the U.S. government. Castro's regime was guilty of severe repression and he created the most violent police state apparatus in the Western Hemisphere. Castro formed "Committees for the Defense of the Revolution" (CDR) which operated in every neighbourhood in Cuba. Large numbers of individuals were imprisoned and hundreds were executed. Countless numbers of Cubans were charged with unspecified 'crimes against the revolution'.

Critics of the CIA invariably fail to examine the assassination plots in the correct context of the times. Castro agents were involved in sabotage on the American mainland.[35] In 1962, three Cuban saboteurs were arrested by the FBI as they attempted to blow up or torch several major targets, including an oil refinery, in New York and New Jersey. The CIA also received an intelligence report that Castro agents intended to murder President Kennedy's children. If Castro had been toppled, the majority of the American people would have rejoiced. And Kennedy had been warned by the CIA's top Russian asset, Oleg Penkovsky, that the President's toleration of Castro was taken as a sign of weakness by Kruschev.[36]

The belief that assassination is acceptable as a last resort in the war to fight terrorism and dictatorship was not confined to this period in modern American history. Assassination of leaders had been considered during the Second World War. It was considered against the Nazis up to 1948, according to ex-British agent, Peter Mason, who maintained that British soldiers were secretly assigned to hunt and kill Nazi war criminals after the war.[37] The assassination question is still debated by American politicians. It is likely that President Reagan knew that Colonel Gaddaffi had been 'targeted' by American fighter planes during the bombing of Libya in 1986. In 1997, some members of the U.S. Congress called for the repeal of President Ford's executive order banning assassination of foreign leaders after Saddam Hussein threatened further conflict in the Middle-East. During Desert Storm, a CIA Directorate of Operations paramilitary unit actively sought to kill Saddam Hussein. Indeed, it was revealed in January 1998 that the United States government had secretly sanctioned and aided dissident groups of Kurds for the express purpose of eliminating Saddam Hussein. In 1999 Henry Kissinger said that U.S. and British forces should concentrate on trying to 'kill' Saddam.[38]

This present day necessity of disposing of tyrants was no different from the climate of the early 1960s. The American government genuinely believed that the Cuban dictator pursued a rigorous and ruthless policy of rooting out anti-revolutionary elements within Cuba. Ridding Cuba of a murderous despot was seen by many as an honourable act. Furthermore, if the American people had known that Castro had urged Kruschev to launch a pre-emptive nuclear strike against the United States during the Cuban Missile Crisis, there would have been no doubt about the morality of attempts to kill the Cuban leader. As Castro's sister, who fled Cuba in 1963, told the House UnAmerican Activities Committee: "Fidel's feeling of hatred for this country (United States) cannot be imagined by Americans. His intention, his obsession to destroy the U.S. is one of his main interests and objectives."[39]

Some authors state that as Robert Kennedy had been informed of the plots to assassinate Castro, then his brother, the President, must also have known. This is true. It is inconceivable that Robert would have kept his brother in the dark about any aspect of governmental operations. But it should be understood in the context of when Robert had been informed and the circumstances of the various plots.

Robert Kennedy had been given direct control of the Cuban project after the disaster at the Bay of Pigs. President Kennedy wanted someone he could trust absolutely. In fact the President had wanted his brother to take over command of the Central Intelligence Agency but Robert had demurred, claiming the Agency should be run by someone less political. It was also felt that the appointment of Robert Kennedy as Head of the CIA would make it impossible to 'plausibly deny' CIA covert operations around the world. Instead the President appointed John McCone to succeed Allen Dulles. But it was Robert Kennedy who, from November 1961 led 'Operation Mongoose'. The oversight group for the project included representatives of the U.S. Information Agency, the Pentagon and the CIA.

RFK wanted a direct, dynamic and vigorous approach to the problem of toppling Castro. In a memo, shortly after the CIA Task Force was set up, he wrote: "My idea is to stir things up on the island with espionage, sabotage, general disorder, run and operated by Cubans themselves...Do not know if we will be successful in overthrowing Castro but we have nothing to lose in my estimate."[40]

Assassination was never officially part of 'Operation Mongoose'. But, as Richard Helms said, RFK was insisting that the top priority of the U.S. Government was the overthrow of Castro and so it would have been natural for the CIA leaders to assume that any means necessary to achieve this end would include assassination.

Helms told the Church Committee that no direct order to kill Castro was needed because Bobby Kennedy's "intense pressure" generated the "kind of atmosphere" in which assassination was authorised implicitly. He told the Committee, "It was made abundantly clear to everyone involved in the operation that the desire was to get rid of the Castro regime and to get rid of Castro...No limitations were put on this injunction...(RFK) would not have been unhappy if (Castro) had disappeared off the scene by whatever means."[41]

The story behind the claims that RFK knew about the assassination plots begins with the CIA recruiting, through intermediary and ex-FBI agent Robert Maheu, mafia boss, Sam Giancana, and his henchman, Johnny Rosselli, to ensure the elimination of Castro. Sam Giancana, in turn, elicited the assistance of Florida mob boss, Santos Trafficante, who had many contacts in Cuba and who could be used to kill the Cuban leader. Payment was offered to the gangsters (150,000 dollars) but they refused to accept the money from the CIA, claiming it was their patriotic duty to assist. This was perhaps a disingenuous move. It is likely these cunning criminals saw a golden opportunity in having some leverage with the Justice Department which was investigating their criminal activities. And, of course, with Castro out of the way, the path would be clear for the Mafia to recover their lucrative and illegal 'businesses'.

Giancana did, however, accept the assistance of the CIA in finding out if his girlfriend, singer Phyliss McGuire, had been having an affair with comedian Dan Rowan (later star of the 'Rowan and Martin Laugh-In' TV series). In order to keep Giancana in Miami to discuss the plots, the CIA offered to go to Las Vegas and bug McGuire's hotel room. Unfortunately, the agents were caught by the local sheriff. The FBI was notified and the CIA had to intervene to prevent a court case which would have publicly disclosed the murder plots. The charges were dropped but by now J. Edgar Hoover had knowledge that the CIA were dealing with the Mafia.

Justice Department Criminal Division Chief, Jack Miller, informed the Attorney-General that "it is clear that the national interest will preclude any prosecution."[42]

On May 22nd 1961, J. Edgar Hoover sent RFK a memorandum: "On May 3rd, 1961 Colonel Sheffield Edwards, Director of Security, Central Intelligence Agency (CIA) furnished the following information- Colonel Edwards advised that in connection with CIA's operation against Castro he personally contacted Robert Maheu as a 'cut-out' in contacts with Sam Giancana, a known hoodlum in the Chicago area. Colonel Edwards said that since the underworld controlled gambling activities in Cuba under the Batista government, it was assumed that this element would still continue to have sources and contacts in Cuba which perhaps could be utilised successfully in connection with CIA's clandestine efforts against the Castro government. As a result Maheu's services were solicited as a 'cut-out' because of his possible entry into underworld circles. Maheu obtained Sam Giancana's assistance in this regard and according to Edwards, Giancana gave every indication of cooperating through Maheu in attempting to accomplish several clandestine efforts in Cuba. Edwards added that none of Giancana's efforts have materialised to date and that several of the plans are still working and may eventually 'pay-off'."[43]

It should be noted that this memo does not explain what these 'efforts' were: intelligence to be used for the Cuban exiles, sabotage, political subversion or assassination?

The memo continued: "Colonel Edwards advised that only Mr Bissell (Deputy Director of Plans, CIA) and two others in CIA were aware of the Giancana-Maheu activity in behalf of CIA's program and that Allen Dulles (CIA Director) was completely unaware of Edwards' contact with Maheu in this connection. He added that Mr Bissell, during his recent briefings of General Taylor and the Attorney-General in connection with other enquiries into CIA relating to the Cuban situation, told the Attorney-General that some of the CIA's associated planning included the use of Giancana and the underworld against Castro."

Some authors infer that RFK must have known about the murder plots at this time (May 1961) rather than May 1962 which has been the conventional view, but there is nothing in the memo to infer that the Mafia were assisting in plans to 'assassinate' Castro. In May 1962, the Attorney General was visited at the Justice Department by CIA General Counsel, Lawrence Houston. Houston briefed RFK about the CIA/mafia plots. Kennedy warned Houston and the other CIA officials present never to use the Mafia again without his specific approval. The CIA told Kennedy that the mafia operation had been shut down. Houston described Robert Kennedy's demeanour during the meeting: "If you have seen Mr Kennedy's eyes get steely and his voice get low and precise, you get a definite feeling of unhappiness...(RFK said)... 'I trust that if you ever try to do business with organised crime again - with gangsters - you will let the Attorney General know.'"[44] However, the CIA ignored the Attorney General. The CIA itself admitted this in the classified study dated May 23rd 1967.[45]

In a memo about a meeting Hoover had with Robert Kennedy after the CIA briefing, Hoover wrote: "The Attorney General told me he wanted to advise me of a situation in the Giancana case which had CONSIDERABLY DISTURBED HIM."(emphasis added).[46]

Hoover later wrote: "I expressed great astonishment at this (CIA/mafia links) in view of the bad reputation of Maheu and the horrible judgement in using a man of Giancana's background for such a project. THE ATTORNEY GENERAL SHARED THE SAME VIEWS." (emphasis added).[47]

FBI Director Hoover intensely disliked Robert Kennedy. Hoover was pleased to see Kennedy lose his powerful position in government after his brother, the President, had been assassinated. It has been said there was nothing in government circles that Hoover was unaware of and it was likely that he would have used any inflammatory information about Robert Kennedy to maintain his position as FBI Director. Evidence that Robert Kennedy and his brother authorised the CIA/mafia plots would have provided Hoover with the 'goods'. And, according to the CIA Inspector General's report of 1967: "It should be noted that the briefing of Kennedy was restricted to Phase one of the operation (the 1960/61 CIA/mafia murder attempts), which had ended about a year earlier. Phase Two (contemporary attempts to kill Castro) was already underway at the time of the briefing, but Kennedy was not told of it."[48]

Robert Kennedy's instructions to the CIA were clear, but they were ignored and the CIA/mafia relationship continued, led by Kennedy's nemesis, William Harvey. Much later, in 1967, when stories of the assassination plots were emerging in the newspapers, Kennedy angrily told his aides: "I didn't start it. I stopped it...I found out that some people were going to try an attempt on Castro's life and I turned it off."[49] Yet the CIA/mafia plotting continued and one of the CIA briefers, Sheffield Edwards, along with William Harvey, falsified the record by saying in a memo that all future plots had to be authorised by the Director of the CIA, John McCone. McCone was not consulted and was deliberately kept unaware.

Some writers, then, have naturally posed the question - why didn't RFK berate the CIA in May 1961 when he first learned of the CIA/mafia ties? There are a number of reasons to explain why this did not happen. Firstly, the FBI May 1961 report did not say the collaboration between the CIA and the Mafia included 'assassination'. It spoke of 'efforts' and 'activities'. He may have been busy dealing with other pressing national issues to bother taking account of the implications of the memo - after all RFK did not take control of the Cuba Project until the Autumn of 1961. Until then he was engaged in trying to put mafia bosses behind bars and the challenges of the Civil Rights movement were taking up a lot of his time. Perhaps it did not grab his attention as something he needed to deal with at this time. RFK possibly assumed that Giancana and others merely had valuable Cuban connections to assist the Cuban exiles with their plans for sabotage.

Seymour Hersh (1997) maintains that Robert Kennedy had his own mafia contact in his desire to get rid of Castro. If this is true then why was the Attorney General trying so hard to put the mobsters in jail? Robert Kennedy's secretary, Angie Novello, disputes Hersh's claim and has stated she has no knowledge of alleged telephone calls made to mafia connected figures.[50] RFK's closest aides, John Siegenthaler,

James Symington, John Nolan and Walter Sheridan, deny any knowledge - and they would have had to have known. They all state categorically that if any direct approach to mobsters had been made, RFK would definitely have worked with Sheridan in particular. Walter Sheridan, shortly before his death, denied the contacts were made. RFK's aides also state that any investigation of mafia activities or any prosecution of mob bosses was never compromised. RFK pushed to get Giancana, Marcello and other crime bosses at any cost.[51] Therefore, it is impossible to imagine how the Attorney General could have made deals with the Mafia in his pursuit of Castro.

The Church Committee eventually concluded that discussions in the White House and between members of the Special Group (Augmented), a group which included Robert Kennedy: "might well have contributed to the perception of some CIA officials that assassination was a permissible tool in the effort to overthrow the Castro regime."[52]

Whether the Kennedys intended it or not, key persons in the CIA, from Helms and Bissell down (but excluding John McCone), all THOUGHT the Kennedys wanted Castro assassinated. After all the Kennedy brothers had placed immense pressure on the CIA to 'do something about Castro' which echoed Henry II's refrain 'Who will rid me of this turbulent priest?' After Kennedy's assassination, according to Harris Wofford (1980), Bissell's deputy for the Bay of Pigs operation, Tracy Barnes: "claimed to have heard the President use that line in connection with Castro."[53] And, if the Kennedys had indeed been consumed by a desire to assassinate Castro, the missiles in Cuba would have provided the perfect pretext. Furthermore, why would the Kennedys risk the lives of the 'Bay of Pigs' prisoners at a time when they were desperately trying to secure their freedom?

A memo released in State Department documents entitled 'Cuba 1961-1962', the then CIA Director of Security, Sheffield Edwards, wrote that knowledge of the plots was "kept to a total of six persons", including himself.[54] We know that the following people have admitted to having had knowledge of the murder plots: Richard Bissell, William Harvey, Desmond Fitzgerald, and Richard Helms. The sixth person could be either Dr Sidney Gottlieb, Samuel Halpern or Allen Dulles. This memo indicates that the White House was likely to have been kept in the dark.

Some authors have averred that because President Kennedy 'signed off' or 'authorised' the assassinations of Dominican Republic dictator, Rafael Trujillo, and South Vietnamese leader, Ngo Dinh Diem, it is likely he conspired also to kill Castro. Seymour Hersh (1997) claims Kennedy knew about and approved of the assassination of Diem. But Hersh's evidence is anecdotal. Government documents released in the late 1990s indicate Kennedy had been unaware of these murder plots. Kennedy Library tapes released in 1998 show that in recordings made in the Oval Office just weeks before his death, Kennedy expressed his concern about his actions preceding the overthrow and murder of Diem. Kennedy said: "I was shocked by the death of Ngo Dinh Diem. He was an extraordinary character, while he became increasingly difficult in the last few months. He has been able to hold his country together for the last 10 months." In the tapes Kennedy expressed regret over sending a cable that preceded the Diem overthrow by Generals who led a coup. The cable gave indirect support for the coup. Kennedy said: "I feel we must bear a good deal of responsibility for it. In my judgement that wire was badly drafted, it should have never been sent on a Saturday. I should have never given my consent to it without roundtable conference." On the tape Kennedy said he sent another cable but the planning for the coup was already in place.[55] General Maxwell Taylor described Kennedy's reaction when he was informed of Diem's murder: "Kennedy leaped to his feet and rushed from the room with a look of shock and dismay on his face which I had never seen before. He had always insisted that Diem must never suffer more than exile."[56] Arthur Schlesinger (1965) wrote: "He was sombre and shaken. I had not seen him so depressed since the Bay of Pigs."[57] And it was Kennedy's anger over Diem's murder that prompted him to tell one Senator that he had to do something to curb the CIA's excessive power.

There is also evidence that President Kennedy did not approve of Trujillo's assassination. At the time of the Bay of Pigs affair, the CIA was giving aid to Dominican Republic dissidents. Weapons were sent by diplomatic pouch which were intended to be used to assassinate dictator Trujillo. However, after the Bay of Pigs, the CIA got cold feet. If another botched attempt was publicised it would be highly embarrassing for the Agency - it could not risk another failure and tried to stop the conspirators from carrying out their act of assassination. The CIA contacted the White House and informed President Kennedy that the weapons had already been handed over. Kennedy ordered the CIA to stop any assistance to the dissidents and a cable was sent to the CIA station in Ciudad Trujillo which read: "We must not run risk of U.S. association with political assassination since the U.S. as a matter of general policy cannot condone assassination."[58] The cable went out on May 29th. On May 30th, Trujillo was assassinated.

An answer to the controversy of whether or not the Kennedy brothers authorised the assassination of Fidel Castro may come from an understanding of the complexities of communications which exist in bureaucracies, especially those engaged in semi-legal activities. It also lies in the Kennedy brothers' support for Cuban exile groups who were planning to eliminate Castro.

Bureaucracies are notoriously inefficient when personnel are new to their jobs and unfamiliar with one another. Words such as 'fair', 'good', 'moderately good' that appear in reports from the Pentagon, State Department and CIA often led to confusion about their precise meanings. Over the years John McCone noted that phrases such as 'dispose of Castro', 'remove Castro', and 'knock off Castro' were always construed to mean the overthrowing of the communist government in Cuba.

CIA official and friend of John Kennedy, Robert Amory, has said: "(Kennedy was) used to dealing with guys...over the years that he knew exactly what they meant by a shrug of their shoulders or the way they phrased a sentence...(But with Dulles, Kennedy said)... 'I can't estimate his meaning when he tells me things.'"[59]

According to Kennedy's assistant, Theodore Sorensen, Dulles would seek tacit approval but speak in a circumlocutious way which confused the President. Dulles would never come out and ask for exactly what he wanted.[60]

Peter Grose (1995) has given a telling clue as to the level of communication between Dulles and Kennedy: "'Now about this Cuban operation...' he might say, to which Kennedy would say, 'Yeah...' in what Allen (Dulles) took as vague impatience. 'If Eisenhower had said that,' Allen explained, 'it would have signified, 'Yes I know all about it and let's go on to something else'. ' Too late, as Allen told it, 'I learned that Kennedy had intended to express, not understanding or assent, but only, 'Yes, I'm listening.'"[61]

Eleanor Dulles, sister of Allen and John Foster, said: "Their (CIA officers) instincts were to protect themselves, to protect each other. They used the same idiom, the same language."[62]

CIA officials themselves were frequently confused as to the meaning of words when communicating ideas to each other. In December 1959, CIA, officer J.C. King, wrote a memo suggesting that "thorough consideration" be given to the "elimination" of Castro. It would "greatly accelerate the fall of the present government". Richard Bissell assumed King meant "incapacitating" Castro.[63] According to author William Breuer (1997), CIA agent, E. Howard Hunt: " always refused to use the term 'eliminate' which had been bandied about in the CIA and interpreted in different ways by various operatives involved in the Cuba project."[64]

McGeorge Bundy, President Kennedy's National Security advisor, said: "There is a terrible danger that if you don't really listen extremely hard and have a relationship of mutual trust that is very close, you can get a situation where what you think you are authorising is in fact rather different from what the agency (CIA) will believe it is free to do under that authorisation. The tendency to believe that 'higher authority' will not mind a little inventive enlargement on what it has intended to authorise is endemic among covert operations, and I repeat that the best way of ensuring that no such liberties are taken is to have a line of authority that guards against them. White House staff supervision is very much a second-best method."[65]

It is easy to see how this misperception on the part of the CIA developed. A president wanting to further his goals with the greatest efficacy, would suggest to the Agency the necessity for covert action, creating a sort of 'carte blanche'. Instead of telling the President of the details of the covert operations they would speak in 'general' terms thus enabling him to 'plausibly deny'.

The Kennedy brothers cannot be accused of "authorising" the murder of Fidel Castro on the evidence available to researchers and historians. Only two 'witnesses' (apart from CIA personnel) say they were definitely aware of Kennedy's so-called knowledge of the assassination attempts - Judith Exner and George Smathers. Judith Exner has contradicted herself so many times that her reliability is unquestionably suspect and her accounts will be examined in a later chapter. Yet how can the statements made by a reliable witness, Senator Smathers, the President expected Castro to be already dead before the Bay of Pigs invasion and his earlier statements to the Church Committee that Kennedy opposed assassination of leaders. The answer may be gleaned in what constituted, at the time, 'American involvement'.

President-elect Kennedy, in the Autumn of 1961, was briefed for two hours and 40 minutes by CIA Director, Allen Dulles, and Deputy Director, Richard Bissell. Available CIA records do not reveal that the

President either authorised the invasion or urged restraint. He was told about the development and support of dissident anti-Castro groups by the CIA's Cuban assets to undertake anti-regime guerilla action inside Cuba. Some authors say Kennedy would likely have been briefed about the assassination attempts and that nothing was put on the record in order to preserve 'plausible deniability'. However 'plausible deniability' had degenerated, according to veteran intelligence officer, Colonel William R. Corson: "to the point where the cover stories of presidential ignorance really are fact not fiction."[66]

However, it is possible that Kennedy knew during the CIA post-election briefing and afterwards as president that Cuban paramilitary groups, acting on their own initiative, but 'controlled' and 'supplied' by the Agency, would naturally try to get the leader of the regime they were trying to topple. After all this has been the natural 'modus operandi' of most insurgent groups around the world; some leaders have been imprisoned after their governments have been overthrown and some have been executed. Whether or not the American government gave aide and assistance to these groups becomes irrelevant - American agencies and personnel were, supposedly, not directly involved in committing the assassination therefore Kennedy could safely conclude that he was not 'authorising' a murder attempt. But in effect both brothers were turning a blind eye to attempts to kill Castro.

Ray Cline (1976) in his book 'Secrets, spies, and scholars' wrote: "There was almost an obsession with Cuba on the part of policy matters." (and it was widely believed in the Kennedy Administration) "that the assassination of Castro BY A CUBAN (emphasis added) might have been viewed as not very different in the benefits that would have accrued from the assassination of Hitler in 1944."[67]

Senator George Smathers confirmed that Kennedy knew about a plot to kill Fidel Castro in an interview with Anthony and Robbyn Summers. "Jack would be (saying)," said Smathers, "all the time, 'If somebody knocks this guy off, OK, that'd be fine...' But Kennedy had to say he could not be a party to that sort of thing with the damn Mafia."[68] As we saw earlier, Smathers is a very credible witness; therefore, we can assume that Kennedy definitely knew that Castro would be assassinated. No mention, however, was made of a CIA plot. Kennedy could have been very well stating the obvious - Cuban exile teams were going to murder Castro.

CIA and Pentagon documents, and statements made by the leaders of a number of anti-Castro groups (as well as statements made by future Secretary of State and former Army General Alexander Haig)[69], conclusively answer the question of whether or not the Kennedy brothers expected Castro to have been targeted for assassination. After the Cuban Missile Crisis, President Kennedy agreed to support 'autonomous' attempts to topple Castro's regime. RFK actively aided and authorised the financing of anti-Castro groups outside the purview of the CIA. In a series of manoeuvres designed to hide U.S. government financial aide, Robert Kennedy sought to distance the Kennedy Administration from these efforts. There is little doubt the Kennedy brothers knew these groups would try to assassinate the Cuban leader. Had a Cuban national succeeded in killing Castro or had a top military officer, turned by the CIA, initiated a coup, the Kennedys would have been pleased. And if the circumstances of the coup d'etat meant the Cuban leader would be killed in the process, it would be a satisfactory outcome if the American role could be kept secret. However, there is no credible evidence to support the contention that the Kennedys directly involved or authorised American agencies to engage in assassination plotting. After all, if the Kennedys had indeed been consumed by a desire to assassinate Castro, the Missiles of October would have been the perfect pretext.

Notes

1. Russo, G. (1998). *Live by the sword - the secret war against Castro and the death of JFK*, Bancroft Press. p. 322.

2. 'Castro death plots set a world record', *The Daily Telegraph*, 21 July 1999, p. 3.

3. Fursenko, A. and Naftali, T. (1999). *One hell of a gamble*, Pimlico. p. 135.

4. Church Committee, *Alleged assassination plots involving foreign leaders*, U.S. Govt. Printing Office, 1975, p. 333-336; Szulc, T. (2000). *Fidel - a critical portrait*, Post Road Press. p. 480.

5. Church Committee, *Alleged assassination plots involving foreign leaders*, U.S. Govt. Printing Office, 1975. p. 330.

6. Thomas, E. (1995). *The very best men - four who dared; the early years of the CIA*, Simon and Schuster. p. 210.

7. *Ibid*, p. 37.

8. Zach Thomas, "Hughes aide: CIA plot to kill Castro a tense time", *Las Vegas Review Journal*, 3 July 1997. (http://www.las vegas.com).

9. Church Committee, *Alleged assassination plots involving foreign leaders*, U.S. Govt. Printing Office, 1975, pp. 93-94.

10. Beschloss, M. R. (1991). *Kennedy v. Kruschev - the crisis years 1960-1963*, Faber and Faber. p. 683.

11. Church Committee, *Alleged assassination plots involving foreign leaders*, U.S. Govt. Printing Office, 1975, pp. 111-112. (Testimony of Richard Bissell).

12. Hilty, J. W. (1997). *Robert Kennedy – brother protector*, Temple University Press. p. 420; Thomas, E. (1995). *The very best men - four who dared; the early years of the CIA*, Simon and Schuster. p. 271.

13. Church Committee, *Alleged assassination plots involving foreign leaders*, U.S. Govt. Printing Office, 1975, pp. 148-150.

14. Hersh, S. (1997). *The dark side of Camelot*, Little Brown and Co. p. 269.

15. Bacon, K. 'An interview with Seymour Hersh', *Atlantic Unbound*, 8 January 1998. (http://www.the atlantic.com).

16. Colby, W. and Forbath, P. (1978). *Honourable men – my life in the CIA*, Hutchinson and Co. p. 186.

17. Church Committee, *Alleged assassination plots involving foreign leaders*, U.S. Govt. Printing Office, 1975, p. 144.

18. Wofford, H. (1980). *Of Kennedys and kings*, Farrar Straus and Giroux. p. 395.

19. Schlesinger, A. M. (1978). *Robert Kennedy and his times*, Houghton Mifflin Co. p. 530.

20. Beschloss, M. R. (1991). *Kennedy v. Kruschev - the crisis years 1960-1963*, Faber and Faber. p. 139.

21. 'CIA'. Produced by Bill Treherne Jones. BBC Television, 1992. (A BBC Production in association with NRK Primetime Television and Arts and Entertainment Network).

22. Thomas, E. (1995). *The very best men - four who dared; the early years of the CIA*, Simon and Schuster. p. 231.

23. *Ibid*, p. 245.

24. *Ibid*, p. 245.

25. Hersh, S. (1997). *The dark side of Camelot*, Little Brown and Co. p. 187.

26. Schlesinger, A. M. (1978). *Robert Kennedy and his times*, Houghton Mifflin Co. p. 516.

27. Thomas, E. (1995). *The very best men - four who dared; the early years of the CIA*, Simon and Schuster. p. 290.

28. *Ibid*, p. 231.

29. *Ibid*, p. 231.

30. *Ibid*, p. 231.

31. Grose, P. (1995). *Gentleman spy - the life of Allen Dulles*, Andre Deutsch. p. 467.

32. Thomas, Z. "Hughes aide: CIA plot to kill Castro a tense time", *Las Vegas Review Journal*, 3 July 1997. (http://www.las vegas.com).

33. Breuer, W. B. (1997). *Vendetta - Castro and the Kennedy brothers*, John Wiley and Sons Inc. p. 11.

34. *Ibid*, p. 238.

35. *Ibid*, p. 3.

36. Andrew, C. (1995). *For the president's eyes only*, HarperCollins Publishers. p. 274.

37. 'British hit squad executed nazis', *Sunday Times*, 28 December 1997, p. 4.

38. 'The great assassination debate', *Pacific News Service*, 9 December 1996. (http://www.pacificnews.org/jinn).

39. Breuer, W. B. (1997). *Vendetta - Castro and the Kennedy brothers*, John Wiley and Sons Inc. p. 244.

40. Schlesinger, A. M. (1978). *Robert Kennedy and his times*, Houghton Mifflin Co. p. 512.

41. Church Committee, *Alleged assassination plots involving foreign leaders*, U.S. Govt. Printing Office, 1975, pp. 195-211, 313.

42. Hilty, J. W. (1997). *Robert Kennedy – brother protector*, Temple University Press. p. 210.

43. Reeves, R. (1993). *President Kennedy - profile of power*, Simon and Schuster. p. 290; Freemantle, B. (1983). *CIA - the 'honourable' company*, Futura. p. 141.

44. Gentry, C. (1991). *J. Edgar Hoover - the man and the secrets*, WW Norton and Co. p. 491; Schlesinger, A.M. (1978). *Robert Kennedy and his times*, Houghton Mifflin Co. p. 531.

45. *CIA Inspector General's Report*, 23 May 1967, pp. 68-69. (http://www.foia.ucia.gov/popdocs/htm)

46. *Ibid.*

47. Schlesinger, A. M. (1978). *Robert Kennedy and his times*, Houghton Mifflin Co. p. 494; Gentry, C. (1991). *J. Edgar Hoover - the man and the secrets*, WW Norton and Co. p. 492.

48. *CIA Inspector General's Report*, 23 May 1967. (http://www.foia.ucia.gov/popdocs1/bayofpigs.htm).

49. Schlesinger, A. M. (1978). *Robert Kennedy and his times*, Houghton Mifflin Co. p. 532.

50. Goldfarb, R. (1995). *Perfect villains, imperfect heroes*, Random House. p. 273.

51. *Ibid.*

52. Church Committee, *Alleged assassination plots involving foreign leaders*, U.S. Govt. Printing Office, 1975, pp. 121-123, 127, 132-133, 324, 330-331.

53. Wofford, H. (1980). *Of Kennedys and kings*, Farrar Straus and Giroux. p. 396.

54. CIA offered Mafia 150,000 dollars to kill Castro - but mobsters said they would do it for free', *Associated Press* Washington, 2 July 1997, (http://www.newsday.com).

55. Kennedy Library Press Release, October 1998. (http://library.kennedy.nara.gov).

56. Newman, J. (1991). *JFK and Vietnam,* Carrol and Graf. p. 415; Schlesinger, A. M. (1978). *Robert Kennedy and his times*, Houghton Mifflin Co. p. 778.

57. Schlesinger, A. M. (1965). *A thousand days - John F. Kennedy in the White House*, Andre Deutsch. p. 848.

58. Reeves, R. (1993). *President Kennedy - profile of power*, Simon and Schuster. p. 141.

59. Grose, P. (1995). *Gentleman spy - the life of Allen Dulles*, Andre Deutsch. p. 517.

60. *Ibid.*

61. *Ibid*, p. 518.

62. Thomas, E. (1995). *The very best men - four who dared; the early years of the CIA*, Simon and Schuster. p. 355.

63. *Ibid*. p. 210.

64. Breuer, W. B. (1997). *Vendetta - Castro and the Kennedy brothers*, John Wiley and Sons Inc. p. 83.

65. Ranelagh, J. (1987). *The agency – the rise and decline of the CIA*, Sceptre. pp. 346-7.

66. Schlesinger, A. M. (1978). *Robert Kennedy and his times*, Houghton Mifflin Co. p. 525.

67. Cline, R. (1976). *Secrets, spies and scholars: blueprint of the essential CIA*, Acropolis Books. p. 209.

68. Summers A. and Summers, R. 'The ghosts of November', *Vanity Fair*, December 1994, p. 100.

69. Russo, G. (1998). Live by the sword - the secret war against Castro and the death of JFK, Bancroft Press. p. 172.

Chapter 5

Vietnam

Was President Kennedy responsible for leading America into the Vietnam quagmire?

"...judging from Kennedy's temperament and record, it is reasonable to assume that, if he had expanded U.S. military involvement in Vietnam, it would have been a restrained escalation that left open the possibility of withdrawal without the appearance of defeat."

Robert Dallek (1998), 'Flawed Giant'

"In view of his death, it must be said that nothing Kennedy was likely to do could have killed the Saigon commitment...nor should it be assumed that...he would have succeeded in sticking to the policy of not sending troops to South Vietnam. It is often overlooked that Lyndon Johnson himself did not go willingly or rapidly down that road...All that can be said is that Kennedy would have been even more reluctant than Johnson to accept it, and might well have looked sooner, harder, and more successfully for an alternative."

Hugh Brogan (1996), 'Kennedy'

Kennedy's role in the Vietnam conflict has been long debated and has been an issue of controversy ever since the question was first asked after his tragic death - would Kennedy have pursued the same policies as his successor and led the United States into the unwinnable and disastrous war in South-East Asia?

A consensus has developed over the past 35 years, if not amongst historians, at least with media opinion-makers, that Kennedy was as much to blame for the national tragedy as the two presidents who succeeded him, Lyndon Johnson and Richard Nixon.

But how fair is this assessment? And how plausible is the notion that Kennedy was not responsible for the national tragedy but instead would have pursued a policy of disengagement had he lived?

By its very nature a hypothetical thesis of this kind is impossible to prove or disprove. However, I believe there is sufficient evidence in the record to make a reasonable judgement as to what Kennedy would have done had he lived. And recently released government documents have helped to clarify this contentious issue.

The issue of Kennedy's supposed culpability for the Vietnam conflict was raised yet again with the publication of Seymour Hersh's (1997) book 'The dark side of Camelot' and of the republication William J. Rust's (1985) book 'Kennedy in Vietnam'. In his best-selling book about the Kennedy presidency Hersh wrote: "John Kennedy's enduring legacy as the 35th President of the United States was not the myth of Camelot or the tragic image of an attractive young leader struck down at the peak of his career. It was the War in Vietnam, a war that in the decade after his death would kill many thousands of the young Americans he had inspired and propel many others to the edge of insurrection."[1] William J. Rust wrote of "the absence of a clear direction to Kennedy's policy."[2]

It is true that President Kennedy subscribed to the now discredited 'domino theory', along with most Republican and Democratic politicians of his era. In 1956 Kennedy said: "Vietnam represents the cornerstone of the Free World in South-East Asia, the keystone in the arch, the finger in the dyke."[3]

It is also true that Kennedy was a product of his generation - men who abandoned the isolationist and pacifist idea - an idea which led to the Second World War. Kennedy and his generation embodied Cold War attitudes which held that peace and economic success depended upon securing alliances and supporting threatened democracies throughout the world. The Soviets were active in promoting international communism and, therefore, should be resisted on all fronts. The subject of collective security was constantly on the minds of post-war American leaders. There was a fear that any lack of will in relation to NATO (North Atlantic Treaty Organisation) and SEATO (South-East Asia Treaty Organisation) would lead to a weakening of European/American and Asian/American relations. And one of the areas of concern was Vietnam.

After the 1961 Bay of Pigs debacle and the settlement of the Laos problem (in which a neutral government had been agreed upon, comprising democratic and communist elements), Kennedy decided that he must take a firm stand against communist encroachment throughout the world and he chose Vietnam as the place to make his point. In May 1961, he told his Vice-President to relay the message to the President of South Vietnam, Ngo Dinh Diem, that the Vietnamese leader had both the support and the respect of Americans and he would take measures to assume responsibility in a joint effort to defeat the Communists in South Vietnam. On May 23rd, he approved a new statement setting out the new approach: "To prevent Communist domination of South Vietnam; to create in that country a viable and increasingly democratic society; and to initiate, on an accelerated basis, a series of mutually supporting actions of a military, political, economic, psychological and covert character designed to achieve this objective...to keep Vietnam free."[4] By the spring of 1963, the number of Americans in Vietnam grew from the original contingent of 600 sent during the Eisenhower Administration to 25,000.

The evidence to support the theory that Kennedy had every intention of remaining in Vietnam is certainly present. Secretary of State, Dean Rusk, said: "(At no time did) Kennedy ever say or hint or suggest to me that he was planning to withdraw troops in 1965."[5] Yet it should be remembered that Kennedy did not have a close working or personal relationship with Rusk. In the period shortly before his inauguration when he was choosing his cabinet, he spoke of his desire to be his own 'Secretary of State' which reflected his own special interest in foreign policy. Kennedy knew that his predecessor, President Eisenhower, had delegated the bulk of foreign policy making to Secretary of State, John Foster Dulles, and he did not want a strong personality to second guess his own decisions. This is one reason why he rejected the advice to appoint Adlai Stevenson as his Secretary of State. Kennedy had also considered replacing Rusk after his re-election in 1964.[6] And he was never close to Rusk. Kennedy referred to many of his Cabinet and advisors by their first names. With Rusk it was always 'Mr Secretary' or 'Secretary Rusk'.

Robert Kennedy contributed to the issue of whether or not his brother would have remained in Vietnam when, in interviews for the Kennedy Library in 1964, he said that there was no such talk of withdrawal and that his brother had reached the conclusion that he would probably stay in Vietnam if only for psychological and political reasons "more than anything else". Robert reiterated his brother's belief in the 'domino theory' that all of South-East Asia would fall if Vietnam was 'lost' to the communists. Robert Kennedy's comments must be respected if only for the fact he was President Kennedy's closest advisor. However, it should be remembered that Robert Kennedy's responsibilities in 1963 were vast. He had been given the job of ousting Castro from Cuba and the growing Civil Rights issue was taking up much of his time. Vietnam was not an issue which monopolised the Kennedy brothers' discussions.

Thomas C. Reeves (1991), a Kennedy critic, believed that Kennedy's behaviour in office and his statements about the conflict indicated he would have followed the same path to calamity as his successor, Lyndon Johnson. Reeves wrote: "Given his belief in the global struggle between east and west, his acceptance of the domino theory, his conviction that Vietnam was the testing ground for combating 'wars of liberation', his often zealous commitment to counterinsurgency (the Green Berets, covert sabotage, strategic hamlets, napalm and defoliation, and his determination never to appear soft on communism, Jack might well have been compelled, as conditions worsened, to commit more American troops to Vietnam. It is clear his harsh public rhetoric made disengagement more difficult."[7]

Kennedy critics have also noted that the escalation figures suggest that Kennedy was in the process of making a total commitment. In early 1961, there were 685 military advisors and by October 1963, there were 16,732. This was in violation of the Geneva agreement of 1954. Aid to the Diem regime increased to 400 million dollars per year. And it was Kennedy's advisors who encouraged Lyndon Johnson to escalate the war. There is little doubt that Kennedy bequeathed to his successor a dangerous situation.

However, Kennedy was convinced that the battle to secure South Vietnam against the indigenous NLF (National Liberation Front) and the North Vietnamese should not be fought with combat troops. He had been advised, wisely, against such measures by World War II, hero

General Douglas MacArthur. Pierre Salinger (1997), President Kennedy's press secretary, wrote in his book, 'John F. Kennedy: Commander-in-Chief': "...the President had been given the advice, from men he respected, to stay out of Vietnam. The first came in a two-hour meeting with General Douglas MacArthur who had come to visit Kennedy in the Oval Office. I was not party to their conversation, but General MacArthur came out and talked to me for a while. He had strongly advised the President never to send troops to Vietnam. He said, in essence, that if you do, it will be a disaster, because the war over there is going to be totally different from any war we have been involved in before. They've got guerrilla experts. America is not set for that kind of war, we'll not win that war, and we will lose a lot of people. It seemed to me that MacArthur, at that particular point, had totally convinced Kennedy that he should not get into a full-time war in South-East Asia."[8]

Kennedy also received advice from French President, Charles De Gaulle, who told him he should avoid getting into Vietnam too deeply. In Paris, in May 1961 he told Kennedy: "You want to rekindle a war that we ended. I predict to you that you will, step by step, be sucked into a bottomless military and political quagmire despite the losses and expenditures that you may squander."[9]

De Gaulle may have played an important role in Kennedy's plans had the President not been killed in Dallas. The nuclear test-ban treaty had initially led to some friction with the French; they had not yet developed their nuclear capability. But in August 1963, De Gaulle had offered to help with the Vietnam problem. De Gaulle arranged a visit to Washington in February 1964. This fact lends credence to the rumours that Kennedy, against the wishes of his State Department, was seriously considering accepting French involvement in devising a settlement. Kennedy told General James Gavin: "Well, I am going to see General De Gaulle in the next few months, and I think that we will be able to get something done together."[10]

There were other telling signs that Kennedy had been growing tired of the Vietnam conflict. 'Sunday Times' journalist Henry Brandon said: "(By this time, 1963) he seemed to be sick of the war and frequently asked how to be rid of the commitment."[11] He hoped that the South Vietnamese would take on the burden of their own war.

Historian Arthur Schlesinger Jnr. (1978), who became a special assistant to the President, reported that during a meeting of the National

Security Council, the chairman of the Joint Chiefs of Staff promised victory in Vietnam if nuclear weapons were allowed. After the meeting Kennedy remarked: "They want a force of American troops. They say it's necessary in order to restore confidence and maintain morale. But it will be just like Berlin. The troops will march in: the bands will play; the crowds will cheer; and in four days everyone will have forgotten. Then we will be told we have to send in more troops. It's like taking a drink. The effect wears off and you have to take another."[12]

According to Schlesinger, Kennedy was absolutely opposed to sending in troops. Cuba and Berlin showed he always preferred negotiation. This was confirmed by Under-Secretary of State, George Ball, who had never been persuaded that South-East Asia had extraordinary strategic importance to the United States. He was never persuaded that the North Vietnamese were the agents of Peking or Moscow. Ball had the ear of President Kennedy and warned him that if the U.S. went down the road of escalation there would be 30,000 men in the jungle. According to Ball, Kennedy replied: "George, you're crazier than hell, it just isn't going to happen."[13]

William Manchester was also privy to some of Kennedy's private musings about the Vietnam situation. Manchester (1983) wrote: "(Kennedy said)..they keep telling me to send combat units over there. That means draftees. Even the French didn't send draftees. I'll never do it...I ask them (his military advisors), 'Why troops?' and they say 'For confidence, for morale.'...As long as it remains their war they should be able to win it. If white soldiers went into action the people would think, 'The French are back'. And then, like the French, we'd lose.' Manchester asked how he would pull the troops out. Kennedy replied, "Oh, that's easy. I'll support a government that'll ask me to leave...We'll never send troops, not on my watch."[14] In 1963, after trouble with the South Vietnamese Buddhists flared up, Kennedy told his close friend, Charles Bartlett: "We don't have a prayer of staying in Vietnam. Those people hate us. They are going to throw our asses out of there at almost any point. But I can't give up a piece of territory like that to the Communists and then get the American people to re-elect me."[15]

Kennedy critics, in defending their position that he had been responsible for the Vietnam quagmire, often seek to dismiss the statements by Kennedy defenders, such as Kenneth O'Donnell, assistant to the President, Mike Mansfield, Senate majority leader, and others close to the President. These statements testify to Kennedy's position on the conflict in the months before his death. Mansfield had visited South Vietnam at the President's request in 1962. On his return he reported to Kennedy: "It is their country, their future that is at stake, not ours. To ignore that reality will not only be immensely costly in terms of American lives and resources, but it may also draw us into some variation of the unenviable position in Vietnam that was formerly occupied by the French."[16] Kennedy had disliked Mansfield's analysis but he told Kenneth O'Donnell, "I got angry with Mike for disagreeing with our policy so completely, and I got angry with myself because I found myself agreeing with him."[17]

In the spring of 1963, Kennedy had invited Mansfield to the White House to discuss the situation. Kennedy told Mansfield that he now agreed with the majority leader's position that a complete withdrawal of American forces from Vietnam was needed but that he could not do it until after the 1964 election. According to O'Donnell (1970) Kennedy said: "In 1965, I'll become one of the most unpopular Presidents in history. I'll be damned everywhere as a communist appeaser. But I don't care. If I tried to pull out completely now from Vietnam, we would have another Joe McCarthy red scare on our hands, but I can do it after I am re-elected. So we had better make sure I am re-elected."[18]

In 1968, General James Gavin said: "There has been much speculation about what President Kennedy would or would not have done in Vietnam had he lived. Having discussed military affairs with him often and in detail for 15 years, I know he was totally opposed to the introduction of combat troops in South-East Asia. His public statements just before his murder support this view. Let us not lay on the dead the blame for our own failures."[19]

Senator Wayne Morse said in 1973 that Kennedy had been changing his Vietnam policy up to the time of his death: "He'd seen the error of his ways. I'm satisfied if he'd lived another year we'd have been out of Vietnam. Ten days before his assassination, I went down to the White House and handed him his education bills, which I was handling on the Senate floor. I'd been making two to five speeches a week against Kennedy on Vietnam...I'd gone into President Kennedy's office to discuss education bills, but he said, 'Wayne, I want you to know you're absolutely right in your criticism of my Vietnam policy. Keep this in mind. I'm in the midst of an intensive study which substantiates your position on Vietnam."[20]

The study Kennedy was referring to was the 'McNamara' study. In an interview in late 1973 Daniel Ellsburg, who had purloined the 'Pentagon Papers' in an effort to inform the public about the national tragedy of Vietnam, said: "A very surprising discovery to me in the fall of 1967, as I began to study the documents of 1961 in connection with the McNamara study project, was that the major decision Kennedy had made was to REJECT the recommendation made to him by virtually everyone that he send combat troops to Vietnam. Kennedy realised that most of the people in the country, whatever their politics, would have said, 'If it takes combat troops, or if it takes heavy bombing or nuclear weapons, it's obviously not worth it for us. We won't succeed.'[21] David Halberstam said, "He knew Vietnam was bad and getting worse, that he was on his way to a first class foreign policy problem, but he had a sense of being able to handle it, of having time to make decisions. In the back of his mind was the idea that it was prudent to delay decisions as the 1964 election approached. If the Vietnamese could hold out so could he."[22]

Kennedy knew that any withdrawal before the 1964 election would strengthen the Republicans and possibly lead to the election of Barry Goldwater, a 'hawk'. Withdrawal may also have split the Democratic party, leading to disaster in election year and inflicting irreparable damage on America's alliances and reputation abroad. Meanwhile, he had to maintain, in public, a commitment which he was growing tired of. In two television interviews shortly before his death he said combat units would not be sent to Vietnam but dismissed talk of disengagement. On September 2nd 1963, two months before he was killed, he told Walter Cronkite: "I don't think that unless a greater effort is made by the government to win popular support that the war can be won out there. In the final analysis, it is their war. They are the ones who have to win it or lose it. We can help them, we can give them equipment, we can send our men out there as advisors but they have to win it, the people of Vietnam, against the Communists."[23]

However, in the same interview he also said: "but I don't agree with those who say we should withdraw. That would be a great mistake." And a week later in an interview with Chet Huntley he said in response to a question asking if he believed in the 'domino theory': "No I believe it. I believe it. I think that the struggle is close enough. China is so large, looms so high just beyond the frontiers, that if South Vietnam went, it would not only give them an improved geographic position for a guerrilla assault on Malaya, but would also give the impression that the wave of the future in South-East Asia was China and the Communists. So I believe it."[24]

It is possible that Kennedy made this comment to prevent any hostile attack from critics on the right who were concerned that Kennedy was too liberal and that the country was in danger of 'losing another China'. Kennedy had been known to hold the view that what was public was propaganda and what was private was policy.

In the final three speeches of his public life, Kennedy reaffirmed his commitment to never send soldiers to solve a problem only the Vietnamese could solve. As his assistant, Theodore Sorensen, said: "All his principal advisors on Vietnam favoured it (sending combat troops) calling it the 'touchstone of our good faith, a symbol of our determination. But the President in effect voted 'no' - and only his vote counted."[25] On October 2nd Kennedy asked the Secretary of Defense, Robert McNamara to announce to the waiting press the immediate withdrawal of 1,000 soldiers and to say the government would probably withdraw all American forces by the end of 1965. As a final thought he called over to McNamara, "And tell them that means all of the helicopter pilots too."[26] However, Kennedy's verbatim instructions, which were preserved in National Security Council records, were misinterpreted by McNamara. McNamara simply told the reporters that in his judgement: "the major part of the U.S. military task (could be) completed by 1965." An October 4th memo from General Maxwell Taylor, Chairman of the Joint Chiefs of Staff, to the other Joint Chiefs, and only released in 1997, confirmed this view: "All planning will be directed toward preparing RVN (S.V) forces for the withdrawal of all U.S. special assistance units and personnel by the end of calendar year 1965."[27]

On the 31st October, Kennedy made sure his decisions would not be misunderstood. He said: "Our object is to bring home every American technician, helicopter pilot, and military advisor by the end of 1965, permitting the South Vietnamese to maintain themselves as a free and independent country."[28] These were clear and unequivocal policy statements.

However, many authors dismiss these statements as optimistic talk which in no way can be interpreted as a definite policy change. Statements by Mansfield and O'Donnell are described as biased interpretations of events emanating from anti-war Senators or 'Camelot apologists'. And there is no doubt that Kennedy had made a number of ambiguous statements about Vietnam. Yet there is a wealth of documentary evidence indicating Kennedy wished to withdraw American forces from Vietnam and it is objective and not dependent on either of these groups.

Before Kennedy left for Dallas he told Mike Forrestal, an assistant to Assistant Secretary of State, Averell Harriman: "...I want you to organise an in-depth study of every possible option we've got in Vietnam, including how to get out of there. We have to review this whole thing from the bottom to the top."[29] However, Forrestal interpreted this statement to mean Kennedy was only playing 'devil's advocate'. Yet Deputy Defense Secretary, Roswell Gilpatric, told journalist, Charles Wheeler: "Before he died, sometime in October of 1963, Kennedy told both McNamara and me that he wanted us to have a plan ready for him early in 1964 to reduce the 16,000 military personnel that were in Vietnam. He wanted to cut back and he felt as he said in a press conference of September of 1963, that if the Vietnamese couldn't provide for their own security no outside power could do so. So, in my judgement, this is purely a hypothesis, Kennedy would not have gone along with an expanded force or deeper involvement of the United States in Vietnam after 1963."[30]

There is no doubt that opinion amongst Kennedy's advisors was polarised. As McNamara (1995) wrote in his memoirs: "...Johnson was left with a national security team that, although it remained intact, was deeply split over Vietnam."[31]

However, John Newman (1991) in his excellent book 'Kennedy in Vietnam' has been able to construct a plausible record of Kennedy's stated and likely intentions over Vietnam had he lived. Newman's analysis has been vigorously contested by a number of historians, including Noam Chomsky, but his work is persuasive. Newman maintains that despite bureaucratic opposition, Kennedy used the memo NSAM 263 to give his authorised disengagement plans "to withdraw 1,000 U.S. military personnel by the end of 1963." This would be a first implementation of a plan that would eventually make it "possible to withdraw the bulk of U.S. personnel ...by the end of 1965."

NSAM 263, published in the 'Pentagon Papers' in 1971, was President Kennedy's last policy directive on Vietnam. It was issued on October 11th 1963. After Kennedy's death, President Johnson issued NSAM 273 and it was designed to show that national policy towards Vietnam had not changed. However, NSAM 273 drastically changed U.S. policy as author, John Newman, has demonstrated.

Newman has shown how the Kennedy Administration were divided over the issue of Vietnam. The 'military' faction which included civilian officials gave priority to winning the war. The 'political' faction had put winning second to international and domestic considerations. NSAM 263, which signalled an avoidance of unlimited commitment to the war by its declaration of withdrawing 1,000 troops, reflected the 'political' faction. NSAM 273 chose the 'military' option of escalation.

Newman has pointed out that Kennedy had long range plans to train the South Vietnamese making it "possible to withdraw the bulk of U.S. personnel...by the end of 1965." These plans were formulated in the top secret 'Military Recommendations to the President' by Defense Secretary, Robert McNamara, and General Maxwell Taylor on October 2nd 1963.

In NSAM 263 Kennedy approved the announcement "in the very near future" withdrawing 1,000 troops "as an initial step in a long-term program to replace U.S. personnel...no formal announcement (should be) made of the implementation."

It was, however, hinted that the details would be made public after a top-level Honolulu conference on November 20th 1963. Two days later President Kennedy was assassinated.

Two days after that tragic event, Kennedy's successor Lyndon Johnson approved a 'new' policy statement, NSAM 273. NSAM said the withdrawal of troops would remain intact. However, the statement included words that McNamara and Taylor had "reported their judgement" that the U.S. could basically complete its military task "by the end of 1965" and "should" be able to withdraw 1,000 men by the end of 1963. This is in stark contrast to the certitude of the NSAM statement which was an unconditional implementation/instruction.

There was, accordingly, from Newman's interpretation of the government files a different and tragic change in Vietnam policy from the Kennedy to Johnson Administrations. The troops of course were never withdrawn. On the surface it looked that way, but the withdrawals were only an 'accounting exercise' and no actual reduction was achieved. Johnson went on to commit the United States government to unequivocal 'victory', as General Taylor stated in January 1964,

"273 makes clear the resolve of the president (Johnson) to ensure victory."

Although there can be no certitude as to which direction Kennedy would have taken America in the Vietnamese conflict, it is reasonable to assume, given Kennedy's philosophy about the Third World and colonialism, his temperament and abiding concerns not to commit ground troops, that he would have done things differently from his successor. He would not have "gotten" himself in the quagmire in the first place. Kennedy had visited Vietnam when it was under French colonial rule and his views then are testament to his belief that America must not repeat the same mistakes as the French. In 1954, as a United States Senator he said: "...to pour money, materials and men into the jungles of Indo-China without at least a remote prospect of victory would be dangerous, futile and self-destructive. Of course, all discussion of 'united action' (to help the French) assumes the inevitability of such victory; but such assumptions are not unlike similar predictions of confidence which have lulled the American people for many years and which, if continued, would present an improper basis for determining the extent of American participation. Moreover, without political independence for the associated states (of Indo-China), the other Asian nations have made it clear that they regard this as a war of colonialism; and the 'united action' which is said to be so desperately needed for victory in that area is likely to end up as unilateral action by our own country."[32]

Kennedy's presidential record suggests that he would never have committed himself to a long drawn out conflict without some foreseeable conclusion. In past problems he had chosen to either force a quick solution, going to the brink, or bring the resolution within a definite time limit - or negotiate a settlement. As Kennedy aide Larry O'Brien told historian Robert Dallek (1998), "...(after the 1964 election) I think he would have found a way of disengaging before it became all-out."[33]

And if Kennedy had expanded military involvement in Vietnam it is likely he would have done it in such a way which allowed for future withdrawal without seeming to suffer defeat. Kennedy, unlike Johnson, did not feel the need to prove himself in the foreign policy arena, certainly not after the successes of 1962/3. His willingness to accept a neutral government in Laos is evidence of his thinking on this matter. This view led McGeorge Bundy to say: "No one can say what JFK would have done. But that it would have been different and it would have been less (than Johnson) are, I think, safe generalisations."[34]

In the final analysis the evidence remains debatable whether Kennedy would have extricated the United States from the war in Vietnam. Kennedy's aides differed sharply on whether he would have followed more or less the same policy as President Johnson. Nevertheless, the preponderance of evidence suggests that a man so different from Johnson would never have allowed the problem to get the better of him. It is quite evident that Kennedy was more self assured than his successor. Johnson was in many ways, according to his biographers, a man who lacked real self-esteem and confidence even though he was brash and overbearing. Johnson was prestige conscious and a Texan through and through. On more than one occasion he likened the Vietnam war to the siege of the Alamo and repeatedly told his advisors that he was not going to be the first president to 'lose a war'. He was unyielding in his desire to pursue his policies and he was confused as to his predecessor's intentions. As Johnson's press secretary, George Reedy, said: "When he first came in (after JFK's assassination), he had a big meeting with all of the top Kennedy people and all his top people. I had the feeling I was sitting in a big poker game. Everyone was trying to hide his cards from the other guy and get a peek at the other guys' hands. He had decided he wanted to continue Kennedy's policies. He was looking to them to find out what Kennedy would have done. They, on the other hand, were looking to him to see what he wanted done. I think a signal got mixed up somewhere. He got the idea that Kennedy was going to prosecute the war in Vietnam to a greater extent than he would have..."[35] Given this state of mind Johnson forged ahead, oblivious to the natural restraints which had been inherent in his predecessor's pursuit of viable solutions to complex problems. Johnson's self-assurance masked a deep-seated insecurity. Kennedy's confidence masked a sophisticated knowledge which sets limits to military-inspired solutions to problems. Former House Speaker, Tip O'Neill, recognised this when he wrote:

> *"(a) misunderstanding about Jack Kennedy is the misinformed notion that he was responsible for getting us into Vietnam. In my view, just the opposite was true. If Jack had lived to serve a second term - and there's no question that he would have creamed Goldwater - he would have pulled out all our troops within a year or two. Certainly the Pentagon would never have exercised the kind of power over Kennedy that it had over Johnson. Lyndon Johnson revered West Point and the military*

leaders who came out of there, and he believed their judgement was infallible. Kennedy, on the other hand, was an Ivy Leaguer who was always sceptical of the military. There was no way he would ever allow them to call the shots."[36]

Kennedy was unaggressive to the point where perhaps only a war hero could have got away with withdrawal. It should be recalled that one of the reasons that Nixon was successful in his China policy was the fact he had been a lifelong anti- communist. Kennedy never came close to asking for war powers, his predecessor and successor sent troops to the Lebanon and the Dominican Republic. Kennedy was content to pursue covert operations linked with diplomatic efforts. And Kennedy refused to pursue an aggressive response in the Berlin Crisis and the Cuban Missile Crisis. During the Bay of Pigs invasion he stood fast against military advice to support the Cuban exiles with American forces. The question must be asked - would John Kennedy have sat still for an endless bloody war which ultimately tore the nation apart?

I believe the record suggests that he would not have allowed the war to get out of hand as Johnson was to eventually do after 1965. It is highly probable, although not conclusive, that he would have extricated America from the conflict and would have concluded that the South Vietnamese were incapable of defending themselves. Shortly after he became President he asked his cabinet to read Barbara Tuchman's 'The guns of August', a book which showed how Europe's leaders had incompetently stumbled into war through their misconceptions and misunderstandings. He said: "I don't ever want to be in that position...We are not going to bungle into war."[37]

Notes

1. Hersh, S. (1998). *The dark side of Camelot*, HarperCollins. p. 412.

2. Rust, W. J. (1985). *Kennedy in Vietnam*, Scribner. p. 117.

3. Giglio, J. N. (1991). *The presidency of John F. Kennedy*, University Press of Kansas. p. 240.

4. Reeves, R. (1993). *President Kennedy - profile of power*, Simon and Schuster. p. 119.

5. Giglio, J. N. (1991). *The presidency of John F. Kennedy*, University Press of Kansas. p. 254.

6. McNamara, R. S. and Vandermark, B. (1995). *In retrospect - the tragedy and lessons of Vietnam*, Times Books Random House. p. 95.

7. Reeves, T. C. (1991). *A question of character - a life John F. Kennedy*, Bloomsbury. p. 411.

8. Salinger, P. (1997). *John F. Kennedy - commander-in-chief*, Penguin Studio. p. 80.

9. Manchester, W. (1983). *One brief shining moment*, Michael Joseph. p. 217.

10. Schlesinger, A. M. (1978). *Robert Kennedy and his times*, Houghton Mifflin Co. p. 744.

11. *Ibid*, p. 772.

12. *Ibid*, p. 761.

13. Hilty, J .W. (1997). *Robert Kennedy – brother protector*, Temple University Press. p. 460.

14. Manchester, W. (1983). *One brief shining moment*, Michael Joseph. p. 220.

15. Reeves, R. (1993). *President Kennedy - profile of power*, Simon and Schuster. p. 484.

16. Karnow, S. (1983). *Vietnam - a history*, Viking. p. 268.

17. O'Donnell, K. P., Powers, D. F. and McCarthy, J. (1973). *Johnny we hardly knew ye*, Pocket Books. p. 15.

18. *Ibid*, p. 16.

19. Gavin, J. M. 'We can get out of Vietnam', *Saturday Evening Post*, 24 February 68, p. 38.

20. *Boston Globe*, 24 June 1973. (http://www.boston.com).

21. *Rolling Stone*, 6 December 1973. (http://www.rollingstone.com).

22. Manchester, W. (1975). *The glory and the dream*, Michael Joseph. p. 994.

23. Brogan, H. (1996). *Kennedy*, Longman. p. 198; McNamara, R. S. and Vandermark, B. (1995). *In retrospect - the tragedy and lessons of Vietnam*, Times Books Random House. p. 61; Reeves, R. (1993). *President Kennedy - profile of power*, Simon and Schuster. p. 589.

24. Brogan, H. (1996). *Kennedy*, Longman. p. 198.

25. 'The Kennedys'. Narrated by John Woodvine, written by Phillip Whitehead and Geoffrey C. Ward. Thames Television, 1992. (A Brook/WGBH Co-production for Thames Television).

26. Manchester, W. (1983). *One brief shining moment*, Michael Joseph. p. 225.

27. 'ARRB JCS Records'. CBS Television News, 22 December 1997. (http://www.cbs.com).

28. Manchester, W. (1983). *One brief shining moment*, Michael Joseph. p. 225.

29. Reeves, R. (1993). *President Kennedy - profile of power*, Simon and Schuster. p. 660.

30. 'The Kennedy legacy'. Narrated by Charles Wheeler. BBC Television, November 1983.

31. McNamara, R. S. and Vandermark, B. (1995). *In retrospect - the tragedy and lessons of Vietnam*, Times Books Random House. p. 97.

32. Nevins, A., ed. (1960). *The strategy of peace by JFK*, Harper New York. p. 59.

33. Dallek, R. (1998). *Flawed giant - Lyndon Johnson and his times 1961-1973*, Oxford University Press. p. 99.

34. *Ibid*, p. 99.

35. Kessler, R. (1995). *Inside the White House*, Pocket Books. p. 27.

36. O'Neill, T. (1987). *Man of the House*, St Martin's Press. p. 208.

37. McNamara, R. S. and Vandermark, B. (1995*). In retrospect - the tragedy and lessons of Vietnam*, Times Books Random House. p. 96.

Chapter 6

The Secret Life of JFK

Did JFK act immorally and recklessly in his private life?

"Do not become archivists of facts. Try to penetrate to the secret of their occurrence, persistently search for the laws which govern them."

Ivan Pavlov

President Kennedy's liaisons with women, other than his wife, have been well reported and written about for 30 years. It all makes titillating reading and gives the impression that Kennedy's affairs of the heart took precedence over affairs of state.

Credible and authoritative sources, too numerous to mention, have confirmed Kennedy's peccadilloes as historical fact - the handsome and fun-loving Kennedy never stopped pursuing attractive women even after entering the White House - nor they him. A number of respected historians have used White House logs, aeroplane logs, government records, FBI files and other archival material to confirm this aspect of Kennedy's lifestyle.

There were two scandals which surfaced during Kennedy's presidency. The first involved a couple, the Katers, who rented a Georgetown, Washington, D.C., apartment to a young girl, Pamela Turnure, who eventually became Jacqueline Kennedy's press secretary in the White House.[1] When John Kennedy was a United States senator he visited

Turnure at her apartment a number of times and was photographed by the landlords, Leonard and Florence Kater, leaving in the early hours of the morning. They also made tape recordings of Kennedy and Turnure's liaisons. During the presidential campaign of 1960, the staunchly Catholic Katers held up placards at rallies and even demonstrated outside the White House protesting that Kennedy was an adulterer. The press, in line with common practice during this period, took no notice.

The second scandal surfaced in 1962 with a rumour that John Kennedy had been married previously.[2] The woman in question was Durie Malcolm, a Kennedy Palm Beach neighbour. When the rumours came to John Kennedy's notice he asked 'Washington Post' friends, Ben Bradlee, and publisher, Phil Graham, to kill the story and deny its truth. He also enlisted the help of top Washington lawyer and former Truman Administration official, Clark Clifford, to look into the matter.

The rumour began with an entry in a little known book, published in 1956, which traced the Blauvelt family roots. Blauvelt was an amateur genealogist who added this item to his list sometime before his death in 1959. It is vague and inaccurate; he did not know Durie Malcolm's birth date or how to spell her name, and he reversed the chronology of her first two marriages. According to FBI memos the surreptitious marriage occurred in 1939 and ended in a Reno court in 1948. It was also rumoured that Kennedy Snr. used his friendship with Cardinal Cushing to have the marriage annulled so John Kennedy could marry Jacqueline Kennedy in 1953. In 1961, J. Edgar Hoover asked Attorney General, Robert Kennedy, about his brother's alleged first wife. According to the FBI memo: "The Attorney General stated the fellow who put (the book) together is dead and the executor of the estate went through the material to find out where he got the information and all he found was a newspaper clipping saying the President had gone out with the girl...once."[3]

At the time the rumours surfaced Durie Malcolm signed an affidavit denying the marriage had taken place. In the mid-1990s she told the 'Sunday Times': "I wouldn't have married Jack Kennedy for all the tea in China. Why? I'll tell you why: if you want to know the truth, I didn't care for those Irish micks and Old Joe was a terrible man...I've always denied it. I knew all those Kennedy kids although Joe (Jnr.) was more my age. I guess there was this time I went with Jack and his father and this whole bunch of other people down to a football game in Miami and some guy wrote this trashy thing for a New York paper.

Then this old guy Blauvelt - apparently he saw it - and because the Blauvelts had never had anyone important for years, he put us together. I guess he was 80 or something and he got it all mixed up. I've always denied it. I kept saying: "Why doesn't the White House deny it?"[4]

The rumour again surfaced with the publication of Seymour Hersh's (1997) book 'The dark side of Camelot'. Hersh got Kennedy friend Charles Spalding to confirm that the 'marriage' took place and that Spalding had destroyed the marriage record. Everything else Hersh wrote was based on rumour. Hersh never bothered to ask why a minor Kennedy friend would be asked to handle such a delicate matter even though Kennedy Snr. was skilled in the art of 'handling' such matters. He had tried and tested operatives who took care of such problems, men like James McInerney and lawyer, Jack Miller. Spalding's veracity is mixed. He has been a strong source for many stories about the Kennedys in the past. However, his veracity in connection with this story is weak. He has admitted his short term memory had been failing him in old age and he miscommunicated the meaning of his statements to other authors like C. David Heymann (1998) to whom he gave the impression that the stories of an affair between Jackie Kennedy and Robert Kennedy were true.[5] Until further research is forthcoming, the story of a John F. Kennedy first marriage cannot be accepted as true.

It was not until the mid-1970s that the great wealth of stories of John Kennedy's philandering entered the public domain. Kennedy's privacy was guarded by Secret Service agents and a number of them revealed information to newspaper reporters. In the 1990s, four agents gave a detailed account of Kennedy's behaviour in the White House to author Seymour Hersh. These accounts were published in Hersh's (1997) book 'The dark side of Camelot' and cannot be dismissed. The agents expressed a fondness for the President and spoke with great discomfit. There is no evidence that they revealed their accounts for monetary gain or through a desire to seek fame.

As his wife, Jacqueline, was often away on vacation and his work involved frequent travel, the opportunities for extra-marital activities were too irresistible for a man like John Kennedy. Moreover, he seemed to enjoy the image and he never tried to hide his attraction for starlets and pretty girls, seeking them out for special attention as he moved into crowds to shake hands or spotting a pretty campaign worker amongst his many supporters. On one occasion he surprised British Prime Minister, Harold MacMillan, during a 1962 conference in

Nassau by casually stating that if he went too long without a woman he suffered severe headaches.[6]

Kennedy was particularly attracted to Hollywood stars and starlets. His 'conquests' are too numerous to give individual accounts. Some of the most recognisable women in show business who submitted to John Kennedy's advances include Marilyn Monroe, Jayne Mansfield and Gene Tierney. All three women admitted they had slept with Kennedy.[7] Credible sources, many of whom had been close friends of Kennedy for most of his life, have confirmed there were many more starlets, both major and minor, with whom Kennedy had affairs. A number of women have given discreet but coy answers to questions posed by reporters. A likely candidate for JFK's affections was actress Angie Dickenson who spent some time with the new President on the evening of his inauguration. She has responded with the reply that her relationship with the President should remain 'private'.[8] On the whole, however, these relationships were only fleeting liaisons and did not add up to any serious interest on Kennedy's behalf.

Most of the women associated with Kennedy were unknown and faceless and were procured for Kennedy from the ranks of government workers, airlines and assorted connections with friends and associates. Most often cited were two secretaries; Priscilla Wear, (an assistant to Kennedy's secretary, Evelyn Lincoln), and Jill Cowan, who worked for Pierre Salinger. Known by their nicknames 'Fiddle and Faddle', they displayed few secretarial skills but nevertheless worked on his staff. Bright and charming, they were attractive but 'bimbo-like'. The two often turned up in the President's entourage when Kennedy was travelling. Although assigned no discernible duties they usually appeared at Palm Beach when JFK was on vacation. They were usually assigned quarters near the President.

Sadly, one young woman who had known Kennedy when he was a senator, had fallen in love with him. When Kennedy became President, she was given a job on the National Security Council staff in the executive office buildings near the White House.[9] It would seem that this affair was a forerunner to another 35 years later when a White House intern fell into the same type of emotional vortex with another handsome and charismatic President.

Mary Meyer

The preponderance of evidence strongly suggests that Kennedy had an affair with Mary Meyer, sister-in-law of 'Washington Post' editor, Ben Bradlee. Meyer was an artist who lived in Georgetown in Washington D.C.. Her affair with the President lasted two years. In 1964, a year after the President's assassination, she was murdered as she walked along a tow-path next to the Potomac river. Meyer's killer, according to police reports, grabbed her from behind and in broad daylight shot the 42 year old just once under the cheekbone. Her killer escaped and Meyer died instantly.

A number of authors have tried to tie the murder in with attempts by government agencies to keep the affair with President Kennedy secret. They have also attempted to explain her death as an effort to silence her because she purportedly knew about a conspiracy to murder the President.

The story gained some credence through the investigation of the case by best-selling author, Leo Damore, and JFK conspiracy author, John H. Davis. They suggest that Mary Meyer had been told by JFK shortly before his death that there was a conspiracy to assassinate him. Kennedy also purportedly told Meyer that the conspirators were people who were close to him. The conspirators allegedly decided Meyer had to be silenced before she could reveal what she knew about JFK's assassination.

The 'Meyer Conspiracy' proponents, Damore and Davis, researched the story in the early 1990s. Damore said he persuaded many government officials to talk for the first time about the case and they agreed that Mary Meyer was murdered because she knew too much. They said that some very powerful people feared that Meyer knew the 'real secret' of the JFK assassination.

One of Damore's sources was a retired police detective who had worked on the case in 1964.[10] He said that the murder was the work of a professional assassin and that the federal government was involved. The federal government, apparently, had put pressure on the police department to close the case quickly.

The simple facts of the case are quite different.[11] An African-American male, Raymond Crump, was spotted near the murder scene, and was arrested and charged with Meyer's murder. The evidence against

Crump was strong. Witnesses near the scene of the attempted rape or mugging heard shots; one of them, Henry Wiggins, identified Crump as the man who stood over Meyer's body shortly after the shots had been fired. Crump had been arrested approximately ¾ of an hour after Mary Meyer had been killed. He had been hiding in some bushes near the scene of the crime. He lied to police officers and had fresh cuts and bruises on his body. However, a jury acquitted Crump in the face of overwhelming circumstantial evidence due mainly to an inept prosecutor. The case came down to a choice between believing Crump who appeared to be a quiet and reverent soul, and witness Wiggins who had been a war veteran and former military policeman. It would appear that the trial had been a precursor to O. J. Simpson's; race had played an important part in the proceedings.

Mary Meyer, who was single at the time of her affair with the President, had been married to CIA officer, Cord Meyer. They divorced in 1956. Ben Bradlee, who was married to Mary's sister Toni, did not know at the time that his sister-in-law was having an affair with his friend John Kennedy.

In his autobiography, Ben Bradlee (1995) relates the story from his viewpoint. On the night of the murder he got a call at his home from Anne Truitt, Mary's artist friend and then wife of James Truitt, 'Newsweek's' Tokyo correspondent. Mary had told Anne to retrieve her diary in which she documented her affair with the President, in case anything happened to her. The next morning Ben and Toni went to Mary's house and once inside they discovered CIA counter-espionage chief, James Angleton, was there. No diary was found. But later in the day the Bradlees found it at Mary's art studio which was directly across a dead-end driveway from the Bradlee's house. They again discovered Angleton who was picking the lock of the studio. Embarrassed, Angleton walked off. Toni found the diary an hour later. The diary confirmed that Mary had been having an affair with JFK even though his name was never mentioned. The diary was given to James Angleton under the assumption it would be destroyed. However the diary was not destroyed until some years later.[12]

There have been contradictory accounts of how the diary was found but there is no credible evidence to support the theory that Mary Meyer had been murdered to silence her. If 'government agents' had indeed killed her then why would they leave a witness at the scene to identify the real culprits? Would the killers not have been afraid that the man arrested for the murder might reveal their true identities?

The Meyer diary has been used by other authors, notably Nelly Bly (1996) in her book 'The Kennedy men', to support one story or another which seeks to label Kennedy as a drug user. In a 'National Enquirer' article in 1976, James Truitt stated that Mary Meyer had revealed her affair with Kennedy to him. He went further and stated that Meyer and Kennedy had smoked marijuana.

Timothy Leary (1983) enhanced this story in his book 'Flashbacks'. Leary embellished it by contending that Mary Meyer was consulting him in 1962 about how to conduct LSD sessions. Meyer had, purportedly, told Leary that she had a friend who was a 'very important man' who also wanted to try the drug. Leary maintained that after the assassination, Meyer talked of people who were upset about a 'peace-loving' president, who were turned on by drugs, and who had been done away with because they could not control him any longer. However, Leary admitted to author, Nina Burleigh, that he had no proof that Meyer had introduced the President to LSD and said he was not sure whether it was true or not. He did claim to have introduced Marilyn Monroe to the drug.[13]

There is a central problem with Leary's story. Leary did not mention Meyer in any of his books until 'Flashbacks' more than 20 years after he had supposedly met her. Leary was a lifelong radical who took every opportunity to challenge the establishment. It stretches the imagination to assume he would not have revealed scandalous events about the American government. Furthermore, many of his books are autobiographical. Given the astounding nature of his revelations, it is simply incredulous that he did not write about these events long before 1983. In short Leary's retroactive storytelling is simply not credible.

There are other reasons why Leary's claims should be rejected. Kennedy's lifestyle throughout his 46 years has been well chronicled by numerous sources, including family friends and others who knew him well. Kennedy did not smoke and was only a social drinker. If Kennedy had taken LSD and smoked marijuana in the White House it would have been totally out of character.

On the other hand there is strong evidence that President Kennedy took amphetamines but it is unlikely he did so knowingly.[14] It was the medical malpractice of the day and not at all unusual. These drugs were perfectly legal in 1963 and steroids were not known to be carcinogenic. According to J. Edgar Hoover biographer, Richard Gid Powers (1987), the FBI Director may have received 'vitamin shots' laced with amphetamines.[15] Dr Max Jacobson, along with others like Dr Janet Travell, was hired by Kennedy to treat his ailing back. Jacobson had invented an elixir and injected his patients with 'vitamin shots'. The shots boosted the patient's energy and confidence and in general filled them with a sense of well-being. The concoction, which was sent by Robert Kennedy for laboratory testing turned out to be a mixture of vitamins, steroids and amphetamines.

Max Jacobson travelled with President Kennedy to the first summit meeting with Kruschev in Vienna in June 1961. At this time Kennedy was having severe pain in his back. He had strained it whilst planting a tree in Ottawa the previous May. When told by his brother that the mixture was dangerous, Kennedy said that he did not care if it was 'horse's piss' as long as it relieved his back pain with no obvious side effects.[16] After years of ineffectual treatment for his back it is no wonder that he insisted on the treatment continuing up to the time of his death in November 1963. And there is compelling evidence from Jacobson's family that the doctor supplied the 'elixir' to Jacqueline Kennedy long after she left the White House.[17]

Marilyn Monroe

Contrary to public perception, President Kennedy's relationship with Marilyn Monroe was neither long-lasting nor deeply emotional and cannot by any stretch of the imagination be described as 'an affair'. Over the years this mythical part of the Kennedy legend has been misunderstood by countless authors and it has been increasingly exaggerated. The truth of the matter is that there was only one intimate rendezvous between Kennedy and the glamorous movie star and it occurred at Bing Crosby's house in Palm Springs on Saturday 24 March 1962. Marilyn Monroe stated this clearly to her close friend and masseur Ralph Roberts.[18]

The only thing that can be definitely stated is that Kennedy and Monroe met five times between 1960 - the year when Kennedy was elected President - and August 1962 - the time of Marilyn's death. This was at a party at Peter Lawford's house in Santa Monica; a dinner party for the President at the home of Fifi Fell in Manhattan; at Bing Crosby's house as stated above; at Madison Square Garden for the President's birthday gala and afterwards at a private party; and finally when Monroe visited the Kennedy compound at Hyannisport which was witnessed by Kennedy's good friend, Charles Spalding. According to

Monroe biographer, Donald Spoto (1993), all other claims for specific meetings were impossible both geographically and chronologically.[19] And why should this be believed against a host of books which delineate the Kennedy-Monroe affair over a period of years? As Spoto wrote:

"Were Marilyn Monroe's characteristic candour on such matters the only evidence - the fact that she never exaggerated nor minimised her romantic involvements - that would be weighty reason to accept her version of the one night of intimacy. There is, however, good external evidence to support her claim. Accounts of a more enduring affair with John Kennedy, stretching anywhere from a year to a decade, come from fanciful supermarket journalists and tales told by those eager for quick cash or quicker notoriety: those who fail to check the facts of history and are thus easily dispatched as reliable sources."[20]

Pierre Salinger, President Kennedy's press secretary, told the 'Daily Mail' in September 1992: "There's got to be one question in your head which is 'If I was so close to Jack, how come I didn't know about his women sneaking in and out of the White House all the time?' But I knew or saw absolutely nothing...Just how Marilyn Monroe could have got in or out without anybody noticing is something isn't it? But I didn't see her and nobody on the staff came to me and said they had or that they knew anything about it and we were with him almost all the time...(They say JFK and Marilyn Monroe used Peter Lawford's house for their rendezvous) But anytime we were in LA it was me who always stayed at Peter's house, always. We were partners in a nightclub. I slept there in his house and, what, am I blind or something that I could not notice Marilyn strolling around in a nightdress?"[21]

Spoto's (1993) well-researched and extremely detailed account of Marilyn Monroe's life did not prevent Seymour Hersh (1997) from writing: "Her affair with Kennedy was by all accounts in full bloom as the presidential campaign was getting under way. Many of the rendezvous were at the Santa Monica home of Peter and Patricia Lawford...who were Monroe's close friends. There has been published speculation that Monroe became pregnant by Kennedy and had an abortion in Mexico; the full story may never be known, but accounts of her affair and abortion have been published again and again since her suicide and his murder."[22]

But do these accounts make the speculation correct? Hersh seems to think so, even though one might expect something better from a

Pulitzer Prize winning writer. Seymour Hersh suggests that many mutual friends of Kennedy and Monroe testified to him about the affair and yet we are only privy to a sample. George Smathers, Kennedy's fellow senator and close friend, told Hersh about the affair but he did not speculate as to the closeness of Kennedy and Monroe nor did he state how long the 'affair' lasted.[23]

Hersh has also misquoted Charles Spalding. Hersh wrote that in 1960, on an occasion when Monroe had been bingeing on alcohol and drugs, Kennedy asked Spalding to go to Los Angeles to quieten Monroe down as he feared she would talk about their 'affair'. Spalding has stated that he did make the trip to Los Angeles but not for the purposes of keeping Monroe quiet. Other writers maintain that railroad lobbyist and friend of Kennedy's, Bill Thompson, had been given that task.[24]

As Donald Spoto (1993) wrote: "The posthumous revelations of Kennedy's philandering revealed the impossibility, for obvious reasons, of pursuing any serious romance with one woman."[25] In his biography of Jacqueline Kennedy (Spoto, 2000), he wrote: "...the purported affair with Marilyn Monroe was a matter of only one afternoon in March 1962, at Bing Crosby's home in the California desert."[26] Marilyn's close friend Susan Strasberg testified to this fact when she denied any long term affair had existed between John F. Kennedy and the Hollywood movie star: "Not in her worst nightmare," Strasberg wrote, "would Marilyn have wanted to be with JFK on any permanent basis. It was okay for one night to sleep with a charismatic president - and she loved the secrecy and drama of it. But he certainly wasn't the kind of man she wanted for life and she was very clear to us about this."[27]

However, there is little doubt that had Kennedy's single sexual liaison with Monroe become public his presidency would have been at risk. It was a period when the American public would not have forgiven a presidential sexual indiscretion. Furthermore, had the revelations about Kennedy and Monroe been released, it would have given a precedent for the media to open up Pandora's box as far as the President's other women were concerned.

Ellen Rometsch

President Kennedy also put his presidency at risk because of his sexual liaison with Ellen Rometsch, a German girl who had married an American soldier.[28] There has been speculation about the story in a number of Kennedy biographies and it was made popular by Seymour Hersh (1997) in his best-selling 'The dark side of Camelot'.

Ellen Fimmel Rometsch was an East German refugee who had married an American Air Force sergeant who was assigned to the West German Embassy in Washington D.C.. As a young adult she had been a member of the communist party and was 'suspected' of being a communist spy even though no evidence has been forthcoming and FBI files show no sinister activities.

By early 1963, Rometsch had become one of Bobby Baker's girls. Baker, the secretary to the Senate and a close colleague Lyndon Johnson, ran the Quorum Club, a private social club situated in a private suite at the Carroll Arms. It was a club for high level officials, congressmen and lobbyists which was situated near the Capitol Building. Many congressmen had liaisons with pretty girls arranged by Baker.

Kennedy friend, Bill Thompson, spotted Rometsch at the club and thought she would be just right for the President. After arranging matters with Baker, Thompson took Rometsch to the White House to meet Kennedy. According to Baker, Rometsch returned 'ten or more times' to meet the President. Baker's position as a source is authoritative and his position as the '51st Senator', as many congressmen called him, would make his stories very credible. Until Baker's statement on an ABC television documentary, the story has been speculated upon by many authors; but Baker's evidence has confirmed it as an historical fact.

The FBI picked Rometsch up in July 1963 with Attorney General, Robert Kennedy's approval and deported her to West Germany. The Rometsch affair was reported in the American papers as a potential scandal involving 'high level' officials and congressmen. It was hinted that she was potentially involved with 'high-ranking' members of the executive branch of government. In fact she had named the President as one of the officials who had called on her services.

Robert Kennedy ordered she be denied a visa if she was ever to apply to return to the United States. When she protested, RFK had an aide, LaVern Duffy, go to West Germany to keep her quiet with a large cash payment. The whole affair threatened to become a major scandal, but was swept under the carpet since it could not only jeopardise the President but also politicians of both political parties.

Jack and Jackie

A number of books have stated that John Kennedy's womanising had a debilitating effect on the John and Jacqueline Kennedy's marriage. Whilst there are elements of truth in these accounts, the relationship was much more complex.

Jacqueline Bouvier Kennedy was a private woman; indeed she cherished her privacy. Above all she was an accomplished actress who could play the part required because she was an astute and intelligent woman. Her breathless and feminine voice fooled many who considered her to be a woman who was less than erudite. Her mother taught her never to appear more intelligent than a man which may account for her adoption of a feminine, whispery voice; a voice which disarmed and charmed. In her television campaign appearances she came across as a young wife who was totally eclipsed by her worldly and intelligent husband. But beneath the surface of her personality lay a woman who could intelligently manage the vicissitudes of the political world which she embraced. Rather than a dull and brainless creature she was instead witty and funny. Indeed she had a well developed and intelligent sense of humour. She was also fiercely independent and steel-willed. John Kennedy was often frustrated by his wife's unwillingness to conform to political demands.

Born into the social elite of east coast America she learned to appreciate the qualities of dignity and tried to maintain it at all times. As a young woman she was often described as well-bred and 'nice'. However, her independent streak developed in her a lifelong hatred of regimentation - a quality not likely to endear her to the Kennedys. Her father, 'Black Jack' Bouvier (he came to the nickname because of his swarthy dark looks and a reputation as a 'womaniser'), had married Janet Lee from an old established and wealthy family. He was a playboy and his wealth was 'old money', but because of his reckless business dealings he did not secure a financially stable lifestyle. His strong reliance on gambling and alcohol ruined his life. The couple divorced when Jackie was a young woman, but Jackie never stopped loving her father. More than one friend thought that when Jackie married John Kennedy she came the nearest to marrying her father.

She was introduced to young Congressman Kennedy by journalist Charles Bartlett. Eventually Joseph Kennedy saw the 'classy' Jackie as an asset to his son's political life and he encouraged their relationship. After a short courtship the couple were married in September 1953 after

Jack's election to the Senate in the 1952 elections. The marriage was one of the social events of the year.

For Jackie the marriage gave her financial security; the Kennedy family wealth had been estimated at over 400 million dollars. The Kennedys liked the idea that Jackie was 'upper class'. Their marriage has often been described as a 'great American love story'. However, it is clear that she would never have married him if he had not been rich and he would never have married her if his father had not said he had to for political reasons.

There were some who said that in a social sense she was marrying beneath herself. However, the marriage was successful at first and Jackie had no illusions as to her husband's fidelity. From accounts of close friends who knew them during this period, it is evident that Jack did not remain faithful and took every available opportunity to play around. Evelyn Lincoln, his Senatorial and Presidential private secretary, has said that he had "a number of girlfriends at this time".[29]

According to Priscilla Johnson McMillan, the marriage became troubled in 1956. Joseph Kennedy, fearful a divorce would damage his son's chances for the presidency, met with her and some accommodation made to smooth over the rift. Speaking on the Thames Television documentary 'The Kennedys' (1992), McMillan said that one of the conditions for Jackie's staying with her husband was that JFK would be discreet and not "fling his affairs in her face...not that he might not roam but he would not do so in a way that was humiliating to Jackie."[30] There have been rumours that a financial settlement had been made but there is no concrete evidence to support this contention. Author Donald Spoto (2000) maintains that Joseph Kennedy offered one million dollars to Jackie as an inducement to stay married to his son but she turned it down.[31]

Surprisingly, Jackie's aloof and regal style did not hinder her husband's political life but instead enhanced it. Voters recognised that she was not sophisticated politically but had a dignified role and was greatly appreciated. She learned how to play the role of the 'princess'. However she never learned to like 'politicians' or politicians' wives and took every opportunity to avoid the day to day schedule of hectic campaigning. But John Kennedy had immense pride in his wife's contributions to his career. She was conversant in a number of languages including French, Italian and Spanish. Speaking to ethnic groups in their language of origin was a definite bonus during the 1960 campaign.

After her husband's election to the White House, Jackie performed well as 'First Lady'. The American people were charmed by her glamour and she impressed many with her job of redecorating the presidential mansion. Her appearance in a special television documentary about the refurbishings confirmed to many, including her husband, that she was a great political asset.

Jackie, however, did not confine her spending powers to the White House alone. Jack was frequently frustrated with his wife's avarice and voiced his anger not only to her but also to many of his aides. One friend described Jackie as the kind of woman you pay for in camels. Frequent shopping sprees and purchases of designer clothes, jewellery and antiques forced Jack Kennedy to request his aides keep a close check on Jackie's spending. Jack's efforts to curb these extravagant spending bouts met with little success.

There are some who were close to the couple who have reasoned that Jackie got away with her spending habits because of her husband's affairs; Jack Kennedy may have reasoned that he could not approach her to complain in the knowledge that his weaknesses were far greater. Others have speculated that Jackie felt confident in her habits knowing she could retaliate by raising the matter of his affairs should he ever challenge her. But this reasoning remains, at best, only speculative.

John Kennedy continued to see other women during his presidency and towards the end, according to Evelyn Lincoln, Jackie had affairs herself.[32] Lincoln saw nothing surprising in this, "All the jet set were like that," she said. There is, however, no piece of authoritative evidence to confirm 'Jackie's affairs' beyond gossip and speculation. Her step-brother, Hugh Auchincloss, vigorously denies them.[33] And it should be noted that Evelyn Lincoln has not given any specific proof that the affairs occurred apart from her belief that they were so. Although she was close to John Kennedy in a professional way (she had been his private secretary), she operated outside the Kennedy's social life.

However, according to the most authoritative accounts given by numerous friends of the couple, it appears that Jackie knew about some of her husband's affairs. One of Nina Burleigh's confidential sources told her that Jackie "felt it was okay. She knew he had this problem."[34]

She internalised it and quietly suffered but dealt with it in a dignified way. She had her own interests and was absolutely taken with being First Lady, and she was proud of her husband. Jackie knew she could not change him and accepted his lifestyle as long as he did not flaunt his women. And, of course, infidelity was nothing new to her, having been raised by a father who saw nothing wrong in taking mistresses. She had loved and admired her father in full knowledge of his way of life and she saw him as a glamorous and exciting figure. John White, one of Jackie's friends from her newspaper days, said: "I don't think Jackie cared much about JFK's morals...more important to her than his morality was that he was at the centre of events and that he acquit himself well and give her a decent role in the drama. It's fair to say they both lived up to their ends of the bargain."[35] Early on in the marriage, Jackie had formed a close relationship with her father-in-law and they confided in each other. She was not shocked by the senior Kennedy's reminisces about his former lovers. He paid her bills and she forgave his son.

Jack Kennedy's lifestyle was made easier by Jackie's frequent trips abroad, her shopping sprees and her interest in equestrian events. She spent many weekends alone at the couple's new home at Atoka. And Jack made sure he did not put his wife in a position where she would be embarrassed or disgraced by him. Secret Service agents have said that the President's swimming pool 'playtimes' occurred only when Jackie was away. Jackie must have felt some assurance in the fact that the press, during this period, would never print personal and scandalous items.

The couple led curiously separate lives. Compatible temperaments were not a consideration when they decided upon marriage. Jack Kennedy once drew a wavy line on a piece of paper and said: "That's Jackie". He then drew a straight line and said: "That's me". Whilst Jackie was given to varying temperament, Jack's personality was on an even keel. However, during his presidency Kennedy made sure that they both spent the early afternoon together in the White House and were committed to one another. A warm family environment was established contrary to some who say the couple must have been at constant war over Jack Kennedy's philandering. They also made a total commitment to their children as far as their lives would allow and both parents protected them from unwanted public attention. One of Jacqueline Kennedy's lasting legacies were her children who, against enormous odds, grew up to be emotionally stable. In the words of Arthur Schlesinger Jnr.: "They were brought up unspoiled, modest, hard-working, well-mannered, friendly to their contemporaries, courteous to their elders."[36]

There were no outward signs of affection between Jack and Jackie and much has been made of the appearance of a lack of affection. Betty Spalding, a close friend of Jackie's, said: "In their strangulated way, Jack and Jackie loved each other but neither was able to relate to the other, and there was never any affection between them at any time. He was always quite diffident towards her. He had a total lack of ability to relate emotionally towards her. He had a total lack of ability to relate emotionally to anyone...(but) both of them were blocked emotionally. (Jackie) had the same emotional block and panics that Jack had."[37] But they did have a full physical relationship. A short time after Jack's death, Jackie told author Theodore H. White, the couple had made love in the Fort Worth hotel the night before the assassination.[38]

Jackie loved and respected her husband, often needled him about his fondness for other women, but she would not have done anything to bring shame on him. She felt her parents had failed her by divorcing and she was convinced she would not travel the same route. She knew Jack deeply loved his children and her admiration, love and respect for his position in life was undiminished and even enhanced as his career flourished.

However, many writers have failed to correctly interpret their mutual 'coldness' toward one another. Jack's and Jackie's parents were distinctly cold toward their spouses and they grew up in a time when public displays of affection were interpreted as brash and vulgar. Jack disdained sentimentality and Jackie's warmth was not something which she believed should be displayed outside her family life. Even before her marriage Jackie told one friend they were both 'icebergs' keeping much of what they felt submerged.

There is evidence to suggest that the marriage became stronger after the loss of their new born son Patrick in August 1963. Jack had been seriously affected by the death of his infant son. At the funeral mass he had been distraught and wept more than anyone had remembered seeing him. To those who knew the couple well, the death brought them closer together. Jack's close friend Bill Walton, who spent the weekend of the funeral with the Kennedys, said: "She hung onto him and he held her in his arms, something nobody ever saw at any other time because they were very private people." Jackie told Jack that, great as the loss of their son was, "the one blow I could not bear would be to lose you."[39]

Jackie herself confirmed to author Theodore H. White that their relationship became much stronger after the death of her baby. It would seem that John Kennedy, late in marriage, was achieving the maturity of full commitment. They found solace in one another and those close to the presidential couple have said the love they had for one another was 'genuine'. Jack had come to see his wife not just as a political asset but more as a 'person'. After her infant son's death Jackie recuperated by taking a trip to Greece. She wrote her husband:

> *"I miss you very much. I think how lucky I am to miss you - I know I exaggerate everything - but I feel sorry for everyone else who is married. I realise here so much that I am having something you can never have - the absence of tension...I wish so much I could give you that...But I can't...so I give you every day while I think of you. (It is) the only thing I have to give and I hope it matters to you."[40]*

The popular myth of Jackie Kennedy (from the 1970s onwards) is one of a 'wastrel shopper' who was in love with money and married billionaire Aristotle Onassis for this reason. The truth is somewhat different. After the death of her husband and later after the tragedy in Los Angeles, Jackie wanted to protect her children and believed her marriage to Onassis would guarantee this. Contrary to reports in various Jackie Kennedy biographies, there was no 170 clause 'marriage contract', nor did Ted Kennedy broker an agreement before her marriage to Onassis. In fact she dismissed ideas of grabbing a large part of Onassis' fortune which could have been her due under Greek law. This is one reason why Onassis' sister liked Jackie and why the billionaire's primary lawyer, Stelios Papadimitriou, confirmed these facts in 1998.[41]

Jacqueline Kennedy never sought publicity and often commented how surprised she was that anyone would see her as a celebrity. She believed that celebrities were people who 'accomplished things'. Jackie eschewed the 'jet set' life during the latter part of her life. She preferred, instead, to commute between her New York City apartment and her retreat on Martha's Vineyard. She travelled frequently and devoted herself to her work in publishing and the Arts. Her primary role was to be fulfilled by work and the nurture of her children. It was work, privacy and family which dominated her life, not riches.

As a corrective to the numerous books written about Kennedy's immoral activities an explanation of why Kennedy acted as he did may be in order: This is not to excuse but to present a balanced understanding of a very complex man.

No serious Kennedy scholar could possibly excuse Kennedy's womanising. It was reckless and immoral and reflected a troubled 'psyche'. Yet it should also be remembered that the milieu in which Kennedy interacted with others, both in a social and a professional sense, was extremely conducive to the lifestyle he adopted. As Nina Burleigh (1988) wrote: "As hard as it might be to imagine it today, Washington was a sexier town in the years of the Cold War...The capital's moral tone was set by Congress, where in the secretly swinging 1950s and early 1960s Senators and Representatives were accustomed to the occasional assignation with a willing woman from the typing pool or reception desk. Private morality rarely matched public appearance."[42]

Some authors have made reference to the 'Don Juan' syndrome to explain Kennedy's womanising. Michael John Sullivan (1991) wrote: "Psychiatrically speaking, the 'Don Juan' complex from which John Kennedy so obviously suffered can be attributed to a blocked personality, from which threatening problems of either a sexual or emotional nature were kept securely hidden in the unconscious by the relentless pursuit and conquest of every woman whom the subject encountered. Of course, any kind of psychic intimacy or emotional involvement was avoided at all cost, this being not only unattractive and undesirable for the Don Juan, but also a complete impossibility because of the problems lurking in the subconscious. Many victims of the 'Don Juan' complex are latent homosexuals, who keep their true desires hidden behind the constant lovemaking performances to display and 'prove' their heterosexuality. There is no evidence that John Kennedy was latently homosexual. Other Don Juans are emotionally crippled early in life and demonstrate hostility and aggression toward women and an inability to form intimate relationships with them...considering the crushingly pernicious influence of his immoral father and acute lack of affection and cold indifference of his mother, it is no surprise that the young Kennedy should have developed exactly such a complex."[43]

John Kennedy's upbringing was vital in the formation of personality and character. The Jesuits are noted for the aphorism, 'Give me a child at age five and I will show you the man'. Kennedy's parents are part of the solution in an understanding of John Kennedy and particularly the example set by his father, Joseph Kennedy Snr.

It is quite evident that Kennedy tried to follow in his father's footsteps in his attitude towards women. Psychologists call this "compulsive repetition"; how family traits are passed on and adapted by each generation; an acting out of the same behaviour. The father often left his family back East when he became a Hollywood mogul in the 1920s, and his personal morality was not formed by his Catholic faith but in the class system prevalent in Boston society which frowned upon the Irish. Joseph Kennedy was scarred by the system which left him wanting to excel and supersede the 'Boston Brahmins'. In so doing he was led to believe that he could snub his nose at convention and, if he was rich enough, live by his own rules.

Joseph Kennedy had a much-publicised business relationship with Hollywood star Gloria Swanson; they often appeared together at parties in New York and California. Eventually, the business relationship turned into a sexual one as well, even though both parties were married. Joe Kennedy even indulged himself with her when the Kennedys took a voyage to Europe. Rose seemed to believe the relationship was platonic although there is a wealth of evidence from sources close to the Kennedy family that Rose had a particular arrangement with her husband, allowing him his sexual conquests as long as it did not embarrass her. It is true they loved one another, but Rose's philosophy seemed to approach the issue of marriage as confined solely to procreation and living the life of a family matriarch. A close sexual relationship did not seem to figure as a large issue in her idea of a successful marriage. Many writers have contended that Rose and Joe were not alone in defining marriage as such - the Eastern establishment families considered such arrangements to be both recognised and not unusual.

But Joe Kennedy's practices were, by most normal standards, highly immoral. He often brought his mistresses home to stay with him at the family home in Hyannisport. Rose, a staunch Catholic, had closed her mind to her husband's philandering, accepting it as a condition of her position in life. The activities of the father were not lost on the sons.

However, despite everything - his womanising and the nakedness of his ambitions - there were many sympathetic attributes to his personality. Joe Kennedy was a strange mixture of good and bad as Kennedy biographer, Doris Kearns Goodwin, realised after researching his life for many years:

"The truth is that he united in his person both inexorable self-will and the capacity for deep attachment, both appalling ruthlessness and unswerving fidelity, the images jostle one another, yet are part of the same complicated character. Deficient in civility, he could be the most disagreeable man in the world; unbounded by convention, his crudeness would betray others again and again. However, when the gates of his passion were opened for those he loved, the love he received in return was past the size of dreaming. Let the world classify him a blackguard, so long as his family and his friends ranked him a king."[44]

It is certainly true that the nine Kennedy children loved and respected their mother and she was the glue that held the family together. However, she had a 'schoolmistress' personality; she was prim and proper and always conscious of her aspirations to be part of a respected eastern establishment with the proper manners and social graces. It was quite evident to the many family friends and acquaintances of John Kennedy that his relationship with his mother was loving but remote. There seemed to be an emotional and physical distance between them. John's attitude towards his mother was one of love but not respect. It was his father who he looked up to and emulated.

A physical distance developed between mother and son when he was sent to boarding schools; a physical distance which developed into an emotional one. He wrote many letters to both parents but those he sent to his mother do not reveal a desperate need for maternal acceptance. Even when he returned home to the family compound, his mother would often retreat to her own little house on the beach where she could read in solitude. Every day she attended Mass in nearby Hyannis and she liked nothing better than to play a round of golf by herself. John Kennedy said more than once to his friends that his mother never approached him to give him a hug or become tactile. This lack of physical affection was to condition Kennedy and all through his life he would balk at anyone who got physically near him or who touched him. He did, however, love his mother, but was frustrated by her stoical stance and the sublimation of her personality to her husband. John Kennedy wanted his mother to stand up for herself.

Charles Spalding, a close friend said: "(Jack) hated physical touching-people taking physical liberties with him - which I assume must go back to his mother and the fact that she was so cold, so distant from the whole thing. Touch! Mrs. Kennedy - she just didn't have the time, you rarely saw her. Maybe the other Kennedy kids would say the same thing. She never touched me, either. I never saw her with her arms up outstretched. I never saw her in any easy, sophisticated position - by sophisticated I mean a woman who knew that her son needs some fondling and so she rumples his hair or something like that. That is not Mrs Kennedy.

I doubt if she ever rumpled the kid's hair in his whole life...It just didn't exist: the business of letting your son know you're close, that she's there. She wasn't. She was with eight other kids and one of them retarded and that husband- she just had problems enough herself if she is going to stay afloat...What is touch? It must come from some deep maternal security - arms, warmth, kisses, hugs...maybe sex is the closest prize there is, that holds the whole thing together. I mean, if you have sex with anybody you care about at all, you feel you've been touched, it seems to me, if there's anything successful."[45]

Both Jack and Jackie were alike in that they balked at displaying emotion or physical affection. At all times they expressed a sense of dignity through their deportment. Friends have sometimes called this 'emotional detachment'.

There is little doubt that John Kennedy never revealed himself fully to others - only a surface affability and friendliness. And it was a singular quality with John Kennedy, as it was with his brothers, that he could never counterfeit his feelings. If he expressed a feeling, it was authentic.

His closest aides have often spoken of how he 'compartmentalised' his life. No one person was able to observe his multi-faceted persona. Historian, Richard Reeves, has observed that: "He was among the most compartmentalised of men, able to separate private and public, a trait we now seem to have lost."[46] Friends never got to know the real John Kennedy. Generally speaking, he could be described as emotionally blocked: deprived of early maternal warmth he developed a narcissistic personality craving attention and affection. There is also strength in emotional detachment. In his conquests he may have enjoyed the physical nature of his relationships with women, but he never connected emotionally allowing him the benefit of not having to clutter his life with emotional baggage. American television personality, Nancy Dickerson, dated John Kennedy in the 1950s and believed that sex to Kennedy was nothing more than 'a cup of coffee'.[47] It is quite clear that Kennedy's emotional development had been stunted.

Other major forces that shaped Kennedy's life were his illnesses and his experiences in the Second World War. Kennedy suffered from a congenitive back ailment known as Addison's disease and other minor ailments, including allergies connected to animal hair and house dust for which he received injections of vaccine. There is little doubt he saw his life differently because of these forces. His experiences during the war contributed to his philosophy that merit and talent should supersede background. It also persuaded him that in moments between life and death hedonistic pursuits were a way of 'grabbing at life'. Anne Truitt, a friend of Mary Meyer's, writing on the men of her generation who had experienced the horrors of the Second World War, said: "Confronted by the probability of their own deaths, it seems to me that many of the most percipient men of my generation killed off those parts of themselves that were most vulnerable to pain, and thus lost forever a delicacy of feeling on which intimacy depends..."[48]

Kennedy's illnesses were to contribute to his 'live every day as if it were the last' attitude and the recklessness with which he pursued his hedonistic conquests, especially in later life. Kennedy believed his illnesses were a mark of feminincy, a weakness. Womanising, on the other hand, was a sign of strength, virility and masculinity.

A Kennedy did not admit illness, but from the time of his youth John Kennedy had extreme lower back pain later requiring the occasional use of crutches and spinal operations in Boston and New York. The degenerative back problem was a birth defect. His doctors gave him frequent shots of procaine to ease the pain. His Addison's disease was an adrenal insufficiency finally diagnosed in 1947 after years of painful testing in the Mayo Clinic and the Lahey Clinic in Boston. Throughout his life he was treated with cortisone and other medication. Joseph Kennedy made sure that supplies of the drugs were readily available for his son and created stores of the drugs in safety deposit boxes throughout the United States in case his son had a 'relapse' at any time during his travels. Later, when he was a public figure, spinal pain, infections, stress and weakness would be obvious to many as he made speeches and campaigned. Many authors have criticised Kennedy for lying to the American public about his Addison's disease. Clearly, Kennedy misrepresented his ailments, but there is a perfectly logical reason why he did so. He wanted to hide a rare and misunderstood disease that he knew his political opponents (such as LBJ in the 1960 Presidential campaign primaries) would distort and exaggerate in order to destroy him. In reality there was no real fear that Kennedy would be unable to discharge his duties as President effectively because of the disease. After 1947, Addison's disease was about as serious as that of a diabetic on insulin.

The history of John Kennedy's ailments cannot give full measure to the intense suffering he endured. Throughout his years he was imbued with the sense that fate would not allow him to live out a full and healthy life. "Almost all his life," Rose Kennedy (1974) wrote in her biography, "it seemed he had to do battle against misfortunes of health."[49] His brother Robert said: "At least one half of the days that he spent on this earth were days of intense physical pain. He had scarlet fever when he was very young and serious back trouble when he was older. In between he had almost every other conceivable ailment. When we were growing up together we used to laugh about the great risk a mosquito took in biting Jack Kennedy - with some of his blood the mosquito was almost sure to die."[50] He never expected to live beyond the age of 45 and this suggests that through his grit and acting abilities he was able to convey an impression of youthful vigour.

October 11th 1954 proved to be a turning point in Kennedy's battle for health. On that day he was admitted to the Hospital for Special Surgery at Cornell Medical Centre in Manhattan. It was decided that back surgery was necessary although Kennedy's personal doctor, Sara Jordan, opposed the idea. She felt that Kennedy's Addison's disease might produce post-operative complications and be life-threatening. No Addisonian had ever survived traumatic surgery. But the back pain was so great he would rather have died than continue with it. His back was operated on October 21st. A double fusion operation was performed on Kennedy's spine in the hope of stabilising and strengthening his back. However, within days infection set in and for three weeks he remained on the hospital's critical list, but he eventually pulled through. Kennedy recuperated at his parent's house in Palm Beach. He had lost 40 pounds and had to endure lying on his stomach every minute of the day for fear of aggravating his open and oozing wound. He was in a great deal of pain. Within two months of leaving hospital he was readmitted for the removal of a metal plate implanted in the previous operation. It took months for the wound to heal. However, he still suffered muscle spasms in the back and neck and he was given regular injections of novocain and oral cortisone to control them. He was, as always, treated for Addison's disease and took DOCA time-release capsules implanted every three months in his thighs. He also took cortisone tablets daily. The cortisone stimulated not only his adrenal glands but also his libido. It likely had the effect of an early version of viagra.

It was Kennedy's ill health which prompted his extreme sense of fatalism. Ever since adolescence he believed he would not live a long, vigorous and healthy life. He became philosophical about his chances for survival and expected every day to succumb to his body's weaknesses. And so he lived every day to the fullest. Judging him by the standards of an ordinary man seems to be unfair. Friends who knew him have testified to his immense courage in dealing with his illnesses. It had to take consistent psychological stamina to go through the trying adversity he faced.

But friends who knew him well say he did not have a morbid sense of fate and that death was not always on his mind. They did, however, sense it was always under the surface; deep and subconscious it did surface on more than one occasion in the final years of his life when he would sometimes move his friends to tears by speaking the words to "September Song". To anyone who has listened to the song made famous by Frank Sinatra, it is clear the lyrics speak of limited time, chances missed and the fickleness of fate. More than once he was quoted as saying: "I take one day at a time and fill it up to the brim." It is apparent to any examiner of his lifestyle that he lived life as a race against death, boredom and a feeling that time was running out.

However, notwithstanding the effect that cortisone had on his libido, it was perhaps Kennedy's psycho-sexual neurosis which may have been the determining factor in his philandering. Kennedy's behaviour was comparable to that found in those people who have an impulse control disorder. In an 'impulse control' disorder a person suffers from an irresistible repetitious weakness to one particular temptation. Kennedy may have found comfort from the pressures of his life by engaging in transitory and frequent sex with women who were, for the most part, strangers. His early role in his dysfunctional relationship with his mother is unlikely to have done much for his emotional self-esteem and may have made him overdependent on sex.

Doctors have argued about the role of the level of testosterone in the blood in determining sexual drive. Various surveys have found it hard to relate definitively high natural levels of testosterone to promiscuity, but there is evidence that it can be linked to those whose testosterone levels are artificially enhanced as John Kennedy's was. The reverse is true - those with low testosterone levels are associated with loss of libido.

Kennedy was also not interested in posterity insofar as his womanising was concerned. He was totally focused on the 'present' which is why he told a friend that his womanising was irrelevant. He believed that the press 'could not touch him' when he was alive and after his death it did not matter. 'Time' magazine correspondent during the Kennedy years, Hugh Sidey, believed the press were culpable in allowing Kennedy to live the way he wished as President. There was little public restraint on the public man. According to Sidey: "It was just a different time and we didn't do that. It just didn't occur, because it was considered to be their life. Also while people had their suspicions, Kennedy was never caught. Perception is part of leadership, and the fact of it is that John Kennedy was a strong leader."[51]

Kennedy had a noblesse oblige view of private matters. He once took exception to a story about one of Russian Leader Lenin's affairs and he had an affinity to the British aristocracy who historically had lived less than moral lives. He had a great deal of sympathy for John Profumo, the Minister of War, who had been scandalised in 1963 for lying to the House of Commons about his relationship to Christine Keeler. Hugh Sidey thought he captured the essence of the man and the reasons for his lifestyle when he asked Kennedy what his favourite book was. Kennedy told him it was 'The Young Melbourne', the story of William Lamb, Queen Victoria's early Prime Minister, who presided at the height of the British Empire. The book described a world in which the British aristocracy served brilliantly in Parliament then on weekends retired to their country home to live a life of near debauchery. Sidey believed this was the lifestyle Kennedy was emulating.[52]

For these reasons John Kennedy was the man he was. But Kennedy's indiscretions have scarred and distorted popular and historical perceptions of his life and presidency. Kennedy's critics may be right. He had to have corrupted many people in order to pursue this lifestyle and his image may always remain that of a rich boy who did whatever he wanted and got others to clean up the mess.

However, there is an alternative prism through which to see President Kennedy. There is no doubt that the term 'womaniser' is an apt description when applied to him. Yet it should be remembered that women, in the words of his secretary, Evelyn Lincoln, "threw themselves at him". "Maniser" has never been adopted as a term for women who pursue men but that may be an apt title for many of the women, including married ones, who knew John Kennedy. This is not to excuse his behaviour but simply to put it in the correct context.

It may also be argued that character is not the mainstay of leadership. We know that President Roosevelt was loved by millions yet he was personally disliked by many who knew him. Many associates disliked his bitterness and the cruel way he humiliated his subordinates. Kennedy was certainly flawed but he was also idealistic and compassionate. President Kennedy put the government on the side of the minority in Civil Rights, he inspired a new generation to believe that government can change society for the better and he changed the image of the United States abroad. If a president is judged as a leader by how he brings about the best or the worst in people, Kennedy must be seen to have succeeded in spite of his personal transgressions. Whatever personal flaws Kennedy had as a private man it cannot be denied that he was a figure of great importance and, in our ignorance, a great role model for a generation.

Notes

1. Hilty, J. W. (1997). *Robert Kennedy – brother protector*, Temple University Press. p. 253.

2. Martin, R. G. (1983). *A hero for our time*, Macmillan Publishing Company. p. 399.

3. FBI Memorandum, 14 November 1961, *Smoking gun.* (http://www.the smoking gun.com).

4. Carroll, T. 'Mystery of the phantom marriage', *Sunday Times Magazine*, 4 October 1996, p. 39.

5. 'Smashing Camelot', *Time*, 17 November 1997, p. 75.

6. Ball, I. 'Kennedy never hid his fondness for women', *Daily Telegraph*, 7 July 1975, p. 8.

7. Martin, R. G. (1983). *A hero for our time*, Macmillan Publishing Company. chapters 3 and 16.

8. Sullivan, M. J. (1991). *Presidential passions*, S.P.I. Books. p. 64.

9. Ball, I. 'Kennedy never hid his fondness for women', *Daily Telegraph*, 7 July 1975, p. 8.

Mary Meyer

10. Burleigh, N. (1998). *A very private woman - the life and unsolved murder of presidential mistress Mary Meyer*, Bantam Books. p. 293; Duffy, D. and Bolton, B. "JFK's secret mistress assassinated because she knew too much", *National Enquirer*, 4 April 1997. (http://www.nationalenquirer.com).

11. Burleigh, N. (1998). *A very private woman - the life and unsolved murder of presidential mistress Mary Meyer*, Bantam Books. pp. 252-282.

12. Bradlee, B. C. (1995), *A good life - newspapering and other adventures*, Simon and Schuster. pp. 266-271.

13. Burleigh, N. (1998). *A very private woman - the life and unsolved murder of presidential mistress Mary Meyer*, Bantam Books. p. 341.

14. Hilty, J. W. (1997). *Robert Kennedy – brother protector*, Temple University Press. p. 249; Gentry, C. (1991). *J. Edgar Hoover - the man and the secrets*, WW Norton and Co. p. 692.

15. Powers, R. G. (1987). *Secrecy and power*, Collier Macmillan Publishers. p. 356.

16. Hilty, J. W. (1997). *Robert Kennedy – brother protector*, Temple University Press. p. 250.

17. Andersen, C. (1998). *Jackie after Jack*, William Morrow and Company Inc.
p. 102.

Marilyn Monroe

18. Spoto, D. (1993). *Marilyn Monroe - the biography*, Chatto and Windus. p. 539.

19. *Ibid*, pp. 538-546. Donald Spoto's investigation of the JFK/Monroe relationship is authoritative and persuasive. He states that the President and the Hollywood actress met 4 times. Yet Charles Spalding's statement to Seymour Hersh - that the President

and Monroe met at Hyannisport - cannot be dismissed, even though Spalding has admitted to 'short term memory loss'.

20. *Ibid*, p. 540.

21. Edwards, J. 'Jackie and the big lies', *Daily Mail*, 22 September 1992, p. 9.

22. Hersh, S. (1997). *The dark side of Camelot*, Little Brown Co. p. 102.

23. *Ibid*, p. 104.

24. Lacayo, R. 'Smashing Camelot', *Time*, 17 November 1997, p. 79.

25. Spoto, D. (1993). *Marilyn Monroe - the biography*, Chatto and Windus. p. 541.

26. Spoto, D. (2000). *Jacqueline Bouvier Kennedy Onassis - a life*, St Martins Press. p. 156.

27. Strasberg, S. (1992). *Marilyn and me - sisters, friends*, Warner Books New York. p. 40.

Ellen Rometsch

28. Branch, T. (1998). *Parting the waters - America in the King years*, Simon and Schuster. p. 149; *see also* Hilty, J. W. (1997). *Robert Kennedy - brother protector*, Temple University Press, for the true facts of the scandal.

Jack and Jackie

29. 'Secret lives - Jackie'. Narrated by Max Easterman, produced and directed by Charles Furneaux. Channel 4 Television, 1995. (A Barraclough Carey production).

30. 'The Kennedys'. Narrated by John Woodvine, written by Phillip Whitehead and Geoffrey C. Ward. Thames Television, 1992. (A Brook/WGBH Co-production for Thames Television).

31. Spoto, D. (2000). *Jacqueline Bouvier Kennedy Onassis - a life*, St Martins Press. p. 118.

32. 'Secret lives - Jackie'. Narrated by Max Easterman, produced and directed by Charles Furneaux. Channel 4 Television, 1995. (A Barraclough Carey production).

33. Towle, P. and Haley, L. 'Bobby Kennedy's secret life of drugs, brawls and sexcapades', *National Enquirer*, 12 December 1997. (http://www.nationalenquirer.com).

34. Burleigh, N. (1998). *A very private woman - the life and unsolved murder of presidential mistress Mary Meyer*, Bantam Books. p. 200.

35. Sullivan, M. J. (1991). *Presidential passions*, S.P.I. Books. p. 24.

36. Schlesinger, A. M. Jnr., 'Brought up to be a good man', *Time*, 26 July 1999, p. 46.

37. Sullivan, M. J. (1991). *Presidential passions*, S.P.I. Books. p. 25; Blair, J. and Blair, C. (1977). *The search for JFK*, Berkeley Medallion Books. p. 329.

38. Klein, E. (1998). *Just Jackie - her private years*, Ballantine Books. p. 10.

39. *Ibid*, p. 333.

40. 'Love letter from Camelot', *New York Daily News*, 27 February 1998. (http://www.nydailynews.com).

41. Spoto, D. (2000). *Jacqueline Bouvier Kennedy Onassis - a life*, St Martins Press. p. 238.

42. Burleigh, N. (1998). *A very private woman - the life and unsolved murder of presidential mistress Mary Meyer*, Bantam Books. p. 14.

43. Sullivan, M. J. (1991). *Presidential passions*, S.P.I. Books. p. 22.

44. Ward, G. C. 'All in the families', *New York Times*, 15 February 1987. (http://www.nytimes.com).

45. Hamilton, N. (1993). *JFK reckless youth*, Arrow. p. 691.

46. Lamb, B. *'Interview with Richard Reeves'*, C-Span, 12 December 1993. (http://www.c-span.org).

47. Sullivan, M. J. (1991). *Presidential passions*, S.P.I. Books. p. 23.

48. Burleigh, N. (1998). *A very private woman - the life and unsolved murder of presidential mistress Mary Meyer*, Bantam Books. p. 191.

49. Kennedy, R. F. (1974). *Times to remember*, Pan Books. p. 470.

50. Meyers, J., ed. (1965). *JFK - as we remember him*, Atheneum, New York. p. 60.

51. 'Smashing Camelot', *Time*, 17 November 1997, p. 80.

52. *Ibid*.

Chapter 7

The Mafia

Did the Kennedys have close ties to the Mafia?

"Integrity without knowledge is weak and useless, and knowledge without integrity is dangerous and dreadful."

Samuel Johnson

"...Yes, he (Joseph Kennedy Snr.) was amoral...I was not shocked in the least. I expected...that politicians and big business men don't have any morals. That is, public morals."

Arthur Krock

Stories that John Kennedy and his father had close ties to the U.S. Mafia have been circulating for more than two decades. Their origins arose from a number of sources: some originated from former mafia bosses who alleged that Joseph Kennedy Snr. had been involved in 'bootlegging' in the 1920s; Congressional investigations revealed that President Kennedy carried on an affair with Judith Campbell Exner, a friend of Chicago mob boss Sam 'Momo' Giancana; and there were rumours that John Kennedy had elicited help from the Mafia through his friend Frank Sinatra or his contacts during his 1960 campaign for the presidency. Many authors accept all or some of these stories as historical fact but the truth is much more complex.

Joseph P. Kennedy - the sins of the father

A number of authors have averred that President Kennedy's father,
Joseph P. Kennedy Snr., was recognised by the Mafia as 'one of their
own'. In 'proving' Kennedy's mob ties, writers have repeatedly made
reference to the senior Kennedy's whisky business, referring to it as
'bootlegging'.

There is little doubt that Joseph Kennedy's acquisition of vast wealth
was the result of a single-minded pursuit of legal loopholes and
exploitation of the stock market. In the world of business today he may
have been referred to as a 'stock market predator'. After leaving
Harvard, Kennedy sought to build up his fortune by securing a position
in banking as president of the Columbia Trust Company and he became
the youngest bank president in the country. Kennedy borrowed 45,000
dollars at the age of 25 to take over the small bank his father had
invested in. He left the bank in 1917 to become general manager of
Bethlehem Steel's Fore River factory in Quincy, Massachusetts. His
next appointment was with the brokerage firm Hayden, Stone and
Company in Boston. He became very successful and was now on the
path to fulfilling his dreams of acquiring a financial fortune by
speculating in the stock market in between those times he looked after
his clients' business. The unregulated stock market was made for Joseph
Kennedy's ambitious financial skills and acute intelligence. He would
boost a stock artificially using accomplices and compliant journalists
and then, at its peak, he would sell the stock to the gullible and reap the
benefit. He made this money before laws were passed which outlawed
such practices.

In 1923, he devoted himself fully to becoming an independent banker
and speculating for himself. By 1927 he had made millions and,
anticipating the stock market crash, he sold his assets for cash whilst his
associates continued to buy. The secret of his success was perhaps the
attitude he adopted early on in life that he would not accept his place in
Boston society as a second-class Catholic or as a grandson of Irish
immigrants. He never wanted anything except money, social approval
and to get even with the Boston Brahmins who had snubbed him.

Kennedy's connection to the liquor trade began long before the
Volstead Act was passed in 1919, outlawing the sale of alcoholic
beverages. Kennedy's father Patrick was a saloon keeper in Boston and
also a local politician. As repeated in most popular biographies of the
Kennedys, the story goes that Kennedy became the largest whisky

distributor in America in the 1920s and used mobsters to distribute it. At the time, rum-running on the east coast from Boston to Philadelphia was financed by a New York gambler named Arnold Rothstein and one of his main operating agents was Frank Costello, later to become a big name in mafia circles. Costello, reminiscing in the later years of his life, said Joe Kennedy had been his partner in bootlegging and had double-crossed him in a business deal. According to writer Peter Maas[1], Kennedy had approached him in the early years of prohibition and asked him to help in smuggling liquor into the United States from England. Kennedy would buy the liquor, mostly Scotch whisky and gin, and lease the ships to carry it across the Atlantic as far as the 12 mile limit. From there Costello and his men would smuggle it into the United States in small, fast boats. Another mobster, Joe Bonanno, also stated that Kennedy's people unloaded whisky during prohibition at Sag Harbour in Long Island, New York.[2] Q. Byrum Hearst, lawyer to gangster, Owney Madden, maintains that Madden had a partnership with Kennedy. Further evidence to support Kennedy's relationship with mobsters was given by Chicago mob lawyer, Abraham L. Marovitz, who said Kennedy was bootlegging in New England and must have had a relationship with the mob otherwise he would not have been in business so long.[3] Mobster Meyer Lansky also alleged that Kennedy had been involved in 'bootlegging'.[4]

Ronald Kessler (1966) believes Joe Kennedy admitted to his bootlegging enterprise when he was United States Ambassador to England during the late 1930s. He quotes Kennedy as saying: "On and off for 20 years I have more or less successfully traded with the English". As Kennedy at this time had no other foreign trade, Kessler maintains, he could only have been talking about the importation of liquor to the United States.[5]

However, Kennedy historian, Doris Kearns Goodwin, maintains that whilst Joe Kennedy did indeed make a lot of money out of the whisky trade it was nonetheless probably 'legal'. The money was made after prohibition ended when he acquired the sole rights to the American distributorship of famous brands of British gin and whisky. He also had knowledge of his uncles' use of medicinal prescriptions for alcohol which could be legally issued during this period. Goodwin (1988) wrote in her best-selling 'The Kennedys and the Fitzgeralds':

"With Rose's uncle as a built in market, it is possible, as some people have claimed, that Joe Kennedy got involved in financing illegal shipments of liquor from Canada or the Bahamas. Over the years countless stories have surfaced from people who claim

to have seen Joe Kennedy standing on the rocky Gloucester shore, watching for his boats to come in, a romantic image of daring - do which links him with the old Yankees whose original money came from the opium trade with China. If the stories are true- and no hard evidence has yet been produced - it is most likely that Kennedy was involved in the early twenties, when a host of small bootleggers and rumrunners competed for the profits of the trade...it is harder to imagine Kennedy still involved during the middle to late twenties, after the large criminal gangs had taken over and fundamentally changed the nature of the illicit trade. For one thing he could scarcely have had time to compete with the big liquor bosses when his mind was preoccupied as it was by Wall Street and Hollywood.[6]

It is true that he supplied his Harvard reunion class with liquor in 1922 and arranged to sell liquor at cost to a large circle of friends, but some of this supply undoubtedly came from his father's private stock which had been stored in his cellar after alcohol was made illegal. He also had access to a stock of liquor which was acquired by the Columbia Trust Company in 1925. And his uncles, who were definitely involved in the illicit trade, supplied their nephew.

Kennedy did not escape scrutiny for his involvement in the liquor trade. House Assassinations Committee counsel and Professor of Law, Robert Blakey (1992), who was Director of the Notre Dame Institute on Organised Crime, thoroughly investigated the rumours of Kennedy's involvement in bootlegging and found them to be without credence.[7]

Seymour Hersh's allegations that a Sam Giancana/Joseph Kennedy alliance had been formed in prohibition days cannot, then, be accepted as historical fact. Hersh gives no solid evidence that Kennedy had been engaged in rum-running with gangsters. He quoted gangsters, who years afterwards, told him they worked with Kennedy. Hersh also maintains that anyone who owned an enterprise like the Chicago Merchandise Mart had to know what the gangsters were up to. However, it remains at best a theory since Hersh lacks credible witnesses and documentary proof.

Yet there are simply too many anecdotal tales to dismiss the allegations that Joseph Kennedy had in some way been involved with mafia figures. According to Richard D. Mahoney (1999), the former Arizona Senator and future Republican presidential nominee, Barry Goldwater, told him that Robert Kennedy had stumbled over evidence of Joseph Kennedy's dealings with the "underworld" in his zeal to destroy the Mafia in the McClellan Committee investigations in the late 1950s. According to Goldwater, the evidence "Just killed him (RFK)."[8]

Contact between national politicians and the Mafia was widespread in the 1950s and 1960s, ergo numerous congressmen who allegedly received generous campaign donations from underworld figures.[9] Richard Mahoney inferred that Joseph Kennedy had been willing to solicit campaign contributions from any source, including the least reputable of donors and that the father had been willing to meet with anyone in order to secure the presidential nomination for his son. Mahoney (1999) wrote: "The implicit understanding was that he (Joseph Kennedy) would put money where it counted, pull the strings, and do the deals. The less Jack and Bobby knew about this, the less they would have to answer for."[10]

It would be curious indeed if Joseph Kennedy had not rubbed shoulders with the underworld during his 40 year mission to acquire vast riches. Dealing with mob-related figures in Hollywood could not be avoided as the movie industry had been virtually held to ransom by the mob. And the Mafia often set themselves up in legitimate enterprises and businesses. The mob's tentacles reached out to practically every area of American industry and commerce and no large business was immune to the dealings of the mob. In this sense the sins of the father had been visited on the sons. Joseph Kennedy had been willing to make a Faustian bargain in order to ensure his own financial success and the political success of his sons. Robert may have finally recognised this fact when, years later, after his brother had been killed and his father was incapacitated by a stroke, read the death speech of Henry the Fourth to poet Robert Lowell. Henry the Fourth's legacy to his children had been, "(T)he cankered heaps of strange-achieved gold." Robert told Lowell, "Henry the Fourth. That's my father."[11]

It is, therefore, entirely possible that Seymour Hersh may very well be correct when he asserted that Joseph Kennedy had arranged meetings with Sam Giancana to solicit help in electing his son, but there is simply no credible evidence, as yet, to assume they occurred.

Sam Giancana

The Chicago mob or 'Outfit' as it was more commonly known, had an illustrious past. First made famous by its legendary boss, Al Capone, in the 1920s, the 'Outfit' as it was called flourished in the 1940s and 1950s due mainly to its reputation as the most violent and corrupting in America. It was also multi-ethnic, absorbing its members from Jewish, Sicilian and other groups. But in the 1940s it became controlled by a mafia 'crime family'.

Capone's successor was Frank 'The Enforcer' Nitti. After Nitti's suicide in 1943 he was succeeded by Paul 'The Waiter' Ricca. Ricca's reign, however, did not last long and he was jailed for extorting money from Hollywood. Antonio Accardo was responsible for having Ricca's jail sentence reduced to three years and he achieved this by bribery and blackmail. For his reward as a loyal and aggressive member of the Outfit he was made boss and reigned until he left to defend himself on charges of evading income tax.

In 1955, Accardo was replaced by Sam 'Momo' Giancana, a 49 year old widower whose reputation stretched back to the days of Capone and whose efforts on behalf of the Mob included intimidation, extortion and the murders of dozens of people. He was a man who developed a strange intimacy with death and torture.

Giancana's rise in the crime organisation began in his teens on Chicago's West Side where he was born in 1908 the son of an immigrant grocer. A school dropout, he joined the Chicago Outfit as a getaway driver and then graduated to mob gunman. Convicted of making illegal whisky in 1939, he turned his four year sentence to his advantage by cultivating Edward Jones, the black illegal gambling king of Chicago's South Side, who was serving time for income tax evasion. From Jones, Giancana learned that the city's 'numbers racket' was a two million dollar enterprise and not the small operation the mob thought it was. Soon after Giancana was released, he and other young members of the mob won control of the numbers through a series of vicious kidnappings, beatings and murders of black racketeers. Giancana, who at first had been Jones' friend, now turned on him and bundled him into a car and made it plain that he had a choice either to hand over control of his criminal enterprise or die.[12]

During World War II Giancana stayed out of the military by being honest; he told his draft board that he stole for a living. The board promptly rejected him for army service describing him as "a constitutional psychopath (with) an inadequate personality and strong anti-social trends."[13]

When Giancana became head of the multi-million dollar outfit, he inherited the control not only of crime activities but also of many legitimate businesses. He ruled a three state empire of some 1,500 Mafiosi who ran gambling, narcotics, prostitution, 'loan-sharking' and other underworld ventures. By 1960 it has been estimated he had ordered the murders of over 600 people. FBI file, No. 25-244122, described him as a man "(who should be) considered armed and dangerous since he allegedly has a vicious temperament, psychopathic personality and has been known to carry firearms."[14]

Giancana controlled some 300 'made members' plus scores of associates. Associates of the Outfit included gangs of professional criminals who gave a percentage of their 'take' and in return received the Outfit's protection and assistance through their ability to control judges, sheriffs, Chicago city policemen and politicians. At the height of his power, Giancana lived modestly in Oak Park with his three daughters but holidayed on a lavish scale: Miami Beach and Europe in the winter, and Paradise Valley, near Las Vegas, in the summer which afforded him opportunities to oversee the Outfit's multi-million dollar stake in the gambling capital of America. The Chicago mob had the lion's share in the money 'skimmed' from the mob-controlled casinos. Giancana also controlled mafia interests west of the Mississippi.

Sam Giancana would have reigned unnoticed by the rest of America if it had not been for the Mafia's 1957 'Apalachin Conference' in upstate New York. The meeting of mafia bosses from across America was called to discuss their criminal interests. Over 62 known mobsters gathered, including Vito Genovese, Joe Profaci, Joe Magliocco, Joseph Barbara, Carlo Gambino, Paul Castellano, Joe Bonanno, Carlos Marcello and Santos Trafficante as well as Sam Giancana. They came from upstate New York, Philadelphia, North-East Pennsylvania, Boston, Cleveland, Kansas City, New Jersey, Illinois, Texas, Colorado, California and even Havana.

Conference members were arrested by a local policeman. This forced J. Edgar Hoover to recognise that there was indeed a National Crime Syndicate which was set up to arbitrate disputes between crime families: until then he had denied the existence of a national organised crime structure. Hoover responded by increasing surveillance of the Mafia (the term Mafia and Cosa Nostra, 'Our Thing' was not officially recognised until mafia informant Joe Valachi gave evidence to the United States Congress in 1963.)

The Outfit's headquarters were in a luxury custom made tailor shop called Celano's at 620 North Michigan Avenue, but Giancana carried out most of his business from the Armory Lounge, a bar-restaurant which was located at 7247 West Roosevelt Avenue in the suburb of Forest Park. Both premises were bugged by the FBI, yielding vast amounts of intelligence on the membership of the Outfit and criminal enterprises in progress. Like a feudal lord, Giancana held court presiding over his 'middle managers'.

According to FBI agent Bill Roemer (1989), who organised the surveillance of the mob boss, Giancana had bombed and killed his way to the top of the organisation. The mob boss, in Roemer's eyes, was 'scum', 'an animal' who had raped, tortured and murdered; a man who had the face of a gargoyle and the disposition of a viper.[15]

Roemer had made Giancana a top target for the FBI and vigorously pursued the mob boss from the late 1950s. He first met Giancana at Chicago's O'Hare airport in 1961. Giancana's girlfriend at the time was Phyliss McGuire of the nationally famous McGuire Sisters singing act. Roemer had been waiting to serve a subpoena on McGuire calling her to testify before a grand jury enquiring into the activities of Giancana and the Chicago mob. Roemer said Giancana had been extremely angry and hysterical, calling Roemer names and making threatening remarks. Roemer, in turn, theatrically announced to the airport crowd that they were in the presence of 'scum'.[16]

It is claimed by many authors that Sam Giancana was instrumental in electing John Kennedy president by controlling the election in Chicago. It is true that Giancana assisted the Kennedy campaign in the 1960 election. Frank Sinatra acted as an intermediary to solicit the help of the mob boss in the West Virginia primary and parts of Chicago in the November presidential election.[17] However, it is untrue that the Mafia as a national organisation supported the Democratic candidate. Carlos Marcello of New Orleans and the mob-controlled Teamsters boss, Jimmy Hoffa, supported Richard Nixon and donated large sums of money to Nixon's campaign.[18]

Seymour Hersh (1997), in his book 'The dark side of Camelot', states that he found a source who confirmed that Joe Kennedy met with Sam Giancana in order to ask the mob boss for help in securing his son's election.[19] The key to understanding Joe Kennedy's involvement in corrupting the electoral process, we are led to believe by Hersh, is Kennedy Snr.'s anger at his sons' participation in a Senate investigation into the corrupt activities of labour unions in the 1950s. Kennedy Snr. believed it would undermine his son's solicitation of union help in the coming 1960 presidential election.

Joe Kennedy no doubt used his money and influence to garner support from labour unions and he also probably used his money to corrupt the electoral process. But it should be remembered that the Kennedys were acting within a political system which was free from the restraints of post-Watergate election laws. Other leading contenders for the presidency, including Richard Nixon, were not without sin when it came to campaign finance.

But Hersh's 'proof' that Kennedy Snr. dealt directly with a leading Chicago mobster in order to corrupt the electoral process is flawed. The first question about the meeting is why would Joseph Kennedy risk meeting with Giancana when he had a 'go-between', Frank Sinatra, readily available? Hersh maintains that Joe Kennedy approached an old friend, William J. Tuohy, Chief Judge of the Circuit Court of Cook County, to set up a meeting with Sam Giancana. The meeting supposedly took place in Tuohy's courtroom unobserved by the judge. However, Hersh's only source for this story, former mob attorney Robert J. McDonnell, is less than credible.

McDonnell was an unsavoury character and an ex-alcoholic who had been disbarred. He was convicted in 1966 of using forged money orders and in 1983 of attempted bribery. McDonnell had been little more than a mouthpiece for the mob. He was married to Sam Giancana's daughter, Antoinette, in 1983 until they divorced in 1995.[20] It is beyond belief that McDonnell would not have told his wife of the meeting in question. Yet her memoirs, which were published in 1984, said not a word of the Giancana/Kennedy meeting. Why, if Kennedy had long ties with the mob stretching back to prohibition days, as Hersh claims, would he need to go to Judge Tuohy for an introduction to Giancana? If he did not know Giancana by this time, surely he would know somebody who did? A judge is constantly in the public eye - why would Kennedy risk using this type of intermediary?

Hersh contradicts his evidence by quoting Frank Sinatra's daughter, Tina, who told him her father admitted eliciting Sam Giancana's help in the 1960 campaign. Tina Sinatra has also commented: "The notion that Joe (Kennedy) would go to Sam Giancana was out of the question for obvious reasons."[21]

Giancana controlled Chicago's West Side bloc and the local politicians were under his influence and control. He made sure these politicians worked hard to turn the electorate out to vote for Kennedy. He had specifically used his own money and connections with politicians like John D'Arco and Pasqualino Marchone (Pat Marcy). It is also likely that he engaged in election fraud on a massive scale. No one would put this past a man like Giancana.

FBI bugs revealed why Giancana had worked to secure Kennedy's election. Mafia member, Johnny Formosa, visited the Armory Lounge and spoke to the mob boss of how the mob had done everything it could to get Kennedy into the White House and in return they were rewarded with the largest crack-down on organised crime ever. The FBI concluded that Giancana was led to believe (probably by Giancana's good friend Frank Sinatra) that the newly-elected president would go easy on the mob.[22] In any case Giancana believed the Kennedys were obligated to him. Giancana also believed his efforts to secure the elimination of Fidel Castro would stand him in good stead with the incoming Administration.

However, the opposite occurred and Giancana became a top target for Attorney-General, Robert Kennedy, and Chicago became the centre of aggressive action against the Mafia. This is proof alone that no deal had been made between the Kennedys and Giancana. Both John and Robert loved and revered their father. It is inconceivable that Robert would have gone against his father's wishes to leave Giancana alone.

In the same bugged conversation between Giancana and Formosa, the latter offered to kill Frank Sinatra in revenge for the singer's lack of success in persuading the Kennedy brothers to lay off Giancana.[23] Giancana turned Formosa down but made sure Sinatra returned favours by appearing at his Villa Venice Club on the outskirts of Chicago.

Another FBI memo reveals the extent of Giancana's belief that he had a relationship with the Kennedys: "(blank) advised yesterday that (blank) was in conference with Giancana yesterday and related to Giancana the story of a recent visit which (blank) had to the home of (blank) in California. (Blank) states he questioned (blank) as to the progress which (blank) has made if any in an attempt to intercede with the Kennedys on behalf of Giancana. (blank) has attempted to persuade (blank) could work on the Kennedys through Kennedy Snr. However, (blank) did not feel that the Kennedys were faithful to Kennedy Snr. In that respect, however, (blank) believed otherwise and was trying to persuade (blank) that he could work on Kennedy Snr. (blank) related to Giancana that Kennedy Snr. called (blank) three times during visit with (blank)...Concerning the next presidential campaign, Giancana indicated that he would not DONATE ONE PENNY (emphasis added) toward any such campaign and furthermore stated that '(blank) better not think of taking this (blank) state.' Giancana claimed that he MADE A DONATION TO THE RECENT PRESIDENTIAL CAMPAIGN (emphasis added) of Kennedy and was not getting his money's worth because if he got a speeding ticket 'none of these would know me'. The informant further related that (blank), in an attempt to persuade Giancana that (blank) had attempted to intercede for Giancana, stated (blank) 'says to me...he (Giancana) ain't being bothered'. Giancana then screamed, 'I got more ____ on my ____ than any other ____ in the country.' he continued raving and stated that everyplace he goes there are 'twenty guys next door, upstairs, downstairs' and he is surrounded."[24]

This memo confirms that, rather than money travelling from Kennedy to Giancana, it was the other way around; Giancana helped the Kennedy campaign by making donations in the hope that he would be rewarded. There is no evidence of a 'deal' having been made as some writers claim. Giancana was using his money to corrupt the voting system in the First Ward. It is possible Mayor Daley knew about this: on the eve of the presidential election he told John Kennedy, "Mr President, with a little bit of luck and the help of a few close friends, you're going to carry Illinois."[25] There is nothing to indicate who those 'close friends' were. Kennedy only knew that the man who had dictatorial power in the city of Chicago was the illustrious Mayor Daley. The city was controlled by Daley not Giancana.

Seymour Hersh said the mob stole the presidency for JFK and that Giancana stole enough votes in a few wards to tip the electoral votes of Illinois to JFK by a margin of 8,000. Hersh's allegations that the Mafia secured the election for Kennedy have been repeated in books and magazines for nearly twenty years and the myth continues. In 1998 Philip Norman wrote: "According to Hersh Sinatra helped fix the mob support that was DECISIVE (emphasis added) in winning Kennedy the presidency."[26] Yet Arthur Schlesinger's review of Hersh's claims have not met with the same publicity. Schlesinger told the 'New York Daily News': "(Hersh's) chapter on the vote in Chicago is total vanity. The idea that Sam Giancana controlled the Chicago unions is ridiculous. The unions belonged to Mayor Daley...He bases his statements on disgruntled Secret Service Agents or mobsters who'll claim anything."[27]

Giancana certainly had power within Chicago's electoral system. Estes Kefauver (1951), the Chairman of a Senate Investigatory Committee looking into the relationship between labour unions and the mob in the 1950s, wrote in his book 'Crime in America': "Everywhere we went the committee found a certain amount of political immorality, but in Chicago the rawness of this sort of thing was particularly shocking...There was no doubt in the minds of any of us, after the sort of testimony we heard in Chicago that organised crime and political corruption go hand in hand, and that in fact there could be no big-time organised crime without a firm and profitable alliance between those who run the rackets and those in political control."[28]

Richard Nixon, in the November presidential election, carried 93 of Illinois' 102 counties and lost Illinois by 8,858 votes. If 4,500 had been switched to Nixon it would have given him the state's 27 electoral votes. However, Kennedy's victory was not due alone to Illinois. Kennedy won Texas by only 46,000 votes - a comfortable majority for Texas. If the combined 51 electoral votes of Illinois and Texas had gone to Nixon, he would have become president with an electoral majority of two. But if Nixon had carried Illinois without Texas, JFK would still have been elected president. The notion that Giancana tipped the balance is absurd. Other more important factors in 'tipping the balance' were Kennedy's appeal to black voters and the confidence voters had that his religion would not interfere with his duties as president.

There was certainly vote-stealing and ballot box stuffing in Cook County, Chicago.[29] But it was controlled by Richard J. Daley and not by Sam Giancana. More important to Daley were the aldermen who were loyal to him. Furthermore, it should be noted that any vote-stealing organised by the Democrats in Chicago was matched by the Republicans downstate. Some writers have countered this explanation by pointing to a later unofficial recount of less than 20% of Chicago's Cook County precincts which showed that Nixon had picked up 4,539 votes. This, however, is not sufficient evidence as the Republicans have traditionally stolen more downstate votes than Daley's machine stole in Cook County. This is why Senator Paul Douglas, who was running for election that year, said he was anxious for the recount if it included the whole state and not just Cook County. When the challenge was finally made, the state election board, which had a 4-1 Republican majority, voted unanimously to certify Democratic electors.

Those writers who claim that the Kennedys made a deal with the mob to steal the 1960 election are naive in their assessments of the political process in Chicago. And they should ask themselves the obvious question - if Robert Kennedy had known that Giancana was instrumental in stealing the election for his brother would he have prosecuted the mobster with such zeal? This is not to say that Joseph Kennedy did not unilaterally solicit the help of unsavoury characters in his desire to get his son elected president. It is likely that he did. The mob was closely tied to the Chicago political machine, but it was Mayor Daley and not Giancana who made the 'deals'.

The Sinatra connection

Frank Sinatra had always been a strong Democrat. He had been influenced by his mother Dolly who had been very involved in New Jersey politics. Sinatra had supported and idolised Franklin Roosevelt and had contributed money to the president's campaigns. He had supported Harry Truman in 1948 and Adlai Stevenson in 1952 and 1956.

In 1954 John Kennedy had met Sinatra when his sister, Pat Kennedy, married Hollywood actor, Peter Lawford, then an established star who had appeared in Hollywood movies since the 1940s. Pat and Peter Lawford bought Hollywood mogul Louis B. Meyer's house in Santa Monica and Kennedy used it frequently on visits to the West Coast. In time Kennedy began to socialise with Sinatra and the 'Rat Pack' often dined at Puccini's, the Beverly Hills restaurant in which Lawford and Sinatra had a part financial interest. Both Sinatra and Kennedy were compulsive womanisers who, strangely, preferred a night out with the boys.

John Kennedy became a close friend of Sinatra who introduced the young senator to Hollywood starlets and other women. Kennedy could not say no to a challenge. His father had associations with Hollywood all through his career. With Kennedy it was all part of his curiosity about life and his fascination with stardom. One of the reasons he liked Sinatra was because the singer turned movie star brought him all the gossip about Hollywood. And, as Charles Bartlett, a close friend of Kennedy's, told author Laurence Leamer (1994), Kennedy confided to him that he kept his friendship with Sinatra because the famous singer was the only person in Hollywood who could give Peter Lawford work. Kennedy believed he could cement Peter and Pat Lawford's marriage by seeing that Peter got jobs by being nice to Sinatra.[30] Appreciative of his help in the election campaign Kennedy turned to Sinatra to organise the inaugural celebrations. Sinatra assembled show business personalities from all parts of the entertainment industry to honour the new President in Washington D.C..

Sinatra's links to mob boss, Sam Giancana, originated with Hollywood. Giancana's source of power in the movie capital was the Chicago mob-controlled film unions which could stop production, terrorise producers and extort money from studios. No doubt Sinatra enjoyed the power he had in Hollywood not only because of his own star qualities but also through his friendship with Giancana.

FBI files confirm that Sinatra, Kennedy and Lawford were seen on a number of occasions visiting the Sands Hotel in Las Vegas during the period in the run up to the presidential election. An FBI report said that "showgirls from all over town were running in and out of the Senator's suite." Another FBI report said: "members of the underworld element...are financially supporting and actively endeavouring to secure the nomination for the presidency of Democratic candidate John F. Kennedy. He (informant) said that Frank Sinatra is going to campaign for him in several primaries."[31]

Rumours that Frank Sinatra was involved with the Mafia have been circulating since the 1940s, but the public have been confused as to the extent of that connection. Was Sinatra a 'made member' of the 'Cosa Nostra'? Did Sinatra make a 'deal with the devil' when his career was on the wane and was he thereafter forced to do the Mafia's bidding? Did Sinatra engage in illegal operations with his mafia friends? And did John and Robert Kennedy know that Sinatra had been enlisting his friend Giancana to help in the presidential campaign?

In the eyes of the American public the stories of Sinatra's ties to the mob seemed to be confirmed with the publication of Mario Puzo's novel 'The Godfather' and the release of the movie by the same name which became a box office success in the early 1970s. One of the book's peripheral characters, singer Johnny Fontaine, was assisted in his Hollywood career by fictional mob boss, Don Corleone, principally by 'persuading' a Hollywood producer to hire the failing star. Many were quick to observe the similarities with Sinatra's career and the movie was used as 'proof' of the allegations that Sinatra was 'mob controlled'.

Sinatra family members naturally decried such rumours, stating that the singer would inevitably have had to deal with underworld characters if he was to pursue his career in the entertainment business.

The truth about Sinatra's connections to the U.S. Mafia lies somewhere between the two contending images: a person who aided, abetted and assisted mafia bosses in their illegal enterprises and was rewarded in return and someone who simply socialised with mob figures without any active participation in their illegal activities.

Sinatra grew up in a tough area of Hoboken, New Jersey which had been dominated since his childhood by leading mafia 'families'. Sinatra, like many young men of his generation, looked up to such figures as 'men of respect'. He had known many criminal characters from his hometown who eventually became mob members. One such character was Joe Fischetti, a cousin of Al Capone, who asked Sinatra in January 1947 if he would like to meet the boss of the Cosa Nostra, Lucky Luciano. Luciano had been in exile in Havana, Cuba since October 1946, but he still controlled the criminal organisation offshore. In 1947, Luciano requested the heads of the mafia families, including top mobsters Albert 'The Executioner' Anastasia, Carlo Gambino, Vito Genovese, Joe Bonanno, Santos Trafficante and Meyer Lansky, to come to Cuba for a convention in which decisions would be made concerning the running of the criminal enterprise. Joe Fischetti and Sinatra journeyed to Cuba and met Luciano who later revealed in his memoirs that the Mafia had helped to sever Sinatra's ties with the Tommy Dorsey band. It is likely that Luciano, along with many others, was laying claim to the Sinatra legend by bragging he had helped Sinatra's career. The evidence suggests otherwise. Old friends of Sinatra from the 1930s and 1940s have revealed that small-time 'hoodlums' did indeed intimidate Dorsey to cancel Sinatra's contract, but this was not the reason why Dorsey relented. It had more to do with Dorsey's own reasoning, believing as he did at that time, that he would still inherit a large percentage of Sinatra's income long after Sinatra left the band.[32]

Sinatra's trip to Cuba was reckless and poor judgement and it was dangerous to his career. His close friends and managers, when they heard about the Cuban meeting between Sinatra and Luciano, told him he had been reckless.[33] Sinatra continued his association with gangsters, but the reasons are less sinister than we have been led to believe by some authors. Sinatra was a Hoboken boy through and through. He liked and admired the 'macho' personalities of the criminals he associated with and he very probably fantasised about becoming a gangster himself. He told singer Eddie Fisher that he would rather be 'a Don' than 'President of the United States'.[34]

Sinatra's links to the Mafia lasted until well into the 1980s notwithstanding the fact that he vehemently denied such associations to reporters, especially during the televised hearings by the Nevada Gaming Board into his application for a gambling licence. He was, of course, lying as he had lied previously when he denied in the early 1960s that he knew Sam Giancana.[35] At that time Sinatra was forced to relinquish his 50% ownership in the Cal-Neva Lodge in Lake Tahoe, Nevada because of allegations he had played host to the Chicago mob boss.

However, common sense would dictate that Sinatra would have had no reason to benefit from any real membership in the criminal organisation. He admired these personalities and often did favours for them, but there is no evidence that he gave over a percentage of his earnings to them or knowingly engaged in any criminal activity (apart from lying to elected officials about his close relationships with mobsters). And, of course, Sinatra had no need to engage in illicit activities to enrich himself.

Sinatra liked to think of himself as a 'made guy'. However, many gangsters who he rubbed shoulders with thought he was too soft, too hot-tempered and too conspicuous to ever fit the profile. He courted their friendship and enjoyed the power he had in Hollywood by associating with men who could close down any film production with a few telephone calls to mob-controlled unions. Producers and Hollywood moguls were aware of the singer's ties to the mob and became very cautious in their dealings with him.

Mobsters, in turn, liked to show off they had a 'big star' pal. But apart from running a few errands Sinatra was never privy to any of the Dons' national crime schemes. But some did relish the opportunity to use Sinatra as a big draw for their nightclubs. However, some gangsters were so contemptuous of Sinatra that they engaged him on occasions in schemes they knew were fraudulent and illegal. Jimmy 'The Weasel' Fratianno took 10,000 dollars from Sinatra during the 1970s for enrolling the singer as a 'Knight of Malta'. The real organisation, of course, had no knowledge of the scam.[36] To many, Sinatra was a joke whose pretentious imitating of the gangsters' style produced derisive scorn.

When Sinatra's career took a downward turn in the late 1940s, mobsters did him a good turn by hiring him to sing at their clubs. Similarly, Dean Martin, although contemptuous of politicians and mobsters, nevertheless accepted the reality that in those days an entertainer could not be choosy about when and where to appear. Nightclubs and the mob went hand in hand. Both Sinatra and Martin sponsored Mafioso Johnny Rosselli for membership of the Friars Club and Rosselli had been a houseguest of Sinatra's. In 1962, Sinatra and Martin performed at the Villa Venice in Northbrook, Illinois, a nightclub owned by Sam Giancana. It was Sinatra's 'thank you' to the mob boss for helping out in Kennedy's campaign.

By the mid-1950s, Frank Sinatra was the most successful male singer in the United States and was a multi-millionaire. His talents alone secured him this position. Many friends and colleagues of Sinatra are convinced his association with the Mafia was only skin deep. Some make reference to the kidnapping of Sinatra's son in December 1963 as proof of this. If Sinatra had indeed been allied closely to the Mafia, as some writers contend, would he not have had the kidnappers executed? Nevertheless, Sinatra's continued association with known Mafia members throughout the 1960s and 1970s, and indeed into the 1980s, only fuelled speculation as to the origins of that connection.

Sinatra was proud to be associated with the Kennedys and did not flinch when Kennedy Snr. asked the singer to help with the Kennedy presidential campaign which began in earnest in 1959. Whilst many Kennedy campaign workers did not like the idea of a controversial character like Sinatra helping out, they at least acknowledged that his mother's connections in the key state of New Jersey was beneficial. Sinatra also recorded his hit song 'High Hopes' changing the words into a campaign song which was played in juke boxes all over America. It was especially beneficial to the Kennedy campaign in West Virginia. There is little doubt that the Hollywood star and world famous singer influenced voters in the presidential campaign. It is also likely that Kennedy knew that Sinatra would ask his good friend, Sam Giancana, to help out in the West Virginia primary election, a vital primary in the battle for his party's nomination. Giancana's friend, Paul 'Skinny' D'Amato, was despatched to the state to influence the sheriffs who controlled the state's election machine. Many of the sheriffs were gamblers at the mob controlled 500 Club in Atlantic City and were more than happy to do Giancana a favour.[37] And FBI wire taps revealed that Sinatra himself had disbursed large amounts of mob donations to assist his friend John Kennedy in the election campaign.

No doubt Giancana assisted his friend Frank Sinatra in helping out in West Virginia, but it is also true that Giancana's contribution has been exaggerated over the years. Seymour Hersh (1997) maintains that Joe Kennedy poured two million dollars into the West Virginia campaign. However, the entire outlay for the national campaign in 1960 has been estimated at around ten million dollars. Hersh is correct in saying that clandestine money was handed around but he never explains how he arrived at this incredible figure of two million dollars. Charles Peters, Editor-in Chief of the 'Washington Monthly', who was chairman of the Kennedy campaign in Kanawha county, told 'Time' magazine that he was interviewed by Hersh five times and when he told the author that the figure of two million dollars was wrong, Hersh refused to back down. Peters said Hersh "just wasn't listening".[38]

And the Kennedy machine was not solely dependent on mob help during the West Virginia primary campaign. Former House Speaker, Tip O'Neill (1987), said: "I told them a story about Eddie Ford (a campaign worker). Eddie Ford went out there (West Virginia) with a pocketful of money, he'd see a sheriff and then he'd say to the sheriff, 'Sheriff, I'm from Chicago. I'm on my way south. I love this young Kennedy boy, he can help this nation, by God he's got the feeling for it, he'll do things for West Virginia. I'll tell you what...here's 3,000 or here's 5,000...you carry your village for him or your county for him and I'll give you a little reward when I'm on my way back'...They passed money around like it was never seen."[39]

It may be true that Sinatra and Giancana disbursed cash to election officials in West Virginia, but there is no evidence that any 'deal' had been arranged which would have secured help to the Mafia in a Kennedy Administration, or that John or Robert Kennedy sanctioned mob assistance. It may be true that John and Robert Kennedy had an inkling of Sinatra's efforts in the area of cash dispersal, but in the manner of all presidential campaigns the candidate distanced himself from campaign finances. On the other hand it is feasible that Joseph Kennedy knew what Sinatra and Giancana were doing. However, there is compelling evidence that the brothers were unaware that any kind of money was being distributed. Lawrence O'Brien admitted disbursing cash to West Virginia county leaders but confirmed that John and Robert Kennedy were not told.[40] And writers who decry the Kennedy campaign for its 'corrupt' practices fail to place the election of 1960 in the correct context. All candidates seeking their party's nomination were engaged in disbursing cash to election officials and poll watchers. West Virginia was notoriously corrupt and advantage was taken by both the Kennedy and Humphrey camps. Humphrey's organisation admitted that giving cash to political leaders was 'common practice' in West Virginia. Theodore H. White, in his excellent account of the 1960 election, wrote: "At this degraded level all were evenly matched."[41] Unfortunately Humphrey did not have a private fortune at his disposal.

The disbursement of money was not decisive in Kennedy's victory over Hubert Humphrey in the West Virginia campaign - a margin of over 22% testifies to this fact. The major factor in Kennedy's success was not money but the brilliant and effective enlistment of President Roosevelt's son, Franklin Rooosevelt Jnr., in the campaign. President Roosevelt was revered in the state and the sight of his son campaigning with John Kennedy swung thousands of voters. Add to this Kennedy's very effective use of television advertising and the appearances of his wife Jacqueline, and the allegation that Kennedy 'bought' the election appears naive.

It is likely that Sam Giancana manipulated Sinatra's friendship with John Kennedy in order to gain an edge in his conflict with law enforcement agencies. This is the reason he acceded to Sinatra's request to help John Kennedy in the corrupt world of Chicago politics. However, John Kennedy's appointment of his brother Robert as Attorney General eliminated any hope that the government would go easy on the Mafia boss or indeed other leading mobsters across the United States. Robert Kennedy's single-minded pursuit of Giancana began almost immediately the President's brother was sworn into office. Sinatra made a show of trying to intervene with Robert Kennedy as a favour to Giancana, but Robert would have nothing to do with it. FBI surveillance tapes recorded how angry the mob boss was with Sinatra and thereafter the singer no longer had much respect from Giancana. According to Sinatra biographer J. Randall Taraborrelli (1997), historians and biographers have over the years got the story of Sinatra's intervention on Giancana's behalf wrong. Tarraborrelli wrote: "...historians and biographers over the years have observed that Frank simply had no influence over Joseph, John and Robert Kennedy where Frank Sinatra was concerned, no matter how hard he tried. It's true Frank didn't have any influence over the Kennedys, but it's also true that at least where Giancana was concerned, HE NEVER TRIED (emphasis added)".[42]

Tarraborrelli maintains that Sinatra had no intention of damaging his relationship with the Kennedys. The relationship was unstable to begin with. The Kennedys appreciated Sinatra's help in the 1960 election campaign and invited Sinatra to the White House to show their appreciation. Yet they wanted to distance themselves from him even during the 1960 campaign because of the singer's unsavoury connections. Publicly they supported him; after all he helped raise 1.3 million dollars for the Democratic Party.

Sinatra's relationship with Giancana and the influence he had with the mob boss can be no better expressed than in the transcripts of a wiretap surveillance of Giancana dated December 6th 1961. Giancana discussed Sinatra with mobster Johnny Rosselli:

"Rosselli: *He (Frank Sinatra) was real nice to me...He says: 'Johnny, I took Sam's name, and I wrote it down, and told Bobby Kennedy, 'This is my buddy, this is what I want you to know, Bob.' between you and I, Frank saw Joe Kennedy three different times - Joe Kennedy the father. He called him three times...He (Sinatra) says he's got an idea that you're mad at him. I says: 'That, I wouldn't know.'*

Giancana: *He must have a guilty conscience. I never said nothing...Well, I don't know who the f... he's (Frank's) talking to, but if I'm gonna talk to...after all, if I'm taking somebody's money, I'm gonna make sure that this money is gonna do something, like, do you want it or don't you want it. If the money is accepted, maybe one of these days the guy will do me a favour.*

Rosselli: *That's right. He (Sinatra) says he wrote your name down...*

Giancana: *Well, one minute he (Sinatra) tells me this and then he tells me that and then the last time I talked to him was at the hotel in Florida a month before he left, and he said, 'Don't worry about it. If I can talk to the old man (Joe Kennedy), I'm gonna talk to the man (President Kennedy).' One minute he says he's talked to Robert, and the next minute he says he hasn't talked to him. It's a lot of shit...Why lie to me? I haven't got that coming.*

Rosselli: *I can imagine...if he can't deliver, I want him to tell me: 'John, the load's too heavy.'*

Giancana: *That's all right. At least then you know how to work. You won't let your guard down then, know what I mean...Ask him (Sinatra) if I'm going to be invited to his New Year's party.*

Rosselli: *I told him that's where I usually go for New Year's with Sam. But he says, 'I have to be in Rome the twenty-seventh.'*

Giancana: *Too f... bad. Tell him the Kennedys will keep him company.*

Rosselli: *Why don't you talk to him (Sinatra)?*

Giancana: *When he says he's gonna do a guy a little favour. I don't give a shit how long it takes. He's got to give you a little favour.*"[43]

Giancana got so angry with Sinatra that he later considered a mobster's plan to 'whack' not only the singer but also the rest of the 'Rat Pack'. In a conversation with Johnny Formosa, overheard by FBI agents and recorded on surveillance tapes, Giancana listens as Formosa says: "Let's show these asshole Hollywood fruitcakes that they can't get away with it as if nothing's happened. Let's hit Sinatra. Or I could whack out a couple of those other guys, Lawford and that Martin, and I could take the nigger and put his other eye out."[44] Giancana told Formosa he had other plans for the 'Rat Pack' which became evident when they performed at Giancana's Villa Venice.

It became apparent that the Mafia had vastly overestimated Sinatra's clout with the Kennedys. In 1961, Santos Trafficante asked Sinatra to intervene to prevent New Orleans boss, Carlos Marcello, from being deported. He was unsuccessful. Rosselli warned Giancana not to rely on Sinatra's help in getting rid of the FBI's constant surveillance of the Chicago mob boss: "He's got big ideas, Frank does, about being ambassador, or something. You know Pierre Salinger and them guys. They don't want him. They treat him like they treat a whore. You f... them, you pay them, and they're through. You got the right idea. Moe (Giancana) go the other way. F... everybody. We'll use them every f... way we can. They (the Kennedys) only know one way. Now let them see the other side of you."[45]

By 1962, the FBI was learning a lot about Sinatra's ties to leading mobsters. J. Edgar Hoover prepared three reports on Sinatra alleging that he had "personal ties to 10 leading figures of organised crime."[46]

President Kennedy read the memos but resisted breaking ties with Sinatra. It was Robert Kennedy who eventually persuaded his brother to stop seeing the singer. A presidential visit to the West Coast had been arranged in early 1962 and the President was expected to stay at Sinatra's Palm Springs house. Sinatra had specially built an extension to house the presidential staff and Secret Service agents. He also had a helipad specially built for the White House helicopter.

Robert Kennedy gave Peter Lawford the job of informing Sinatra that the President would now be staying at Bing Crosby's house instead. The reason given was concerns about security, but Sinatra saw through this excuse and became livid. According to Sinatra's valet, the singer was so angry he took his rage out on the helipad and smashed it to pieces. Sinatra did not blame John Kennedy but shortly afterwards he broke his ties with Peter Lawford and seethed about Robert Kennedy's role in the affair. However the Sinatra/JFK relationship never recovered.

Judith Campbell Exner

In 1975, during hearings held by the United States Senate Intelligence Committee, the world learned that President Kennedy had had a friend who was also the friend of a mafia gangster. The person's name was not revealed during the hearings and anonymity was protected. But not for long. The press was naturally curious as to who the 'friend' was and it was not long before her name was revealed to the American public. It was Judith Campbell Exner, a beautiful dark-haired Elizabeth Taylor look-alike, who confessed that she had had a long-standing sexual relationship with John Kennedy, beginning when he was a presidential candidate and terminating in 1962. She also confessed she had been a close friend of mob boss, Sam Giancana, although her relationship with the gangster did not include sexual relations, at least not whilst she had been seeing the President. After the publicity surrounding the Church Committee hearings subsided, she published her memoirs in 1977.

Exner's story about her relationship with President Kennedy has been used by writers and historians for over 20 years. There is no doubt that her claims that she had an intimate relationship with the President are true. Her visits to the White House were confirmed by White House logs. However, aspects of her constantly changing story have created suspicions that she embellished the original facts with salacious details in order to benefit financially. Historian, Herbert S. Parmet (1984), called her stories 'simple-minded and tedious' and 'specific items lack(ed) authority' and James DiEugenio (1997) in his excellent 'Probe' magazine article, 'The Posthumous assassination of JFK', helped to highlight her contradictions. However, until now, no-one has been able to disprove her allegations, depending as they do on her word and her word alone. For the first time, in this book incontrovertible evidence is presented which conclusively proves that Exner not only embellished her story about her relationship with President Kennedy but also lied about it.

The revelations that John Kennedy had been having an intimate relationship with a mafia-linked woman emerged during the Senate Church Committee investigation into the CIA plots against Fidel Castro. The Committee's report said:

"As elaborated in the previous sections of this report, all living CIA officials who were involved in the underworld assassination attempt or who were in a position to have known of the attempt have testified that they never discussed the assassination plot with the President. By May 1961, however, the Attorney General and Hoover were aware that the CIA had earlier used Giancana in an operation against Cuba and FBI files contained two memoranda which, if simultaneously reviewed, would have led one to conclude that the CIA operation had involved assassination. There is no evidence that anyone within the FBI concluded that the CIA had used Giancana in an assassination attempt. The Committee has uncovered a chain of events, however, which would have given Hoover an opportunity to have assembled the entire picture and to have reported the information to the President.

Evidence before the Committee indicates that a close friend of President Kennedy had frequent contact with the President from the end of 1960 through mid-1962. FBI reports and testimony indicate that the President's friend was also a close friend of John Rosselli and Sam Giancana and saw them often during this same period.

On February 27, 1962, Hoover sent identical copies of a memorandum to the Attorney General and Kenneth O' Donnell, Special Assistant to the President. The memorandum stated that information developed in connection with a concentrated FBI investigation of John Rosselli revealed that Rosselli had been in contact with the President's friend. The memorandum also reported that the individual was maintaining an association with Sam Giancana, described as 'a prominent Chicago underworld figure'. Hoover's memorandum also stated that a review of the telephone toll calls from the President's friend's residence revealed calls to the White House. The President's secretary ultimately received a copy of the memorandum and said she believed she would have shown it to the President.

The association of the President's friend with the 'hoodlums' and the person's connection with the President was again brought to Hoover's attention in a memorandum preparing him for a meeting with the President planned for March 22, 1962. Courtney Evans testified that Hoover generally required a detailed summary of information in the FBI files for drafting important memoranda or preparing for significant meetings...The FBI files on Giancana then contained information disclosing Giancana's connection with the CIA as well as his involvement in assassination plotting...

On March 22, Hoover had a private luncheon with President Kennedy. There is no record of what transpired at that luncheon. According to the White House logs, the last telephone contact between the White House and the President's friend occurred a few hours after the luncheon.

The fact that the President and Hoover had a luncheon at which one topic was presumably that the President's friend was also a friend of Giancana and Rosselli raises several possibilities. The first is, assuming that Hoover did in fact receive a summary of FBI information relating to Giancana prior to his luncheon with the President, whether that summary reminded the Director that Giancana had been involved in a CIA operation against Cuba that included 'dirty business' and further indicated that Giancana had talked about an assassination attempt against Castro. A second is whether Hoover would then have taken the luncheon as an opportunity to fulfil his duty to bring this information to the President's attention. What actually transpired at that luncheon may never be known, as both participants are dead and the FBI files contain no records relating to it." [47]

From the period of the Senate Report's release to Exner's interview with author Seymour Hersh in the mid-1990s, Judith Exner added to her original story. The simple facts of her engaging in a sexual relationship with the President of the United States became embellished with tales of abortion, of ferrying documents about CIA murder plots against Fidel Castro to mob boss Sam Giancana and of meetings with both President Kennedy and Robert Kennedy in the White House.

Judith Exner was born in Los Angeles in 1933, the daughter of wealthy parents. As a young woman she gravitated towards Hollywood and an acting career that never got off the ground. At 18 she married an ambitious actor, William Campbell, who later starred in the television series 'Cannonball'. He would, years later, give his views about the allegations that his ex-wife had carried important intelligence documents between Sam Giancana and President Kennedy. According to Campbell he "couldn't imagine her being privy to any kind of secret information...she wouldn't understand it anyway. I mean...they weren't dealing with some kind of Phi Beta Kappa."[48] The marriage was unsuccessful and she settled down to a single life in Beverly Hills supported by an inheritance from her father who had made his money as an architect.

The young Judy Campbell (she changed her name to Exner after she married a golfer Dan Exner) had a brief affair with Frank Sinatra. She had met Sinatra in 1959 after she had been introduced to the singer by Nick Sevano. After the affair was over, she still maintained a friendship with Sinatra and it was through Sinatra she met presidential candidate John F. Kennedy at a Las Vegas casino, the Sands Hotel, on February 7th 1960. Kennedy was en route to Oregon for a campaign stop and decided to detour to Las Vegas to meet his friend Sinatra.

The month after she had been introduced to the presidential aspirant, a meeting was arranged in New York and a sexual relationship ensued between the glamorous party girl and the next President of the United States. A week after the New York meeting Exner was invited to Miami by Sinatra to see him perform at the Fontainebleau Hotel. It was here that the singer introduced Exner to Sam Giancana. At the time Giancana was using one of his many aliases ('Sam Flood') and Exner was unaware of his criminal background.

Exner stated in a 1988 interview with Kitty Kelley that she was initiated into a 'courier' role by John Kennedy at his Georgetown home in 1960. She said that Kennedy arranged for her to carry 'packages' to Sam Giancana and also to set up a meeting between the mob boss and the presidential candidate. Exner told Kelley: "I was not present (at the meeting) but Jack (Kennedy) came to my suite afterward, and I asked him how the meeting had gone. He seemed very happy about it and thanked me for making the arrangements. He then stayed with me for an hour or so, and we talked about the campaign."[49] According to Exner, Kennedy handed her an envelope with 2,000 dollars in cash for gratitude for her services. Later Exner maintained that she not only carried money from the Kennedy campaign to Giancana but she also carried documents dealing with the murder plots against Castro.

There is little doubt that Exner did indeed have an affair with the President. White House logs prove that she had contact with him on a number of occasions, by telephone and by visits to the White House. But her story has changed so many times over the years and has been embellished each time that her credibility is weak when it comes to recounting how Kennedy personally requested the aid of the Mafia in the 1960 election and how the President arranged meetings with Giancana to discuss the murder plots against Castro.

In the 1970s, Exner admitted only to affairs at different times with Kennedy and Giancana. No mention was made of the meetings or her role as a 'courier'. Then in the 1988 Kelley interview, she told of how she could now speak freely and reveal more. Apparently, she had been fearful that the mob or the CIA would kill her, suggesting that this is what happened to Giancana and Rosselli after they testified, or were about to testify, before the Senate Intelligence Committee. Exner now maintained that Kennedy and Giancana had prolonged meetings, using her as a 'go-between'. She told Kelley that she never knew what was in the packages when she acted as a courier and that Kennedy did not explain what was going on.

In 1991, in an interview with Anthony Summers, Exner further embellished her story by stating that Kennedy had told her the packages contained 'intelligence material' pertaining to the murder plots against Castro and that she had also carried money from Kennedy to Giancana to assist in the Kennedy primary campaign in West Virginia.[50] She had carried the money in a satchel from Kennedy's Georgetown house, boarding a train for Chicago and handing the money over to Giancana.

However, this part of her story is fraught with problems and it begs the question - why would John Kennedy risk exposure through this act when he had his brother and numerous intelligence personnel to do his bidding? Furthermore, Sam Giancana's daughter, Antoinette Giancana, has vigorously denied Exner had acted as a courier for her father.[51] She said her father had "utter contempt" for JFK and never mentioned any contact with the President during his time in the White House. G. Robert Blakey, former counsel to the House Assassinations Committee which investigated the links between the CIA and the mob, said to Larry King that neither JFK nor Sam Giancana would have confided in Judith Exner as she would not have been "creditable".[52]

The personal dispersal of funds for the presidential campaign would seem to be a risky venture for the ambitious senator - why would Kennedy, a man who had literally hundreds of people working for him in the campaign, allow himself to be compromised by disbursing large sums of money? Furthermore, it has been accepted by all historians that what John Kennedy knew his brother also knew. Why would Robert Kennedy pursue the Mafia with such zeal if he was aware that Giancana could blackmail the President at any time?

Contradictions are everywhere in Exner's stories. If Kennedy had been meeting personally with Sam Giancana, why would he need Sinatra to act as a conduit? It is true that Sinatra had, through the kind auspices of his mob friends, disbursed large amounts of Kennedy Snr.'s cash to pay off election officials. FBI wiretaps indicate this. Sinatra had asked his friend Giancana to help win the vote in the West Virginia primary and the mob boss sent his colleague, Paul 'Skinny' D'Amato, to the impoverished state to meet with the sheriffs who controlled the political machine.

Judith Exner further embellished her story about Kennedy corruption in 1997. After the interviews with Kelley (1988), Summers (1991) and Hersh (1994), she spoke to gossip reporter Liz Smith (1997).[53]

In her 1997 version, Exner tells Liz Smith of 'Vanity Fair' that she had never slept with Giancana. There are another two new 'revelations' in this version. She states that President Kennedy made her pregnant and that she subsequently had an abortion. But there are obvious problems with this version and it was apparent that reporter Liz Smith did not investigate her claims fully. In 1977, Exner stated there was no abortion - it was made-up by the FBI in order to embarrass and harass her. Exner (1977) wrote: "He (FBI agent) turned and there was the most hideous leer on his face. If I could have killed that man, I would have on the spot. There is nothing heinous about an abortion today, but in 1963, my God, it was the sin of the century. They knew precisely what they were doing when they falsely accused me of something like that. As far as I know, they never talked to Dr Jacobson or to my gynaecologist. It was just another ploy in their vicious cat-and-mouse game."[54] But she told author Seymour Hersh that when she became pregnant with Kennedy's child she and the President decided she must have an abortion. Kennedy allegedly asked: "Would Sam (Giancana) help us?" We are thus asked to believe that the President wants to incur a debt to a mafia boss. The whole idea stretches credulity but this fact seems to escape Hersh. And Hersh never asks the question - why would Kennedy risk this venture when he had his 'fixer' father and numerous powerful connections to arrange the purported 'abortion'.

However, it is a comment Exner made to Larry King which conclusively proves she has repeatedly lied about the extent of her relationship with President Kennedy. It also proves she has repeatedly embellished her story, rendering her unfit as a reliable source for historians. The following discrepancies in her story cannot be dismissed as faulty memory or the fear of Mafia retaliation.

On February 4th 1992, Judith Exner was interviewed by Larry King at her home in California. She had been suffering from cancer for many years and she wanted to set the record straight, believing that she did not have many more years to live. (She eventually succumbed to the disease in September 1999). King asked Exner what relationship she had had with Bobby Kennedy:

"Exner: *None.*

King: *None at all? You never spoke to him?*

Exner: *I noticed in my testimony (to the Church Committee) which I've only just received...and I noticed, with my trying to cover everything up (Exner is referring to her fears of retribution from the mob or the CIA), they do ask me about Bobby and, luckily this was testimony that wasn't sworn to, and I said yes I had met him and I think that probably I met Bobby at a couple of parties. I know there was a fundraiser out here at (movie actor) Barry Sullivan's house and I think probably that's what was in my mind. But I didn't know him well."[55]

However in 1997, she completely contradicts this statement made to King in an interview with Liz Smith. Talking about supposed White House meetings between Sam Giancana and President Kennedy she said:

"You know I used to be at the White House having lunch or dinner with Jack (Kennedy), and Bobby would often come by. He'd squeeze my shoulder solicitously and ask 'Judy, are you O.K. carrying those messages for us to Chicago? Do you feel comfortable doing it?'"[56]

This is not a nuance of language but a direct contradiction and renders her stories false.

Apart from the obvious contradictions in her statements to King and Smith there are other controvertible facts about the whole White House scenario. Bobby Kennedy at this time had such heavy surveillance on Giancana that the mobster went to court to prevent six FBI agents from following his every move. Bobby Kennedy hated Giancana as much as he hated Jimmy Hoffa and he was vigorously trying to put both men in prison.

It now seems evident that Judith Exner has embellished a simple truth - that she had been the mistress of JFK - into a story of gross exaggeration. Consequently, the fallout damage to historical truth is inestimable.

The Kennedy/Mafia connection

Many writers have been taken in by the braggadocio of prominent mobsters who have claimed that Joseph Kennedy Snr. had been 'one of us' meaning he engaged in illegal 'bootlegging' activities in his whisky business. However, they ignore evidence which suggests that, at best, the links were nothing more than a slight association. Joseph Kennedy had been thoroughly investigated in the 1950s by the FBI (when he received a minor government position with the Eisenhower Administration) and the Anti-Trust Division of the Justice Department investigated him. The probes turned up nothing to substantiate the rumours. But, in the financially unregulated world of American politics in the 1950s and 1960s, it is not surprising that Joseph Kennedy may have solicited the help of legitimate and quasi-legitimate sources to help his son become President. After all other national political figures were doing the same. There is no credible evidence, however, that would suggest John and Robert Kennedy had anything but a suspicion that mafia elements were assisting in the 1960 campaign. RFK must have felt uncomfortable with the knowledge that his father had skirted the fringes of the underworld in his rise to financial success or that he may have condoned the assistance of questionable figures during the 1960 election. Yet it did not make him cautious in his desire to bring the Mafia to justice. RFK, as Attorney General, tried to distance the Kennedys from Frank Sinatra who had too many gangster associates. He believed that any connection to hoodlums, however slight, would tarnish the Kennedy presidency. JFK, on the other hand, had a much more easygoing and, some say, reckless style when it came to associating with others in his pursuit of the presidency. JFK felt no foreboding in being in the same room as Sinatra's mob-related friends and would, like his father, accept campaign help from any quarter.

Most biographies of Frank Sinatra show that he was a talented man from humble origins who craved 'class'. This is no more revealing than the bad associations he kept whilst soliciting the friendships and acknowledgement of eastern establishment 'high society' types. Sinatra was proud of his mafia friendships and may have been culpable of aiding and abetting with their nightclub enterprises. In reality he was a 'gangster groupie'. In return he received the dubious respect of the Hollywood elite who recognised who his friends were and accordingly became very wary of crossing him. But there is no evidence that he personally engaged in any illegal mob enterprises or received illegal payments. He was, after all, a multimillionaire because of his talents not his connections.

It would seem likely that on the evidence available Frank Sinatra enlisted his friends in the Mafia to support John Kennedy's campaign for the presidency. There is no credible evidence to support the contention that John Kennedy asked Sinatra to enlist the mob's help in the campaign. Joseph Kennedy Snr. was the power behind John Kennedy's campaign even though Robert Kennedy was the nominal campaign manager. The elder Kennedy knew that whatever deals he made to secure campaign finances and assistance would have to be distanced from the candidate. So Joseph Kennedy may well have asked Sinatra to bring in whatever help was necessary in the West Virginia primary campaign - help which included bribing sheriffs and the like. The most reasonable conclusion to draw is that Sinatra, without John or Robert Kennedy's knowledge, insinuated to Giancana that the Outfit's assistance would be reciprocated after Kennedy became President. Mobster, Paul D'Amato has stated that the price for the Kennedys to pay was the return of mobster, Joe Adonis, who had been deported. This quid pro quo was not forthcoming. Robert Kennedy would have nothing to do with Sinatra's pleading for his friend Giancana or any support for the return of Adonis.

There is no doubt that a close personal relationship existed between Judith Campbell Exner and President Kennedy - it has been well established over the years. However, we can only guess at Exner's reasons for embellishing her original story. Her credibility can now only be regarded as poor in terms of historical truth.

The myth of a close relationship between the Mafia and the Kennedys has been fed by unscrupulous writers whose trust in the veracity of known killers and liars is evident. No credible evidence of a close relationship can, however, be established.

Notes

1. "Peter Maas interviews Frank Costello", *New York Times*, 9 September 1973. (http://www.nytimes.com)

2. Bonanno, J. and Lalli, S. (1983). *A man of honour: the autobiography of Joseph Bonanno*, Simon and Schuster. p. 44; *see also* '60 minutes' with Mike Wallace, CBS, 1 May 1983. (http://www.cbs.com).

3. Hersh, S. (1997). *The dark side of Camelot*, Little Brown and Co. p. 50.

4. *Ibid*, p. 51.

5. Kessler, R. (1996). *The sins of the father*, Hodder and Stoughton. p. 38.

6. Goodwin, D. K. (1988). *The Fitzgeralds and the Kennedys*, Pan Books. pp. 441-443.

7. Blakey, G. R. and Billings, R. (1992). *Fatal hour: the assassination of President Kennedy by organised crime*, Berkeley New York. pp. 407-408.

8. Mahoney, R. D. (1999). *Sons and brothers*, Arcade Publishing. xv.

9. In 1969, leading government organised crime expert Ralph Salerno estimated that the votes of 25 Congressmen could be corrupted by mob influence (*Time*, 22 August 1969). Congressmen Cornelius Gallagher, Frank Annunzio, Roland Libonati and Daniel Flood had close dealings with the Mafia ('The Congressman and the Hoodlum', *Life*, 9 August 1968). Richard Nixon reportedly received (perhaps unknowingly) campaign contributions from mob figures during his Congressional and Senate campaigns. [Moldea, D. (1978). *The Hoffa wars*, Paddington Press Ltd. p. 352]. In February 1961 the 'Los Angeles Times' reported that Nixon bought a house lot from Teamsters boss Jimmy Hoffa 7,000 dollars below its real value [Ambrose, S. (1987). *Nixon - the education of a politician, 1913-1962*, Simon and Schuster. p. 629]. The 'New York Times' called Nixon's pardon of Jimmy Hoffa "a pivotal

element between the Administration and the two million-member truck union, ousted from the rest of the labor movement in 1957 for racketeer domination."(*New York Times*, 24 December 1971) The 'Los Angeles Times' demonstrated how the Nixon Administration intervened to stall prosecutions and investigations of Teamster criminal activity in its editorial 'Nixon, the teamsters, the Mafia' (*Los Angeles Times*, 1 June 1973). 'Time' disclosed in 1977 that the Nixon White House had received a 1 million dollar bribe. (*Time*, 8 August 1977). 'Time' reported Allen Dorfman, Teamster pension fund advisor, provided half of the bribe for Nixon on Teamster president Frank Fitzsimmon's orders. The FBI called the information on the million dollar transaction "solid" [Moldea, D. (1978). *The Hoffa wars*, Paddington Press Ltd. p. 320]. It is possible Nixon wanted the money to pay off the Watergate burglars - one of Nixon's most famous statements on the Nixon Tapes, (23 March 1973) was "We could get that...You could get a million dollars. You could get it in cash. I know where it could be gotten." In 1960 mafia boss Carlos Marcello funnelled 500,000 dollars in cash to Nixon through Jimmy Hoffa [Moldea, D. (1978). *The Hoffa wars*, Paddington Press Ltd. p. 108]. Lyndon Johnson's campaigns for the Senate were backed by Texas Oil baron Clint Murchison Jnr. who was involved with the Teamsters through I. Irving Davidson in Washington (*Life*, 2 May 1969)

10. Mahoney, R. D. (1999). *Sons and brothers*, Arcade Publishing. p. 39.

11. Stein, J. and Plimpton, G., eds. (1970). *American journey - the times of Robert Kennedy*, Harcourt Brace Jovanovich. p. 36.

Sam Giancana

12. 'Reputations - Sam Giancana', BBC Television Documentary, 1998.

13. 'The demise of a don', *Time*, 30 June 1975, p. 31.

14. FBI File No: 25-244122. (http://foia.gov/giancana.htm).

15. Roemer, W. (1989). *Man against the mob*, Fine New York. pp. 130-133.

16. *Ibid*, p. 133.

17. Taraborrelli, J. R. (1997). *Sinatra - the man behind the myth*, Mainstream Publishing Projects. p. 205.

18. Sheridan, W. (1972). *The fall and rise of Jimmy Hoffa*, Saturday Review Press; Moldea, D. (1978). *The Hoffa wars*, Paddington Press Ltd. p. 260; Goldfarb, R. (1995). *Perfect villains, imperfect heroes*, Random House. p. 193.

19. Hersh, S. (1997). *The dark side of Camelot*, Little Brown and Co. pp. 135-137.

20. Wills, G. 'A second assassination'. *New York Times*, 18 December 1997. (http://www.nytimes.com).

21. Hersh, S. (1997). *The dark side of Camelot*, Little Brown and Co. p. 138.

22. Goldfarb, R. (1995). *Perfect villains, imperfect heroes*, Random House. p. 137; Gentry, C. (1991). *J. Edgar Hoover - the man and the secrets*, WW Norton and Co. pp. 490-491.

23. *Ibid*, p. 491.

24. FBI Memo. (http://www.the smokinggun.com/about.shtml).

25. Martin, R.G. (1983). *A hero for our time*, Macmillan Publishing Company. p. 219.

26. *Sunday Times*, 14 June 1998, p. 10.

27. 'Book depicts JFK as reckless and immoral', *New York Daily Times*, 9 November 1997. (http://www.nydailynews.com).

28. Kefauver, E. (1951). *Crime in America*, Doubleday. p. 35.

29. Schlesinger, A. M. (1978). *Robert Kennedy and his times*, Houghton Mifflin Co. p. 237.

The Sinatra connection

30. Leamer, L. (1994). *The Kennedy women*, Villard Books. p. 562.

31. FBI Airtel Memo to J. Edgar Hoover, 23 March 1960, Smoking Gun. (http://www.thesmokinggun.com).

32. Taraborrelli, J. R. (1997). *Sinatra - the man behind the myth*, Mainstream Publishing Projects. pp. 84-92.

33. *Ibid*, p. 84.

34. Kelley, K. (1986). *His way*, Bantam Press. p. 265.

35. "Crime Inc. Interview with Aladena 'Jimmy the Weasel' Fratianno. Thames TV Documentary, 1984; Short, M. (1984). *Crime Inc*. Thames Methuen. p. 229.

36. *Ibid*.

37. Mahoney, R. D. (1999). *Sons and brothers*, Arcade Publishing. p. 54; Taraborrelli, J. R. (1997). *Sinatra - the man behind the myth*, Mainstream Publishing Projects. p. 205.

38. 'Smashing Camelot'. *Time*, 17 November 1997, p. 78.

39. O'Neill, T. (1987). *Man of the House*, St Martin's Press. p. 106.

40. Hilty, J. W. (1997). *Robert Kennedy – brother protector*, Temple University Press. p. 144.

41. White, T. H. (1978). *In search of history*, Jonathan Cape. p. 466.

42. Taraborrelli, J. R. (1997). *Sinatra - the man behind the myth*, Mainstream Publishing Projects. p. 222.

43. FBI Transcript and Memo, 6 December 1961. (http://www.thesmokinggun.com).

44. Gentry, C. (1991). *J. Edgar Hoover - the man and the secrets*, WW Norton and Co. p. 491.

45. FBI Memo, 21 December 1961.
(http://www.thesmokinggun.com).

46. Hilty, J. W. (1997). *Robert Kennedy – brother protector*, Temple University Press. p. 208.

Judith Campbell Exner

47. U.S. Senate Select Committee to Study Governmental Operations with Respect to Intelligence Activities. (1975). *Interim report: alleged assassination plots involving foreign leaders' 94th congress, 1st session*, U.S. Government Printing Office. P. 194. (Church Committee).

48. Schlesinger, A. M. (1978). *Robert Kennedy and his times*, Houghton Mifflin Co. p. 532.

49. Kelley, K. "The dark side of Camelot", *People*, 29 February 1988. (http://www.people.aol.com).

50. Summers, A, "The unmaking of a myth', *Sunday Times*, 6 October 1991, p. 18.

51. Balsamo, W. and Carpozi, G. Jnr. (1997), *The Mafia – the first 100 years*, Virgin Books. xiv.

52. 'Larry King live'. Interview with Judith Campbell Exner. CNN, 4 February, 1992. (video and transcript on http://www.cnn.com/transcripts).

53. Summers, A. 'The unmaking of a myth', *Sunday Times*, 6 October 1991, p. 18.

54. Exner, J. (1977). *My story*, Futura Publications Ltd. p. 282.

55. 'Larry King live'. Interview with Judith Campbell Exner. CNN, 4 February, 1992. (video and transcript on http://www.cnn.com/transcripts).

56. Smith, E. 'The Exner files', *Vanity Fair*, January 1997, (http://www.condenet.com).

Chapter 8

Hoover

Did FBI boss J. Edgar Hoover blackmail the Kennedys?

"Nam et ipsa scientia potestas."
(Knowledge itself is power)

Francis Bacon

Anthony Summers (1993) in his best-selling biography of J. Edgar Hoover, 'Official and confidential' and Seymour Hersh (1997) in his book 'The dark side of Camelot', amongst many others, claim that J. Edgar Hoover blackmailed the Kennedys. The allegations have been made repeatedly for the past 35 or more years and Hoover's reputation has diminished as a result. Seymour Hersh claims to provide further evidence that the FBI Director conspired with Senate Majority leader, Lyndon B. Johnson, to blackmail Democratic presidential nominee, John F. Kennedy, to place the Texas senator on the Democratic ticket. Anthony Summers believes that Hoover resisted efforts to tackle the national problem of organised crime because he himself was blackmailed by the Mafia. But what is the truth concerning the relationship between J. Edgar Hoover, President Kennedy and Attorney-General Robert Kennedy? And if J. Edgar Hoover had been blackmailed by the Mafia, how did he respond to Robert Kennedy's zealous quest to rid the country of the insidious national crime syndicate?

Hoover's rise

J. Edgar Hoover became Director of the FBI at its inception in the 1920s. The FBI's origins lie in the crime-ridden 'Roaring Twenties' when America became a nation of lawbreakers. It was against the law to make or consume alcohol and yet millions of Americans refused to recognise this fact. The distillation and distribution of alcohol became big business involving millions of dollars and corruption of public officials on a scale unheard of either before or since.

Criminal gangs competed for the business of supplying the public what it wanted. Violence was inevitable as gangsters moved into territories owned by competing gangs. The violence and corruption was significant in the growth of the American Mafia.

The United States had no national police force at this time, but Congress decided in the early 1930s that a federal force was necessary to deal with a law-breaking situation which was becoming too big for state and city police forces. Congress chose a small department within the Justice Department headed by an unknown professional bureaucrat by the name of J. Edgar Hoover.

When Hoover took over the newly-formed Federal Bureau of Investigation its resources were limited and Congress had not yet passed laws to strengthen the authority of its agents. Under the leadership and persuasive skills of Hoover, the department expanded to become a world-famous and internationally renowned institution. Hoover's 'G-Men' (Government men) became national heroes as they captured notorious criminals like John Dillinger, Ma Barker, Machine-Gun Kelly and leading members of criminal gangs. The titles 'Public Enemy No. 1' and 'The Ten Most-Wanted' list originated with the Bureau. J. Edgar Hoover became a national hero, in part because of his publicity skills and his ability to persuade politicians and presidents to expand the authority of the Bureau. Hoover did everything in his persuasive powers to see that Congress was generous with the Bureau's budget. Hoover also strictly monitored anything which extolled the virtues of the FBI, from books and radio serials to Hollywood movies.

Hoover was partly successful because he changed crime-fighting into a science. He instituted fingerprint files and laboratories to analyse forensic evidence. During the Second World War, the Bureau successfully fought efforts at sabotage and subversion by the Germans and they could proudly point to the fact that not one instance of sabotage on the American mainland was successful. After the war the FBI was also successful in detecting and arresting many Soviet spies. Hoover was convinced there was an international left-wing conspiracy to take over the world and, during the late 1940s and 1950s, most of his energies were devoted to rooting out anything which smacked of 'communism' or 'socialism'. Recent research has suggested that the idea of subversion by the Soviets was not all in the imagination of right-wing politicians or the conservative FBI Director. There is a wealth of evidence to confirm that the Soviets were using every means available to infiltrate the American government and any other institution in America which had influence within the body politic. Hollywood was a particular target for communist cells, but many lives were destroyed because of the paranoiac hysteria which often accompanied right-wing Congressional efforts to 'clean up' the movie industry.[1]

During this period of anti-communist fervour Hoover had been blind to the existence of a national crime syndicate even though a 1950s Congressional investigating body led by Senator Estes Kefauver had produced a mountain of evidence proving this fact. However, it was not until the early 1960s and the Congressional testimony of top mafia member, Joseph Valachi, that the country learned the real names of this criminal organisation, 'Cosa Nostra' (translated 'Our Thing') and Mafia (from the Italian heritage of Sicilian gangs). After the nationally televised Kefauver hearings, Hoover still insisted that there was no such thing as the Mafia and as a consequence there was a period of consolidation of the criminal organisation and a period of growth for mafia 'families' in every city across America.

Hoover and the Mafia

Anthony Summers (1993) claims Hoover deliberately refused to crack down on organised crime because he was blackmailed by the Mafia for living a secret life as a homosexual. Summers believes that Hoover was blackmailed after Meyer Lansky, a mafia associate of Frank Costello and the most powerful American Godfather, obtained photographs of the FBI boss in a compromising position with his friend, Clyde Tolson. Summers' 'proof' about Hoover's homosexuality comes from a number of witnesses who told the writer that they had seen photographs. Former members of the Mafia or mafia associates told of how Lansky pressured the FBI Director into leaving the criminal organisation alone. Summers' strongest source for Hoover's homosexuality is Susan Rosenstiel, the fourth wife of Lewis Solon Rosenstiel, a mobster and distilling mogul. She claims to have witnessed Hoover in drag at two orgies at New York's Plaza Hotel in 1958 and 1959. Senator Joseph McCarthy's former aide, Roy Cohn, a known homosexual, was also present. Rosenstiel's story could not be corroborated as all the participants present at the parties are now deceased. Summers himself has not seen the photograph purportedly used to blackmail Hoover.

Hoover's sex life was a mystery. It was quite obvious he was not interested in women and there are no stories of courtship. He was raised mostly by his disciplinarian mother who rewarded obedience and punished disobedience within a strict code. In high school, Hoover was recognised by his peers as a boy who had strict ideas about morality and celibacy and friends averred that Hoover was in love with his school's cadet corps. In the school's yearbook he was described as "a gentleman of dauntless courage and stainless honour." He developed a stutter and this may account for his bashfulness with girls. To those who knew Hoover at this time it was obvious he had a fear of becoming too personally involved with people. He gave a lot of affection to the dogs he owned over the years and in later life he doted on his pets. He had only two close friends throughout his life, Frank Baughman and Clyde Tolson, but after Baughman married the friendship diminished.

Those who knew Hoover throughout his life are divided in their judgements of the man. To some Hoover was a dedicated public servant who was neither arrogant nor a megalomaniac. He was friendly, a man of great humour who enjoyed being with people. The actor, James Stewart, is typical of this group of acquaintances who described Hoover as a man who: "...liked to be with people, and I thought always that he was very easy to be with and it always surprised me...he was so easy to be with and so easy to talk to....I had the feeling that I was with a very strong, determined man, always."[2]

Others have described Hoover as a man who had a lot of prejudices. He hated Jews, African-Americans and "pseudo-liberals"; he was a conservative in the truest sense of the word, disliking any change at all in a society whose foundations were built on the ability to constantly renew itself. Hoover's detractors generally describe him as a man who spent too long in the job, becoming increasingly senile, angry and personally corrupt, having accepted gratuities from Dallas millionaires, Clint Murchison and Sid Richardson. Hoover and Tolson frequently stayed at their hotel without paying. Hoover also used FBI personnel to write his books and do odd jobs around his home. To Hoover enemies of the state were everywhere and it was his God-given right to protect the nation.

However, like accounts of the Kennedys, Hoover's motives and character have often been misrepresented. His reputation has consequently suffered. Allegations of misuse of office certainly ring true. Yet the context of Hoover's transgressions has been missing. Hoover did not see himself as personally corrupt. He had been head of the FBI for decades and considered himself above reproach in giving himself some leeway in accepting relatively small gratuities. There is no evidence that he enriched himself to the tune of millions of dollars through his position as head of the FBI. Indeed, he had been offered a lifetime job by billionaire, Howard Hughes, but turned it down. Hughes told Hoover that he could set his own salary. Instead, Hoover wished to remain with his true love - the directorship of an institution which he had personally built. In later years he worried that he would not be financially secure in his old age and accepted what was common and legal up to the 1970s - 'honorariums' accompanied by large cheques.

Neither his friends nor many of his detractors have ever considered Hoover's friendship with Tolson as anything but chaste. To those who knew both men, Cartha 'Deke' Deloach, George Allen and Charles Spencer are representative in their understanding of Hoover's relationship with his friend. Allen said: "Tolson was sort of Hoover's alter ego. He almost ran the FBI. He's not only a brain, but the most unselfish man that ever lived. He let Hoover take all the bows all the credits...They were very, very close because he needed Clyde so much. He couldn't have done the things he did without Clyde."[3] Spencer said, "Oh, Christ I heard rumours about them a thousand times. All around, every place, and I think it's just the result of people unable to believe that two men could be as dedicated to their country as those two were. It wasn't just speculation and it was worse than rumours. It had to be developed by jealous and enviable people that were out to do somebody in. Their demeanour was always flawless. Very businesslike. The best way I can put it is that Clyde Tolson was the Associate Director of the FBI. He lived 24 hours of every day, seven days a week for the full year as Associate Director of the FBI. It was a Director and Associate Director relationship."[4] Cartha Deloach worked closely with Hoover for over 20 years and became the 3rd ranking FBI agent. Deloach dismissed stories about Hoover's alleged homosexuality stating: "I think it's significant to note that no one who knew Hoover and Tolson well in the FBI has ever even hinted at such a charge. You can't work side by side with two men for the better part of 20 years and fail to recognise signs of such affections."[5]

President Truman's top military aide, General Harry Vaughn, worked closely with Hoover during the Truman Administration and was convinced the rumours about Hoover and Tolson were untrue. Writer Ovid Demaris (1975) asked Vaughn if the two men were homosexuals: "Oh, no", Vaughn replied. Demaris asked him why he was so positive: "Well, because he (Hoover) was a red-blooded virile individual. I can imagine that I might be in a job like that, having an old college classmate of mine associated with me, and we'd be living together. In fact one time I heard a member of the press say that the reason that Harry Truman and his staff spent two weeks down at key West without their wives was because 'most of those bastards are homosexuals'."[6]

However, even Hoover's agents speculated about their boss' sexual preference and noted how, from the 1920s up to the time of their deaths in the 1970s, Hoover and his friend, Clyde Tolson, went everywhere together. They vacationed together and shared an interest in horse racing. Throughout the decades together they took lunch together at the Mayflower Hotel in Washington D.C., always sitting at the same table. Hoover and Tolson shared affectionate nicknames. Hoover was known by his childhood name, 'Speed'; Tolson was 'Junior'.

In 1928 Tolson joined the FBI eventually ending up as an Associate Director. Both men were 'loners' and appeared bashful in social situations. Each morning Hoover arrived at Tolson's apartment and the two men journeyed to the FBI offices which were situated in the Justice Department building on Pennsylvania Avenue in the centre of the nation's capital. During periods when Tolson was ill he would stay at the Director's house in N.W. Washington. Throughout Hoover's tenure as Director he was accompanied on leisurely 'inspections' of FBI offices around the nation, usually choosing Southern cities. Tolson was the only person, other than Hoover's secretary Helen Gandy, who the Director allowed unlimited access to secret files. The two men were eventually buried side by side. Hoover preceded Tolson in death by three years. After Hoover's death in May 1972 the bulk of his estate went to his friend.

Throughout his period in office J. Edgar Hoover used the FBI to squelch rumours that he was homosexual. He was vigorous in his approach because he believed the allegations impugned his good name and integrity. His detractors were often intimidated by FBI agents.

Hoover ordered them to demand that the rumour mongers 'put up or shut up'. It is clear that Hoover was confident no evidence existed of any indiscretions.

Anthony Summers' 'evidence' of Hoover's homosexuality lacks veracity according to two of Hoover's most acclaimed and authoritative biographers. Richard Gid Powers[7] and Athan Theoharis both believe Summers' sources are not credible. Athan Theoharis said that the popularisation of Hoover's homosexuality was the result of "shoddy journalism".[8] A third acclaimed biographer, Curt Gentry, offers no evidence for or against Summers' allegations and remains neutral. He has written that: "There was always a rumour within the Bureau but never any evidence." He does however, quote Roger Baldwin, founder of the American Civil Liberties Union (no friend of the Director's). Baldwin had known Hoover since 1924 and his integrity and political courage has been commented upon by a number of authoritative historians. Gentry (1991) wrote: "...more important...was that he (Tolson) was J. Edgar Hoover's only true close friend. Roger Baldwin, in an interview shortly before his death, saw nothing unnatural in this. It would have been unnatural, Baldwin thought, had someone in such a high and solitary position not had at least one 'buddy', someone he could confide in, trust."[9]

Richard Gid Powers, commenting on Summers' book which was released in 1994, said: "Summers has tracked down more rumours more assiduously than any other biographer, but getting someone to give you a quote about rumour does not make it true...This is a hell of a good read. It weaves together all the rumours about Hoover but the difficulty is connecting the web of rumours to the facts. Hoover is a lost cause as far as his reputation is concerned even before this...book."[10]

Powers also questioned the reliability of many of Summers' witnesses quoted in the book. Powers said that Hoover was such a hated figure that many people were prepared to believe the worst about him and to 'badmouth' him. As an example of the witnesses' unreliability, Powers cites John Weitz, a former wartime secret service officer, who, according to Summers, was at a dinner party in the 1950s when the host showed him a picture and identified Hoover having sex with another man. Weitz did not himself recognise Hoover and he refuses to identify the party host.[11]

It was Athan Theoharis (1995) who successfully demonstrated, in his book 'J. Edgar Hoover, sex, and crime', that Summers' claims were not believable. Theoharis believes there is no evidence that Hoover and Tolson were sexually involved and that there is evidence to suggest that Tolson was strongly heterosexual, citing reports by a number of Tolson's associates. Theoharis believes that the likelihood is that Hoover never knew sexual desire at all.

Of Rosenstiel's claim that Hoover was homosexual, Theoharis wrote: "Susan Rosenstiel...was not a disinterested party. Although the target of her allegations was J. Edgar Hoover, she managed as well to defame her second husband with whom she had been involved in a bitterly contested divorce which lasted ten years in the courts. Her hatred of Lewis Rosenstiel had led her in 1970 to offer damaging testimony about his alleged connections with organised crime leaders before a New York state legislative committee on crime."[12] Throughout Theoharis' book fact after authoritative fact is presented which demolishes Summers' thesis. His research is supported by Cartha Deloach (1997) who said Rosenstiel blamed Hoover for supplying her husband with damaging information used in her divorce trial. Furthermore, according to Deloach, she had been peddling the Hoover 'drag' story to Hoover's critics for years without success - until Anthony Summers came along.[13]

And Susan Rosenstiel's credibility is weak which is evident from her story given to a BBC documentary team. When questioned by Anthony Summers about her observations at the Plaza Hotel she said the person in drag "LOOKED LIKE J. EDGAR HOOVER. (emphasis added)" After a prompt by Summers she agrees that it was definitely Hoover. It is clear that Rosenstiel's story is less than convincing especially when her claims are considered; Hoover was allowing himself to be observed by someone who could have destroyed his career and compromised him for the rest of his life. Her story simply lacks credibility.[14]

Summers' account of mafia blackmail cannot be taken seriously. It would have been impossible for Hoover to prevent the prosecution of mafia bosses. This act would have required a conspiracy involving FBI agents and officials, leading members of Congress, senior officials in the Justice department, senior White House officials, as well as state and local law-enforcement officials.

The real reason why Hoover did not investigate the Mafia throughout the 1930s, 1940s and 1950s is that he had a genuine fear that his agents would be corrupted by the criminal organisation. The FBI was the only love of Hoover's life and he protected and defended it as a father does with a son. On more than one occasion he made reference to the fact that state and local law officers had been corrupted by the mob. There was also a self-serving reason. Throughout his leadership of the Bureau, Hoover had been unwilling to tackle any major initiative unless he had been assured of success. Fighting organised crime, to Hoover, did not provide that guaranteed success. As Arthur Schlesinger (1978) wrote: "Former FBI agents laid great stress on Hoover's infatuation with statistics. He liked to regale Congress with box scores of crimes committed, subjects apprehended and crimes solved. Organised crime did not lend itself to statistical display. It required a heavy investment of agents in long tedious investigations that might or might not produce convictions at the end. The statistical preoccupation steered Hoover toward the easy cases - bank robbers, car thieves, kidnappers and other one-shot offences."[15]

Most importantly, it was Hoover's obsession with 'communist subversion' which drew his complete attention and he was aided and abetted in this by successive post-war administrations and congresses. He believed communism to be the main threat to the 'American way of life'. It was this desire to keep the fight against communism at the top of the political agenda which led to his clash with the first Attorney-General, Robert Kennedy, who saw the Mafia as public enemy number one.

Hoover and the Kennedys

The Kennedys were the most compelling of J. Edgar Hoover's targets. For over 30 years he dug into the lives of the Kennedys for political leverage. Beginning with Joseph Kennedy Snr., Hoover knew that information about the family would eventually benefit the power conscious FBI Director. As Ambassador to Great Britain during the Second World War, Kennedy Snr. had an important position in President Roosevelt's Administration and when the ambassador fell out with the President, Roosevelt turned to Hoover to provide him with details of Kennedy's private life.

However, Kennedy maintained his friendship with the FBI Director and jumped at any opportunity to praise Hoover publicly. FBI files also record that Joe Kennedy acted as an FBI informant providing the FBI with names to investigate.[16]

Hoover compiled a file on John Kennedy from the moment the young naval intelligence officer engaged in a relationship with a married woman, Inga Arvad, whom the Bureau suspected of being a Nazi spy (a number of FBI memos confirm that there was no truth to the allegations). One of the hotel rooms where Kennedy and Arvad met was bugged by the FBI, but no proof was found that either Kennedy or Arvad had been engaged in spying activities. However, the fact that Ambassador Kennedy's second son had been conducting a scandalous relationship with a married woman was more than enough information to hold against Kennedy Snr.

Over the years John Kennedy's career moved from the House of Representatives to the Senate then the presidency in 1960. By that year Hoover had become the symbol of law and order in the United States. Hoover's file on John Kennedy grew, delineating liaisons with women other than the politician's wife. The file also recorded campaign contributions from mafia bosses.

Hoover ordered the accounting of files in the Spring and Summer of 1960 when it seemed likely Kennedy would be the Democratic nominee for president. On July 13th 1960, FBI official Milton Jones prepared a nine page memo for Assistant Director Cartha DeLoach: "...The Bureau and the Director have enjoyed friendly relations with Senator Kennedy and his family for a number of years...Allegations of immoral activities on Senator Kennedy's past have been reported to the FBI over the years...they include...data reflecting that Kennedy carried on an illicit relationship with another man's wife (Inga Arvad) during World War Two; that (probably January 1960) Kennedy was 'compromised' with a woman in Las Vegas; and that Kennedy and Frank Sinatra have in the recent past been involved in parties in Palm Springs, Las Vegas and New York City."[17]

After Kennedy was elected President, Hoover realised that a good way of keeping check on his amorous activities was to cover Peter Lawford's activities. Lawford was Hoover's link between Hollywood and Washington. Throughout the period of Kennedy's presidency, FBI agents had been ordered to keep surveillance on Lawford's comings and goings and to make a written record of any liaisons the President had.

As a law enforcement agency, the Bureau had all the resources needed to eavesdrop and wiretap citizens suspected of breaking federal laws. Those same resources were used to find and collate information about public servants, especially presidents. Hoover knew all about the private lives of leading members of Congress and anyone engaged in public policy. G. Gordon Liddy, ex-FBI agent from 1957 to 1962 (and Watergate burglar), said:

> *"Mr Hoover would send someone such as I up to Capitol Hill, knock on the Senator's door, to apologise for the intrusion on his privacy and to assure him that Mr Hoover had seen to it that that bit of information had been removed from the files and say that 'Mr Hoover counsels you, sir, with all due respect that if we could stumble upon this then so might your political enemies.' Then the fellow would sort of wipe his brow, thank Mr Hoover and I would return."* [18]

Congressional disgust with Hoover's tactics came to a head in 1971 when House Democratic leader, Hale Boggs, spoke out against Hoover on the floor of the House of Representatives: "When the FBI taps the telephones of members of the Senate, when the FBI adopts the tactics of the Soviet Union and Hitler's Germany, then it is time that the present director no longer be the director." [19]

Hoover's snooping was not confined to public officials. Actors, actresses, journalists and church officials were fair game for targeting if Hoover had the slightest intimation they were engaging in 'subversive' activities. Hoover had set himself up as the moral guardian of the nation and kept files on John Lennon (hardly surprising in light of recent disclosures concerning Lennon's financing of subversive groups like the IRA), Elvis Presley and a host of other celebrities who he considered were subverting the morals of the nation's youth. FBI files reported that Elvis Presley: "is of the opinion that the Beatles laid the groundwork for many of the problems we are having with young people in this country. He advised that the Smothers Brothers, Jane Fonda and others in the entertainment industry of their ilk have a lot to answer for the way they have poisoned the minds by disparaging the United States." [20] Notwithstanding Elvis' role as an informant, Hoover considered Presley to be as bad as the people he informed on.

However, Hoover's practices were often condoned by his superiors. President Roosevelt encouraged the FBI Director to supply him with details about his political enemies. Although Eisenhower disdained Hoover's methods he made no attempt to curb the awesome power the bureaucrat had accumulated. President Johnson always appreciated the information Hoover supplied him. And it was clear to many that Hoover's practices must have been condoned by Johnson. During his years in the White House President Johnson included in his private conversations references to the private lives of Congressmen which could only have come from surveillance.

On taking office, President Kennedy knew that the FBI Director had become a national institution who held a great deal of information about millions of citizens, including himself. It would take a brave president to get rid of him. On more than one occasion Kennedy responded to queries about why he did not get rid of the ageing bureaucrat by saying: "You don't fire God."[21] One of the first acts of his new Administration was to reappoint Hoover.

Throughout the Kennedy presidency the new Attorney General, Robert Kennedy, was constantly reminded of Hoover's secret files. Hoover made a point of sending RFK memos containing scurrilous information about family members or colleagues as a way of telling the Kennedy brothers that the Director should be treated with respect.

Hoover hated the Kennedys believing them to be moral degenerates. The situation did not improve when RFK became Hoover's new boss. However, there was never any direct confrontation between the 35 year old Attorney General and the 65 year old FBI Director. And as Hoover was protective and respectful of the Office of the Presidency he was at all times civil and obedient to President Kennedy. Although he was irked at orders from RFK he never challenged the Attorney-General. Hoover's bureaucratic instincts told him that it would be futile to challenge the President's brother and closest confidante.

In the past Hoover's relationships with Attorneys General had been founded upon an unwillingness to challenge Hoover's autonomous position within the Justice Department. Attorneys General under previous presidents had allowed Hoover to govern the Bureau without interference. Hoover had been allowed direct contact with the president, circumventing the Attorney General of the day. The situation changed after the appointment of Robert Kennedy and Hoover was forced to deal directly with the President only through the office of the Attorney General. RFK placed a direct telephone link on Hoover's desk and made it plain that the Director was his subordinate. When Robert Kennedy took office at the age of 35, Hoover was 65 years old and knew he did not have to retire until January 1st, 1965 when he would have reached the age of 70.

On one occasion Hoover said to an aide: "They call him 'Bobby'!". It was evident to those close to the FBI Director that Hoover would not enjoy working with a young activist like Kennedy. FBI headquarters guides used to point out that Hoover took over the Bureau a year before the Attorney-General was born. Hoover was the quintessential bureaucrat who lived by rules. The young Attorney General frequently broke the 'rules' by appearing at meetings in shirt-sleeves, bringing his dog into the office and lounging in his chair whilst meeting with subordinates. Kennedy generally encouraged a relaxed and informal atmosphere within the Justice Department. Hoover, on the other hand, frequently remonstrated with subordinates who did not adhere to the appropriate dress code. If an agent was found to have had extra-marital relations he was immediately transferred to a less prestigious posting.

FBI Agent, Courtney Evans, who was appointed by the Kennedys to be the FBI liaison with the White House, felt that Hoover and RFK were too much alike to be effective colleagues: "When I looked at Bob operating in 1961, I figured that's the way Hoover had operated in 1924...the same kind of temperament, impatient with inefficiency, demanding as to detail, a system of logical reasoning for a position, and pretty much of a hard taskmaster."[22]

There was probably an element of jealousy in Hoover's relationship with RFK. Hoover believed that nationally organised crime did not exist and felt there was no evidence that it did. He also refused to recognise the term 'Mafia'. The FBI extended no cooperation to Congressional investigating committees on organised crime beyond giving them criminal record sheets. For seven years Hoover ignored the Kefauver Committee Hearings into Organised Crime until in 1957 a national mob boss meeting was discovered in Apalachin, New York. Hoover was forced to act. And, Agent, William Roemer, uncovered the existence of a Mafia national crime commission in 1959 after bugging the Chicago mob. It was an important breakthrough, but Hoover still refused to recognise that there was a national commission which acted as the ruling body of organised crime.

When Robert Kennedy became Attorney General, those agents who had been assigned to investigate organised crime were immensely overjoyed. They knew Robert Kennedy was a committed crime fighter who would throw all the resources of the Justice Department behind fighting the Mafia. Because of his previous work as a counsel to Senate investigating committees, Kennedy understood, as few officials did in the 1950s, the true nature of the mob. It was not a loosely knit band of non-violent criminals who served the public's harmless appetite for gambling but instead a powerful and insidious organisation in American society. In fact Kennedy knew that the Mafia, through its control of many labour unions, greatly affected the welfare of every man woman and child in America.

The scope and success of RFK's campaign against organised crime was unprecedented. As Arthur Schlesinger (1978) wrote: "Subversion was out. Organised crime was in. Hoover grudgingly went along." Between 1960 and 1963 there was:

- A 200 percent increase in the number of attorneys - from 17 to 60.

- More than a 900 percent increase in days in the field - from 660 to 6,172.

- A 1,250 percent increase in days in grand jury - from 100 to 1,353.

- A 1,700 percent increase in days in court - from 61 to 1,081.

- A 500 percent increase in defendants indicted - from 121 to 615.

- A 400 percent increase in defendants convicted - from 73 to 288. [23]

There were a number of other reasons why the relationship with the Kennedys got off to a bad start. Although Hoover had been friendly with Joseph Kennedy he had little respect for his sons who he considered to be upstarts. Hoover knew about John Kennedy's womanising and took the view that he was unfit for public office and that his character was weak. Hoover had been a lifelong bachelor, mother-dominated and raised with strict puritanical and Calvinist strictures. Kennedy's liaisons, faithfully reported on by Hoover's agents, obviously upset the FBI Director's moral equilibrium.

Hoover's knowledge of John Kennedy's affair with the Danish beauty, Inga Arvad, had been useful in his relationship with Joseph Kennedy. However, it was not until the presidential election of 1960 that Hoover began to take a deep personal interest in the Senator's private life. He became disgusted with reports emanating from Las Vegas, a favourite Kennedy stop-over in the presidential campaign. A report in 1960 to the

Director described orgiastic goings-on during the filming of the Sinatra Rat Pack's movie "Oceans 11". The report stated, in part: "Show girls from all over town were running in and out of the Senator's suite."[24]

Hoover also had a photo of Kennedy leaving the home of his wife's secretary, Pamela Turnure, in the early hours of the morning. It was the secretary's landlords, the Katers, who informed the Director and the couple began a vigorous campaign to reveal Senator Kennedy's adulterous acts. However, the media largely ignored their campaign. An extreme right-wing magazine called the 'Thunderbolt' published their story and this gave Hoover the excuse to bring it to the attention of the Kennedys. This is an excellent example of how Hoover operated. Hoover could not use his subtle blackmailing techniques by referring to his agents' reports. The Kennedys would have been outraged that the FBI Director had been snooping on them. However, if scandalous material had been disseminated through other organs, Hoover could righteously say that he was bringing the offending material to their attention and 'protecting' them.

A number of authors have alleged that the Director instructed FBI agents to assist RFK in removing any evidence of the Attorney General's supposed affair with Marilyn Monroe. There is no evidence within FBI records that confirm this allegation. If Hoover did have any incriminating information he would assuredly have used it, especially after RFK was elected to the Senate in 1964; a time when the second Kennedy brother had criticised Hoover on a number of occasions. Authors who have made these allegations have little knowledge of the way Hoover operated. If RFK had asked for Hoover's assistance in hiding any evidence proving the Monroe/RFK affair the FBI Director would have made a complete record for the files; each and every time the Attorney General asked for assistance from Hoover, even down to the most mundane matters, a record was kept. Hoover's assistants have testified that RFK never asked for help from the FBI Director for any personal or political matter.

Hoover knew he could act contemptuously at times. He well understood the respect and admiration that leading groups in the United States held for him. Kennedy's close victory also meant the new president could not act boldly in changing the status quo. As Robert Kennedy said: "It was important as far as we were concerned that (Hoover) remained happy and that he remain in his position because he was a symbol and the President had won by such a narrow margin and it was a hell of an investigative body and he got a lot of things done and it was much better for what we wanted to do in the South, what we wanted to do in organised crime, if we had him on our side. "[25] Even though Hoover maintained a civil attitude to the Kennedys during John Kennedy's presidency, he and the Kennedys worked together in an atmosphere of hatred and mistrust.

It was the knowledge of one of President Kennedy's girlfriends that led Hoover to believe he could intimidate and embarrass the President. FBI reports indicated that Judith Campbell Exner had frequent contacts with President Kennedy from the end of 1960 to mid-1962. (They actually met earlier when Kennedy was running for President and were introduced by Frank Sinatra.) The reports said that Campbell was a close friend of gangster, Johnny Rosselli, and Chicago mob boss, Sam Giancana, and saw them often during this period. Hoover became concerned that the Mafia would use this connection to gain influence with the President. He also no doubt felt that this was a golden opportunity make Kennedy aware that he knew about the affairs under the guise of keeping track of criminal figures. Hoover sent identical copies of a memorandum, dated 27th February 1962, to Robert Kennedy and Kenneth O'Donnell, assistant to President Kennedy. The memo stated that information developed in connection with an FBI investigation of Johnny Rosselli revealed that Rosselli had been in contact with Campbell. Hoover's memo also stated that a review of the telephone calls from Campbell's residence revealed calls to the White House.[26]

On the 22nd March 1962, Hoover had a private luncheon with President Kennedy. There is no record of what transpired but, according to White House logs, telephone contact between Campbell and Kennedy occurred a few hours after the luncheon. Historians are in agreement that it is likely Hoover used this meeting to apprise the President of how reckless and dangerous it was to be connected to a woman who was also friendly with members of the Mafia. Although Hoover was not blackmailing the President, he was subtly reminding him that he had information that could endanger his presidency.

In the two years and 10 months of Kennedy's presidency, Hoover had only been invited to White House functions a dozen times. Hoover was also unhappy that he could no longer contact the President directly as he had done under previous presidents. His relationship with both RFK and JFK was parlous to say the least. Yet there is nothing in the record that Hoover tried to harm President Kennedy by leaking information that could have diminished him even though he relished the opportunity to show Kennedy that he knew a lot of secrets.

The term 'blackmailer' cannot be accurately applied to describe Hoover's dealings with the Kennedy brothers. In the final analysis there is no evidence that Hoover, unlike the typical blackmailer, was ever willing to reveal his secrets if backed into a corner. Hoover's techniques were subtler than that. As Walter Mondale, Vice-President under Jimmy Carter and United States Senator during the 1960s said: "We do know from other Congressmen and Senators that had been through this (meetings with Hoover) that he'd (Hoover) always say 'Don't worry about it. I know about it but you're O.K.' I think it was subtle blackmail and they did too. One of the reasons I think Hoover stayed on years after the Civil Service rules said he should retire is, I think, a lot of presidents were afraid to drop the hammer on him."[27] Athan Theoharis has described Hoover as an 'astute bureaucrat' who "recognised that a direct attempt at blackmail could compromise his tenure as Director. So he volunteered information only after it was already public...or had been obtained incidentally to a wiretap installed during an authorised criminal investigation (such as the information involving Kennedy's contacts with Judith Campbell, obtained through a wiretap on organised crime leader Johnny Rosselli). A sophisticated blackmailer, Hoover only hinted at the FBI's ability to monitor personal misconduct."[28]

In effect there was a 'stand-off' between the President and the FBI Director. Hoover's secret files contained information that could have done irreparable damage to the Kennedy administration: JFK's womanising, CIA/mafia attempts to kill Castro, Sinatra's links to mob bosses, and Sinatra's efforts to enlist the Mafia to help in the 1960 presidential campaign. Kennedy on the other hand could have fired Hoover at any time during his 1,000 day presidency. Kennedy could also have embarrassed the Director for not recognising the importance of organised crime and not responding, initially, to equal rights directives within the FBI. Neither man was going to create problems for the other if they could help it.

However, during the summer of 1963 Robert Kennedy, in his efforts to protect his brother, solicited the help of Hoover in persuading Congressional leaders to desist in pursuing the Bobby Baker scandal. Baker, a Senate aide, was accused of influence peddling and during the investigation of his affairs it was revealed he had been supplying leading Congressmen with 'party girls'. One particular girl was in the position to bring down Kennedy's presidency, Ellen Rometsch, (discussed in chapter 6). Hoover and Robert Kennedy talked to congressional leaders. The investigation continued but without reference to the Quorum Club which was the centre of Baker's enterprise.[29]

Hoover was now assured he had enough information to hold the upper hand in his dealings with the Kennedys and this may account for RFK's acquiescence in Hoover's request to tap the telephones of Martin Luther King. It now became impossible for Kennedy to get rid of Hoover. He would have to wait until his re-election in 1964 and Hoover's statutory retirement in January 1965 before he could rid himself of a dangerous subordinate.

Hoover and Johnson

Throughout the 1950s, the FBI Director had a close professional and personal relationship with Senate Majority leader, Lyndon Johnson. Johnson and Hoover were neighbours living in the affluent middle class neighbourhood of North-West Washington. The bachelor, Hoover, would often be invited over to Johnson's house for dinner and Mrs. Johnson and her daughters liked and respected their famous guest.

Lyndon Johnson told Senate aide, Bobby Baker, that Hoover loathed and despised John and Robert Kennedy.[30] He also informed him that J. Edgar Hoover had admitted holding extensive files on John Kennedy which showed the leading presidential contender as a 'womaniser'.

After Kennedy won the 1960 Democratic nomination in Los Angeles, a period of confusion reigned for the next 24 hours as Kennedy and his closest advisor Robert debated who should be offered the vice-presidential nomination. The question of why Johnson was chosen over others became a matter of great controversy for years. Many in the Democratic Party were shocked that Kennedy had chosen a man who had personally insulted the presidential nominee during the primary election campaign and who was an anathema to leading liberal elements within the Democratic Party. Authors Anthony Summers (1993) and Seymour Hersh (1997) claim that Johnson, with the assistance of J. Edgar Hoover, blackmailed himself on to the ticket.

Summers quotes Kennedy's secretary, Evelyn Lincoln, who told him: "And when I came in (to the Kennedy suite in the Los Angeles Biltmore Hotel) they (John and Robert Kennedy) were huddled together closely on the bed discussing this tremendous issue about Lyndon Johnson being on the ticket. Bobby would get up, look out the window and stare. Kennedy would sit there and think. It was intense. In fact they hardly knew I came into the room they were so engrossed in their conversation. That went on for 30 minutes trying to figure out how they could manoeuvre to get it so he wouldn't be on the ticket...One of the factors that made John F. Kennedy choose Lyndon B. Johnson for Vice-President were the malicious rumours that were fed to Lyndon B. Johnson by J. Edgar Hoover about his womanising and so that's one of the reasons that pushed him to go down and offer him the Vice-Presidency. Lyndon B. Johnson and J. Edgar Hoover had boxed them into a hole. They were boxed in."[31]

Seymour Hersh uses Summers' interview with Lincoln in his book 'The dark side of Camelot' and adds the clincher to the story by making reference to Kennedy aide Hyman Raskin's unpublished memoir and interviews he held with him. Raskin said that, in a meeting with Johnson and House Speaker, Sam Rayburn, Kennedy was made an offer he could not refuse. "What made Johnson more attractive than the other candidates?", Hersh wrote. His answer is that Johnson, together with Rayburn and Hoover, blackmailed Kennedy into giving him the nomination. Hersh maintains that the fact that Kennedy had wanted Johnson all along was a cover-up to mask the blackmail. Hersh quotes leading Democratic Party stalwart, Clark Clifford, as saying that the real nominee chosen by Kennedy was Stuart Symington.[32]

In her interview with Summers, Evelyn Lincoln does not indicate when and how Johnson or Hoover relayed the talk of blackmail to Kennedy on the night of the nomination. She was not privy to any discussions about Hoover and her statements indicate what was already known about the prevarications in choosing the vice-presidential nominee. Robert Kennedy was against the selection of Johnson. He had already made commitments to union leaders and liberals that Johnson would not be chosen. He tried to persuade his brother not to choose Johnson.

Evelyn Lincoln worked closely with John Kennedy when he was a United States senator and her work place was situated outside the Oval Office throughout the Kennedy Presidency. There is no doubt that she knew a great deal about Kennedy. However, she had encountered credibility problems in the past. When she wrote her memoirs in 1968 she stated flatly that Kennedy told her he intended to drop Johnson from the ticket in 1964 and replace him with North Carolina Governor, Terry Sanford.[33] When Robert Kennedy heard about the allegations he responded: "Can you imagine the President (Kennedy) ever having a talk with Evelyn about a subject like this?"[34] Charles Bartlett, a close friend of JFK, said: "In the swimming pool (not) too long before the assassination I said to Kennedy, 'Why don't you get another vice-president in 1964?' Kennedy turned on me...furious...and said, 'Why would I do a thing like that? That would be absolutely crazy. It would tear up the relationship and hurt me in Texas. That would be the most foolish thing I could do.'"[35] Jacqueline Kennedy was unequivocal in her statement that her husband never intended to replace Johnson.[36] And Kennedy's closest aides Ken O'Donnell and Theodore Sorensen confirm this fact.[37] In any event the rewriting of history should not depend upon a single source whose observations included a lot of guesswork.

The logical explanation for Lincoln's ruminations is that she had observed both Kennedys in the period between the time Kennedy offered Johnson the nomination (some say in the hope he would refuse it) and the period when they were having second thoughts, worried as they were that a floor fight would erupt over the nomination, led by Union leaders and liberals. At 11 a.m. on the morning of the 14th July 1960, Kennedy went to see Johnson to offer him the Vice-Presidential nomination (solely as a gesture, according to Robert Kennedy, and to placate Johnson). Johnson, surprisingly, accepted. There then followed a period when the brothers were huddled together and "talked and talked and talked" according to Edward Kennedy. Robert said they changed their minds seven times during the following hours "(trying to figure out) how could we get out of it."[38]

Robert Kennedy said that there had been no disagreement with his brother over wanting Johnson to reject the offer of the Vice-Presidential nomination. It is likely that John Kennedy allowed his brother to show misgivings about the choice of LBJ as a way of getting out in the open the hostility to Johnson which began brewing after liberal delegates heard about the offer. The astute and detached John Kennedy was thus playing a game. It may also be true that both Kennedys were exhausted from the events of the previous day. Arguing back and forth about the choice they became confused and, in a moment of weakness, JFK agreed that RFK should see Johnson and tell him his presence on the ticket would be problematical. In the meantime, Kennedy had been assured that objections to Johnson's appointment would be minimal.

In reality Kennedy had had Johnson at the top of his list all along (together with Stuart Symington). Kennedy aide, Theodore Sorensen, told author Merle Miller (1980): "...I ranked Johnson at the top (of the

Vice-Presidential list)...I think it is true to say that Kennedy did not expect Johnson to say yes, and it would be inaccurate to say that he was hoping Johnson would say no. Johnson was the logical person to ask. He was the runner-up at the convention. He was the leader of that segment of the party where Kennedy had very little strength-the South, and to some extent the West. He was the leader of the party in the Senate. He was a man with whom Kennedy had worked and knew he could work. Compatible. And he was a man whom Kennedy admired. Had the greatness, the stature."[39]

The evidence suggests that Kennedy had decided on Symington by the morning of his own nomination and told Clark Clifford of his decision. But columnist, Joe Alsop, and 'Washington Post' publisher, Phil Graham, both said Kennedy agreed when they argued with him not to nominate Symington. However, by the following morning Joseph Kennedy had persuaded his son that he could not win the November election without Johnson on the ticket.

And Kennedy had ample advice that Johnson would not turn down the offer. Tip O'Neill, who later became speaker of the House of Representatives, was one of those who advised Kennedy that Johnson would accept. O'Neill told Kennedy on the eve of the presidential nomination that Johnson's mentor, Sam Rayburn, had changed his mind about Johnson taking the Vice-Presidential nomination if offered. That night O'Neill informed Kennedy what Rayburn had said. Kennedy replied: "Of course I want Lyndon. But I'd never want to offer it and have him turn me down."[40]

Of all the people involved in this hornet's nest of decision - making only Phil Graham recorded a contemporaneous account. And, as historian Richard Reeves maintains, it is the contemporary sources which provide the most truthful account of events. Graham wrote his account as a long memorandum to himself within a few days of the event:

> "On Thursday, about 1.45 p.m., I went to Johnson's suite in the Biltmore. The Los Angeles papers and the press in general were prophesying Symington. On entering Johnson's suite, he seized my arm and took me into his bedroom, alone with Lady Bird (Johnson's wife). He said that Bobby Kennedy was with Sam Rayburn in another part of the suite and he had to make a decision.

We sat on the bed, the three of us, about as composed as three Mexican jumping beans. Lady Bird tried to leave. Johnson and I lunged after her, saying she was needed on this one. I tried to duck LBJ's inquiry, but finally said I felt he had to take it. Lady Bird was somewhere between negative and neutral. At this point Sam Rayburn entered and said Bobby wanted to talk directly to LBJ. Lady Bird intervened, apologising by saying she had never yet argued with Mr Sam, but saying she now felt LBJ should not see Bobby.

LBJ asked my advice-the while all of us were pacing around the bedroom, in and out of the bathroom, etc. 'No', I said, 'you shouldn't see him. You don't want it, you won't negotiate for it, you'll only take it if Jack drafts you, and you won't discuss it with anyone else.'

Mr Sam seemed to think LBJ should see Bobby, but he also seemed to think he should turn down the V.P. Finally, in that way decisions leap out of the melee, it was decided. Mr Sam was to tell Bobby LBJ's position and why he wouldn't see Bobby. I was to phone Jack LBJ's position.

About 2.30 (p.m.) I got Jack on the phone and told him LBJ's decision. He said something to the general effect that he was in a general mess because some liberals were against LBJ. He said he was in a meeting with others right then and that people were urging that 'no one had anything against Symington.' He and I had discussed this earlier in the week and he made some reference conceding Symington had no affirmative qualifications. He then asked me to call back for a decision 'in three minutes'.

About 2.40 or 2.45 I phoned back. Jack was utterly calm. It's all set, he said. Tell Lyndon I want him and will have (Governor) Lawrence nominate him, etc. He said he'd be busy getting Lawrence and the seconders and preparing his statement and also putting out fires of opposition, and so he asked me to call Adlai (Stevenson) and tell him the decision and ask him for full support.

My memory is vague, but I believe I called Adlai first because of the need to get his support in such a short time. In any event, I talked to him first and then went down the hall to LBJ's bedroom. He and Lady Bird naturally quizzed me in detail about the conversation with Jack. Also Lady Bird was especially curious about Adlai's reaction. I remember shrugging and saying, Oh, you know, sort of as you'd expect.

Bobby Kennedy had been back down to see Rayburn some 20 minutes before (say, roughly, 3.00) and had said Jack would phone directly. No call had come and LBJ was considerably on edge. I wrote down the private numbers in his bedroom...and said I'll call Jack.

About 3.30 I got Jack, who said he had assumed my message would suffice. I explained what Bobby had told Sam, and he said he'd call at once. He then again mentioned opposition to LBJ and asked for my judgement. I said something to the effect that the Southern gains would more than offset liberal losses, and added that anyway it was too late to be mind-changing. He agreed about the finality of things and asked what Stevenson had said. I said he was wobbling about but would be all right and he asked me to call Stevenson back and ask him to issue a statement shortly after Jack issued his at 4.00.

I told LBJ Jack would be phoning him and then returned to call Adlai. In our prior talk he had argued for Symington on pure expediency grounds and I had been a bit testy in pointing out that any V.P. was likely to be President.

I got Adlai on the phone again after some delay and found him still brimming over with an account of his difficulties. He had spent the time since our last call in 'canvassing' various people's reactions. After I listened to a recital of this for some time, I interrupted and with (I hope) polite firmness said, 'the nominee' had asked me to ask him to please issue a supporting statement as soon as Kennedy made his statement on TV, which should be very soon. Stevenson then quickly agreed.

Sometime around this point (approximately 3.40) I went back into LBJ's bedroom and listened to Senator Kerr and Governor Daniel objecting to LBJ's taking the VPship. By now Rayburn, originally against the idea, was supporting Lyndon's decision and Kerr was soon able, very articulately, to change his mind. But Daniel remained opposed-and very loudly so. On the assumption that 'Yankee faces' might create more furore, I left.

Shortly after 4.00 LBJ's appointment secretary, Bill Moyers, rushed into our room to say Lyndon wanted me. 'I'll be along in a minute.' 'That won't do', Moyers yelled, and, grabbing my arm, dragged me down the hall through a solid jam of press people and into the entrance hall of the suite.

LBJ was in a state of high nerves and said we must talk alone at once. His bedroom was still packed with Daniel et al, so we headed into the adjoining room, which in proper pure farce setting was full of about 15 Hawaiian delegates. Johnson called out that he was sorry he had to have the room and they solemnly filed out, bowing their serious Oriental faces in turn to all of us at the door (LBJ, Lady Bird, Rayburn, Connally, Rowe and me), with LBJ loudly chanting, 'Thank you, boys, thank you. Thank you for all you did.'

In a minute they were gone and the six of us swept into the bedroom, joined by Bobby Baker. LBJ seemed about to jump out of his skin. He shouted at me that Bobby Kennedy had just come in and told Rayburn and him that there was much opposition and that Lyndon should withdraw for the sake of the party.

There was considerable milling about and hubbub, and finally Mr Rayburn said, 'Phil, call Jack.' The only phone was a regular Biltmore extension and it took a minute which seemed an hour to get the operator, then another series of hourlike minutes as we got Kennedy's switchboard, then his secretary, and finally Kennedy. 'Jack', I said, 'Bobby is down here and is telling the Speaker and Lyndon that there is opposition and that Lyndon should withdraw.'

'Oh', said Jack, as calmly as though we were discussing the weather, 'that's all right; Bobby's been out of touch and doesn't know what's been happening.'

'Well, what do you want Lyndon to do?', I asked.

'I want him to make a statement right away; I've just finished making mine.' (I believe he was reported to have made his statement downstairs in the Biltmore Bowl at 4.05)

'You'd better speak to Lyndon,' I said.

'Okay', he said,' but I want to talk to you when we're through.'

I was standing between twin beds, and as I handed the phone to LBJ he sprawled out across the bed in front of me, lay on his side, and said, 'Yes...Yes...Yes...' and then, 'Okay, here's Phil,' as he handed the phone back to me.

At this point Kennedy chatted along to me as though we were discussing someone else's problems. He said Alex Rose was threatening not to list him on the Liberal Party ticket in New York because of Johnson and that 'this is a problem we'll just have to solve.' I heard myself saying, 'Oh, don't worry, we'll solve that.' And then, returning closer to sanity, I said, 'You'd better speak to Bobby.' So Baker dashed out to fetch Bobby, who walked in looking dead tired.

'Bobby, your brother wants to speak to you,' said I (in what at once seemed to me the silliest line in the whole play). Bobby took the phone, and as I walked out of the room I heard him say, 'Well, it's too late now,' and half slam down the phone.

In the hall of the suite LBJ and Lady Bird were standing, looking as though they had just survived an airplane crash, with Lyndon holding a typed statement accepting the VPship. 'I was just going to read this on TV when Bobby came in, and now I don't know what I ought to do.'

With more ham than I ever suspected myself of, I suddenly blurted: 'Of course you know what you're going to do. Throw your shoulders back and your chin out and go out and make that announcement. And then go on and win. Everything's wonderful.'

This soap opera thrust was somehow wonderfully appropriate, and Bill Moyers echoed loud approval while swinging open the doors and pushing Johnson out into the TV lights and the explosion of flashbulbs. Someone else propelled Lady Bird, and from the hall I could watch them rising to stand on some chairs, and as they rose their faces metamorphosed into enthusiasm and confidence.

One other incident I cannot place exactly in time and so have left to a postscript, but I think it occurred just before Johnson asked

> *me to call Kennedy (i.e. about 2.15), Rayburn told me the details*
> *of Bobby's visit to offer the VP (which must have been around*
> *1.30). He said Bobby came in and sat down with Rayburn (and I*
> *believe Connally), with Rayburn waiting for the obvious. Bobby*
> *said he wondered if Johnson would like to be National*
> *Chairman. 'Shit', answered Rayburn, whereupon Bobby offered*
> *the Vice Presidency."[41]*

Phil Graham's account remains the most authoritative of all the accounts of Lyndon Johnson's selection. Graham's first hand account also reveals the unreliability of Hersh's description of events.

There are obvious problems with Hersh's account. If Johnson had blackmailed himself on to the ticket why did he and many of his advisors prevaricate? One of Johnson's closest friends and advisors, Representative Homer Thornberry, was against LBJ's acceptance of the Vice-Presidency and told Johnson so. Johnson told him: "Well, here's my problem. If I refuse it and go back as majority leader and Kennedy chooses somebody else, and he loses, they'll blame me for it, and then my position as Majority Leader might be in jeopardy. If he wins, they'll say, 'He won without your help', and then I'll have some problems. Finally, I may owe a responsibility to try to carry this country for the Democratic Party." Thornberry thought about it and became convinced that Johnson should accept if the Vice-Presidency was offered. Johnson then asked Thornberry, "Well, what do we do about Mr Rayburn?" Thornberry replied, "That's not your job. That's up to Kennedy. If he asks you to do it and you accept then it's up to Kennedy to talk to Mr Rayburn."[42]

If Hersh's account is correct, and Rayburn conspired with Johnson to blackmail Kennedy, why would Johnson be so anxious about breaking the news to Rayburn? Rayburn had phoned Johnson the previous night to extract a promise that Johnson would not accept the nomination offer under any circumstances. However, Rayburn was persuaded by Hale Boggs that Johnson was needed on the ticket to prevent a Nixon victory in the November election. Rayburn was an avid Nixon-hater and would do anything to prevent his election. Rayburn said, on the morning after Kennedy's nomination, "I'm a wiser man this morning", and urged Johnson to accept the nomination.[43] Bobby Baker, Johnson's close aide, implored Johnson to accept if offered: "And I said, 'Mr Leader', let me tell you, John Kennedy knows that no Catholic has ever been elected President in the history of this country. He knows the only chance in hell he has to be President of the United States is if you run as Vice-

President. And I said the Vice-Presidency is the worst job in the country...but you're one heart beat away from the Presidency."[44]

Seymour Hersh's strongest source for his allegations of blackmail is Kennedy aide, Hy Raskin. Hersh begins his tale with a well-known fact - there was a tense night after JFK was nominated. Stuart Symington was the front-runner for the Vice-Presidential offer and Johnson was only a second option. But Johnson then emerges as the front-runner and this comes as a shock to many who were close to John Kennedy and many delegates who disliked Johnson. "What made Johnson more attractive than the other candidates?" Hersh wrote, "...Johnson was not being given the slightest bit of consideration by any of the Kennedys.". Hersh's answer is that Johnson, together with the powerful House Speaker, Sam Rayburn, and with information supplied by J. Edgar Hoover, blackmailed Kennedy into giving him the nomination.[45]

In support of his thesis, Hersh relies on Hyman Raskin's unpublished memoir and interviews he held with the Kennedy aide in 1994/5. Raskin told Hersh that it was always Stuart Symington who was going to be Vice-President.[46] This is partly confirmed by Clark Clifford. However, this constructed scenario does not take into account the fluctuating conditions which always existed in the short period of time when a decision about the Vice-Presidency had to be made. It does not allow for the fact that Kennedy needed Texas and the South (especially Florida) if he was to win. Kennedy knew that Johnson was the key to carrying the South in the November election.

Hersh maintains that in a meeting with Johnson and Rayburn, Kennedy was made an offer he could not refuse. But in Hersh's account Raskin does not make clear what that offer was. Raskin quotes Kennedy as saying, "...Those bastards (Rayburn and Johnson) were trying to frame me. They threatened me with problems and I don't need more problems."[47]

In Hersh's account the assumption is that Kennedy is making reference to blackmail attempts in connection with the candidate's 'womanising'. Hersh goes on to explain in his own words: "In other words, Raskin ASSUMED (emphasis added by present author), Johnson blackmailed his way into the Vice-Presidency."[48] Hersh thus uses, unconditionally, the term 'blackmail' leading the reader to assume conclusions which are dark and dramatic.

Although Hersh puts Raskin's statement within a sinister context historian, Michael Beschloss, who used Raskin as a source, does not. In his book, 'Kennedy v. Kruschev', Beschloss (1991) wrote: "But when Johnson snatched up his pro forma offer (of the Vice-Presidential nomination), Kennedy would not or could not summon the political courage to retrieve it...That day he (Kennedy) told his aide Hy Raskin, 'Lyndon Johnson forced me to name him. You know we had never considered Lyndon, but...he and Sam Rayburn...reminded me that there would undoubtedly be a session of Congress between now and the election. If Lyndon was not the Vice-Presidential candidate, there was a likelihood that some difficulties were in store for me. There was no time to try to figure it out or debate it...Nixon will give us enough problems. There is no sense in inviting more from those Texas bastards."[49]

Thus Beschloss puts Raskin's statement in the correct context - if Johnson returned to the Senate as Majority Leader legislative difficulties might ensue. Kennedy knew that it "wouldn't be worth being President" if Johnson stayed on as Majority Leader. The 'threats' Kennedy had been referring to in his conversation with Raskin could also have been a threat by Johnson to hold a Convention 'floor fight' which could have disunited the Democrats.

Furthermore, the idea that Rayburn and Johnson would go ahead with a threat to leak details of Kennedy's 'womanising' is ludicrous. If they had carried out their threats, Johnson's career would have been destroyed. The Democratic Party would have been unforgiving and Johnson would have destroyed any future chance he might have at the Presidency. And Sam Rayburn was devoted to the Democratic Party. He would not have considered any move which would have destroyed the Democratic Party nominee's chances in the November election. It was also highly dangerous for Johnson and could have made him extremely vulnerable. It was common knowledge among leading politicians and the press that Johnson had enjoyed many extra-marital affairs. As historian Robert Dallek (1998) wrote: "(Johnson had)..an affinity for womanising...". Dallek quotes Johnson as saying: "Why, I had more women by accident than he (Kennedy) ever had by design."[50] And Gil Troy (1997), in his book 'Affairs of state', showed how Johnson carried on a 30 year affair with Alice Glass.[51] So it is unlikely Johnson would have engaged in a suicidal gesture of blackmailing the Kennedys when his own extra-marital liaisons were known to many.

If Hersh is correct in stating that Johnson used his blackmailing skills to ensure a place on the Democratic ticket we cannot accept close aide John Connally's version of Johnson's reaction to Kennedy's phone call asking to see the Majority Leader. Connally said, shortly before his death, that on the morning after Kennedy's nomination, Johnson had told him: "Jack Kennedy just called. He's coming down to see me. What do you think he wants? And I said he's going to offer you the Vice-Presidency. He said, 'No, he wouldn't do that, he's probably just going to ask me to manage the campaign. I said, 'No, he's going to ask you to be Vice-President. He said, 'Well, what should I say to him?' I said, 'You don't have any choice, you'll have to say Yes.'"[52]

Notes

Hoover's rise

1. Powers, R. G. (1995). *Not without honour: the history of American anti-communism*, Yale. pp. 239-240.

Hoover and the Mafia

2. Demaris, O. (1975). *The director - an oral biography of J. Edgar Hoover*, Harper's Magazine Press. p. 20.

3. *Ibid*, p. 30.

4. *Ibid*, p. 31.

5. DeLoach, C. D. (1997). *Hoover's FBI*, Regnery Publishing Inc. p. 63.

6. *Ibid*, p. 106.

7. Powers, R. G. (1987). *Secrecy and power*, Collier Macmillan Publishers. p. 172.

8. Theoharis, A. G. (1995). *J. Edgar Hoover, sex, and crime*, Ivan R. Dee. p. 9.

9. Gentry, C. (1991). *J. Edgar Hoover - the man and the secrets*, WW Norton and Co. p. 192.

10. *Sunday Times*, 8 February 1994, p. 11.

11. *Ibid*.

12. Theoharis, A. G. (1995). *J. Edgar Hoover, sex, and crime*, Ivan R. Dee. pp. 39-43.

13. Deloach, C. D. (1997). *Hoover's FBI*, Regnery Publishing Inc. p. 77.

14. 'Timewatch - the secret file on J. Edgar Hoover'. Narrated by Andrew Sachs, produced by Stephanie Tepper, written and directed by Andrew Cran. BBC Television, 1993. (An In Vision Production for BBC and WGBH, Boston).

15. Schlesinger, A. M. (1978). *Robert Kennedy and his times*, Houghton Mifflin Co. p. 284.

Hoover and the Kennedys

16. Gentry, C. (1991). *J. Edgar Hoover - the man and the secrets*, WW Norton and Co. p. 470.

17. FBI Memo, *Smoking Gun*, (http://www.thesmokinggun.com).

18. 'Timewatch - the secret file on J. Edgar Hoover'. Narrated by Andrew Sachs, produced by Stephanie Tepper, written and directed by Andrew Cran. BBC Television, 1993. (An In Vision Production for BBC and WGBH, Boston).

19. 'Bugging J. Edgar Hoover', *Time*, 19 April 1971, p. 17.

20. Nash, A. (1995). *Elvis Aaron Presley - revelations from the Memphis Mafia*, HarperCollins Publishers. p. 503.

21. Schlesinger, A. M. (1978). *Robert Kennedy and his times*, Houghton Mifflin Co. pp. 275-280; Gentry, C. (1991). *J. Edgar Hoover - the man and the secrets*, WW Norton and Co. 1991. p. 472.

22. Hilty, J. W. (1997). *Robert Kennedy – brother protector*, Temple University Press. p. 224.

23. Schlesinger, A. M. (1978). *Robert Kennedy and his times*, Houghton Mifflin Co. p. 289.

24. FBI Memo, *Smoking Gun*, (http://www.thesmokinggun.com).

25. Guthman, E. O., ed. (1988). *Robert Kennedy in his own words*, Bantam Press. p. 125.

26. Hilty, J. W. (1997). *Robert Kennedy – brother protector*, Temple University Press. p. 208.

27. 'Timewatch - the secret file on J. Edgar Hoover'. Narrated by Andrew Sachs, produced by Stephanie Tepper, written and directed by Andrew Cran. BBC Television, 1993. (An In Vision Production for BBC and WGBH, Boston).

28. Theoharis, A. G. (1993). *From the secret files of J. Edgar Hoover*, Elephant Paperbacks. p. 35.

29. Hilty, J. W. (1997). *Robert Kennedy – brother protector*, Temple University Press. p. 256.

Hoover and Johnson

30. Schlesinger, A. M. (1978). *Robert Kennedy and his times*, Houghton Mifflin Co. p. 227; 'Timewatch - the secret file on J. Edgar Hoover'. Narrated by Andrew Sachs, produced by Stephanie Tepper, written and directed by Andrew Cran. BBC Television, 1993. (An In Vision Production for BBC and WGBH, Boston).

31. 'Timewatch - the secret file on J. Edgar Hoover'. Narrated by Andrew Sachs, produced by Stephanie Tepper, written and directed by Andrew Cran. BBC Television, 1993. (An In Vision Production for BBC and WGBH, Boston); Summers, A. (1993). *Official and confidential - the secret life of J. Edgar Hoover*, Victor Gollancz. p. 272.

32. Hersh, S. (1997). *The dark side of Camelot*, Little Brown and Co. p. 123.

33. Lincoln, E. (1968). *Kennedy and Johnson*, Holt Rinehart and Winston. p. 205.

34. Schlesinger, A. M. (1978). *Robert Kennedy and his times*, Houghton Mifflin Co. p. 652.

35. Miller, M. (1980). *Lyndon - an oral biography*, Ballantine Books. p. 397.

36. Sidey, H. "The presidency - Jackie Onassis' memory fragments on tape", *Time*, 24 April 1978, p. 15.

37. O'Donnell, K. P., Powers, D. F. and McCarthy, J. (1973). *Johnny we hardly knew ye*, Pocket Books. p. 3.

38. Guthman, E. O., ed. (1988). *Robert Kennedy in his own words*, Bantam Press. p. 304.

39. Miller, M. (1980). *Lyndon - an oral biography,* Ballantine Books. p. 328.

40. O'Neill, T. (1987). *Man of the House*, St Martin's Press. p. 109.

41. Phil Graham's account is taken from "A go-between's memo on the wild day LBJ was named Vice-President." *Life Magazine*, July 1965, p. 56.

42. Miller, M. (1980). *Lyndon - an oral biography*, Ballantine Books. p. 330.

43. *Ibid*, p. 331.

44. 'Timewatch - the secret file on J. Edgar Hoover'. Narrated by Andrew Sachs, produced by Stephanie Tepper, written and directed by Andrew Cran. BBC Television, 1993. (An In Vision Production for BBC and WGBH, Boston).

45. Hersh, S. (1997). *The dark side of Camelot*, Little Brown and Co. p. 123.

46. *Ibid*, p. 126.

47. *Ibid*.

48. *Ibid*, p. 123.

49. Beschloss, M. R. (1991). *Kennedy v. Kruschev - the crisis years 1960-1963*, Faber and Faber. p. 511.

50. Dallek, R. (1998). *Flawed giant - Lyndon Johnson and his times 1961-1973*, Oxford University Press. p. 408.

51. Troy, G. (1997). *Affairs of state*, The Free Press. pp. 146-147.

52. 'Timewatch - the secret file on J. Edgar Hoover'. Narrated by Andrew Sachs, produced by Stephanie Tepper, written and directed by Andrew Cran. BBC Television, 1993. (An In Vision Production for BBC and WGBH, Boston).

Chapter 9

RFK

Was Robert F. Kennedy a ruthless opportunist or a committed idealist?

"John Kennedy was...a realist disguised as a romantic; Robert, a romantic disguised as a realist."

Arthur M. Schlesinger

"Everyone is broken by life and afterward some are stronger in the broken places."

Ernest Hemingway

There had always been contradictory images of Robert Kennedy. Ever since RFK managed his brother's campaigns for the Senate and then the presidency, politicians and the press often talked as if there were two Robert Kennedys - the 'Good Bobby' and the 'Bad Bobby' - as immortalised in the famous Jules Feiffer cartoon. The latter could, on occasions, be tough, nasty, even ruthless. The 'Good Bobby' was too good for the world and was almost obsessively concerned with ghetto poverty which sprung from a moral purity that most politicians of his era lacked. The 'Good Bobby' was man with a passion for helping the poor and underprivileged; he wanted to right the wrongs of the world and he believed in what he was preaching. Unlike his brothers, his commitment to his Catholic faith was strong and he was a 'puritan' who frowned on moral transgressions even though he protected his brother from sexual scandal.

With the publication of Arthur Schlesinger's (1978) book, 'Robert Kennedy and his times', RFK's position as a liberal icon seemed to be assured. Schlesinger admitted he was biased in favour of Kennedy; he worked for him and cared deeply about the man. However, notwithstanding these biases, his book faithfully recorded the life of a special type of politician who had become a hero to a generation. Schlesinger's Kennedy was a man devoted to his family, passionate about the ailments of his country and courageous in his quest to seek the presidency and change American society for the better.

For the past 15 years this image has come under attack from a number of authors bent on putting the record straight and demolishing the image of RFK as the most human of post-war American politicians. According to these authors the 'Good Bobby' had been a false description. The 'Bad Bobby' was much more apt. The debunking began with the publication of Anthony Summers' biography of Marilyn Monroe, 'Goddess'. Summers (1985) raised a number of questions as to Robert Kennedy's relationship with the movie star. He posited the theory the Attorney General may have had a hand in her death, perhaps abusing his power by enlisting the aide of J. Edgar Hoover in covering up the circumstances of her demise. (RFK's relationship with Marilyn Monroe is discussed in chapter 10). The book also raised questions as to Kennedy's faithfulness to his wife Ethel and intimated that, throughout his life, Robert had had a string of affairs with other women. Summers did not give any value judgements as to RFK's character as a politician. This area of revisionism and debunking of apparent myths was left to anti-Kennedy authors like C. David Heymann (1998) and Nelly Bly (1996). The image of RFK as a committed and idealistic politician was changed by these books. To Heymann and Bly, RFK's image had been false. The authors took the view that RFK had a rapacious sexual appetite; was a ruthless 'hitman' for his brother, the President; an opportunist politician who was not at all sincere in his beliefs; and was a ruthless Attorney General who made racist remarks, wiretapped indiscriminately and frequently lied to the press. This view of RFK shocked many Americans who had previously seen the President's younger brother as a liberal icon, a family man and a dedicated politician devoted to changing American society.

We are thus left, 33 years after the Senator's death, with a contradictory and controversial image of Robert Kennedy, both as a man and as a politician.

Robert Francis Kennedy was born in the fashionable Boston suburb of Brookline, Massachusetts on November 20th 1925. He grew up as the 'runt of the litter' and throughout his childhood he compensated for his slight build through will and determination. Of the four sons Robert was most like his father who said later that his son "Resembles me much more than any of the other children"[1]. Robert reflected his father's character mainly in the way he had an iron will and an exaggerated sense of competitiveness. Kennedys did not come last and the father often told his children that to win was a moral obligation - "We don't want any losers around here. In this family we want winners...Don't come in second or third - that doesn't count - but win." Edward later recalled: "His personality was so strong, his ideas so definite, his views and outlook so determined, that he dominated our home and our lives."[2]

When Robert was born, his brother Joseph Jnr. was ten and John was eight. Edward was born seven years later. Robert lived in his older brothers' shadows but gradually emerged as an independent minded member of the family. He reflected his mother's qualities in that throughout his life he was a devout Roman Catholic, differentiating himself from his brothers who had only a passing relationship with their faith. At one period in his youth he considered becoming a priest. It was not until his brother John's assassination that in the personal soul-searching that always accompanies grief and tragedy, he began to question his faith. But he did not abandon it. Robert frequently annoyed his siblings by making moralistic judgements about their personal behaviour. He commented about their romantic affairs outside the faith. They considered him to be a moody prude. As a young man he rejected the habits of alcohol and cigarettes and confined himself to soft drinks. Later as an adult he drank moderately.

Like most men of his generation he wanted to see action in the waning months of the Second World War but instead was assigned to the USS Joseph Kennedy Jnr., named after his older brother who heroically died when his bomber blew up over the skies of England. After his discharge in 1946, Robert worked on his brother's Congressional campaign and later went to Harvard and then set his sights on a law degree at the University of Virginia Law school. During his time there he was appalled at the loose sexual morals of some of the students. In June 1950 after a long courtship, Robert married Ethel Skakel in her home town of Greenwich, Connecticut.

Later that year, Robert was admitted to the Massachusetts bar and took his first job investigating corruption and income tax evasion cases for the Justice Department, which ten years later he would direct. He gave up the job in 1952 to manage his brother's campaign for the Senate. John Kennedy won the election due mainly to Robert's effective management of the campaign. His ruthless side showed when he stepped on the toes of leading local politicians by his abrasive and single-minded approach to getting his brother elected. They considered him an inexperienced, rude upstart, but his methods worked. It was the beginning of his role as 'brother protector'; a role which would haunt him throughout the rest of his life, resulting in accusations that he was aggressive, abrasive, arrogant and ruthless in his will to power. Many writers have also assumed that because Robert's father and brothers were notorious womanisers, the rumours about his affairs must also be true. Robert's role as protector of his brother, the President, also brought him under suspicion for his own foibles. Yet the relationship between the brothers has been grossly misunderstood. As a committed Catholic, Robert was not pleased with his brother's behaviour in relation to women. But he forgave his brother knowing he was unable to change him. He also understood his brother's complex nature - John Kennedy's fatalism and need to live every day as if it were his last - he understood him, in short, as a man. There is no doubt the brothers were close and loved one another but on an emotional level there was a distance; one reason being the fact that Robert had a moralistic, prudish attitude. The time they spent together socially has often been exaggerated. The more Robert learned of his brother's private life, often through the good auspices of J. Edgar Hoover after John became President, the more he must have wondered how reckless his brother was in his relationships. Close friends have said that their close relationship was based more on political considerations than anything else.[3]

After John's Senate campaign, Robert went to work for the Senate Subcommittee on Investigations which was headed by the controversial senator from Wisconsin, Joseph McCarthy. Although later in his career this move was to cause Robert Kennedy to lose the support of many liberals, he never felt the need to answer his critics or deny his association with Senator McCarthy. The roots of McCarthy's association with the Kennedy family were superficial. McCarthy, like the Kennedys, was an Irish Catholic politician who was revered in Massachusetts. And RFK's Catholic faith was consistent with a vehement anti-communism. As William Shannon wrote: "...only Catholics can fully grasp the sinister nature of communism, an avowedly anti-religious movement. Communism was the work of Satan in politics; one should not compromise with Satan in politics any more than one should compromise with sin in one's private life."[4] However, RFK came to see McCarthy's insidious efforts as 'madness'. While he was Attorney General Robert Kennedy completely repudiated the myth of McCarthyism by stating, "It is such a nonsense to have to waste time prosecuting the (U.S.) Communist Party. It couldn't be more feeble and less of a threat and besides its membership consists largely of FBI agents."[5]

After six months on the Subcommittee staff, Kennedy became disillusioned with the ways the investigations were conducted and resigned, blaming the Committee's chief counsel, the notorious Roy Cohn, who Robert detested. Cohn would later be disgraced when he tried to blackmail the army into giving a friend specialist treatment after he was drafted. Ten years later Cohn was indicted for perjury. He died of AIDS many years later.

Robert moved to the Democratic minority coalition on the same Committee, which hoped to oust McCarthy from within. Several times during the Army-McCarthy hearings, in which the Committee tried to find communist influence and corruption, Robert nearly came to blows with Cohn in the hallways of the Senate building. McCarthy was eventually disgraced because of the manner in which he conducted his 'witchhunts' and died from an alcohol-related ailment in 1957.

Robert remained on the Committee as chief counsel until 1957 when he resigned to head the newly-formed Senate Rackets Committee, from which he proceeded to investigate the mob-controlled leader of the Teamsters Union, Jimmy Hoffa. His headline-making inquiries into the corruption of labour unions caused many to consider Robert Kennedy anti-labour. In reality Kennedy was supporting working Americans in ridding the unions of mafia influence and control. His work took him to cities across America. His life was threatened on numerous occasions and his staff feared that one day he would be murdered by mobsters. His 'vendetta' against Hoffa would last until the Teamsters boss was imprisoned for jury tampering in 1967.

When Robert's brother John announced his candidacy for the presidency in 1960, Robert resigned his position to manage the campaign. It was during this campaign that the description 'ruthless' really stuck. If it bothered him he did not show it. He explained: "I'm not running a popularity contest...I don't try to antagonise people, but somebody has to be able to say no."[6]

After John Kennedy was elected, he appointed Robert Attorney General in charge of the Justice Department. Because of his experiences of investigating mobsters and corrupt union officials for the government in the 1950s, he was well equipped to take on the role of chief law enforcement officer, but at first Robert did not want to accept the post. He thought the general public would regard the appointment as nepotism. But Joe Kennedy convinced his son, the President, that he needed someone in Government he could trust without reservation. John Kennedy acceded to his father's wishes and the furore over the appointment died down. It was eventually seen as one of the wisest appointments the President made.

By the time Robert Kennedy became Attorney General he was widely regarded as power-hungry and ruthless, an impression that the public eventually found to be deceptive, at least until the new biographies of the 1990s. Arthur Schlesinger Jnr. said: "I do not know of any case in contemporary American politics where there has seemed to me a greater discrepancy between the myth and the man."[7] Arthur Garrity, who helped RFK secure JFK's nomination for the Senate in 1952, believed the idea that RFK was ruthless stemmed from this period: "...I remember how terribly shy he was...he rarely made eye contact with us...It was a strange combination of shyness, directness and intensity...he was tough and direct and yet you had a sense of a certain gentleness underneath."[8]

Robert Kennedy increasingly became a symbol of hope to a new generation who identified with the demands of African-Americans for basic civil rights and with the call of the disenfranchised poor who had been ignored by an affluent society. John Kennedy was the larger symbol and Robert Kennedy stood in his shadow. But Robert was the force behind the Administration's decision to throw its support for the Civil Rights movement. This was a gradual approach in the three years of the Kennedy Administration; the Kennedys were aware that they had a slender majority and could not damage their whole programme without shoring up support from Southern Democrats. He was also the force behind the fight to eliminate organised crime throughout America.

His fight to eliminate organised crime was extremely risky. Death threats from mobsters became an everyday fact of life. During the period of his Attorney Generalship indictments of mobsters increased to incredible proportions. FBI agents were ecstatic. They now had a head of the Justice Department who knew what he was talking about; an Attorney General who knew how far the criminal organisation reached into the lives of every American.

Robert Kennedy's role in the government was not confined to heading the Justice Department. He was, in effect, the 'Assistant President', President Kennedy's most important advisor. His brilliant participation in the Cuban Missile Crisis deliberations would alone earn him a place in the history books, for without RFK's wise counsel events may have resulted in nuclear war. Robert McNamara, Kennedy's Secretary of Defense, said: "Throughout the entire period of the crisis, a period of the most intense strain I have ever operated under, he remained calm and cool, firm but restrained, never nettled and never rattled."[9] British Prime Minister, Harold MacMillan, believed RFK's role in the crisis proved he was a "great man".[10]

After his brother's assassination, however, all his power within the Administration evaporated. Lyndon Johnson and Robert Kennedy despised each other; a conflict which had its origins in the role Robert played in the selection of Lyndon Johnson as the Vice-Presidential Democratic candidate in 1960. Robert was upset at the unseemly haste with which the new President took over the Oval Office the day after the assassination. He also believed that Johnson was in some way a 'usurper'. Johnson on the other hand was frightened of the emerging Kennedy myth and even had nightmares that Robert would challenge him for the presidency. Johnson, rightfully and naturally, wanted to govern in his own right. Robert became a thorn in his side probably of Johnson's own making. There was a strong feeling that Lyndon Johnson should accept Robert Kennedy as his running mate in the 1964 elections. This was the last thing that Johnson wanted - the possessor of the Kennedy legend only one heartbeat away from his job. The new President was also concerned that Robert's popularity, in the wake of the Kennedy legend, would surpass his. Johnson was also fearful that Kennedy would be a constant irritant in his desire to force the new President in carrying out those policies which had been his brother's concern. As it happened Lyndon Johnson also believed in many of the Kennedy policies and one of his first acts as President was to push a Civil Rights Bill through Congress. Eventually domestic policies, such as the War on Poverty and Voting Rights, became cornerstones of Johnson's 'Great Society'.

Johnson's 'trick' in getting rid of the RFK threat was to issue a statement to the press ruling out the consideration of any Cabinet member as a possible running mate in the 1964 election. Disillusioned at not being selected as Vice-President, Kennedy resigned the Attorney Generalship and established residence in New York. He ran for the Senate and won. Now he was his own man and was not tied to the Johnson Administration. However, he was still tied to the Democratic Party and therefore supported President Johnson.

It was during this period in his life, beginning with the assassination of his brother and his run for the Senate, that Kennedy's beliefs and ideology took a radical turn. Sensing a lapse in his early education - unlike John he had never been bookish - he was rarely seen without a book, as if he were required to pass his own course in self-improvement. He would borrow Jacqueline Kennedy's 'Plutarch', a gift from poet Robert Lowell, peruse the biographies Lowell had marked for her to read and then himself mark some for her. Robert became very conscious of the 'nobility and danger of pride and fate', one of Plutarch's overriding concerns. He had an intense sense of mortality after his brother's death and became aware of the uncertainties of life. It was a period of deep depression and gloom yet he was also aware that he had inherited his brother's legacy and it was incumbent upon him to fulfil it. He kept on going because he thought he could make a difference. This change in personality and temperament was recognised by John Kennedy's close aide, Theodore Sorensen, who said, in 1966: "When I first met him (RFK) thirteen years ago I would not have voted for him for anything. He was much more cocky, militant, negative, narrow, closer to his father in thinking than to his brother. Today I have no serious doubts about him...I would vote for him for anything."[11]

In the Senate, Robert Kennedy continued to fight for the minority groups he had so long championed. But his passion to help became more intense. The celebrated Kennedy charisma added more force to his every activity but he began to differentiate himself from his brother in the way he called for more radical programmes to help the poor and the less powerful in society. In his first two years in the Senate, Robert Kennedy inspired a number of projects in New York State of which even veteran legislators were proud. They included assistance to underprivileged and emotionally disturbed children; the establishment of a corporation to bring industry to Brooklyn slums; and the setting up of regional development councils for upstate New York. Nationally, he spoke out for jobs, housing and education. Whereas John Kennedy's call for action was disinterested and remote, RFK became personally involved in his work. As his father said: "Bobby is soft, soft on people. He has the capacity to be emotionally involved, to feel things deeply."[12] He was moving beyond liberalism yet he was still conservative in many ways, believing as he did in the rule of law, the work ethic and the family. During the 1964 election campaign, liberals were still suspicious of Kennedy. They remembered his support and association with Joseph McCarthy and his aggressiveness in riding roughshod over anyone in his quest to get his brother elected president. Liberal icons, Eleanor Roosevelt and Adlai Stevenson, had disliked him.

However, while the job of senator offered him a new sense of direction, it was not enough for someone who had been near the centre of power. He began taking frequent trips across the nation, speaking out on national and international issues. He experienced first hand the plight of Native Americans whilst visiting Indian reservations. He appealed to the consciences of many Americans by reminding them that the children of California migrant farm workers and of Indians on South Dakota reservations were all fellow Americans. Many felt as if a saint had visited the reservations. He went to the grubbiest children and hugged and kissed them. His visits to the ghettoes of American cities and to the rural areas of the Mississippi Delta, where poverty was endemic, enraged him.

When he toured the Mississippi Delta he went into a foul smelling room and found a starving child with a distended stomach. He held the child and, talked to him while rats and cockroaches scattered around the floor. Robert Kennedy sat with tears running down his cheeks. The night he came back from Mississippi, he told his startled children how families were living in houses smaller than their dining room. He told them they had a responsibility to give something back. Driving them around Washington D.C.'s black neighbourhoods, he pointed out to them how poor people lived in such appalling conditions.

Robert Kennedy's power lay in the manner in which he expressed these national ills. Somehow he was able to communicate to people that he understood their troubles and sympathised, not as a politician but as a human being. Many Americans of this generation find it very difficult to imagine such a politician, but dozens of people who knew Robert Kennedy will testify to this fact.

Robert Kennedy was a politician who carried out his duties without the glib, poll-driven responses which politicians manufacture these days.

He was no saint; he lost his temper on many an occasion and he made people angry. But he pursued policies and goals that were not simply based upon opinion polls but on what he genuinely believed were on the interests of natural justice and American values regardless of political consequences. He advocated giving blood to the Viet Cong, not because he was aiding and abetting the enemy, but because his religious faith instructed him.[13] When he spoke at the University of Oklahoma and on other campuses in 1967, Kennedy challenged the students who supported the war in Vietnam by asking those who favoured escalation of the war to raise their hands. Then he asked those who favoured the current policy of giving students a deferment from the draft to raise their hands. The vast majority did so. "Let me ask you another question, " Kennedy said, "How many of you who voted for escalation of the war also voted for exemption of students from the draft?"[14] It was the kind of challenge unheard of from politicians.

Kennedy spoke for the family of an American communist who was also a war veteran and who was refused burial at Arlington National Cemetary. Alone amongst senators, he said that this was wrong: "I don't think anyone now buried in Arlington would object to having (Robert) Thompson buried there," he said, "so I don't see why all these living people are objecting."[15] His doubts, his emotions and his regrets were all too exposed. He was also, however, torn between the politics of the old and the politics of the new; the radicalism of what he wanted to do and the realism of what was possible.

Robert Kennedy experienced real growth and change in the years after his brother's assassination, change which was to lead him to an extraordinary advocacy of policies to end war, poverty and social injustice, far removed from his party's positions on the issues. He experienced real inner change and growth. He wanted to understand everybody from the inside, particularly people who suffered in society. He had deep feelings and could be transformed by the experience. His journey was an unimaginable leap: from his beginnings as the son of an anti-semitic father to working for Joseph McCarthy, and from his upbringing in a world of privilege and wealth to embracing the right actions on Civil Rights, the Mafia, racism and the War in Vietnam. As author Brian Dooley (1995) put it: "Prophet or not, Kennedy's journey from Cold Warrior to radical liberal was a transformation which took the main body of American liberalism 30 years to complete."[16]

Kennedy was also a politician who was actually affected and influenced by writers and philosophers like Aeschylus, Sophocles, Camus,

Emerson and Jefferson, and he frequently quoted them in his speeches. He was also influenced by his experiences as a politician who deliberately sought out opinions from diverse groups of Americans. He had a pivotal meeting, for example, in 1963 when he met Civil Rights leaders and black writers and activists at his New York apartment in 1963. He had expected a reasonable meeting with a group that included writer James Baldwin, actor Harry Belafonte, pacifist Jerome Smith and social psychologist Kenneth Clarke. It became, however, very heated and he was shocked at the animus present during the discussion. As recounted by Arthur Schlesinger(1978), Baldwin asked Smith whether he would fight for his country. Smith replied he would not. Robert was stunned and accused Smith of treason, and this put everyone on Smith's side. It went on for three hours. Afterwards, Clark called the meeting: "one of the most radical, violent, emotional verbal assaults that I have ever witnessed before or since." Robert, until then, had never heard an American say he would never fight for his country. Back in Washington - and this is an example of how he had the ability to learn, change and grow - Robert said: "I guess if I were in his shoes, if I had gone through what he's gone through, I might feel differently about the country."[17]

Robert Kennedy, then, became a different man and a different politician after his brother's death. He metamorphosed into a committed seeker of change and he was able to transcend the myth of Camelot, the dark secrets of government complicity in attempts against Castro's life and the private life of his brother. He did not seek glamour and style in his pursuit of the presidency but instead sought to enlighten the American people to the injustices hidden in the underbelly of American life - white hatred for African-Americans, innocents dying in Vietnam and poor Americans living in squalor.

At the same time Robert Kennedy tried to work within a system he truly believed in. Paradoxically, he was a conservative in the sense that he held deep beliefs about his Catholic faith and the American Constitution. Faith, family and country did not become alien concepts to him. He was patriotic and convinced about the efficacy of American power around the world. Yet in the later years of his life he was also committed to radical programmes of change to help the have-nots in society. His ability to change and develop as he experienced the wrongs in society testified to his experiential and existential nature.

Was Robert Kennedy a hero? Perhaps the answer lies in the nature of the word. Joseph Campbell said: "A hero is someone who has given his or her life to something bigger than oneself." Ronald Goldfarb, a Justice Department lawyer who worked closely with Robert Kennedy has no doubt: "If to be a hero one must...perform acts that are extraordinary and have public, rather than personal, influence, of course, Robert Kennedy would qualify. In about a decade in public life - from the McClellan Committee to the Justice Department to the Senate - Robert Kennedy grew exponentially, in wisdom, in breadth of influence, in impact for the public good. Few public figures have grown better as their power increased; this Robert Kennedy did."[18]

Bobby and Ethel

Ethel Skakel was born in Chicago, the sixth of seven children to George and Anne Skakel. George was a self-made former railway clerk who came from humble origins and used to tell his family that their riches should not be taken for granted. He owned the multi-million dollar Great Lakes Carbon Corporation, eventually moving it to New York. He bought a 16 acre estate for his family in Greenwich, Connecticut.

Ethel's mother was very religious, a staunch Catholic, and she passed on this abiding faith in God to her daughter Ethel. However, both parents were alcoholics, according to Ethel's biographer, Jerry Oppenheimer (1994). But there is no evidence that the family home was a strife ridden environment and Ethel grew up a stable and happy child. Like the Kennedy's, the Skakel family had their share of tragedy. Ethel's parents were to die in a plane crash in 1955 after Ethel's father asked her mother to fly with him on a business trip to Los Angeles in his company-owned plane. The plane exploded in mid-air killing everyone on board. Eleven years later Ethel's brother George Skakel Jnr. was killed in plane crash along with Bobby's close friend Dean Markham.

Ethel's strong faith helped her to deal with the tragedies of her parents and brother. However, there is some evidence that she naturally suffered depression as a result of the tragedies and turned to alcohol for relief. There was nothing superficial about her faith (at one time she considered becoming a nun) and it was this rather than a dependence on alcohol which brought her through. Ethel engaged in spiritual reading every day. Athletics was her passion and she also excelled in swimming, skiing and horsemanship.

The Skakel and Kennedy families first came together around 1940 when the children met at school. Seventeen year old Ethel and 20 year old Bobby met in 1945 at Mont Tremblant, a Canadian ski resort near Montreal. Ethel was introduced to Bobby by Jean Kennedy. She was instantly attracted to Jean's brother but the feeling was not mutual at first. Bobby was attracted to Ethel's sister Pat. He asked her out and the relationship lasted for approximately two months. Pat became interested in someone else and so Ethel's mother discreetly brought Bobby and Ethel together. Bobby was shy and introverted but Ethel had the right temperament to bring him out of his shell. She had a strong personality, vivacious and intelligent, and she was more than a match for the rest of the highly competitive Kennedy family.

Bobby asked Ethel to help with his brother's campaign for Congress in 1946 and she threw herself into the challenge. In 1950 they were married in Greenwich and settled down to raise a family. From the beginning they had an extraordinary relationship. Bobby's sister Eunice Shriver would reminisce years later that: "I hear him on the beach, in his home, on his boat, on the front lawn playing football, at the tennis court - always with the same question: 'Where is Ethel?' He grew out of this slowly. He was a lonely and unfulfilled youngster. He met Ethel and all the love and appreciation for which she seemed to have an infinite capacity came pouring down on him. How he blossomed."[19] The couple eventually had 11 children, the last child was born six months after Robert's death.

Their first homes were in Charlottesville, where Bobby was studying law, and in Georgetown, Washington D.C.. In 1956 Jackie Kennedy, after suffering a miscarriage, decided that she no longer wished to live in their mansion, Hickory Hill, and gave the property to Bobby and Ethel. It was a short car ride across the Potomac river and it was large enough to house Bobby and Ethel's growing family and near enough to the young government lawyer's work in the capital.

Bobby and Ethel never lost the love, respect and dependency they had for one another. Throughout Bobby's work in Government and during his time as Attorney General, Ethel was always near to him often bringing the children to his place of work.

After the assassination of President Kennedy, Ethel found it difficult to see her husband in such a miserable state and supported him in his desire to continue in politics. During the campaigns for the Senate and the Presidency she was always at his side. It was during this time that

Robert felt a compelling need to be close to his brother's widow Jackie. Their closeness developed because of their mutual pain after the assassination and Robert's role as the surrogate father to John and Jackie's children, John Jnr. and Caroline. He took her out for meals and at one time accompanied her on vacation to Antigua. 'Look' magazine reporter, Stanley Tretrick, who was a friend to both Robert and Jacqueline, told author, Jerry Oppenheimer: "Bobby was getting a lot of criticism for spending so much time with Jackie. Once, he looked at me and said, 'She's lonely'."[20]

During the late 1990s, assessments of Robert Kennedy's character in relation to his private life have been challenged by a number of authors, notably Christopher Andersen (1998), Jerry Oppenheimer (1994) and C. David Heymann (1998). Heymann and Oppenheimer maintain that Robert and Jackie had an affair. Andersen claimed that shared grief provoked Jackie and Robert Kennedy to begin a romance shortly after President Kennedy's assassination. He quoted Charles Spalding, a Kennedy family friend, who said: "Bobby and Jackie were definitely an unit, a twosome. She relied on him for everything, and he adored her. There was definitely an intimacy."[21]

However, in an interview with the 'New York Daily News', Spalding said the relationship between Jackie and Bobby was benign: "Her husband was gone and Bobby spent time with her...It's anything you or I would do but there was nothing salacious."[22] Jackie's step-brother, Jamie Auchincloss, told the 'National Enquirer': "They became emotionally close after JFK was killed. A romance would have shattered the friendship they had and valued."[23]

As evidence of the 'affair', Andersen cites Secret Service files 'showing' that Jackie and Bobby were in each other's constant company throughout the latter half of 1964. He also found 'evidence' that Jackie and Bobby dined at the Four Seasons restaurant and then spent the 'night together' at brother-in-law Stephen Smith's Fifth Avenue apartment. However, Peter Duchin, a close friend of Jackie's, dismissed this 'proof' as nothing less than lies. He said: "If they spent the night, I would bet it wasn't in the same room. It's such an idiotic thing to intimate. I know they were very close friends, but I never saw any indication of romance."[24]

As additional 'evidence', Andersen quotes four 'sources', including one he took from another book. Two more 'sources' - Nancy Dickerson and Clare Booth Luce - are now dead. Dickerson's husband, however, said his wife never told him of the 'affair': "I'm very doubtful that she did believe it," he said, "She certainly didn't use that kind of language."[25] In the same book, Andersen also alleged an affair between Jackie and the actor Marlon Brando. Brando's co-author, Robert Lindsay, vigorously denied it, saying: "They didn't sleep together. I think it was a one-night stand where Marlon and a friend went to Jackie's apartment in Georgetown. They danced and that's as far as it went. There was no sleeping together. Marlon would have told me if there was."[26] And, of course, Brando has never been shy when it comes to discussing his many affairs.

The truth of the matter is that both RFK and Jackie were emotionally damaged after JFK's assassination. They both needed each other as a 'link' to the dead brother and husband. The relationship was deep and intense but chaste. Robert Kennedy was a committed Catholic who would have considered an intimate relationship with his brother's widow sacrilegious.

The scurrilous allegations have been repeated by C. David Heymann who has gone further than any other author in his promiscuous literary attack on Robert Kennedy. Heymann has relied on second hand gossip to paint a picture of Kennedy as a rapacious sexual predator and an unfaithful husband. Like Andersen his case is weak and many of the people he interviewed have been shocked that they have been so misquoted.

Heymann maintained that Robert Kennedy had an affair with Barbara Sinatra before her marriage to the famous singer. She denied ever having a relationship with him: "I was never that lucky. But I got even luckier than that when I married Frank Sinatra in 1976."[27] Furthermore the same allegation, from the same source, was to be used in a Kennedy-trashing book in 1991. When the source's lawyer found out about the impending book he threatened legal action. The lawyer, Barry Slotnick, said his client "put everyone on notice that if she was named as a source for this information she would utilise the courts to the fullest extent."[28]

Peter Lawford's third and last wife, Pat Lawford Stewart (Patricia Seaton Lawford), was also quoted by Heymann as having had an affair with Robert Kennedy. She has vehemently denied it and called for a complete retraction. Stewart also contacted a lawyer, so incensed was she by the made-up story.[29]

Heymann also claims in his book that Robert Kennedy had an affair with an 'American Heritage' magazine reporter. Heymann wrote: "The last great romance of Robert Kennedy's life was with Kristi Witker, a bouncy, buoyant twenty-one year old with long blonde hair, hypnotic blue eyes, and a beguiling figure."[30] Heymann goes on to say that Witker told him she fell passionately in love with the senator from the moment they met and she was idealistic and in love.

Yet again Heymann has been irresponsible with his facts. Witker told 'USA Today' that the story was a total fabrication and that it was "utterly untrue". She denied having a sexual relationship with Robert Kennedy saying: "Absolutely not! How could I? I was always in a plane with everybody...I was crazy about Bobby, I admired him enormously, I was a bit star-struck and flattered he spent so much time talking to me."[31]

The most sensational of Heymann's tales about Robert Kennedy's private life concerns a so-called intimacy with the ballet star, Rudolf Nureyev. Kennedy apparently had been seen kissing Nureyev passionately at a New York nightclub. Heymann used ballerina and TV producer, Janet Villela, for this ridiculous story[32]; and probably much to his regret as Villela contacted the media. She told the 'New York Post's' Cindy Adams the story was 'hogwash'. Like Pat Lawford Stewart and Kristi Witker she hired a lawyer to rebut the allegations.[33]

Jamie Auchincloss dismissed Heymann's allegations telling the 'National Enquirer':

> "All this talk about Bobby doing drugs and playing around is rubbish. I don't believe any of it is true...It is all a figment of the imagination. I knew Bobby well. He was the original Mr Go Get 'Em...like a top cop. He was a straight arrow."[34]

In the meantime, however, Heymann's best-seller distorts the picture for a generation of Americans.

It is virtually impossible to disprove a negative. An allegation without substantial proof has a way of entering the national consciousness even though it has been vehemently denied. However, it cannot be said with any measure of certitude that Robert Kennedy remained faithful to his wife throughout his married life. It is an area that biographers are often not privy to. It is also true that unsubstantiated and scurrilous gossip should not be published unless it has been rigorously scrutinised and supported by documentary and reliable and authoritative witness evidence. Gossips have linked Robert Kennedy to many women. Most, like Barbara Sinatra, have denied the allegations. Jerry Oppenheimer wrote: "The women who were named as having had flings with Bobby offered vehement denials. After making their denials each would then point the finger at another woman, claiming that that woman had been involved with Bobby."[35] No biographer of Robert Kennedy has discovered anyone who has admitted to an affair with him. Heymann, Oppenheimer and Andersen have all relied on second-hand accounts of what sources say they 'knew'. A number of named women, like Polly Bussell, have described RFK's flirtations as 'innocent'.[36]

Two credible sources, both of whom were close to Robert Kennedy, believe he indulged in some extra-marital activity but it was nowhere on the scale of his brother John. Arthur Schlesinger Jnr. and Clark Mollenhoff have indicated, without elaboration or attribution, that RFK was less than faithful to his wife.[37] However, no woman has come forward with a credible and substantiated story confirming the suspicions. As author James W. Hilty (1997) wrote: "Assignations and affairs would not only have been wildly out of character for Robert Kennedy, they would have been wholly inconsistent with the roles thrust upon him by his place in the family and would have further complicated his already difficult task as his brother's protector."[38] It would also have been completely out of character for the deeply religious Robert to commit adultery. RFK took his faith seriously and any moral transgressions would have caused him considerable personal grief.

Taking Robert Kennedy's life as a whole it can be said that he was true to his wife and family and that this commitment was real. In any event if Robert Kennedy had indeed experienced intermittent lapses in spousal fidelity, it did not detract from the strong loving bond he had with his wife. Ethel Kennedy heard the rumours of her husband's alleged affairs even when he was alive but she never believed them. She was as certain of Robert as any woman can be of a husband. After Robert's assassination Ethel never remarried. "How could I?", she often said to friends, "with Bobby looking down from heaven." Her love for her husband was never relinquished and she could never share her love for her husband. As her mother-in-law, Rose Kennedy wrote: "She and Bobby loved each other deeply - they loved being together, shared everything; they had a perfect life."[39]

Notes

1. Hilty, J. W. (1997). *Robert Kennedy – brother protector*, Temple University Press. p. 167.

2. 'The Kennedys'. Narrated by John Woodvine, written by Phillip Whitehead and Geoffrey C. Ward. Thames Television, 1992. (A Brook/WGBH Co-production for Thames Television).

3. Hilty, J. W. (1997). *Robert Kennedy – brother protector*, Temple University Press. p. 493; Beran, M. K. (1998). *The last patrician - Bobby Kennedy and the end of American aristocracy*, St Matrin's Griffin. p. 61. "All this business about Jack and Bobby being blood brothers has been exaggerated". (Eunice Kennedy Shriver quoted in Beran)

4. O'Donnell, H. (1998*). A common good*, William Morrow and Company. p. 101.

5. Schlesinger, A. M. (1978). *Robert Kennedy and his times*, Houghton Mifflin Co. p. 281.

6. *Ibid*, p. 230.

7. *Ibid*, xv.

8. O'Donnell, H. (1998). *A common good*, William Morrow and Company. p. 86.

9. Schlesinger, A. M. (1978). *Robert Kennedy and his times*, Houghton Mifflin Co. p. 573.

10. Wofford, H. (1980). *Of Kennedys and kings*, Farrar Straus and Giroux. p. 408.

11. 'The Bobby phenomenon'. *Newsweek*, 24 October 1966, p. 22

12. Hudson, J. A. (1969). *RFK*, Scholastic Book Services. p. 36.

13. Newfield, J. (1970). *Robert Kennedy - a memoir*, Jonathan Cape. p. 121.

14. Schlesinger, A. M. (1978). *Robert Kennedy and his times*, Houghton Mifflin Co. p. 834.

15. *Ibid*, p. 790.

16. Dooley, B. (1995). *RFK - the final years*, Keele University Press. p. 41.

17. Schlesinger, A. M. (1978). *Robert Kennedy and his times*, Houghton Mifflin Co. pp. 355-359.

18. Goldfarb, R. (1995). *Perfect villains, imperfect heroes*, Random House. p. 327.

Bobby and Ethel

19. 'The Kennedy of Hickory Hill'. *Time*, 25 April 1969, p. 42.

20. Oppenheimer, J. (1994). *The other Mrs Kennedy*, St Martin's Paperbacks. p. 361.

21. Andersen, C. (1996), *Jack and Jackie - portrait of an American marriage*, William Morrow and Company Inc. p. 102.

22. Schwartzman, P. 'In fact it's fiction'. *New York Daily News*, 22 February 1998. (http://www.nydailynews.com). Authors, mistakenly, continue to use Charles Spalding as a source for allegations that RFK and Jacqueline Kennedy had an affair. In 'USA Today' excerpts from Sarah Bradford's (2000) book "America's queen", Viking, Spalding is quoted as having told Kennedy biographer Nigel Hamilton that "Jackie and Bobby were lovers". Her other 'sources' for the allegation remains anonymous. (*USA Today*, 17 October 2000, p. 11B)

23. Towle, P. and Haley, L. 'Bobby Kennedy's secret life of drugs, brawls and sexcapades'. *National Enquirer*, 14 February 1998. (http://www.nationalenquirer.com).

24. *New York Daily News*, 22 February 1998. (http://www.nydailynews.com).

25. Schwartzman, P. 'Book: it's Jackie oh!'. *New York Daily News*, 11 February 1998. (http://www.nydailynews.com).

26. *Ibid*.

27. Johnson, R. 'RFK linked to Frank's Barbara'. *New York Post*, 8 December 1997. (http://www.nypostonline.com).

28. *Ibid*.

29. 'Battle stations over RFK tell-all'. *New York Post*, 16 September 1998. (http://www.nypostonline.com)

30. Heymann, C. D. (1998). *RFK – a candid biography*, William Heinemann. p. 472.

31. Williams, J. 'RFK biographer, woman are at odds.' *USA Today*, 9 October 1998. (http://www.usatoday.com)

32. Heymann, C. D. (1998). *RFK – a candid biography*, William Heinemann. p. 419.

33. *New York Post*, 16 September 1998. (http://www.nypostonline.com).

34. Towle, P. and Haley, L. 'Bobby Kennedy's secret life of drugs, brawls and sexcapades'. *National Enquirer*, 5 April 1998. (http://www.nationalenquirer.com).

35. Oppenheimer, J. (1994). *The other Mrs Kennedy*, St Martin's Paperbacks. p. 321.

36. *Ibid*, p. 323

37. Summers, A. (1986). *Goddess - the secret lives of Marilyn Monroe*, Sphere Books. p. 285; Giglio, J. N. (1991). *The presidency of John F. Kennedy*, University Press of Kansas. p. 309.

38. Hilty, J. W. (1997). *Robert Kennedy – brother protector*, Temple University Press. p. 249.

39. Kennedy, R. F. (1974). *Times to remember*, Pan Books. p. 512.

Chapter 10

The RFK/Monroe 'Affair'

What was Robert Kennedy's true relationship with Marilyn Monroe?

"No one gossips about other people's secret virtues"

Bertrand Russell

Ever since the publication of Anthony Summers' bestselling biography of Marilyn Monroe (Summers, 1986) and a complementary television documentary based on the book's findings, the American and British publics have become convinced that President Kennedy's brother Robert had a brief affair with the movie actress in the months leading up to her death. The story of the 'affair' has been so ingrained in popular consciousness that news programmes, books, television documentaries and television talk shows continually refer to the story of the RFK/Monroe relationship as a given fact.

The story has been repeated in many books and documentaries but the account differs from author to author. However, there are common threads: President Kennedy began a romance with the Hollywood actress then passed her on to his brother Robert who soon tired of her obsessive nature and unstable personality. In the weeks leading up to her death, RFK issued instructions to his aides that he did not wish to communicate with her. Fearing Monroe was about to reveal her relationships with the Kennedy brothers to the press, Robert and his brother-in law, Peter Lawford, decided to pay Monroe a visit. A violent argument resulted in Monroe physically attacking RFK and threatening him with her intention to tell all. Discarded and emotionally wrought over the break up, she took her own life. Some authors go further and state, preposterously, that she was murdered by either the CIA or the Mafia or the Kennedys with the FBI assisting in the cover-up. As 'proof' author after author referred to audio tapes which supposedly recorded the fatal bedroom death scene in which RFK's voice could be heard.

The story of the alleged RFK/Monroe affair began a few years after her death in August, 1962. There had indeed been rumours of her affairs with both Kennedy brothers while John Kennedy and Marilyn Monroe were alive, but published stories of her affair began in 1964 with a pamphlet by a right-wing extremist, Frank Capell. Cappell's allegations were supported by ex-convict, Lionel Grandison, a former coroner's aide who said that the police falsified Monroe's autopsy, and by Los Angeles police sergeant, Jack Clemmons, who was the first policeman to arrive on the scene after Monroe's death. It was also given credence by author, Norman Mailer (1973), who stated in his book 'Marilyn' that there may have been some truth to the story. He later apologised for his baseless ruminations in a CBS '60 minutes' interview with Mike Wallace. Mailer's excuse was that he 'needed the money'.[1]

Frank Capell was the person responsible for starting the rumour but he had assistance from those people who hated RFK. One of the Kennedy-haters who pushed the story was right-wing columnist, Walter Winchell, aided and abetted by Kennedy nemesis, J. Edgar Hoover. As FBI Assistant Director, William Sullivan, noted in his memoirs: "The stories about Bobby Kennedy and Marilyn Monroe were just stories. The original story was invented by a so-called journalist, a right-wing zealot who had a history of spinning wild yarns. It spread like wildfire, of course, and J. Edgar Hoover was right there, gleefully fanning the flames."[2]

After Norman Mailer's allegations, Robert Slatzer (1975) was next in line to push the story of the Robert Kennedy/Marilyn Monroe relationship. In 1972, Slatzer had approached a writer named Will Fowler with an idea for a book detailing the 'murder of the Hollywood actress'. Fowler read it and found it to be without merit. He told Slatzer that if he had been MARRIED to the actress then it would make a good story. Shortly afterwards Slatzer got in touch with Fowler again and stated that it had slipped his memory but he had indeed been married to Monroe for a period of 72 hours. It allegedly happened in Mexico on October 4th 1952. Unfortunately, Slatzer could not produce corroborative evidence or a marriage certificate, but he nevertheless stuck to his story and published his book. For the following 30 years he appeared on television talk shows, documentaries and videos ['Say goodbye to the President' (1985), 'Marilyn Monroe - the final day', (2000)] without any solid proof to his claims except for nine photographs of himself and the Hollywood actress taken in the late forties.

The genie was out of the bottle and authors lined up to benefit from the dramatic story which had been sparked by inconsistencies in the police investigation and anomalies in witness statements. Slatzer was followed by Tony Sciacca (1976) and Milo Speriglio (1982 and 1986), whom Slatzer hired as an investigator, and both took their lead from Slatzer. In the 1980s and 1990s, Anthony Summers, Seymour Hersh (1997) and C. David Heymann (1998) followed. They gave credibility to the story by their own reputations as gifted investigative journalists as well as the fact they interviewed hundreds of people connected to the case. Unfortunately, the reliance these authors placed upon some questionable sources is a weak point in both of their books.

Up to the time of the publication of Summers' (1986) book, the story of RFK's relationship with Monroe was based on scurrilous gossip and the second-hand accounts of what really happened at Monroe's house originating, supposedly, with Kennedy-in-law Peter Lawford. When U.S. Justice Department records were released in the 1980s, telephone calls from Monroe to Robert Kennedy were interpreted in the worst light by many authors who believed that the Attorney General and the movie actress had had an intimate relationship. The records, however, proved nothing more than the two knew each other. For the most part the calls were taken by RFK's secretary, Angie Novello. The telephone records show very brief calls - a total of eight in the summer of her death - and they were innocuous dealing with mundane matters. These calls and four meetings were the sum total of RFK's relationship with Monroe. As Ed Guthman, RFK's close aide, said: "Ethel was the woman in his life, and he seemed uninterested in any other except in the normal, socially acceptable and public way of doing things. That summer (of 1962) Marilyn did indeed call (Kennedy) several times at his Washington office. Bobby was a good listener and he took an interest in her questions, her life, even her troubles. But the truth is that for me, for Bobby and for Angie the calls became something of a joke and certainly nothing secret or whispered...And to have an affair? Well, frankly it wasn't in his character."[3]

Historians had, until Summers' book was published in 1985, accepted that the President had had a brief and shallow 'affair' with Monroe and that it was possible that RFK had, at some stage, been despatched to the West coast with instructions to ask Monroe to remain quiet about the relationship with the President. Many assumed RFK was distancing the President from a woman who was becoming obsessive and irrational in thinking there was anything more to the JFK/Monroe affair than a brief liaison.

Arthur Schlesinger (1978) wrote about Robert Kennedy's relationship with Monroe in his book 'Robert Kennedy and his times'. However many accused him of covering up the real truth about their relationship. Schlesinger wrote: "(Bobby met her when she sang at the celebration of John Kennedy's 45th birthday and again at Peter and Pat Lawford's Los Angeles house). She called him thereafter in Washington using an assumed name. She was often distraught. Angie Novello, his secretary, talked to her more often than the Attorney General did. One feels Kennedy came to inhabit the fantasies of her last summer."[4]

Summers' book forced many respectable writers, journalists and authors to take another look at the Monroe/Kennedys relationship. Summers' research led him to conclude that Robert Kennedy was with Marilyn Monroe on the day of her death and that it was likely she was romantically involved with the President's brother.

According to Summers, there was sufficient evidence to suggest the mafia and/or Teamster boss, Jimmy Hoffa, were attempting to gather evidence to blackmail the President and the Kennedys and Monroe were targets of electronic eavesdropping. Summers related how Monroe in 1962 had entered her final year involved with the Kennedys. She spent her final months as a highly unstable and volatile actress who was not in control of her life and was dependent on alcohol and drugs which were a vital ingredient in her desire to sleep. Upset that President Kennedy was distancing himself from her, she began an affair with his brother. When JFK dispatched Robert to the West Coast to stop Marilyn from talking about her affair with the President, an angry and bitter argument occurred. Marilyn was either murdered to keep her quiet or she committed suicide and the evidence of the Kennedys relationship with the actress was disposed of. Robert was squirreled out of Los Angeles and the Los Angeles Police Department and the FBI initiated a cover-up.

The original story released after Monroe's death began with housekeeper, Eunice Murray, becoming worried that Monroe's bedroom light was still burning at 3 'o' clock in the morning of 4th August 1962. Alarmed, she pounded on the bedroom door but Monroe did not answer. Murray hurried outside and peered into the bedroom from the French windows. She saw Monroe sprawled motionless across her bed the telephone receiver clutched in her hand. Panic-stricken Murray phoned Monroe's psychiatrist. Dr Greenson rushed over, broke a window and climbed into the room. He telephoned Dr Hyman Engelberg, Monroe's doctor, who arrived ten minutes later and pronounced the Hollywood actress dead of an apparent sleeping pill overdose.

However, reporters and writers soon saw inconsistencies in the timing of events and the forensic evidence. Consequently writers used these errors to construct alternative scenarios of how Monroe died. By the 1980s rumours of a cover-up involving the Los Angeles Police Department, the CIA, the FBI and the Mafia spread. It was alleged that on the afternoon of her death, either with Peter Lawford or alone, Robert Kennedy arrived at Monroe's house and a shouting match over their love affair took place. Monroe became upset and her psychiatrist was called to calm her down. The others left and Monroe remained in a narcotic haze. Robert Kennedy was squirreled out of Los Angeles and a cover-up ensued. Some writers intimated that Monroe may have been murdered to silence her. The reasons for her demise centred around her desire to hold a press conference to tell of her affairs with the Kennedy brothers and her possession of a supposed diary the star kept detailing her relationship with the Kennedys and her knowledge, through conversations with Robert Kennedy, of the CIA/mafia plots to assassinate Castro. It is telling that all the books claiming Monroe knew about the plots to murder Castro were published AFTER the well-publicised Congressional hearings into the CIA's illegal activities.

As the revelations about President Kennedy and the CIA/mafia plots were publicised in the 1970s, they became linked in the minds of many writers with the death of Marilyn Monroe. Further reports of Monroe's connections with the Mafia, through her friendship with Frank Sinatra, led some to believe the Mafia intended to blackmail the President. They had apparently wanted proof of the star's affairs and by July 1962 Monroe's house, according to some sources, had numerous bugging devices installed where every word she uttered was recorded. Jimmy Hoffa supposedly sent his wiretapper, Bernie Spindel, to bug Monroe's house and the mob deployed Fred Otash to make tapes. It was also alleged that Monroe had installed her own recording device to get proof of her relationship with the Kennedy brothers, if and when she decided to tell her story. When JFK and RFK learned about this they allegedly decided the Monroe affair had gone too far. Monroe responded by telling 'intimates' that she planned to hold a press conference.

Bernie Spindel, a known boaster, had stated as early as December 1966 that he had conducted electronic surveillance of Monroe's home and obtained material "which.. strongly suggests that the officially reported circumstances of (Monroe's) demise are erroneous".[5] However, he made this statement after a raid by the Manhattan District Attorney's office in which evidence of illegal wiretapping had been seized resulting in the arrests of 28 people. Days later Spindel claimed the tapes had been stolen. The District Attorney's office concluded that Spindel's story had been a fraud. Manhattan Assistant District Attorney, Ronald Carroll, wrote in his report: "Spindel's asserted desire to have the tapes made public appears to have been a ploy...The (Spindel) tapes were in fact heard by staff investigators and none of the tapes contained anything relating to Marilyn Monroe."[6]

Reason and logic seems to escape those authors who believe the tapes actually existed. If Robert Kennedy had been compromised by tape recordings which had been made for Kennedy's enemy, Teamster boss Jimmy Hoffa or Hoffa's mafia colleagues, then they would have surely been used to prevent the corrupt union official from going to jail. And if the Mafia had come into possession of the tapes they would have used them to prevent the Attorney General's crackdown on organised crime. Nothing of the sort happened because the tapes never existed.

Sam Giancana's godson (1992), also named Sam Giancana, and Chuck Giancana, the mobster's brother, claim in their book 'Double cross' that when Monroe threatened to tell the world about herself and the Kennedys, "...the CIA requested that Marilyn Monroe be eliminated. And Sam Giancana accepted the contract." According to the Giancanas four, hired mob killers waited until darkness then entered Marilyn's room around midnight and performed the perfect undetectable crime. The killers held Monroe down and taped her mouth shut: "She struggled at first. Calmly, and with all the efficiency of a team of surgeons," they then inserted into Monroe a rectal suppository filled with the barbiturate Nembutal in a dose strong enough to kill. The chemical would be impossible to trace in the colon and would kill quickly because it is speedily absorbed into the bloodstream.[7]

The Giancana book is typical of how a story can be embellished in the interests of greed and notoriety. The Giancanas attempted to reveal how Sam Giancana was responsible for the assassination of President Kennedy but research has indicated the book was constructed from hearsay and innuendo and had no basis in truth.[8]

Most conspiracy accounts of Robert Kennedy's relationship with Marilyn Monroe rely on four crucial 'witnesses': Peter Lawford, brother-in-law to the Kennedy brothers; Robert Slatzer, a supposed ex-husband; Jeanne Carmen, a supposed friend and neighbour; and Fred Otash who, allegedly, had Peter Lawford's Santa Monica beachhouse wiretapped. Many others, including Marilyn's housekeeper Eunice Murray, have told writers and investigative reporters that they saw Kennedy and Monroe together, but they have not testified to an intimate and close relationship.

Authors have built their stories around these 'witnesses' and, in most cases, have accepted their stories as true even though inconsistencies, absurdities and changed versions occur in their accounts. For the past 12 years the four critical 'witnesses' have been used by conspiracy authors and yet their veracity has never been challenged.

Matthew Smith (1996) in his book 'The men who murdered Marilyn' and Donald H. Wolfe (1998) in his book 'The assassination of Marilyn Monroe' are the latest conspiracy authors who give credence to the four 'witness' accounts.

Smith, Wolfe and Summers believed Slatzer and stated that they had interviewed a number of people who could testify to Slatzer's friendship with Monroe. But author Donald Spoto discovered that none of the people who were close to the actress had even heard of him: "…not one of Marilyn's friends, relatives, business associates, colleagues, spouses or lovers could even recall meeting him (much less Marilyn ever mentioning him) nor is he to be found in any of her personal telephone or address books."[9]

In his research, Spoto (1993) discovered that Slatzer's claim he had been married to Monroe was invented. Spoto found out that Monroe was in Beverly Hills on the day of the 'marriage' on a shopping spree and she signed a cheque dated October 4th to pay for articles she purchased. Since Slatzer says that the couple left for Mexico on October 3rd and stayed for the following weekend, this successfully demolishes the story which should have been investigated by authors like Anthony

Summers. Spoto also demolished the story of the 'red diary', a pure invention and embellishment of the story of Monroe's simple address book which had been found on the table next to her bed.

Authors Summers, Hersh, Smith, Wolfe and RFK biographer, C. David Heymann (1998), place heavy reliance on Jeanne Carmen. A late-surfacing, supposed intimate of Marilyn Monroe, she professes to have been a neighbour and, at one time, a flatmate of Monroe's when the actress lived in Doheny Drive before she bought her home in Brentwood. Carmen began to tell her story after Robert Slatzer published his ridiculous story. However, Donald Spoto discovered that Monroe's neighbours at Doheny Drive and her other friends of the stated time period have no knowledge of Carmen. Spoto wrote: "The residents of a nearby house had a wild party the night before, and knowing of their famous neighbour they stood under her window and shouted her name, calling her to join them...Marilyn never knew the name of the woman who had led this group, nor did they ever meet; she was a former bit-part actress who sometimes used the name Jeanne Carmen. Like Robert Slatzer, Carmen emerged from obscurity many years later to transmute her geographical proximity to Marilyn Monroe into something of a career. Claiming that she was Marilyn's roommate at Doheny drive, she began, in the 1980s, to invent an imaginative series of scurrilous tales for which there is simply no basis in fact: a wild romance between Marilyn and Robert Kennedy, for example, including indiscreet assignations, joyrides to Malibu beaches and nude swims...Like that of Slatzer, however, Carmen's name is nowhere to be found in Marilyn's address books, nor did anyone who knew Marilyn ever hear of (much less see or meet) her."[10]

Conspiracy authors bought into Carmen's uncorroborated stories because she was the person who could provide details of the RFK/Monroe romance. She is the source for their often repeated story of how RFK and Monroe visited a nudist beach and RFK was disguised in a wig and dark glasses. It was a total fabrication yet the salacious story has been used in nearly every book which purports to reveal the RFK/Monroe romance.

In 1991, Donald Spoto successfully demonstrated how Carmen should not be used as a reliable or credible source and yet eight years later she still spins her yarns to gullible listeners. Her most recent Kennedy story was given to author, C. David Heymann (1998), who should have realised that what she had to say about President Kennedy was preposterous. For two decades or more she had forgotten to tell all the authors and documentary makers about her 'relationship' with the President. One would have thought that this aspect of her story would not have escaped her memory, considering it was, after all, the President of the United States who she now claims she had been sleeping with. In Heymann's book 'RFK - a candid biography' Carmen says: "To John Kennedy, Marilyn was just another f... I don't think he ever really cared about her the way Bobby did, and I don't think she was ever really in love with him. And he wasn't even good in bed; I can tell you that one firsthand, because I had him too. I don't know too many women out here who didn't sleep with Jack. He was a two-minute man. I think sex to him was just about another conquest."[11]

In the sources section of Heymann's book, the author stated that some interviews were held whilst researching his book about Jackie Kennedy, entitled 'A woman called Jackie', which was published in 1989. Again the question must be asked about the veracity of these sources - why didn't he reveal this sensational anecdote at the time he published his earlier work?

Carmen herself produced no factual and verifiable evidence to support her story. She maintained that Monroe had sent her a birthday card shortly before Monroe's death and yet it has never been produced. One would have expected the card would have been kept as a treasured memento especially since it would have been the last correspondence Monroe had sent. Furthermore, no photographs exist of Carmen and Monroe nor any documentary evidence to prove they were friends. And despite Spoto's (1993) book, authors still use her as a credible 'witness'.

Donald H. Wolfe found someone who could testify to the fact that Carmen had known Monroe. He was actor and friend of Frank Sinatra, Brad Dexter. However, Dexter could go no further than to say they knew each other and there is no indication in Wolfe's book that the actor thought the Carmen/Monroe friendship was anything other than an acquaintainship. In any case Carmen's scurrilous statements should not have been accepted without corroborative evidence. And if Carmen had really been a close friend then why did mutual friends not come forward to support her allegations?

The third main witness to the RFK/Monroe alleged relationship is Fred Otash who claims to have heard tape recordings of RFK and Monroe together. In 1985, the former Hollywood private investigator told the 'Los Angeles Times' that on the night of Monroe's death he had received a panicky late-night phone call from Peter Lawford saying Monroe was dead. Lawford told Otash that Monroe and RFK had a screaming fight about their relationship that evening. Otash said RFK arrived at Lawford's house, nervously telling Lawford: 'She's ranting and raving. I'm concerned about her and what may come out of this.'

Otash went on to tell the 'Los Angeles Times' that Lawford begged him to rush to Monroe's house and 'pick up any information that linked her to the Kennedys' before it could get into the wrong hands. Otash said he sent an assistant to do the sweep. (The assistant has never been named and has not come forward to corroborate Otash's statement.)

Later, in 1991, Otash told author James Spada (1991): "He (Lawford) told me that Bobby Kennedy had broken off the affair with Marilyn and that she was hysterical and calling the White House and the Justice Department and Hyannis Port, insisting that Bobby get in touch with her. And that the Department of Justice had called Bobby in San Francisco and told him, 'You'd better get your ass down to LA because she's out of control.'"[12]

However, a close friend of Otash, acclaimed novelist, James Ellroy and author of 'American Tabloid', said Otash had confided in him his belief that the RFK/Monroe affair was bogus. Ellroy told the 'Richmond Review': "As much research as I've done, one fact stands fast - I think Robert Kennedy was a great man, perhaps the chief crime fighter of the twentieth century in America, and a paragon of moral rectitude. Parenthetically he did not play bury the brisket and pour the pork with Marilyn Monroe...I used to be friends with Shakedown Freddy Otash, private eye to the stars in LA circa 1955 to 1965. God bless him, Freddy died recently at the age of 71...Freddy told me he is convinced that Bobby never had an affair with Marilyn Monroe that, at the time of Marilyn's death, Bobby was interceding on Jack's behalf, trying to get this crazy woman to quit calling the President of the United States at the White House. She just kicked off coincidentally."[13]

The motives of 'witnesses' like Jeanne Carmen, Robert Slatzer and Fred Otash can be understood as they all had a vested interest in promoting the RFK/Monroe affair. However, Peter Lawford is an authoritative source simply because he was the President's brother-in-law and his story cannot be dismissed easily. Unfortunately, there have been so many versions of 'his story' that it is difficult to sort fact from fantasy. In the final few years of his life, Lawford was dependent on drink and drugs and was altogether destitute. Perhaps he saw the embellishments to his story as a way of resurrecting his failing career. No one will ever really know. A number of authors claim to have interviewed some of Marilyn's friends who said Peter Lawford had told them about the supposed RFK/Monroe affair. C. David Heymann (1998) claims he spoke to Peter Lawford a year before the actor's death in 1984. He said that Lawford described, in full detail, the RFK/Greenson 'conspiracy' to subdue Monroe on the afternoon of the star's death. According to Heymann, Lawford told him: "I certainly think Marilyn would have held a press conference. She was determined to gain back her self-esteem. She was unbalanced at the time - and Bobby was determined to shut her up, regardless of the consequences. It was the craziest thing he ever did - and I was crazy enough to let it happen."[14]

If Lawford's comments are correct - and until this time he had consistently denied RFK was anywhere near Monroe's house on the day of her death - then the scenario changes. But this does not mean that the Kennedys had a hand in her death or that RFK was having an affair with the actress. It only means that RFK took the opportunity, on his West Coast trip, to visit with the actress and tell her to stop contacting himself and his brother. There is no credible evidence available which would lead to the conclusion that RFK had engaged in an affair with Monroe or that the Kennedys had her killed in order to 'silence' her.

The first issue to consider in examining Lawford's remarks to Heymann is why the actor chose to make his statements to this particular author one year before his death. During this same period Lawford had been interviewed by author Anthony Summers. Heymann had apparently succeeded where Summers failed. Summers told an IPC Magazines reporter: "I have to admit that I never did do an interview with Lawford (about Monroe) because as soon as I referred to the night of Marilyn's death he burst into tears...real tears. That wouldn't normally have prevented me from asking him a lot of tough questions later, but it was early in my research and I expected to see him again. His death came before I was ready."[15]

And if Peter Lawford opened up to Heymann it would have been a definite change of heart. Lawford consistently refused to talk about the Kennedys even when he had been snubbed by them after his divorce from Pat Lawford. On his deathbed on Christmas Eve 1984, he told a 'Los Angeles Times' reporter: "Even if these things were true (Monroe's relationship with the Kennedys) I wouldn't talk about them. That's just the way I am."[16]

In the years before his death, drink and drugs had taken their toll on the President's brother-in-law. Lawford frequently said things in a drunken state to his wives and friends which he later regretted. Deborah Gould, Lawford's third wife for a brief period of time, stated to a reporter that Lawford had informed her that RFK had indeed been at Monroe's house the day of her death and that RFK and Monroe had been having an affair.

Her statement is contradicted by Lawford's last wife, Patricia Seaton Lawford (1988). She had been a common law wife to Lawford for 11 years and married him on his deathbed. In statements made to the 'New York Post', Patricia Seaton Lawford said that Gould had invented the stories about the Monroe/RFK relationship. She also told the 'Post's' Neal Travis that C. David Heymann fabricated stories about RFK and Monroe in his book, 'RFK: a candid biography'.[17]

According to Patricia Seaton Lawford, her husband discussed the Kennedys and Monroe with her on many occasions. Her account of the Kennedy/Monroe story is credible and authoritative precisely because she was close to the actor for 11 years, unlike Gould who had a stormy and superficial relationship with Lawford for a brief period of time - their relationship lasted for only a few months. But why do murder conspiracy authors choose Gould over Seaton as a credible source for Lawford's RFK/Monroe story? Simply stated, it is because Gould's account supports the murder conspiracy theory.

Patricia Seaton Lawford is adamant that the RFK/Monroe stories have no basis in truth: "Although there would be rumours of Bobby Kennedy's infidelity, Peter frequently told me they were not true...Peter said that in most instances where Bobby was linked to some woman it was because of Jack...the situation (of the RFK/Monroe connection) started when Bobby had a talk with Marilyn concerning her constant calls to the private quarters of the White House. She was told she was not going to be First Lady. She was not even a serious affair for the President."[18]

According to author Donald Spoto, all of Peter Lawford's closest friends, including William Asher, Milton Ebbins and Joseph Naar: "insist the Monroe/Kennedy friendship was platonic".[19]

To deal with sources whose credibility is unsound is one thing. Much more difficult is tracking the changes these sources make to their stories. Surprising new details emerge in the re-telling. One can only speculate that memory improves with age - or that some sources have an inherent difficulty in sticking to the truth. For example, hairdresser Mickey Song told James Spada (1991) for his book, 'The man who kept the secrets': "While I was working on Marilyn she was extremely nervous and uptight. The door (to the backstage dressing room) was open and Bobby Kennedy was pacing back and forth outside, watching us. Finally he came into the dressing room and said to me, 'Would you step out for a minute?' When I did, he closed the door behind him, and he stayed in there for about fifteen minutes. Then he left and I went back in. Marilyn was all dishevelled. She giggled and said, 'Could you help me get myself back together?'"[20]

We are thus left with the impression that Robert Kennedy spent an intimate 15 minutes with the Hollywood actress. However, three years later Song gave an interview to Donald Wolfe (1998) and a different impression is gained as to what exactly happened: "While I was working on Marilyn, she was extremely nervous and uptight. The dressing room door was open and Bobby Kennedy was pacing back and forth outside, glaring at us. Finally he came into the dressing room and said to me, 'Would you step out for a minute?' When I did, he closed the door behind him for about 15 minutes." So far there is nothing different in this version until Wolfe writes: "While waiting in the hall outside the dressing room, Mickey Song could hear Kennedy and Marilyn having an argument. The Attorney General's voice was growing louder and louder, and he was using expletives. When Kennedy came out he said to Song, 'You can go in now', and then unexpectedly grabbed Song by the arm and demanded 'By the way do you like her?'. Song recalled nodding enthusiastically that he did. 'Well I think she's a rude f...... bitch! Kennedy exclaimed as he stormed down the hall."[21] The implication from this account is that Robert Kennedy was angry at Monroe for her tardiness in keeping the President waiting.

Confusion arises when authors also misstate the facts. Matthew Smith (1997) in his book 'The men who murdered Marilyn', stated that Peter Lawford, worried about Monroe, telephoned a friend, Joe Naar, at approximately 11 p.m. on the night of Monroe's death. Smith relates that Lawford asked him to check on the actress. Before he left the house, however, Naar received another call from Lawford telling him it was a false alarm and there was no need to go after all. However, it was not Lawford who made the second phone call to Naar but Lawford's manager, Milt Ebbins, who countermanded Lawford's request saying everything was fine.[22]

With this simple conscious or unconscious error, Smith leads the reader into a sinister scenario with a list of questions: "What did he (Lawford) learn which prompted him to ring Naarr (sic) in the first place and what happened to make him cancel everything a few minutes later? Did he obtain information he was not revealing? Was he being updated on events at Marilyn's? And was he trying to establish witnesses to a timescale which suggested that all was well with Marilyn at 11.30 p.m.?"[23]

Smith's credibility as a Kennedy scholar was evident when he stated that RFK received the Democratic nomination for president - (he didn't).[24] The reader's confidence in Smith's ability to understand the circumstances of Monroe's death is not enhanced by this inaccuracy.

Smith and Wolfe also misinterpret quotes they find in other works. In 'The men who murdered Marilyn', Smith (1997) states: "When Marilyn spoke to journalist Sidney Skolsky on the telephone on Saturday morning (the day of her death) she told him she was going to see Robert Kennedy that evening."[25] Smith provides no source for the statement but Donald Wolfe does. Wolfe wrote (1998): "During the morning Marilyn spoke on the phone to Sidney Skolsky and mentioned that she planned to see Bobby Kennedy later that day."[26] Wolfe gives as his source page 305 of Anthony Summers' (1986) book 'Goddess'. What Summers actually wrote was: "From his home across the city, reporter Sidney Skolsky made his regular weekend call to Marilyn. He had been alarmed by her confidences about the Kennedy family and, as on other recent occasions had his daughter Steffi listen in on an extension. He felt he wanted a witness. 'What are you doing tonight?', Skolsky asked cheerily. By now Marilyn appeared to have a plan for the evening. She replied, 'Maybe I'll go down to the beach. Everyone's going to be there.' As Skolsky's daughter remembers it, Marilyn said she expected to be seeing one of the Kennedys at the Lawford house."[27]

We can see how the indiscriminate use of this quotation by two authors has been used to prop up their versions of events, 'proving' that Robert Kennedy had been in Los Angeles that day. Summers did not interview Sidney Skolsky for his book. He interviewed his daughter who had been reminiscing about events which occurred twenty years earlier. It should also be remembered that Peter Lawford's wife, Pat, was also 'one of the Kennedys'.

Furthermore, both Smith and Wolfe fail to tell their readers that Sidney Skolsky and all of Peter Lawford's closest friends, including William

Asher, Milton Ebbins and Joseph Naar, insisted that the Monroe/RFK friendship was platonic. Skolsky said: "As for Robert Kennedy, she never mentioned him...".[28] The statement made by Skolsky's daughter: 'He had been alarmed by her confidences about the Kennedy family', refers to Skolsky's knowledge that Monroe had been intimate with John Kennedy.

Wolfe also uses Patricia Seaton Lawford, Eunice Murray and Murray's son-in-law handyman, Norman Jefferies, as sources for the mythical June 23rd dinner party at the Lawfords and RFK's subsequent visit to Monroe's house the next day. Wolfe writes: "On Saturday June 23rd...Bobby Kennedy flew to Los Angeles and Peter Lawford arranged for Marilyn and Kennedy to meet. Kennedy was to attend a dinner party at the Lawford beach house, and Marilyn was invited...According to Patricia Seaton Lawford, the purpose of Bobby Kennedy's visit was to stop Marilyn from trying to contact the President...The following day (Sunday 24th June 1962) Bobby paid a visit to Marilyn's home..."[29]

There is certainly no mention of that particular weekend visit in Patricia Seaton Lawford's memoirs. Eunice Murray later retracted her story about Robert Kennedy's 'visit'. In any case Murray's only statement about an RFK visit to Monroe's house was in connection with the day the actress died - a statement which she retracted before her death. Wolfe's singular source must, therefore, be Norman Jefferies who related his story about the death of Monroe for Wolfe's 1998 book 'The assassination of Marilyn Monroe'. They must be suspect coming as they do 36 years after Monroe's death and, more importantly, many years after his mother-in-law's 'confession'.

However, the unreliability of Wolfe's sources are irrelevant when various pieces of documentary evidence is considered which prove that RFK's whereabouts during 1962 speak for themselves. Desk diaries, telephone logs for 1961 and 1962 and FBI files (Hoover recorded everything RFK did and even had his FBI agents 'spy' on the Attorney General in the hope of gathering discreditory information) show that RFK and Monroe met three times at large dinner parties at Peter Lawford's Santa Monica house - 4th October 1961, 2nd February 1962 and 26th June (he arrived in Los Angeles that afternoon for a dinner party the next evening, returning to Washington D.C. the morning of 28th June 1962). On two other occasions in 1962, when RFK was in Los Angeles (24th and 25th March and 26th July), Monroe was in Palm Springs and Lake Tahoe. Telephone records document a telephone call on Monday 25th June 1962 that Monroe made to RFK's Washington office to confirm Kennedy's presence at the Lawford's on the following Wednesday evening; she spoke to RFK's secretary Angie Novello and the call lasted about 1 minute.[30]

If RFK had been with Monroe the previous Sunday then why would she need to call him on the Monday to remind him about the Lawford's party? And why would RFK make two journeys to the West Coast with only a one day interval in Washington D.C.?

'Sightings' of Robert Kennedy in Los Angeles on the day of Monroe's death have been included in every book which purports to show sinister reasons for her death. Many are credible coming as they do from sources which cannot be dismissed. Daryl Gates and Tom Reddin, ex-Los Angeles Police Chiefs, said that RFK had been seen at the Beverly Wiltshire Hotel on August 4th 1962.[31]

However, from the evidence obtained from FBI files and from statements made by RFK's host, the host's family and ranch workers, it is impossible that the Attorney General could have been in the city that day. Robert and Ethel Kennedy flew to San Francisco on Friday 3rd August 1962 and were met by their friend John Bates, his wife and family. They all insist that RFK had been in full sight of one member of the family or ranch workers for the full day. Dinner ended at approximately 10.30 p.m. and the party retired to bed shortly afterwards. On the Sunday morning they all attended Mass in the town of Gilroy. The Bates family stories have been rigorously researched and, unlike many tales about this sorry event, have the ring of truth.[32]

FBI Director, J. Edgar Hoover, who hated Robert Kennedy had kept a file on Monroe ever since she married Arthur Miller (Hoover viewed the playwright as a left-wing subversive). According to Ed Guthman, a close aide to the Attorney General: "It would have been impossible for Hoover not to have known about such goings-on had they occurred and he certainly would have used this information during Bobby's later campaign for office."[33]

Hoover biographer, Curt Gentry (1991), said the FBI knew no more than the average person about the connection between Monroe and Robert Kennedy: "Had he (known more), Hoover would almost certainly have used this information against Kennedy at a later date, when he ransacked his files for every bit of derogatory material he could find."[34] And had RFK contacted Hoover to have the FBI retrieve telephone company records, Hoover would have created a record to protect himself and to use as leverage.

Gentry said Hoover learned about the RFK/Monroe connection two weeks after the Hollywood star's death when Attorney General Kennedy confided to a Hoover aide. As noted in an FBI memo: "...he (RFK) was aware there had been several allegations concerning his possibly being involved with Marilyn Monroe. He said he'd at least met Marilyn, since she was a good friend of his sister, Pat Lawford, but that these allegations just had a way of growing beyond any semblance of truth."[35]

Some writers have used FBI documents to 'prove' Robert Kennedy had been having an affair with Monroe but they fail to discriminate between those reports emanating from agent observations and those which are the result of 'informant information'. It was an informant who prompted agents to report that: "Robert Kennedy was deeply involved emotionally with Marilyn Monroe and had repeatedly promised to divorce his wife to marry Marilyn. Eventually Marilyn realised that Bobby had no intention of marrying her."[36] It was the same type of 'informant information' that resulted in an FBI memo concerning John Kennedy's relationship with Inga Arvad to report her as a 'German Spy'. This information, of course, was erroneous.

Ed Guthman travelled all around the country with the Attorney General. He was with Robert Kennedy and Marilyn Monroe on at least two occasions. Guthman told author James Hilty, "I KNOW there was no affair."[37]

There is no credible evidence which shows that Monroe and the President's brother had an affair and, contrary to the claims made by author Anthony Summers, no part of the FBI files can safely substantiate an RFK/Monroe affair. The truth of the matter is that RFK had only a passing acquaintance with the Hollywood actress. Documentary evidence in the form of court transcripts, letters or phone records 'proving' such a relationship do not exist. A letter from Jean Kennedy Smith, RFK's sister, is the only piece of documentary evidence which can be possibly misinterpreted. It refers to Marilyn Monroe and Robert Kennedy as an 'item'[38], but Jean Smith has gone on record as saying the phrase was used as a 'joke'[39], no doubt in reference to Monroe's admiration for the President's brother and her determination to impress him with her knowledge of current affairs. Similarly, C. David Heymann (1998) wrongly used notes/letters passed between RFK and Pat Newcomb to substantiate an affair between those two.[40] The letters can only suggest a light-hearted communication between friends.

Correctly, some authors and newspaper reporters questioned the accounts of Monroe's death given to police investigators and official enquiries by the three people who were with Monroe when she died or who arrived at Monroe's house shortly afterwards - Dr Ralph Greenson, Dr Hyman Engelburg and Eunice Murray.

As Spoto (1993) recounts, Dr Greenson, Dr Engelburg and Monroe's housekeeper, Eunice Murray, are the keys to an understanding of what went on that night. What they did explains all the anomalies and inconsistencies in the evidence and testimony gathered at the time of Monroe's death. In their accounts to investigators of the early hours of the Sunday morning when the police were called to Monroe's home, these three witnesses put the time of Monroe's death at 3 a.m. At this time, according to Murray, she saw a light shinning from beneath Marilyn's bedroom door. This was the first inconsistency in Murray's story - a new thick-pile carpet had only recently been laid and it was impossible to see light emitting from the room. Thus began the chain of inconsistencies which eventually led to the bizarre and untruthful 'murder scenarios'. If Murray had been lying, what was she covering up?

Spoto paints a picture of Dr Ralph Greenson as a Svengali-like figure who had an unhealthy control over his famous patient. In turn his ego depended on his relationship with the actress. But Greenson, in the name of 'therapy', was cutting Monroe off from those people she considered her friends, not least Joe DiMaggio whom she intended to re-marry. Monroe was determined to rid herself of both Murray and Greenson. She guessed that Murray had been placed with her to 'spy' for Greenson.

Monroe told Murray that she was not needed anymore and there is strong evidence that she was angry and upset with Greenson and saw no place for him in her new life with DiMaggio. This fact alone makes a supposed relationship with RFK preposterous. On the Thursday before her death Monroe told store owner Bill Alexander: "...I'm so happy because I'm going to be married to someone I was married to once before."[41]

As Monroe's masseur and close friend, Ralph Roberts, said: "She deeply resented Greenson's use of her...He had tried to get rid of almost everyone in her life. But when he tried it with Joe (DiMaggio) - I think that's when she began to reconsider the whole thing."[42] Monroe was rebelling against Greenson who had controlled her life for too long not least in the way he used drugs as a control mechanism.

During her last day alive Monroe engaged in what amounted to a day's therapy session with Greenson, starting at 1 p.m. and lasting until about 7 p.m. with a break between approximately 3 p.m. and 4.30 p.m. By 4 p.m. when she visited the Lawford beach-house she appeared drugged and nervous. From the evidence Donald Spoto accumulated it appears likely that in the all-day session with Greenson she discussed the termination of her therapy with him.

At 5 p.m. Monroe took a call from Peter Lawford who was trying to assemble friends for a Saturday night supper. She declined but he said he would call back later. Around this time Greenson contacted Hyman Engleburg to come and give Monroe an injection which would help her sleep. Engleburg declined and Greenson was left to cope on his own. At 7.15 Greenson departed asking Murray to stay over at Monroe's house that night because he 'didn't want Marilyn to be alone'.

Over the years Greenson and Murray have given inconsistent accounts and the truth has escaped investigators mainly because of their repeatedly changing accounts of what exactly happened. But two telephone calls, according to Spoto, provide important clues to a final resolution of the Monroe mystery. The first call was from Joe DiMaggio Jnr., son of Monroe's second husband, baseball legend, Joe DiMaggio at 7 to 7.15 p.m. The conversation was pleasant and Monroe seemed in good spirits. The second call came from Peter Lawford at 7.40 or 7.45 p.m. Her speech was now slurred and almost inaudible. She said "Say goodbye to Pat, say goodbye to the President and say goodbye to yourself because you're a nice guy." Lawford tried to call back but the line was engaged. Frantic he telephoned his manager, Milt Ebbins. Ebbins told him not to go over to Marilyn's - how would it look, 'You're the President's brother-in-law'.

Within the space of half an hour Monroe had changed from laughing and chatting to a state of dying. Ebbins called Milton Rudin, Marilyn's attorney. Rudin then telephoned Eunice Murray who told him she had checked on Monroe and everything was fine. However, Rudin had the feeling she had not checked at all. Rudin then called Ebbins who reported to Lawford that all was well but still Lawford was worried. Rudin then received a call from Greenson well before midnight to say the actress was dead. He drove to Monroe's house and encountered Greenson and Murray. It is likely an ambulance was called around midnight, but by this time the actress was dead and, as California law prohibited the transport of corpses by ambulance, it returned to base.

But the police were not called until much later - around 4 a.m. - why? According to Greenson it was because they had to get permission from the publicity department of Monroe's studio - an absurdity. When the police arrived Eunice Murray was operating the washing machine - yet another bizarre event in this sorry tale.

Donald Spoto maintains that the most logical reasoning for these strange events that Saturday night was that Greenson had asked Murray to sedate Monroe with an drug laden enema - this would account for the purple discolouration of the star's colon. He could not reach Dr Engleburg and, therefore, he had used Murray to carry out the process. The reason for sedating Monroe was to end the conversation Monroe had been having with Greenson - Greenson perhaps hoped that when Monroe awoke the next morning she would have changed her mind about ending Greenson's services. However, in asking Murray to carry out the act of sedating the Hollywood star, Greenson was committing an unprofessional act and if it was ever revealed it would be the end of his career. Both Murray and Greenson thus had something to hide.

Unaware of exactly how many Nembutal pills Monroe had ingested (she had probably been taking them throughout the day), Greenson sedated Monroe with chloral hydrate. The coroner who actually performed the autopsy found no pills in Monroe's stomach and so it was unlikely she committed suicide. Furthermore, there were no signs of needle marks. What the coroner did find was a colonic discolouration consistent with the use of an enema. Monroe frequently used them but, unfortunately, her enema contained chloral hydrate which is potentially lethal when taken with Nembutal - a fact which would not have been known to Monroe. But because Greenson was unaware of how many Nembutal the actress had taken, he was not in the position to make an informed judgement when the sedative was administered.

Greenson and Murray needed time to consider the awful circumstances they found themselves in and this would account for the 'lost' time between Monroe's death and the arrival of the police.

The only rational alternative reason for Monroe's demise is to consider her addiction to drugs as fundamental to the anomalous occurrences in the state of her body at the time of her death. Monroe was a drug addict and drug addicts tend to increase the dosage in their bodies, developing a tolerance for the drug. As the dosage increases the addict feels no different from when he/she started with the original dose (ably demonstrated with reference to Elvis Presley's drug taking). But now the effects become dangerous or perhaps fatal. Monroe increased her levels to the point where it would not have been difficult for her to cross the danger line. And how can we account for the lack of drug residue in Monroe's stomach? An addict's stomach becomes used to the drug of choice and it easily passes into the intestines. Addicts routinely die with no trace of the pills in the stomach and, in Monroe's case, this is entirely consistent with the Coroner's report. An empty stomach does not preclude the possibility that she digested the pills over a number of hours and the high levels of barbiturates found in Monroe's liver testifies to this.

It has not helped matters when authors of popular biographies or murder conspiracy books have deliberately or unconsciously ignored, manipulated or used facts to pursue their investigation into Marilyn Monroe's death. But matters are not improved when authoritative historians enter the field giving credence to incredible theories. Writing in the 'Sunday Telegraph' British historian, Paul Johnson reviewed C. David Heymann's biography of RFK, and he said: "When Jack wanted to discard Marilyn Monroe he passed her on to Bobby, who used her and discarded her in turn. He clearly bears some responsibility for her suicide..."[43] Thus the waters again become muddied and murder conspiracy authors are given credence by a reputable but unwitting historian.

Key sources like Patricia Newcomb, friend and assistant to Marilyn Monroe, and Ralph Roberts, Monroe's masseur, who was constantly in her company have been ignored. This is a central weakness in books which try to 'prove' a Robert Kennedy/Marilyn Monroe affair or seek to popularise murder conspiracies involving the Kennedys. As Newcomb told author, J. Randall Taraborrelli (1997): "I knew Bobby very well, better than Marilyn did in a lot of ways. However, you didn't even have to know him well to know that he would never have left Ethel. And with all those children? Come on. I think she may have come on to him, but I don't believe anything happened between them; just from the little things he said to me about her, I don't think so."[44]

Arthur Schlesinger (1978) interviewed Roberts for his book 'RFK and his times': "In other moods she (Monroe) spoke more reasonably. She once mentioned the rumours about Robert Kennedy to her masseur Ralph Roberts, with whom, according to (Norman) Mailer she had a 'psychic communion that is obviously not ordinary'...'It's not true,' she said to Roberts, 'I like him (RFK), but not physically'."[45]

Perhaps the final words on the Kennedys/Monroe affair should be left to Robert Kennedy's closest friend, Ken O'Donnell, and author, James Hilty (1997), whose excellent book 'Robert Kennedy – brother protector' should stand as a literary monument which meets the highest standards required of historical writing and research. O'Donnell told Lester David (1988): "I knew this man as well as anybody. I was intimately associated with him for years and knew everything he ever did, and I know for a fact that this Marilyn Monroe story is absolute bullshit."[46] Hilty (1997) wrote: "Perhaps the Marilyn-Bobby story has gained undeserved credibility in the popular culture because in today's intellectual and cultural climate, sophists regard knowledge as socially or culturally constructed, values and truth are subjective, and history has multiple meanings, none definitive. Perhaps its credibility springs from the popular attraction to conspiracy theories fed by tabloid journalism, where shocking allegations and personal opinion carry more weight than the thoughtful evaluation of historical sources. And some people simply will insist on their right to their opinion that the story was so...No amount of exculpatory evidence, correction of historical error, or logic will dissuade them, as long as others with a stake in perpetuating the story loudly and persistently assure them it was so. Finally, any historian who criticises the Marilyn-Bobby story risks being labelled an adjunct of the 'Camelot School' or, as one Kennedy critic charged of being 'obsessed with protecting the Kennedy image.'"[47]

Notes

1. Spoto, D. (1993). *Marilyn Monroe - the biography*, Chatto and Windus. p. 669.

2. Sullivan, W. (1967). *The Bureau - my 30 years in Hoover's FBI*, Little Brown. p. 56.

3. Spoto, D. (1993). *Marilyn Monroe - the biography*, Chatto and Windus. p. 545.

4. Schlesinger, A. M. (1978). *Robert Kennedy and his times*, Houghton Mifflin Co. p. 636.

5. Spoto, D. (1993). *Marilyn Monroe - the biography*, Chatto and Windus. p. 672.

6. *Ibid.*

7. Giancana, S. and Giancana, C. (1992). *Double cross*, MacDonald. p. 313.

8. *see* Chapter 9 'The conspiracy theorists' In Ayton, M. (1999). *Questions of conspiracy*, Horseshoe Publications.

9. Spoto, D. (1993). *Marilyn Monroe -* the biography, Chatto and Windus. p. 250.

10. *Ibid*, p. 523.

11. Heymann, C. D. (1998). *RFK – a candid biography*, William Heinemann. p. 313.

12. Spada, J. (1991). *The man who kept the secrets*, Bantam Press. p. 5.

13. Duncan, P. 'Call me dog - an interview with James Ellroy', *Richmond Review*, July 1997. (http://www.richmondreview.co.uk).

14. Heymann, C. D. (1998). *RFK – a candid biography*, William Heinemann. p. 322.

15. Thomas, S. 'Marilyn', *Woman Magazine*, 26 October 1985, p. 11.

16. Spada, J. (1991). *The man who kept the secrets*, Bantam Press. p. 330.

17. Travis, N. 'Battle stations over RFK tell - all', *New York Post*, 16 September 1998. (http://www.nypostonline.com).

18. Lawford, P. S. (1988). *The Peter Lawford story*, Carrol and Graf Publishers Inc. p. 87.

19. Spoto, D. (1993). *Marilyn Monroe - the biography*, Chatto and Windus. p. 546.

20. Spada, J. (1991). *The man who kept the secrets*, Bantam Press. p. 303.

21. Wolfe, D. H. (1998). *The assassination of Marilyn Monroe*, Little Brown and Company. p. 410.

22. Smith, M. (1997). *The men who murdered Marilyn*, Bloomsbury. p. 33.

23. *Ibid*, p. 33.

24. *Ibid*, p. 234.

25. *Ibid*, p. 53.

26. Wolfe, D. H. (1998). *The assassination of Marilyn Monroe*, Little Brown and Company. p. 453.

27. Summers, A. (1986). *Goddess - the secret lives of Marilyn Monroe*, Sphere Books. p. 305.

28. Spoto, D. (1993). *Marilyn Monroe - the biography*, Chatto and Windus. p. 546.

29. Wolfe, D. H. (1998). *The assassination of Marilyn Monroe*, Little Brown and Company. p. 430.

30. Hilty, J. W. (1997). *Robert Kennedy – brother protector*, Temple University Press. p. 554.

31. *Ibid*, p. 455.

32. David, L. and David, I. (1986). *Bobby Kennedy - the making of a folk hero*, Sidgwick and Jackson. p. 177; Hilty, J. W. (1997). *Robert Kennedy – brother protector*, Temple University Press. pp. 245 and 554; Spoto, D. (1993). *Marilyn Monroe - the biography*, Chatto and Windus. p. 622.

33. *Ibid*, p. 546.

34. Gentry, C. (1991*). J. Edgar Hoover - the man and the secrets*, WW Norton and Co. p. 494.

35. FBI Case File No. 105-40018, FBI. (http://foia.fbi.gov/monroe.htm).

36. *Ibid*.

37. Hilty, J. W. (1997). *Robert Kennedy – brother protector*, Temple University Press. p. 247.

38. Beran, M. K. (1998). *The last patrician - Bobby Kennedy and the end of American aristocracy*, St Matrin's Griffin. p. 179.

39. Oppenheimer, J. (1994). *The other Mrs Kennedy*, St Martin's Paperbacks. p. 317.

40. Hilty, J. W. (1997). *Robert Kennedy – brother protector*, Temple University Press. p. 248.

41. Spoto, D. (1993). *Marilyn Monroe - the biography*, Chatto and Windus. p. 622.

42. *Ibid*, p. 619.

43. Johnson, P. 'RFK - The Star Report', *Sunday Telegraph* (Sunday Review), 20 September 1998.

44. Taraborrelli, J. R. (1997). *Sinatra - the man behind the myth*, Mainstream Publishing Projects. p. 244.

45. Schlesinger, A. M. (1978). *Robert Kennedy and his times*, Houghton Mifflin Co. p. 637.

46. David, L. (1988). *JFK - the wit, the charm, the tears*, Paperjacks. p. 176.

47. Hilty, J. W. (1997). *Robert Kennedy – brother protector*, Temple University Press. p. 244.

Chapter 11

The Lost President

How close did Robert Kennedy come to winning the Presidency?

"A man does not show his greatness by being at one extremity but rather by touching both at once."

Albert Camus, 'Resistance, Rebellion and Death'

For the past 30 years political scientists and historians have debated the question of whether Robert Kennedy would have secured the 1968 Democratic presidential nomination and would have gone on to win the presidency against his Republican rival, Richard Nixon. William Manchester, Arthur M. Schlesinger Jnr. and others believed Robert Kennedy would have become president had he not been killed in Los Angeles. Manchester wrote: "There can be little doubt that, had he been spared, he, not Hubert Humphrey, would have been the Democratic nominee in 1968, and that Bob would have defeated Richard Nixon."[1] American historian, James T. Patterson (1996), was typical of those historians who took a different view. Patterson concluded that it was unlikely Kennedy would have secured the Democratic nomination against his main rival Vice-President, Hubert. H. Humphrey. Patterson wrote: "Could Kennedy have won the nomination if he had lived? That became one of the most frequently asked questions in the history of modern American politics. When he was killed, he needed 800-odd additional delegates to win the nomination. Some of them might have come from McCarthy - if McCarthy, an unpredictable man, proved willing to let them go. Others might have abandoned Humphrey, whose chances then seemed hopeless for November. Still, the Johnson-Humphrey forces maintained a firm hold on the party machinery, which they manipulated without qualm at the convention. Johnson hated Kennedy as much as Kennedy hated him. All these political realities would have worked against Kennedy's chances for the nomination."[2]

In adopting their positions without concrete evidence, both Schlesinger and Manchester failed to 'prove' their contentions, relying instead on intuitive speculation based on their knowledge of the candidate and their own understanding of the American political system. And whilst Patterson's critical assessment of Kennedy's chances are based on political realities of the time, it is also evident that he has ignored a great deal of evidence which suggests his conclusions are wrong. Historians are rightly split on the subject. No one can say for sure what would have happened: a hypothetical study of this nature is fraught with problems since any number of unseen events could have derailed Kennedy's campaign. However, it is the opinion of the present author that a substantial body of evidence has been ignored in the negative assessments of Kennedy's chances. This evidence suggests that, on the balance of probability, forces were moving in Kennedy's favour and would have ensured his nomination by the Democratic Party and, ultimately, a successful campaign against the Republican nominee, Richard Nixon.

Robert Kennedy's constituency

Robert Kennedy became a different kind of man and a different kind of politician after his brother's death in 1963. He inherited the national grief over his brother's death which afforded him something of a charismatic image in politics. But he became, in a personal way, metamorphosed by the tragedy. He began to read the Greek philosophers searching for answers to the tragic elements of life. This sense of tragedy and suffering forced him to empathise with those groups in society who had been alienated by the American experience. He began to visit Indian reservations, poor areas in the Mississippi delta, the city ghettos and farming regions where Hispanic-Americans were exploited. Experiencing pain himself, it was easy for him to identify with their position in American society. He also began to realise that the war in Vietnam was tearing the nation apart as the increasing number of body bags arrived on American shores.

Kennedy drew great support from anti-war students across the nation. The radicalism of 1968 had been split between three groups. The counter-culture was made up of thousands of young 'drop-outs' who believed America had become corrupt and arrogant depending, as it did, on the acquisition of wealth as a measure of greatness. There were the anti-war dissidents who opposed the war for reasons of humanity or national interest. And there were the hard-line ideological groups like the Black Panthers, Students For a Democratic Society and the terrorist 'Weathermen' who rejected any form of association with the 'System'.

The group which supported Robert Kennedy and Eugene McCarthy in the 1968 election was the nucleus of the 'Movement' against the War in Vietnam, made up primarily of young people and the disillusioned middle classes who believed that President Johnson must be replaced if the nation was not to self-destruct. They did not interpret the war as a metaphor for a hopeless capitalistic, imperialistic and technocratic society.

This anti-war majority was itself split between the supporters of McCarthy and the supporters of Kennedy and included the old and new left, militant Christians, intellectuals and moderate African-Americans. However, the real opposition to the War in Vietnam came from campuses across America. According to the Commission on Student Disorders, headed by Archibald Cox, the University was: "The surrogate for all the tensions and frustrations of American policy in Vietnam."[3]

As marginal members of society, students as a group, like African-Americans, were more likely than other groups to be attracted to areas critical of society. This was the basic sociological criteria that gave rise to the student Left and the new radicalism in general. More immediate influences in the 1960s were John Kennedy's presidency, coming as it did after the quietude of the Eisenhower years, and the Civil Rights movement, which initiated a generation of students into protest politics. The vast majority of students were predisposed to work within the system and recognised that power lay with the 'unblack, unpoor and unyoung' and their strength was in their ability to be activist campaigners for anti-war candidates.

The majority of the young student campaigners supported Robert Kennedy although many thousands still remained loyal to McCarthy after Kennedy's entry into the presidential race in March 1968. They supported Kennedy because he was both radical in his policy positions and, as an established and charismatic politician with a nationwide following, he was more likely to fulfil their ambitions to end the war.

Kennedy also drew support from the students because of his empathy with the young. In speech after speech on college campuses, in the years after his election as Senator from New York, he said that the present generation was the most idealistic and generous of all generations. In a speech he gave at Kansas University, Kennedy had opened with a quote from William Allen White: "If our colleges and universities do not breed men who riot, who rebel, who attack life with all the youthful vision and vigour then there is something wrong with our colleges. The more riots that come on college campuses the better the world for tomorrow."[4] No other politician in America could have 'gotton' away with giving this speech.

Kennedy often quoted the existentialist philosopher, Albert Camus, in his speeches to college students. In the 1968 campaign it appeared that Camus' themes merged with his own - man must be neither a victim nor an executioner. A man must rebel but with a sense of limits and moderation. Men are not happy and they must die. Action and courage are everything.

In the years shortly before his candidacy, Kennedy's staff accepted more invitations from student groups than from religious or civic organisations. During February 1967 Kennedy met with the New Left radical leader, Tom Hayden, because he wanted to open up a line of communication to the student Left. Hayden came away from the meeting admiring Kennedy and sympathetic to his radical liberalism. 20 years after RFK's death, Hayden wrote about Kennedy in his book 'Reunion' and argued that Kennedy would have won the nomination and election, retaining Hubert Humphrey's basic vote, taken votes from George Wallace and inspired large numbers of disaffected voters that Humphrey found it difficult to rouse.[5]

It had been accepted all along that McCarthy's strength was limited and based upon a narrow middle-class constituency. And it was the judgement of most political observers that McCarthy could never solidify the differing elements within the Democratic Party. Nevertheless, Kennedy did need McCarthy's support if he was to secure the Democratic nomination. After his victory in the June 4th California primary, Kennedy believed McCarthy could be swayed by the offer of Secretary of State in a Kennedy Administration.[6]

Robert Kennedy was also supported by the vast majority of African-Americans who turned out in droves to vote for him in the primary campaigns. In a survey published in the July 29th 1968 edition of 'New York' magazine, 92% of the residents of Harlem said the assassination of Robert Kennedy affected them as much, if not more, than the assassination of John Kennedy. In the California primary campaign, there were dozens of African-American districts where the turnout exceeded 90% and with Kennedy getting more than 90% of the actual vote. Furthermore, Gallup polls frequently gave him high ratings amongst the African-American districts across the nation. When asked about their choice for president against all the leading contenders, Kennedy came out top every time.[7]

There is also evidence to conclude that Martin Luther King was ready to throw his support behind Kennedy shortly before the Civil Rights leader's tragic assassination in April 1968. King's aide, Stanley Levinson, said:"...his mind was made up. He had decided that he (King) would support Bobby Kennedy...No question: if he had lived, he would have supported Bobby Kennedy."[8] Walter Fauntroy, another close King associate quoted King as saying: "We've got to get behind Bobby now that he's in."[9] Andrew Young said: "...Bobby Kennedy had been with us in Atlanta at Martin's funeral. And many of us began to see in him a hope for the future. We kind of transferred a little of our loyalty, a little of our trust, and a little of our hope to him, and now he was gone too."[10]

Paradoxically, Robert Kennedy was also supported by American working class whites, many of whom were racists. Their support was forthcoming not simply because of the family name and the charisma Robert Kennedy had inherited from his brother the President. They responded to Kennedy because he talked to them and expressed their views and needs even while addressing himself directly to the grievances of African-Americans, Hispanics and Native-Americans. They responded to his call for decentralised government and grass roots democracy. Many, of course, voted for Kennedy for the same reasons they voted for McCarthy in the New Hampshire primary - not because he was an anti-war candidate especially or saw the war as immoral - but because they did not like the Administration's indecisiveness about the war. They would have equally applauded an all-out effort to win the war or a withdrawal of troops.

Writing in the 'Village Voice' magazine after Kennedy's death, Paul Cowan summed up the importance of Kennedy's candidacy: "I realised for the first time how important Kennedy's candidacy had been (for) he was the last liberal politician who could communicate with white working-class America."[11]

Because of the growing social and political dissatisfaction with the American government the role of Robert Kennedy became crucial. He was at the exact median point of American idealism and American power. He understood the potency of America's idealism as a domestic if not an international force and yet he had also exercised power whilst a member of the executive branch of government. He was also a bridge. In a transitional period in American politics when old coalitions were crumbling, Kennedy's knowledge of the country's mood, of the new political forces at work and of the old politics equipped him uniquely to practice this transitional politics. He was in harmony with the anti-establishment resentment toward participatory democracy and yet he knew that the old power brokers still held sway over the nominating process. And Kennedy knew how to enter the 'smoke-filled' back rooms.

Kennedy's chances in winning the Democratic nomination and the November 1968 election

Robert Kennedy was the most popular politician within the Democratic Party.[12] In the Harris poll published in the 23rd April 1968 edition of 'Newsweek', Kennedy led by 37% to Humphrey's 24% and McCarthy's 22% amongst the Democratic 'rank and file'. He also had an impressive string of primary victories with the exception of Oregon. And he was the acknowledged leader of the 'new politics'. Kennedy was a radical-liberal supported by the young, black and working class, but unlike George McGovern in the election of 1972, he never left the mainstream of the Democratic Party.

In order to influence the party 'bosses', Kennedy's strategy had been to beat both Humphrey and McCarthy so clearly in the primaries that there would be no doubt that he would be the man who could win for them in November against the likely Republican candidate, Richard Nixon. Kennedy clearly accomplished most of his goals, climaxing in the California victory on the day he was killed.

After California, Kennedy's image as a winner was set; he had beaten McCarthy and Humphrey not only in California but also in South Dakota - Humphrey's 'backyard'. This was perhaps the least noted political event of the year and yet its significance was undeniably great. Kennedy was ready to carry off his next set of convention delegates in the state he represented in the Senate - New York.

The most important 'party boss' in 1968 was Mayor Richard J. Daley of Chicago. Kennedy needed Daley's support for a number of reasons; Daley held the Illinois State party machine in his pocket and, as the convention was due to be held in Chicago, the mayor's influence within the party had been enhanced. Kennedy had long known that Daley's position on the Vietnam war was 'dovish'. In April 1968, Daley's hand-picked candidate for the United States Senate, Illinois Attorney- General William G. Clark, declared his "grave concern" over the conduct of the war [13] - a sign that Daley was deciding a possible shift from his previous position of support for President Johnson. At that time Kennedy had remarked, "Dick Daley is the Ball-Game." It was also known that, as Robert Kennedy's son, Maxwell, said many years later, "Mayor Daley was like a father to him." [14]

Some time after Clark's remarks, Daley had told Kennedy that he thought Johnson's Vietnam policy was wrong; that Johnson should have "cashed in his chips a long time ago." [15] But Daley did not want to make a break with Johnson or have Kennedy split the Democratic Party. Daley made no move to support Kennedy during the primary campaigns but there were signs that his support was forthcoming. Daley acknowledged this fact after Kennedy's death when he said that Robert Kennedy had been his first choice.[16] This was confirmed after the presidential election when Hubert Humphrey remarked to the press that Chicago had been a "tragedy" and that: "Mayor Daley didn't exactly break his heart over me." Daley responded to these reports by saying his preference in the first place had been "the name of a former president".[17]

Other signs of Daley's support were less evident but nonetheless important. Daley and Kennedy were both Catholics and the Mayor had supported John Kennedy's presidential bid in 1960. President Johnson, one of the most astute politicians in the post World War II America, thought as early as April 1968 that Daley's support would eventually go to Kennedy. He told his Vice-President that Daley and (political boss) Hughes would probably come out for Bobby.[18]

The lynchpin for Kennedy's strategy after the California victory was to challenge Hubert Humphrey to debate over the key issues in the campaign: the War in Vietnam, growing discord in American cities and the War on Poverty. McCarthy had been effectively neutralised after Kennedy's victory. He would need to persuade the McCarthy forces that they had nowhere else to go. This was eventually demonstrated during the Chicago convention in August when McCarthy was willing to throw his support behind Edward Kennedy. And two of McCarthy's strongest supporters, John Kenneth Galbraith (famous economist and author) and Allard Lowenstein (who had started the 'Dump Johnson movement in 1967) after the California victory, indicated to Kennedy aide, Richard Goodwin, that they were ready to transfer their allegiance to Kennedy.[19]

Robert Kennedy had just beaten Humphrey in the state in which he was born, South Dakota. Kennedy told his advisors: "I'm going to chase his ass all over the country."[20] He believed that debating Humphrey in Rhode Island in the coming month would result in a Kennedy victory. Beyond that he would need to wrest support for Humphrey from the big city bosses and the big industrial states that had no primaries.

In the 'Newsweek' delegate poll published the week before the California primary, 989 delegates were perceived as leaning towards Humphrey, 713 to Kennedy and 280 to McCarthy. 349 were uncommitted. According to 'Newsweek' if Kennedy did not win California and South Dakota and if Humphrey could win delegates in Pennsylvania, Ohio and Michigan and gain Daley's support, Humphrey could win on the first ballot. This sequence of events, of course, did not happen. Kennedy won the primaries and was ready to receive Daley's support. A second ballot would have been more favourable to Kennedy than Humphrey due to the logical assumption that McCarthy would have to throw his support behind Kennedy. Throwing his support behind Humphrey would have left the image of McCarthy as a traitor to the cause and he was unlikely to do that.

Robert Kennedy's likely, and some say assured, opponent in the November election believed Kennedy would win the Democratic nomination. Writing in his memoirs Richard Nixon (1978) said: "It was clear that Bobby was gaining back the initiative he had lost to McCarthy in Oregon. I believed that Hubert Humphrey had waited too long before declaring his candidacy and I saw no way a Kennedy juggernaut could be stopped once it had acquired the momentum of a California victory. As I went to bed (on the night of the California primary) I said, 'It sure looks like we'll be going against Bobby.'"[21]

Robert Kennedy, unlike Hubert Humphrey, would most likely have been the healer of a disunited Democratic Party. Kennedy would have, as McCarthy said: "got this party under control on Vietnam."[22] He would have been the unifying leader of a party split between the 'old' and the 'new' politics. And eventually it is likely that Labour Union support would have rallied behind Kennedy in the November election (with the exception of the Teamsters Union) even though they had initially supported Humphrey.

The Democratic Party had, ever since Roosevelt's 'New Deal', become the majority party in the United States. Even Hubert Humphrey, leader of a disunited party, very nearly won the November election against Nixon because of this vast registered voter majority. It was evident, therefore, that a more charismatic presidential candidate in the form of Robert Kennedy would have beaten Nixon. And as Arthur Schlesinger informed the present author: "(American Independent Party candidate) George Wallace received about 12.5% of the popular vote (in the November election) and may well have taken enough votes from Humphrey to bring about Nixon's victory. Indications are that many Wallace voters, especially in the North, would have voted for Robert F. Kennedy."[23]

Notes

1. Manchester, W. 'Recapturing bobby', *New York Times,* 7 August 1988. (http://www.nytimes.com).

2. Patterson, J. T. (1996). *Grand expectations,* Oxford University Press. p. 694.

3. Manchester, W. (1975). *The glory and the dream,* Michael Joseph. p. 1134.

4. Newfield, J. (1970). *Robert Kennedy - a memoir,* Jonathan Cape. p. 232.

5. *Ibid,* p. 136.

6. Goodwin, R. N. (1988). *Remembering America,* Little Brown and Company. p. 537.

7. Newfield, J. (1970). *Robert Kennedy - a memoir,* Jonathan Cape. p. 75.

8. Schlesinger, A. M. (1978). *Robert Kennedy and his times*, Houghton Mifflin Co. p. 938.

9. *Ibid*, p. 938.

10. Hampton, H. and Fayer, S. (1995). *Voices of freedom*, Vintage. p. 480.

11. *Village Voice,* 18 July 1968. (http://www.villagevoice.com).

12. 'Can Hubert Humphrey stop RFK?', *Newsweek*, 29 April 1968, p. 21.

13. 'Choosing sides', *Newsweek*, 8 April 1968, p. 19.

14. Minzesheimer, R. *Gentle memories of Robert F. Kennedy*, (http://www.usatoday.com).

15. White, T.H. (1969). *The making of the President* 1968, Jonathon Cape. p. 159.

16. *Newsweek*, 6 September 1968, p. 16.

17. *Time*, 14 March 1969, p. 14.

18. Schlesinger, A. M. (1978). *Robert Kennedy and his times*, Houghton Mifflin Co. p. 934.

19. Beran, M. K. (1998). *The last patrician - Bobby Kennedy and the end of American aristocracy*, St Matrin's Griffin. p. 205.

20. Rogers, W. (1993). *When I think of Bobby*, Harperperennial. p. 149.

21. Nixon, R. (1978). *RN - the memoirs of Richard Nixon*, Sidgwick and Jackson. p. 305.

22. *Time,* 6, September 1968, p. 12.

23. Letter to the author, 9 April 1979.

Chapter 12

Vietnam II

Would RFK have ended the War in Vietnam?

"The abrupt extinguishing of any life before it reaches a natural apogee is an irresistible occasion for speculation about what might have been. When the life was that of a formidable politician with a large and passionate following, such speculation becomes an important civic act, clarifying the nation's trajectory and the possibilities that may have been closed by the person's death."

George F. Will

1968 opened with the United States polarised between "hawks" and "doves". Opposition to American policy in Vietnam had developed almost immediately after the initiation of the U.S. bombing of North Vietnam in 1965. At first only a small minority of the American people were critical, but over the next three years it grew into a deluge persuading some commentators to aver that America was on the brink of civil war. By November 1967, 46% felt it was a mistake to send U.S. troops to Vietnam in the first place.

'Dove' arguments ranged from objections based upon abstract ethical principles to arguments about America's role as an international 'policeman'. Some Americans believed the 'guns and butter' theory and that the war was using money that could be used for Great Society programmes. Others withdrew support for President Johnson's war effort because they wanted an all-out effort to win. In the 1968 New Hampshire Democratic primary election, for example, Eugene McCarthy received 42% of the vote as a 'peace' candidate. However, some of the votes were not based on moral or pacifist principles but were a protest against Johnson's 'weak' effort.

However, the peace movement generally attracted pacifists, intellectuals opposed to America's 'imperialist' foreign policy, religious leaders, secular leaders, students, African-American leaders and middle class anti-war liberals. Humane considerations played a large role in much of their arguments. Extraordinary numbers of non-combatant Vietnamese, both North and South, were killed or wounded by American bombing and civilian casualties were almost certainly greater than military ones. Large numbers of South Vietnamese peasants became refugees. Anti-war sentiment also grew out of the fact that the list of American soldiers killed in action was growing month by month.

Alternatively the 'hawks' reasoned that a 'dirty' war was inevitable in order to stop communist aggression. They believed that anti-war demonstrations gave succour to the enemy and postponed a settlement because outward dissent made it appear that America might eventually abandon their war effort without any concessions on the North Vietnamese side. This idea was adopted by President Lyndon Johnson and Republican presidential candidate, Richard Nixon, who both did not want to be the first president to 'lose a war'. Indeed, President Johnson frequently compared the Vietnam war to the Alamo.

In January 1968, to the surprise of most Americans who believed the communists were virtually beaten, Viet Cong and North Vietnamese troops carried out major attacks throughout South Vietnam including the capital, Saigon. The 'Tet' offensive illuminated truths in the minds of Americans - the government had lied to them as to the efficacy of the American effort in Vietnam and there was no 'light at the end of the tunnel' as Johnson Administration officials had been stating.

In their narrow-minded way the U.S. military, after the communist forces had been pushed back, proclaimed victory. What they could not understand was that the United States had suffered a great 'political' defeat. The immediate effect was that between February and March 1968 the numbers of Americans who stated a desire for a swift negotiated settlement jumped from 25% to over 40% and those supporting President Johnson's Vietnam policies dwindled from 40% to 26%.[1]

On February 8th 1968, Robert Kennedy made a bitter attack on the Johnson Administration criticising it for holding out for total victory in a war which could only be solved by political and not military means: "Our enemy savagely striking at will across all of South Vietnam has finally shattered the mask of official illusion with which we have concealed our true circumstances from ourselves...the time has come to take a new look at the war...the events of the last week (are) not simply a tragedy but a lesson...First, that a total victory is not within sight or 'around the corner', that, in fact it is probably beyond our grasp; and that the effort to win such a victory will only result in the further slaughter of thousands of innocent and helpless people...".[2] With this speech it appeared that the anti-war movement had something to be optimistic about - a mainstream politician had made a devastating attack on the Administration's war policies and if he became a candidate he had a real possibility of becoming president.

Robert Kennedy's politics had a consistent moralistic root and it was for this reason he opposed what was happening in Vietnam. As a man who thought in terms of moral purpose he called war and bigotry 'indecent' and meant it. As President it was clear he would use these ethical precepts in conducting foreign policy. Kennedy began expressing his doubts about the war long before the 'mask of illusion' speech. In December 1966, he confessed to writer Jack Newfield: "I said in Berkeley recently that the bombings were not immoral. They were just counter-productive; now I just don't know."[3]

Until this time he had generally supported President Johnson in the war effort. However, by the start of 1966, Kennedy had become deeply troubled by not only the moral considerations but also the larger dimensions of the war and the price it was exacting on domestic poverty programmes. In February 1966, he gave a speech proposing that a reasonable compromise on Vietnam would have to involve "a share of power and responsibility" with the National Liberation Front (Viet Cong) in the future political life of South Vietnam.[4] To an Administration which thought that victory was possible and communist participation unthinkable, the speech was seen as a deliberate effort by Kennedy to further his own political ambitions.

The feeling that the speech did no good kept Kennedy quiet on the issue for the remainder of the year. This was to be the most pressing problem when he wished to speak out on the war - how to make his feelings known without reducing the argument to a clash of personalities between himself and President Johnson.

Throughout 1966 the war continued to escalate: 150,000 more American troops were committed to Vietnam bringing the total by the end of the year to 350,000. The air war was expanded and new targets added, many of them population centres. At the beginning of 1967, the Johnson Administration deliberately ignored a peace move by the North Vietnamese, prompting Kennedy to decide that the President did not really want peace.[5] Kennedy knew that he could not influence Johnson; their mutual contempt had been simmering ever since Kennedy opposed Johnson for Vice-President in 1960. He did however try to use his influence with Secretary of Defense, Robert McNamara. According to Lyndon Johnson, Kennedy would: "every day...call up McNamara telling him that the war was terrible and immoral and that he (McNamara) had to leave (the Administration)."[6]

After a meeting with President Johnson in February 1967, Kennedy became convinced that Johnson believed strongly in victory without concessions to the enemy and in doing so was prolonging the war. He then began a frontal assault on the Johnson Administration and gave anti-war speeches throughout the country. He called the war "immoral" and accused the President of calling upon "the darker impulses of the American spirit". He criticised him for setting an example "where integrity, truth, honour...seem like words to fill our speeches rather than guiding beliefs." His language gave the anti-war dissenters that certain respectability they had previously lacked.

Kennedy felt he had a clear cut choice - whether to make an irretrievable break and stand against Johnson in the 1968 elections or fall into the ranks of those who fail to act in times of moral crisis. Whilst grappling with this problem, Senator Eugene McCarthy announced his candidacy on November 30th 1967. It left Kennedy in a quandary for he believed McCarthy was vain, lazy and ineffective and that the entire peace movement was in jeopardy. Kennedy believed that the McCarthy movement, based as it was on a narrow middle class constituency, would flounder because it was unable to sustain the momentum gathered in the anti-war and African-American protest movements.

However, Kennedy announced at the end of January, at a National Press Club breakfast sponsored by the Christian Science Monitor, that he would not run for president under any "foreseeable circumstances". This was one day before the Tet Offensive. Many writers have used this statement to support the notion that Kennedy only entered the Democratic Party presidential race because Eugene McCarthy had made a good showing as an anti-war candidate.[7] The truth, however, is more complex. It is frequently overlooked that the original phrase in Kennedy's prepared statement to the press was going to be "conceivable circumstances". After reporters consulted Kennedy's Press Secretary, Frank Mankiewitz, a subtle change was made on the instructions of Kennedy. The report now read "foreseeable circumstances", indicating that the senator was engaged in a debate with himself and his staff about whether or not to challenge Johnson. And he told his aide, Peter Edelman, a few days before the New Hampshire Primary: "Yes, I'm going to do it. If I can, I've got to try to figure out a way to get Gene McCarthy out of it, but, if I can't, I'm going to do it anyway."[8] It was the Tet Offensive, in which targets all across South Vietnam were attacked and the United States Embassy in Saigon was fired upon, convinced Kennedy he must stand against President Johnson. However, by declaring his candidacy after the primary, Kennedy left himself open to charges of opportunism. The chronology of Kennedy's decision making in this respect has been examined by Jack Newfield (1969), Jules Witcover (1969), David Halberstam (1968) and Arthur M. Schlesinger (1978). They all agree that Kennedy would have announced his candidacy whether or not McCarthy received a decent showing in the primary election. Robert had asked his brother Edward to convey to the McCarthy team his intention to run. However, Edward failed to deliver the message. Furthermore, Richard Goodwin, a Kennedy loyalist who had been working for McCarthy's campaign told McCarthy of Kennedy's intentions one day before the primary.

After announcing his candidacy on March 16th 1968, he gave his last speech in the Senate and according to Jack Newfield (1969): "all his inhibitions were gone when he rose to speak spontaneously on Vietnam, confessionally in moral terms and still obsessed by the suffering of innocents."[9] From this speech Kennedy's approach to the war, if elected president, can be clearly gauged: "Every time we have had difficulties over the last seven years over the period during which I was in the executive branch and since I left...the answer has always been to escalate the conflict...the fact is that victory is not ahead of us. It was not ahead of us in 1961 and 1962 when I was one of those who predicted there was a light at the end of the tunnel. There was no light in 1963 or 1964 or 1965 or 1966 or 1967. And there is not now. Moreover, there is a question of our moral responsibility. Are we like the God of the Old Testament and we can decide in Washington D.C. what cities, what towns and what hamlets in Vietnam are going to be destroyed? Do we have that authority (to kill) tens of thousands of people because we say we have a commitment to the South Vietnamese people? But have they been consulted - in Hue, in Ben Tre and in other towns that have been destroyed? Do we have that authority? As to our own interests in Vietnam could not the Germans have argued the same thing before the beginning of World War II, could they not have suggested that they had the right to go into Poland, into Estonia, into Latvia and into Lithuania because they needed them as a buffer. I question whether we have that right in this country...what we have been doing is not the answer, it is not suitable and it is immoral and intolerable to continue it."[10]

A swift end to the war is evident in Kennedy's words. There is no talk of an 'honourable' end to the war which became the guiding phrase of the Nixon Administration. And unlike Nixon, who kept repeating that he had a 'secret' plan to end the war, Kennedy during the 1968 campaign made the policies he would enact as president explicit. Kennedy stated he would halt the bombing of North Vietnam completely as a first step in changing the direction of the war, thus complying with North Vietnam's insistence that substantial peace talks could not be held unless the bombing was unconditionally halted. He would have ordered the American military in South Vietnam to pull back from forward positions to protect the populated areas and he would have withdrawn American troops over a brief amount of time giving the burden of the fighting over to the South Vietnamese. Finally he would have given the National Liberation Front a political role in South Vietnam.[11]

The implications of these policies suggest a conclusion to the war long before Nixon's actual 'peace' in 1973. Although Robert Kennedy did not actually come out for unilateral withdrawal, it is significant that after February 8th he no longer came out against it. Basing his policy on the 'enclave strategy' would have meant that military escalation was not an option without a massive air and land offensive. This would have been unlikely to happen under a President Robert Kennedy as it would have been a betrayal of Kennedy's anti-war constituency and it would not have been in character. The only logical conclusions we can draw, therefore, is that Kennedy would have immediately aimed for 'Vietnamisation' of the war followed by a withdrawal of American forces within months and not years of his inauguration.

In July 1965, Kennedy had said that the history of the previous 20 years had demonstrated beyond doubt that: "...our approach to revolutionary war must be political first, political last, political always. Victory in a revolutionary war is won, not by escalation, but by de-escalation."[12]

Robert Kennedy would have been supported in his withdrawal efforts by the American public. It became quite evident later that the support for the war during the crucial years 1964-1970 had been grossly overestimated by many politicians. Elite policy, according to James D. Wright (1976), was towards continued escalation yet popular opinions was against the war. In 1970, Richard Nixon was asserting that Vietnam had been the nation's "finest hour", but in the same year 62% of the population believed that it was a mistake to send forces to Vietnam in the first place and about 75% rejected the escalation option. The 1970 survey asked people to rate themselves on a seven point 'hawk-dove' scale. About 40% placed themselves on the side of 'immediate withdrawal' and less than 33% chose 'complete military victory'. Wright's other findings showed that in the entire period of American involvement public opinion was consistently more 'dovish' than official policy.[13]

A successful election victory in November 1968 would have convinced Robert Kennedy that his anti-war positions were correct. He would have used his election victory as a mandate for swift and complete withdrawal of American forces from Vietnam thus saving the country from another five years of dissent and turmoil. "He was an activist", Kennedy's press Secretary, Frank Mankiewicz, said after the senator's death, "and those who disliked him were not concerned that if he got power he wouldn't do what he said; they feared that indeed he would."

Notes

1. Bernstein, I. (1996). *Guns or butter*, Oxford University Press. p. 477.

2. *Congressional Record*, 114(19), 8 February 1968.

3. Newfield, J. (1970). *Robert Kennedy - a memoir*, Jonathan Cape. p. 127.

4. *Ibid*, p. 125.

5. Witcover, J. (1969). *85 days - the last campaign of Robert F. Kennedy*, Ace Books. p. 38.

6. Goodwin, D. K. (1977). *Lyndon Johnson and the American dream*, Andre Deutsch. p. 321.

7. 'Campaign'. By Emile de Antonio. CBS Television, 1969. Video.

8. Schlesinger, A. M. (1978). *Robert Kennedy and his times*, Houghton Mifflin Co. p. 910.

9. Newfield, J. (1970). *Robert Kennedy - a memoir*, Jonathan Cape. p. 140.

10. *Ibid*.

11. *Saturday Evening Post*, 5 June 1968, p. 20.

12. Schlesinger, A. M. (1978). *Robert Kennedy and his times*, Houghton Mifflin Co. p. 787.

13. Wright, J. D. (1976). *Dissent of the governed*, Academic Press. p. 39.

Chapter 13

The RFK Assassination

Was Robert Kennedy assassinated as the result of a conspiracy?

"I now realise that even law-enforcement officials...DO make mistakes...if one does not account for occasional mistakes and incompetence, then nearly every...political murder could appear to be a conspiracy, particularly if a civilian investigator - with limited access and resources - is looking for one."

Dan Moldea

Five years after the assassination of President Kennedy a similar tragedy befell his brother Robert. Since that moment of madness in a kitchen pantry of the Los Angeles Ambassador Hotel on June 5th 1968, opinion polls have consistently shown that a majority of Americans believe that Robert Kennedy died at the hands of conspirators.

On the night of his death, Robert Kennedy had journeyed to the Ambassador Hotel from the Malibu home of his friend the movie director, John Frankenheimer. Results had been coming in which indicated that the Senator from New York had won the Democratic California State primary election, which was vital in his struggle to win the Democratic presidential nomination to be held in Chicago the following August. In his 81 day campaign for the nomination, he had won enough momentum to persuade many Americans that he would eventually be elected the next President of the United States.

Robert Kennedy went straight to his fifth floor room of the Ambassador Hotel, which acted as his California election headquarters. By midnight Kennedy's supporters were convinced of victory. Amongst his family and friends were the astronaut, John Glenn, and writer, Budd Schulberg. Jesse Unruh, the California State assembly speaker, persuaded Kennedy it was now time to speak to his supporters who had assembled in the Embassy ballroom downstairs. Unruh led the way to warm the crowd up for Kennedy's victory speech. A short time later Kennedy, with his wife Ethel by his side, descended to the ballroom accompanied by a crowd of aides and supporters. On reaching the ballroom podium, he began his speech by thanking all of the people who had made his victory possible. He then spoke about looking forward to the Democratic convention in Chicago where he hoped he would persuade enough of the remaining delegates to the convention that they should choose him over his two rivals, Vice-President Hubert Humphrey and Senator Eugene McCarthy.

Kennedy was not supposed to go through the hotel pantry on completion of his speech. The original route was organised so that the Senator would leave the platform and travel through the Embassy room doors to the waiting press conference in the Colonial room. His single unarmed bodyguard, ex-FBI agent Bill Barry, wanted to go that way in spite of the crowds which had formed in the ballroom. Instead, Kennedy said it was alright to use the back passageway to the press room. It should be remembered that this was a time when Secret Service protection was not afforded to presidential candidates who were seeking their party's nomination for president through the state primary elections. The law was changed to give this protection after Robert Kennedy's assassination.

Kennedy, his wife and aides went directly behind the speaker's platform through a gold curtain towards a serving kitchen that led to the press room. Kennedy was led through double pantry doors where he was met by hotel workers who were eager to shake his hand. Hotel maitre 'd, Karl Uecker, and Ambassador employee, Edward Minasian, led the way. Ethel had been separated from her husband in the crush.

Seconds after entering the pantry, as Kennedy paused to shake hands with a dishwasher, Jesus Perez, a hand came up clutching an Iver-Johnson .22 revolver. Brushing past Uecker's head the gun fired rapidly. Kennedy reeled backward and all around people ran, fell and surged. Pandemonium broke out as people began to respond to the flurry of gunshots. Uecker grabbed the gunman's neck under his right arm and grappled for the gun with his left hand. Although Uecker clutched the gun and pounded it on the table, the gunman refused to give up the struggle and continued firing until the chambers were empty.

Uecker and Minasian were now aided by Kennedy supporter and ex-football star, Roosevelt Grier, who eventually managed to subdue the gunman. Other onlookers, Rafer Johnson, George Plimpton and Kennedy's bodyguard, Bill Barry, piled on. During the mayhem the bullets found five other human targets. One bullet was recovered from each of the five bystanders, two bullets were recovered from Kennedy - one, shattered, from his head and the other from his neck. Thus seven of the eight bullets that Sirhan could have fired were recovered. An eighth bullet was officially described as having been "lost in the ceiling interspace".[1]

Rafer Johnson finally managed to knock the gun out of the shooter's hand. The assassin screamed: "I can explain, let me explain."[2] A voice in the crowd shouted: "Let's not have another Oswald", making reference to President Kennedy's assassin Lee Harvey Oswald who had been gunned down by self-appointed executioner, Jack Ruby. Later, in a statement to his lawyer Sirhan said: "I was almost killed in that kitchen."

Kennedy lay critically wounded, lying flat on his back in the middle of mayhem. His eyes were open and staring. One bullet had pierced an armpit and lodged near the base of his neck. A second had entered the back of the right armpit and had exited in the front of the right shoulder without striking any bone structure. The fatal bullet had entered the mastoid bone behind his right ear and exploded into fragments that spread through his brain. His final words were to ask if everyone was alright, especially his good friend, Paul Schrade, who had also been wounded. A doctor who had been summoned from the victory celebration, Dr Stanley R. Abo, said: "He was holding a crucifix with some beads in both hands, moving both legs, contorting his body from time to time and moaning. He immediately recognised his wife. He looked up at her and reached out with his right hand. He said: 'Ethel, Ethel'. She murmured, 'It's all right, it's okay'. They just kept looking at each other. When they picked him up to put him on the stretcher, he said: 'No, no, don't'. He was obviously in pain. He said: 'Am I all right?' Ethel looked at me. I said to him: 'You're in good shape. Everything will be all right. An ambulance is on its way. Don't worry.'"[3]

Kennedy was taken to the Central Receiving Hospital for emergency treatment before his transfer to the Good Samaritan Hospital where he was operated on. The wound to the head, however, was fatal. The bullet had shattered and fragments were scattered through the lower right side of the skull, some very deep. It was believed that the bullet had also penetrated or torn the lateral sinus, a large blood vessel and that the bullet's fragments were scattered in the brain. Kennedy never regained consciousness and at 1.44 a.m. the following day he died.

Outside the Ambassador Hotel, Los Angeles police officers bundled the gunman into a squad car and took him to Ramparts police station. The gunman told Jesse Unruh: "I did it for my country."[4] He remained unidentified for the next 12 hours as detectives tried in vain to coax the assassin to reveal his identity. He told his interrogators: "I prefer to remain incommunicado."[5] Police officials found him to be a cool character, not at all nervous. He would not talk about his background or the events at the Ambassador but engaged the interrogating officers in conversation about the stock market, an article he had read recently on Hawaii, his liking for gardening and his belief that the justice system discriminated against the 'underdog'. When a representative from the American Civil Liberties Union, Abraham Lincoln Wirin, arrived at the jail to interview Sirhan and to offer assistance, the accused assassin told him: "You know I did it, I shot him." Sirhan then mimed the shooting of a gun repeating: "I shot him."[6]

Gradually the assassin's background emerged. He was Sirhan Bishara Sirhan. Los Angeles police had traced the gun from an elderly man, Albert L. Hertz, who had bought it during the Watts riot of 1965. He subsequently gave it to his daughter. Not wishing to have a gun in the house as she had children, she gave the gun to an 18 year old boy who in turn had sold it to "a bushy haired man named Joe who worked in a department store." 'Joe' turned out to be Munir Sirhan, the gunman's brother. It was Munir who had gone to the police station when he had spotted a picture of his brother on a television newscast. The identification was confirmed by a check of fingerprints taken when Sirhan applied for a state racetrack job in 1965. He did not, however, have a police criminal record.

The gun was a snub-nosed Iver Johnson eight shot revolver, model 55 SA which sold for 32 dollars. The serial number had been registered with the State Criminal Identification and Investigation Bureau. Several witnesses had seen him practice rapid firing on a target range on June 4th, the day before the assassination. Police also found a David

Lawrence newspaper column cutting on Sirhan. The column noted that Robert Kennedy was a dove on Vietnam and a strong defender of Israel. Other items in his possession included a sum of money, four 100 dollar bills, a 5 dollar bill and some singles, a car key and 3.22 cartridges.

Sirhan (the name means wanderer in Arabic) was born in Jerusalem in 1944. An investigation into his background showed he was an unstable and unhappy man who had entered the United States with his family in 1957 when he was 12 years old. His father had returned to Jerusalem shortly afterwards disillusioned with the independent ways of American wives who, he suspected, had influenced his wife. Unable to hold down a job, Bishara Sirhan returned to his homeland taking 500 dollars which his sons earned. Mary Sirhan and her sons had moved to Pasadena, California, but remained Jordanian citizens with 'permanent resident' status in the U.S..

It was discovered that Sirhan had been beaten viciously by his father when he was a child. Investigators later found out that Sirhan had often gone into blind rages against 'Israel and the Jews'. Sirhan's mother also detected a change in his personality after he took a fall from a horse when he was a racehorse exercise boy in 1966. A doctor who had treated him a year after the accident described him as a "fairly explosive personality".[7]

In 1969 Sirhan Sirhan was found guilty of the murder of Senator Kennedy and was sentenced to be executed. Later his sentence was commuted to life imprisonment. During the trial he said he had taken alcohol on the night of the assassination and had no memory of the events at the Ambassador hotel.

In many ways it was inevitable that the assassination would not, eventually, be considered the act of a single, lone assassin. Beginning in the mid 1960s, a 'JFK Assassination' industry had developed which sought to prove that the President had been assassinated by a conspiracy and that Lee Harvey Oswald had likely been innocent. Many writers rightly criticised the findings of the Warren Commission which had been instituted to investigate the President's murder. The report was found to be inadequate and flawed. Although the Warren investigation was rigorous it had failed to answer many questions about the assassination.

Two months before Robert Kennedy's death, the African-American Civil Rights leader Dr Martin Luther King had been murdered. Many saw connections between the assassination of the President and King's assassination. As with the JFK assassination, investigative reporters and writers had reason to suspect there was more to the King killing than at first appeared. Mistakes in the collection of forensic evidence, anomalies in the test firing of the rifle used in the assassination and the failure of the FBI to pursue promising leads, led some to suspect a conspiracy had been involved. The assassins of Dr King and President Kennedy both professed their innocence. Later, after his arrest and trial, King's killer said he had not fired the rifle, implying he had been part of a wider conspiracy.

In the 1970s, a congressional investigating committee decided that both the assassinations of President Kennedy and Martin Luther King were the results of conspiracies. Although the House Assassinations Committee did not investigate the assassination of Robert Kennedy (for budgetary reasons) their conclusions persuaded many writers and investigative journalists that evidence in the Sirhan case pointed also to a conspiracy.

Several legislative and judicial panels had investigated the circumstances surrounding the murder of Robert Kennedy and they found serious problems with the original LAPD investigation (code-named SUS for Special Unit Senator). The panels found disconcerting inconsistencies in testimony and physical evidence:

- The assassin's gun held eight bullets and all of these were discharged in a few moments of pandemonium as Sirhan Sirhan fired at point blank range hitting Robert Kennedy three times, one fatally, and wounding another five bystanders. A couple of shots ricocheted off ceiling tiles before striking their victims. Each of the eight shots were supposedly accounted for by Police expert, DeWayne Wolfer. However, photographs of the crime scene and the recollections of some witnesses suggested that two more bullets or bullet holes had been found in the wooden frame panels of the kitchen swing doors. And if there were two more bullets than Sirhan's gun could possibly hold then another gun had to have been used.

- When the courts reopened the case in the 1980s, it was found that the LAPD had destroyed the wooden frame panels and hundreds of photographs and documents pertaining to the murder. The reason they gave for destroying the panels was that they were too bulky and the filing cabinets could not contain them.

- The autopsy report revealed, and the coroner Dr Noguchi stated, that burn marks around the wound to Kennedy's head indicated the fatal shot had been fired approximately one to three inches away. Dr Noguchi had found soot in Kennedy's hair around the head wound.[8] When a gun is fired the bullet and metallic fragments exit; the gas which contains the soot is very light and can only travel a few inches; the unburned powder grains which are heavier travel farther, one or two feet. After conducting further tests he believed he knew the precise location of the murder weapon at the moment it was fired: one inch from the edge of his right ear, only three inches behind the head. Yet a number of key witnesses stated that at all times during the shooting the gun had been no closer to Kennedy than a foot and a half. Some important witnesses stated that Sirhan had been at least nine feet from Kennedy. Others stated that Sirhan had at all times been in front of Kennedy and, therefore, a shot to the rear of Kennedy's head was impossible.

- A number of conspiracy authors suspected a security guard, Thane Eugene Cesar, had participated in the shooting. He had been the only other person with a gun and he had been situated close behind Senator Kennedy. The autopsy report described all bullets that hit Kennedy as travelling sharply upwards as though fired from below. Conspiracy authors noted that Cesar had testified he had crouched down when the shooting began and pulled his gun - the only other gun known to be in the pantry at that time. As the bullets retrieved could not be identified as having come from Sirhan's gun some authors pointed to the fact that Cesar had admitted owning a .22 pistol and he could have substituted his .38 for that gun before the shooting began. Some authors attempted to prove that Cesar had links to organised crime. Cesar himself admitted he was a George Wallace supporter and disliked the Kennedys.

- Sirhan has maintained throughout the past 30 years that he has had no memory of the shooting and some witnesses testified he was in a "disassociated" state when he shot Senator Kennedy. His eyes were glazed and after his arrest he showed no signs of nervousness. This evidence led some writers to suggest that Sirhan had been hypnotised into killing Kennedy. This theory was first popularised by Robert Blair Kaiser (1970) in his book "RFK must die". Kaiser had assisted in Sirhan's trial defence and had obtained exclusive interviews with him. Kaiser had observed on a number of occasions how Sirhan's psychoanalyst had hypnotised Sirhan into performing acts which he could later not remember. Kaiser wrote: "On February 8th (1969), during the trial, Dr Diamond programmed Sirhan, under hypnosis, to climb the bars of his cell. Sirhan had no idea what he was doing up on the top of the bars. When he finally discovered that climbing was not his own idea, but Dr Diamond's, he was struck with the plausibility of the idea that perhaps he had been programmed by someone else, in like manner, to kill Kennedy." However, to Dr Diamond, "that was a crackpot theory".[9]

- Some writers suggested the CIA may have 'programmed' Sirhan. The CIA had indeed investigated the possibility of using hypnosis as an assassination tool. The CIA programme was called 'Operation Artichoke'. This theory was popular with those who believed the CIA and organised crime had conspired to assassinate President Kennedy.

- A special court-appointed firearms panel re-fired Sirhan's gun in 1975 and produced bullets with markings different from the bullets retrieved after the shooting. This fact argued strongly for the presence of a second gunman.[10]

- Some witnesses had observed Sirhan standing next to and conversing with a girl in 'a polka-dot dress' shortly before the shooting. This evidence argued that Sirhan had had accomplices.

- One witness, Sandra Serrano, told police she had been out on the terrace of the hotel taking a breath of fresh air when, suddenly, "a girl in a white polka-dot dress ran out of the hotel shouting: 'We shot him, we shot him'."[11]

Over the years it became apparent that concerns about these controversial aspects of the case were not the result of wild conjecture and speculation by conspiracy theorists. There were enough anomalies and inconsistencies in the evidence to suggest that the LAPD had carried out a less than adequate investigation. To add to the confusion police experts disagreed with one another, evidence disappeared and, to the critics at least, the LAPD looked as if it was engaged in a cover-up as year after year officials refused to release files they considered 'confidential'.[12] Sirhan's 1969 trial answered none of the questions and Sirhan's lawyers and the prosecuting lawyers had failed to adequately address them during the trial. But the police mishandling of the investigation set the precedent for much of the later conspiracy conjecture.

By the 1980s and 1990s, leading academics, writers and journalists called for the re-opening of the investigation. Books by conspiracy authors like Donald Freed (1977), Robert D. Morrow (1988), Philip H. Melanson (1991), Sam Giancana Jnr. (1992) and William Klaber (1998) all intimated that Robert Kennedy had been killed by a second gunman. Sam and Chuck Giancana's book (1992), 'Double cross' was typical of the many theories which purported to 'prove' that the Mafia had a hand in the killing of Robert Kennedy: "In April 1969 Chuck (Chicago mobster Sam Giancana's brother) met (mobster Chuckie) Nicoletti by chance. What he had to say about Mooney (Sam Giancana) captured Chuck's attention completely. 'One more Kennedy out of the way, huh?' said Nicoletti smiling broadly. 'So Mooney did it again. Goddam, your brother's a genius. And settin' up that guy Sirhan to take the rap, hell, didn't it work like a charm...You know... Oswald didn't really fire a shot. At least Sirhan did that much. But even if he couldn't hit a barn it didn't matter, 'cos Mooney had another guy to do the job on Bobby.'...Another mobster Tommy Payne would later tell Chuck that the 'Outfit' had controlled everything at the Los Angeles hotel where the hit on Bobby Kennedy had occurred and that the other gunman, an 'Outfit' man, was a last-minute replacement for a security guard."[13]

Thirty years after the assassination the controversy still raged. Internet sites flowered, most of them designed to emulate the JFK sites purporting to prove conspiracy. In 1997, a CBS News Special Assignment publicised some "key evidence" that "may have been suppressed".[14] Sirhan's lawyer, Lawrence Teeter, filed 200 pages of Court documents with the California Supreme Court. Teeter was demanding a new trial for his client stating that there was evidence of a second gun at the crime scene. He said that this proved someone else was shooting at Kennedy. Teeter said he had found a photo of the second gun in police files in 1996 and the gun was similar to the .22 calibre revolver police listed as Sirhan's weapon in the shooting.[15] Unfortunately for Teeter, no one has been able to link this weapon with the shooting. At the time of the original investigation into the shooting of Senator Kennedy the police investigating unit had accumulated thousands of pieces of evidence in their investigation including weapons which were used in tests. This may very well account for the supposed photograph of the 'second gun'. Police officers engaged in the original investigation denied that a 'second gun' had been found. William Klaber (1998), in his book 'Shadow play' argued that Sirhan did not shoot Kennedy and used the photograph of the second gun as proof of a conspiracy.[16]

In 1997, Sirhan insisted he was innocent. At his parole hearing at Corcoran State Prison, Sirhan told his parole board that the true facts of the case have never been revealed and that he should be set free.[17] His parole was denied but his then lawyer, Lawrence Teeter, stirred the flames of conspiracy thinking by proclaiming: "Dr Herbert Spiegal, a New York psychiatrist who teaches at Columbia University and who is widely regarded as among the country's leading experts on hypnosis, has concluded that Sirhan was probably acting out hypnotic commands when he fired a gun in Senator Kennedy's presence that fateful day. Sirhan himself was so disoriented following his arrest that he did not even know he had yet to be arraigned. During pre-trial psychiatric examinations in his cell, Sirhan proved to be the ideal hypnotic subject, climbing the bars of his cell without knowing that he was carrying out post-hypnotic commands. Expert trial testimony established that notebook passages containing repetitions of the phrase 'RFK must die' were written in a hypnotic trance, and Sirhan spontaneously reproduced this phrase under hypnosis when asked in his cell for a description of the Senator. Sirhan's amnesia about the crime was unshaken by hypnosis and has consistently remained intact."[18]

It was evident that conspiracy groups, Sirhan and his lawyer were bent on pursuing the conspiracy line even into the late 1990s. With the publication of Dan Moldea's (1995) book 'The killing of Kennedy' this should not have been the case for, in 1993/94, Moldea carried out a full and thorough investigation of Kennedy's murder and solved many of the puzzles connected with the crime. If there had been a conspiracy to assassinate Robert Kennedy, Moldea, a reformed conspiracy advocate, would have found it. Moldea courageously admitted that he had been wrong in believing that Kennedy may have been killed as the result of a conspiracy.

Investigative reporter, Dan Moldea, had excellent credentials to investigate Kennedy's murder. He had written a number of books which enquired into the activities of the mob-controlled Teamsters Union and organised crime. In 1987 he had written an article for 'Regardies' magazine demanding that the Robert Kennedy murder case be reopened because of mounting evidence that a second gunman had been involved.

Moldea did what no other researcher had done - interview the police officers, over a hundred of them - in order to learn why so many anomalies, inconsistencies and contradictory evidence existed. He separated good leads from bogus ones, eliminated key suspects and successfully sorted hearsay and speculation from the true facts of the case. His conclusions are sound and cannot be challenged easily.

I acknowledge Moldea's contribution and I have relied heavily on his investigation in my descriptions and explanations of the puzzling events that took place that tragic evening, and in formulating my conclusions as to what exactly happened. However, the conclusions drawn are my own. And whilst I do not disagree with Moldea's description of Sirhan's motives in killing Kennedy, I believe that more events and circumstances in Sirhan's life interacted resulting in his decision to commit murder.

The controversy about the supposed bullet holes probably began, as Dan Moldea suggests, very soon after the assassination, when police officers investigated the crime scene. A police officer saw a man trying to recover a souvenir of the shooting by trying to remove a 'bullet' from the pantry door frame. Because the police officer was inexperienced in the subject of firearms, he erred on the side of caution and marked what he believed to be 'bullet holes' in the frame. The 'holes' were most likely 'nail holes'. Over the next few days a number of police officers saw the marked 'holes' and believed they were looking at holes made by bullets. None of these police officers were experienced in the collection of evidence relating to firearms identification nor were they expert criminalists. After the crime scene had been secured, DeWayne Wolfer of the Scientific Investigation Division of the LAPD began his investigation of the crime scene and observed the circled holes. He knew they were too small to be the base for .22 calibre bullets. Moldea's investigation into this controversy was much more complicated but he did trace how most of the 'eyewitnesses' to the 'ninth bullet' had got their accounts from second and third hand tales built on the initial mistake of Officer Tew who had not been trained to know what a bullet hole looked like.[19]

The discrepancies in eyewitness testimony as to the distance of the gun from Senator Kennedy can be explained by considering the pandemonium that existed after the first shot was fired. People were screaming, shouting, pushing and throwing themselves to the floor. It is surprising that any sense was made at all of the positioning of witnesses and Kennedy when the shooting began. Dr Noguchi (1983) believes that Sirhan may have lunged forward unseen by eyewitnesses. In his book 'Coroner to the stars' he wrote: "I have always believed it is perfectly possible that Sirhan could have made that lunge back and forth without being seen by any of those witnesses. My experience with homicides as a medical examiner has shown me over and over again how, and why, witnesses in a crowd in such a situation don't always see the truth. Their eyes are totally glued to the celebrity. It is only reluctantly, and as realisation of something wrong sets in, that they move their eyes away from the celebrity and look elsewhere. In other words, the witnesses may not have seen what actually happened that night."[20]

However, Noguchi continues by using eyewitness testimony and forensics to challenge his own thesis pointing out that witnesses may indeed have had time to observe Sirhan when Kennedy was reeling. He quoted Karl Uecker who said he was positive that Sirhan never got close enough for a point-blank shot. However, as Dan Moldea has stated, estimates by eyewitnesses concerning the distance between Sirhan's gun and Kennedy were based on the first shot only.[21] Witness Edward Minasian had testified that Paul Schrade fell first then Kennedy. Because Kennedy said: "Is Paul alright?" as he lay dying on the kitchen floor, it is likely Kennedy had seen Schrade hit by the first bullet. Moldea, then, maintains that Kennedy had not been hit by the first shot and so he was still standing. It is likely that Kennedy jerked backwards then forwards after the first shot. He then came into point blank range of Sirhan's gun after the crowd surged and he was being manhandled by Karl Uecker. Sirhan himself explained how he shot Kennedy in the back of the head when he blurted out to one of his defence team, Michael McCowan, that he had looked Kennedy in the eyes. When McCowan asked why he did not shoot Kennedy between the eyes Sirhan said: "That son of a bitch turned his head at the last second."[22] This would explain how Sirhan could be in front of Kennedy and still shoot him in the back of the head.

Former Police Chief, Darryl Gates, who was acting police chief the night of Kennedy's murder, believes the paths of the bullets can be explained. Speaking to CBS news in July 1997, he stated that he was convinced that Sirhan killed Kennedy alone. "It's not strange," he told reporters, "once you look at the physical facts. A bullet goes very, very quickly. But a slight turn, a change in movement, can cause a trajectory to be entirely different than what you would anticipate." Unfortunately, Gates' statements were instantly dismissed by many conspiracy theorists who maintain that the cover-up had been instituted by the LAPD. Yet there is an inherent logic in Gates' remarks in dismissing this notion. Gates' said: "Why would we want to do anything except solve this case? What purpose would there be in our suppressing evidence or changing the evidence?"[23]

Dan Moldea solved the puzzle of the bullets that could not be matched with Sirhan's gun during the firearms panel investigation in 1975. Moldea discovered that, after the original investigation was over, police had fired the gun privately several times to get souvenir bullets. These shots created a residue in the chamber that gave the bullets fired in 1975 different markings from the bullets fired in the kitchen of the Ambassador on the night of the assassination.[24]

There is no credible evidence to support the contention that security guard Cesar had anything to do with the shooting of Robert Kennedy even though conspiracy theorists have tried for years to establish this fact. No credible witness has testified to seeing him shoot Kennedy and there are a number of other reasons which suggest he played no part.

Cesar himself volunteered the information that he owned a .22 pistol. It is implausible that a co-conspirator would willingly offer this information to police investigators. Furthermore, Cesar had only been given instructions to be in the vicinity of the Kennedy party a short time before the event. He had no way of knowing where his supervisor would require him to be that night. Other 'Ace' security guards could have been given the assignment. Cesar did not want to work that night in the first place but had been persuaded to by his supervisor. In interviews with Cesar, Moldea could find no evidence in his background which would suggest he had been hired by the Mafia or any other conspiratorial group.[25] Cesar's lifestyle and employment over the past 30 years have been accounted for and there is nothing to suggest that he had come into any large sums of money.

Sandra Serrano's story about the girl in the polka-dot dress is not credible for a number of reasons. She had told police officers that she had heard 'backfires' which were naturally taken by the officers to mean 'shots'. Ballistics tests proved she could not possibly have heard the sounds of the shots from her position outside the hotel. Serrano's statement that she had been seated on an outside staircase (she had changed her location at the time of the shooting from a corridor inside the hotel) was challenged by Captain Cecil R. Lynch of the Los Angeles Fire Department who said that on the night of the assassination he had been assigned to enforce occupancy and fire regulations at the Ambassador Hotel. During the time Kennedy made his victory speech Lynch began checking various stairways and exits for possible violations. He said that he checked the stairs Serrano alleged she was sitting on moments before Kennedy was shot and no one was there. Serrano also failed a lie-detector test. According to Robert Blair Kaiser (1970) Serrano admitted she was confused about her original statement she gave police: "(Detective) Hernandez asked her when she first realised her story was getting out of hand. It was, she said, when she went to the Rampart Street Police Station. Hernandez wondered why she hadn't corrected the story then. She said she had told the police what she thought they wanted to hear.. 'I was sitting there hearing descriptions and descriptions of these people, of these people, of these people. Oh, God, maybe that's what I'm supposed to have seen. It messed me up, that's all; and I figured, well, they must know what they're doing.'" Serrano's credibility was further damaged when it was found out that she had asked another witness, Vincent DiPierro, at the police station, to embellish his story to fit in with her own. Whilst it is difficult if not impossible to disprove her statement the preponderance of the evidence suggests the girl she saw most likely shouted 'They killed Kennedy' and not 'We killed Kennedy'. It is also likely that the couple who noticed the girl running past them also misheard her.[26]

A girl who had worn a polka-dot dress that night did come forward. Her name was Valerie Schulte, a student and campaign worker, and also an eyewitness to the shooting. She voluntarily contacted the LAPD and investigators proved she had nothing to do with the shooting.

Dan Moldea believes the girl in the polka-dot dress could have been one of the anti-Kennedy group who were at the Ambassador Hotel that night, who, after hearing that Kennedy had been shot, became gleeful and decided to claim responsibility but were not in collusion with Sirhan. Moldea points out that it is simply not logical to assume that members of a conspiratorial group would run around the hotel proclaiming their guilt.[27]

There is no authoritative evidence which would suggest that it is possible to programme someone to commit murder if it goes against the subject's own desires. Many medical, psychology and psychiatry experts dismiss these claims. The CIA programmes (including 'Project Artichoke') which had been looking into the possibility of psychologically constructing a 'Manchurian Candidate' type assassin were simply a waste of taxpayers money and CIA doctors who were involved in the programme have stated that it was never brought to fruition.[28] The 'robotic assassin' defence, which Sirhan had encouraged, was found to be bogus by Dan Moldea when, in prison interviews with Sirhan, the assassin confessed to him that the idea had been concocted by his lawyers.[29]

The question of Sirhan's motive for killing Kennedy became a moot point for conspiracy authors. If he had indeed been set up as a 'patsy' or had been programmed to shoot the Senator he would have no intrinsic reason for committing the act. Some authors speculated he had killed Kennedy for money and that perhaps Kennedy's arch-nemesis Jimmy Hoffa or the Mafia supplied payment.[30] But an examination of Sirhan's finances showed he had received no extraordinary payments either before or after the assassination.

Dan Moldea believes that Sirhan killed Kennedy because of 'personal problems'; he had "become a desperate young man losing all hope...a loser...(who had) lost his nerve...humiliated...a clown." Moldea believes that Sirhan's "unilateral motive consisted of nothing more than his desire to prove to himself and those who knew him that he still had his nerve. He wanted everyone to know his name and be forced to recognise him."[31] Ever since the 1970s, Sirhan had been trying to get parole. Knowing that Moldea and others were sympathetic to his case he deliberately courted them hoping they would dig up enough controversial facts in the case that a parole board would err on the side of caution and set him free. In interviews with Sirhan, Moldea heard how the assassin had got drunk and accidentally ended up at the Ambassador Hotel and, therefore, could not have killed Kennedy with any premeditation. But with persistent questioning, Moldea saw Sirhan unravel. When Moldea asked point-blank whether he had committed the crime, Sirhan tried to give a clever answer: "I would not want to take the blame for this crime," he replied, "as long as there is exculpatory evidence that I didn't do the crime." Moldea concluded: "With that reply, I finally began to understand Sirhan's entire strategy: as long as people like me continued to put forth supposed new evidence, he still had a chance to experience freedom. I had been helping to keep his case alive with all of my supposed new revelations...As I sat there, I became furious with myself for having nearly been hoodwinked by Sirhan."[32]

I agree with Moldea's conclusions but there was something more in Sirhan's background which contributed to his feelings of injustice and his desire to seek revenge against a society which had placed him as a misfit and failure. Although a disturbed individual, Sirhan still had the capacity to act duplicitously and cunningly. He was and still is a monstrous fake. For 30 years he pretended he had no knowledge of the shooting yet he confessed to one of his defence team he had looked Kennedy in the eye just before he shot him. In 1981 Los Angeles District Attorney, John Van de Kamp, gave evidence to Sirhan's parole board which indicated Sirhan was still a dangerous man. According to Van de Kamp, an inmate of Soledad Prison had been talking to Sirhan about the 1980 Presidential campaign when the question of Edward Kennedy's risk of assassination arose. Sirhan said: "I know he would (be assassinated)...If I get out of here in 1984 and he's still President I'll take care of him myself."[33]

In one way Sirhan's memory of his actions may have been blurred. He did, after all, consume alcohol that night, no doubt summoning up the courage to commit his cowardly deed. However, one of Sirhan's psychiatrists, Dr Eric Marcus, was not impressed by the accused's claims to suffer amnesia through the effects of alcohol. He had interviewed too many criminals who claimed liquor-induced amnesia, only to discover later that other witnesses had described them as fully cognisant before and after the crime. Sirhan had used this defence as a convenient and unsophisticated way to escape blame. Sirhan maintained he had suffered amnesia because he had no choice in the matter. The idea that he had no memory of the shooting had been placed in his mind by one of his defence lawyers. After his incarceration his only chance for freedom would be to hope that conspiracy theorists would keep hammering away at the idea that Sirhan had been only a pawn manipulated by conspirators. If enough doubt about his culpability was placed in the minds of the American people his eventual release from prison would one day be considered. If he admitted that he had premeditatively murdered Kennedy that hope would be lost.

Conspiracy authors explain away Sirhan's notebooks, which refer to his desire to kill Kennedy, as writings which were stimulated by conspirators who had been hypnotising him. Yet they ignore the fact that Sirhan had assassination on his mind as far back as 1964, four years before the assassination. An examination of his college textbooks revealed he had underlined important passages which made reference to violent, anarchic political acts. In one particular book, 'Readings for college writers', which he purchased in 1964, three months after the assassination of President Kennedy, he had marked a passage which read: "The enemy is not necessarily a bad man. Indeed he may be a man of high character and considerable good will." In an American history text he had written next to a passage about the assassination of President McKinley "and many more will come."[34]

In my book 'Questions of conspiracy' (Ayton, 1999), I stated my belief that Lee Harvey Oswald murdered President Kennedy for a number of reasons, not least because of the unstable nature of his personality which had its roots in the fact that he grew up fatherless. He had no role model and his surly and violent personality misfortunes as Oswald, in no small measure, because of this fact. Sirhan had experienced the same after the age of 12, when his father deserted the household. And there is evidence that even before then Sirhan's father had left his son with negative experiences of a paternal role model. Acquaintances of the family have spoken of Bishara Sirhan's cruelty and indifference to his son. Neighbours in Jerusalem talked of how the father once put a hot iron to Sirhan's feet.

Lessons learned in childhood are lessons learned well. It was evident to many who had known Sirhan that he had grown up a disturbed and embittered individual. Robert Blair Kaiser, who had been on Sirhan's defence team, asked the accused assassin about some of the happy moments he spent with his father: "Sirhan thought long and hard, squinting, trying to remember. 'I was on a bike,' he said, 'with Adel (Sirhan's brother). And I had my arms out like a bird and my father was laughing. Oh, there was laughing. Oh, he got a kick out of it.' I waited. Silence. 'Some more?' Sirhan could not think of any other happy moments."[35]

Clinical psychologist, Dr Martin M. Schorr, believed Sirhan's relationship with his father lay at the core of the assassin's maladjustment. He was backed up by another three psychologists and two psychiatrists. At Sirhan's trial Schorr told the court: "By killing Kennedy, Sirhan kills his father, takes his father's place as the heir to his mother...Essentially, the more he railed and stormed, the more the mother protected Sirhan from his father, and the more he withdrew into her protection. He hated his father and feared him. He would never consciously entertain the idea of doing away with him but somewhere along the line the protecting mother fails her son. The mother finally lets down the son. She, whom he loved, never kept her pledge and now his pain had to be repaid with pain. Since the unconscious always demands maximum penalties, the pain has to be death. Sirhan's prime problem becomes a conflict between instinctual demand for his father's death and the realisation through his conscious that killing his father is not socially acceptable. The only real solution is to look for a compromise. He does. He finds a symbolic replica of his father in the form of Kennedy, kills him, and also removes the relationship that stands between him and his most precious possession - his mother's love."[36]

Sirhan's capacity for violence is often overlooked by those searching for an understanding of how a supposedly mild-mannered individual could commit such a violent act. Yet the evidence exists that he frequently erupted into fits of temper. John Weidner, Sirhan's boss at the health food store where he worked for a short period of time, spoke of how he had to call the police after an altercation with Sirhan.[37] And one of Sirhan's neighbours believed the assassin 'hated' people with money.[38] Sirhan's brother, Munir, had been in trouble with the police and another brother, Sharif, the second oldest of the Sirhan brothers, had an uncontrollable temper. Once he had been caught tampering with the brakes of a car belonging to an ex-girlfriend. Sharif was arrested for attempted murder.[39]

In the year prior to the assassination, according to those who knew him, Sirhan developed no close friendships and he was nervous and self-conscious when he was around girls. His brothers began to think: "There was something wrong with him."[40]

Sirhan's deteriorating self-esteem can be seen in the way he solicited the friendship of the 'garbage man'. According to one of his brothers: "the minute he sees the man, he goes out there and says, 'How's the weather out here? Don't go.' And he goes back and makes coffee and cake and he gives them to him." The same garbage man gave evidence at Sirhan's trial and said Sirhan told him two months before the shooting, "I am planning to shoot him (Kennedy)".[41]

There is also evidence that Sirhan had feelings of racial inferiority. At the time he arrived in the United States in January 1957, he said to his mother: "When we become citizens will we get blond hair and blue eyes?".[42] Later as an adolescent and young man he became conscious of the fact that he did not fit in to the California culture. According to an acquaintance of the family: "They were treated like Negroes...most people didn't know or care...they were really displaced people."[43]

Like many poor single-parent mothers who have low self-esteem, Mary Sirhan had little understanding of her son's personality, character and abilities. She believed Sirhan was a 'genius' at school and that the teachers 'knew this'. Sirhan, however, had achieved only average grades and no teacher testified to the fact that he stood out. At 17 his IQ had been tested as 89.

At Junior High School Sirhan became aware of the differences between himself and the other students - he was a 'have-not they were 'haves' with their different cars, different looks and different cliques. One way of propping up his self-esteem was to embrace left-wing politics and left-wing literature. JFK's assassin, Lee Harvey Oswald, thought he could impress people with his knowledge of left-wing ideas and his pretentious revolutionary persona. Likewise, Sirhan believed he could forge an identity by speaking out for the Arab cause though most people knew he did not take the issue seriously.

In the year before the assassination Sirhan's life was falling apart. Unemployed, uneducated and finding his finances were stretched, he needed to act boldly to prop up his self-image and prevent a sense of failure. He was a small man of 5 feet 2 inches with a personality to match. Many now saw him as a 'loser' and 'clown'. He had a burning desire to show that he was capable of making people pay attention to him. Within the act of murder he was taking revenge against a world which had relegated him to the bottom of the heap. His notebooks, mostly an ad-hoc mixture of stream of consciousness thoughts and meanderings, frequently referred to his lack of power within society. He wrote of having nothing. He identified strongly with the character 'Perry' in Truman Capote's book 'In cold blood', the story of two misfits who murdered a family in Kansas in the 1950s. Perry was small, with a dark complexion: he had been deserted by his father and who became one of life's 'losers'.[44]

By stalking and then killing Robert Kennedy, Sirhan became a somebody. After his arrest he excitedly told a sheriff's deputy: "I was on television." He told one of his defence team during the trial: "...Hell, I gained something. They can gas me. But I am famous. I achieved in a day what it took Kennedy all his life to do." Sirhan premeditatedly killed Robert Kennedy. And he stalked the Senator in the weeks leading up to the shooting. Dr Joseph Sheehan, a professor of psychology at UCLA and his wife Margaret, observed Sirhan, who looked 'malevolent' to them, at a political rally on May 24th 1968.[45] He carried out his infamous deed, not by having been hypnotised by others but by autohypnotism. As witness to the shooting, George Plimpton, said: "He had a look on his face of intense concentration."[46]

By choosing such a great victim Sirhan hoped to rise to a similar high level, if only for a moment.

Notes

1. LAPD Memo to Lt. D. W. Mann, Officer-in-Charge, Criminalistics Section S.I.D, 8 July 1968 In Kaiser, R. B. (1970). *RFK must die*, Grove Press Inc. p. 542.

2. 'A life on the way to death', *Time*, 14 June 1968, p. 10.

3. Kaiser, R. B. (1970). *RFK must die*, Grove Press Inc. p. 30.

4. 'Bobby's last, longest day', *Newsweek*, 17 June 1968, p. 14.

5. 'There just hasn't been a nicer boy', *Newsweek*, 17 June 1968, p. 16.

6. Kaiser, R. B. (1970). *RFK must die*, Grove Press Inc. p. 92.

7. 'There just hasn't been a nicer boy', *Newsweek*, 17 June 1968, p. 17.

8. Noguchi, T. T. (1983). *Coroner to the stars*, Corgi Books. pp. 83-103.

9. Kaiser, R. B. (1970). *RFK must die*, Grove Press Inc. p. 536.

10. Melanson, P. H. (1991). *The Robert F. Kennedy assassination*, Shapolsky Publishers Inc. p. 62.

11. Kaiser, R. B. (1970). *RFK must die*, Grove Press Inc. p. 47.

12. Melanson, P. H. (1991). *The Robert F. Kennedy assassination*, Shapolsky Publishers Inc. p. 45.

13. Giancana, S. and Giancana, C. (1992). *Double cross*, MacDonald. p. 345.

14. 'The assassination of RFK', CBS Special Assignment Broadcast, 31 July 1997.

15. *Ibid*.

16. Klaber, W. and Melanson, P. H. (1997). *Shadow play*, St Martin's Paperbacks. p. 337.

17. 'The assassination of RFK', CBS Special Assignment Broadcast, 31 July 1997.

18. Pease, L. 'The RFK assassination', Real history archives assassination collection.
    (http://www.webcom.com/1pease/index2.htm).

19. Moldea, D. (1995). *The killing of Robert Kennedy*, WW Norton and Co. pp. 313-318.

20. Noguchi, T. T. (1983). *Coroner to the stars,* Corgi Books. p. 100.

21. Moldea, D. (1995). *The killing of Robert Kennedy*, WW Norton and Co. pp. 310-311.

22. *Ibid*, p. 326.

23. CBS News Special Assignment Broadcast, 31 July 1997.

24. Moldea, D. (1995). *The killing of Robert Kennedy*, WW Norton and Co. p. 321.

25. *Ibid*, pp. 199-216, 280-290.

26. Kaiser, R. B. (1970). *RFK must die*, Grove Press Inc. p. 144.

27. *Ibid*, p. 298.

28. *Ibid*, p. 134-135. The LAPD's expert on hypnosis, Michael Nielsen, said: "There is no such thing as mind-control hypnosis."

29. *Ibid*, p. 300.

30. An investigator on Sirhan's 1968 defence team, Michael A. McCowan, said Sirhan talked about extorting 150,000 dollars from Jimmy Hoffa, threatening that if he did not get the money he would tell the world. Robert Blair Kaiser said, "I laughed. Sirhan had been using the same story for months now; first it was Lyndon B. Johnson, then Richard Nixon, now James Hoffa. There was no

reason to suppose Sirhan knew that in actual fact a fellow prisoner of Hoffa's in the Lewisburg, Pennsylvania federal penitentiary had told the FBI that he overheard Hoffa and his cronies in prison talking in May 1968 about a 'contract to kill Bob Kennedy'. Hoffa would not even discuss the matter with the FBI and his friends in prison denied ever hearing of such a contract. It is almost absolutely certain, however, that even if Sirhan was chosen as a hired gun, he would be the last person to know the identity of the man at the top." [Kaiser, R.B. (1970). *RFK must die*, Grove Press Inc. p. 469.]

31. Moldea, D. (1995). *The killing of Robert Kennedy*, WW Norton and Co. p. 322.

32. *Ibid*, p. 302.

33. Farr, B. 'Sirhan threatened to kill Ted Kennedy told', *Los Angeles Times*, 13 August 1981. (http://www.latimes.com); *see also* 'Another Kennedy death threat', *Newsweek*, 24 August 1981, p. 29.

34. Kaiser, R. B. (1970). *RFK must die*, Grove Press Inc. p. 169.

35. *Ibid*, p. 196.

36. *Ibid*, p. 443.

37. *Ibid*, p. 436

38. *Ibid*, p. 98.

39. *Ibid*, p. 132.

40. *Ibid*, p. 133.

41. 'Eye of the hurricane', *Newsweek*, 3 March 1969 p. 20.

42. 'The notebook that read Robert Kennedy must be killed', *Life*, June 1968, p. 30.

43. *Ibid*.

44. Kaiser, R. B. (1970). *RFK must die*, Grove Press Inc. p. 514.

45. *Ibid,* p. 534.

46. 'Eye of the hurricane', *Newsweek*, 3 March 1969, p. 20.

Chapter 14

The Last Brother

Did Edward Kennedy destroy the Kennedy legacy?

"Show me a hero and I will write you a tragedy."

F. Scott Fitzgerald, 'The crackup'

"Mankind is made up of inconsistencies, and no man acts invariably up to his predominant character. The wisest man sometimes acts weakly, and the weakest sometimes wisely."

Lord Chesterfield

During the 1980s and up to the time when Edward Kennedy testified at his nephew's rape trial in 1991, the media have questioned the last Kennedy brother's fitness to hold public office and have severely criticised his private life. During his run for the presidency in 1980 the Chappaquidick incident was resurrected and speculated upon endlessly throughout the campaign. His campaign ended in failure and his rival, President Carter, went on to campaign in the November election without success.

In 1981, the Senator divorced his alcoholic wife, Joan, and he began what can only be described as a shameful journey into political oblivion, at least as far as the national arena was concerned. Liaisons with single and married women, drunken behaviour in public restaurants and an unwillingness to curb his gregarious and fun-loving lifestyle met with stinging disapproval throughout the United States. The tabloid press were quick to track the Senator's private life and the stories made it inevitable that the Senator could no longer be considered as a possible presidential candidate.

Edward Kennedy finally reached the nadir of notoriety in 1991 when he woke up his son and nephew to go drinking at a bar in Palm Beach, Florida. It was the Easter weekend holidays and Kennedy had been reminiscing about his brother-in-law, Stephen Smith, who had died the previous year. Feeling morose and introspective about the family's tragedies, he sought solace in the company of Smith's son, William, and Kennedy's youngest son, Patrick. The invitation to his son and nephew would eventually land him in court as a witness to William Smith's behaviour that night. More than a few believed that Kennedy was finished as a politician. Even in Massachusetts, where faith in the Kennedy legend was deep, a post Palm Beach poll showed that two-thirds of the voters thought he should be replaced. At the Clarence Thomas hearings in the Senate, Kennedy was forced to sit in embarrassed silence as Anita Hill testified to Thomas' alleged sexual harassment.

With the pre-publication publicity surrounding an ex-Kennedy aide's memoirs of his time spent working for the Senator, Kennedy was forced to say something about the lack of public trust in him. Rick Burke's allegations about women and alcohol shocked the American public. Although the book (Burke, 1992) had been written by a man who had serious financial debts and who had been hospitalised for mental illness, the book nevertheless confirmed to many that Kennedy was unfit to be a United States senator.[1]

Kennedy was advised to meet the allegations head on. It was a clear change in the way the Kennedy's had dealt with criticisms of the family: there had always been the belief that a challenge to every rumour and allegation about the Kennedys would set a precedent; spending time and money on such attempts would be futile; cut off one of the Hydra's heads and another one would replace it. However, Kennedy knew that the Palm Beach incident and the stories about his private life were now beginning to affect his leadership abilities in the Senate. Even 'Time' and 'Newsweek' joined in the tidal wave of criticism. 'Time' said he was: "a Palm Beach boozer, lout and tabloid grotesque."[2] Newsweek termed him: "the living symbol of the family flaws."[3] No longer could he take consolation in the American public's willingness to dismiss tabloid stories. Persuaded that public virtues cannot be disassociated from private misbehaviour Kennedy confronted the charges head on.

On October 24th 1991, Kennedy gave a speech at the Institute of Politics at the John F. Kennedy School of Government in Cambridge Massachusetts. During the speech, he took the opportunity to apologise for his behaviour during the 1980s which led many writers to describe him as a drunkard and debaucherer: "I am painfully aware that the criticism directed at me in recent months involved far more than honest disagreement with my positions," he said, "or the usual criticisms from the far right. It also involved the disappointment of friends and many others who rely on me to fight the good fight. To them I say: I recognise my own shortcomings - the faults in the conduct of my private life. I realise that I alone am responsible for them, and I am the one who must confront them. I believe that each of us as individuals must not only struggle to make a better world, but to make ourselves better too."[4]

But what is the truth about Edward Kennedy? Was he the playboy Senator who arrogantly broke the rules in the belief that his power and money would protect him? Or was he a complex individual, who tried to balance the demands of family and public life and whose character and behaviour has been grossly misunderstood?

Edward Moore Kennedy was born in 1932. His arrival as the last of the Kennedy children made him the baby of the family. His brothers and sisters doted on him and he was the apple of his father's eye. For Joe Kennedy, who the world saw as an isolationist and greedy capitalist, was a father to whom his children meant everything. And they loved him without reservation.

Growing up in such a large, demanding and ambitious family was a pleasant experience for the young 'Teddy'. If his parents were absent he had surrogate parents in the form of his siblings whose ages were far removed from his own. The age gap between Teddy and his brothers was too great for them to share a childhood. He was born seven years after Bobby and the two would become the closest of friends only after John Kennedy's death. Ted was only 12 when his older brother Joseph was killed in a bombing raid during the Second World War.

From most accounts of the Kennedy family there is a consensus that the demands and pressures which were placed upon the older Kennedy brothers did not apply to Edward. Being the youngest, Ted missed the heart of the competition in the family. He developed less of an instinct for ruthlessness than any of his brothers. It appears from most accounts of the Kennedy family that the father's love fell mostly on the oldest son Joe, of whom the most was expected, and on the youngest, Ted, of whom the least was expected. Many authors have described Ted as having been 'spoilt'. But although he was treated differently and as the 'baby' of the family he did not become a surly, selfish and demanding 'rich brat'. By all accounts he had a balanced, friendly and positive personality. He had an affable temperament, open with everyone he met and whose 'smile lit up the room.'

Later, many who knew the Kennedy brothers as children would recognise how their childhood personalities were reflected in their adult careers. John Kennedy was like his father in that he was disciplined in what he wanted to do, a creature of self-will, brilliant and hard but also understanding. He was impatient as a senator and became bored with the Senate as an institution. He felt he needed to go where the 'action was', the presidency. Bobby was very religious, but much more emotional. He saw issues in black and white terms and on entering the Senate became impatient with the archaic methods of getting things done. It was evident that to Bobby the Senate was only a stepping stone to higher office. Ted's character traits were a combination of his father's and brothers; and he inherited some of the softer qualities from his mother. He had less of the competitive instinct about him and was less driven to accomplish his goals. These qualities were better suited to the role of a senator; the role requires patience, compromise and an ability to nurture relationships with colleagues. This may help explain why Ted eventually became a 'Senate insider' at a relatively young age.

As the youngest of the Kennedy brothers, Ted was not confronted with open or implicit demands that he would inherit the political ambitions of his father. That role was first mapped out for Joseph and then after Joseph's death John was expected to enter the political arena. Ted, therefore, grew up knowing that the expectations for political success lay with his brothers and not him.

In the Autumn of 1950, Ted entered Harvard which was his father's and brothers' alma mater. The affable youngest brother fitted easily into the culture of the University. Six foot two and weighing 200 pounds, he became successful on the Harvard football team and he was a 'middling' student. However, the first of his adult transgressions occurred when he asked a friend to take a Spanish exam for him. Both students were caught out and suspended for a year. If they showed 'constructive and responsible citizenship' during that period they would be readmitted. The fall from grace at the age of 19 was to follow Ted when he entered politics 10 years later.

According to his mother Rose, Ted said: "When I got into that mess at Harvard in my freshman year at eighteen and was suspended, and called to tell him (Joseph Kennedy), his initial reaction was very calm. What exactly was the situation I'm involved in? What impact could this have on my life and relationships? And then about eighteen to twenty-four hours later, after he had got a 'feel' for what it meant, he was absolutely wild and went up through the roof. For about five hours. From then on he was calm. It was just 'How do we help you?' And he never brought the thing up again."[5]

Years later John Kennedy said: "The toughness (of his father) was important. If it hadn't been for that, Teddy might just be a playboy today. But my father cracked down on him at a crucial time in his life, and this brought out in Teddy the discipline and seriousness which will make him an important political figure."[6]

Shamed, Ted decided to join the Army following in the footsteps of his brothers who had enlisted in the Navy during the War. His father reacted with anger when he saw that the enlistment papers indicated a four year tour of duty. He got the enlistment changed to two years and saw to it that his son would be assigned as an MP to NATO Headquarters in Paris. Thus Ted avoided service in Korea. The Kennedy parents evidently felt they had sacrificed enough. Ted felt later that the Army had helped him to mature.

Edward Kennedy returned to Harvard in the Autumn of 1953. His grades improved and the staff of the University found him to be a more mature student. Despite this maturity, he also became tenaciously competitive and a risk-taker. He broke his shoulder in a skiing accident and had a leather brace made so he could be back on the ski slopes in two weeks. He bravely skied down steep slopes and was fearless on the football field.

Ted graduated from Harvard in 1956 and was admitted to the University of Virginia Law School. However, the playboy image became the visage with which many of his contemporaries viewed the youngest Kennedy brother. He was popular with the other students and was well liked for his genial, friendly personality. But he did not flaunt his wealth and avoided references to his more famous brothers. His behaviour, however, was less than perfect. His youthful indiscretions caused serious concern with his father. The young and handsome millionaire engaged in drinking bouts and recklessly drove his convertible around campus. He was arrested for speeding after trying to outrun a Charlottesville police officer. He was convicted twice more for traffic offences during his time at the University.

Ted Kennedy was 26 and still at law school when he managed his brother John's re-election campaign for the U.S. Senate in 1958. It was vital experience for Ted although it was his father and Kennedy aides Lawrence O'Brien and Kenneth O'Donnell who were really running things. Two years later in 1960, Ted was given a role in his brother John's presidential campaign and successfully campaigned in the western States. It became evident to many that Ted was a 'natural born politician'.

After John Kennedy's election as President of the United States, Joseph Kennedy decided that his youngest son should have the opportunity to join his brothers in government service. In 1962, Ted ran for his brother's old Senate seat and entered the United States Senate in January 1963. During the election campaign he had come under severe criticism for his age - he had just turned 30, the minimum age for a senator - and his lack of political experience. However, he acquitted himself well, took his brother Jack's advice not to react to his opponents' charges during debates and the people of Massachusetts took to him.

Unlike his brother Robert, who was elected as a United States senator from the State of New York in the November 1964 elections, Ted became respectful of the Senate as an institution, carefully biding his time and respecting the seniority of his colleagues. He learnt the rules carefully and became a better legislator than his two brothers. In time his power grew and he became an effective powerhouse for great liberal causes. Edward and Robert Kennedy did everything together during this period and called each other by their childhood names, Eddie and Robbie. They sat next to each other at Congressional hearings and engaged in mock debates as to who made the better senator.

After Robert's assassination Ted began drinking heavily and his mood was one of despair, guilt and a feeling that fate had dealt another terrible blow to his family. Many in the period after the assassination and before Chappaquiddick saw a man who was suffering a delayed reaction to his brothers' assassinations and the awful burden of responsibility they imposed. There was evidence that Kennedy was also suffering from tension and fatigue. To many who observed him during this period he was an accident about to happen.[7] In 1969 he went to Alaska, a trip his brother Robert, as a member of the Indian Education sub-committee, had promised to make. He journeyed to one village after an other deploring the plight of the Eskimo. On the plane ride back home he began drinking heavily. Reporters heard him say: "They're going to shoot my ass off the way they shot Bobby." John Lindsay of 'Newsweek' magazine sent a memorandum to his editors indicating Kennedy was headed for a nervous breakdown.[8] Three months later the Chappaquiddick tragedy occurred. On one occasion he drove his car to his Senate office, sat for a while, then turned around and went home. He spent a great deal of time sailing off the coast of New England, losing himself in solitude. He took solace in what one friend said afterwards was: "the freneticism of booze and sex. Afterwards there were times of guilt."

He was 36 years old when he inherited the mantle of the Kennedy legacy and it was obvious he had not matured enough to take on the burden of the presidency even though many friends and aides urged him to 'pick up the torch'. He refused to challenge Hubert Humphrey for the Democratic presidential nomination of 1968 and turned down Humphrey's offer of the Vice-Presidency. In 1970 after the Chappaquiddick tragedy, he decided against a run for the presidency against Richard Nixon.

But Kennedy was always a threat to the Republicans. He was the most charismatic politician of his generation and was constantly under pressure to take up the fallen standard. Family concerns, which included his son Patrick's severe asthma, his son Teddy's struggle with cancer and his wife's alcoholism, always prevented him from making the run.

Contrary to popular myth the legend has created Ted Kennedy, not the other way around. Unlike his brother John, Ted was not in control of his destiny. He was pushed towards the presidency by his inheritance and by the idea that he had to take up a fallen standard from his brothers. He was also influenced by those who became the Kennedy Administration-in-waiting, confident that his name would take them once more to the pinnacle of power.

In 1979, disillusioned with President Carter's lack of leadership and aware of the urgings of close friends and advisors, he ran for president.

But Ted's heart was never in it. As the most gifted politician and natural legislator of the three brothers, he always suspected that his destiny lay in the Senate. And lesser men would have left politics after seeing their brothers cut down by assassins' bullets. This act alone demonstrates the false tabloid descriptions of Edward Kennedy. Ted knew throughout the decades after Dallas that an assassin could strike at any time. Someone out there was waiting to kill the third and last Kennedy politician. Throughout this period there were many scares as he went about his business as the senior senator from Massachusetts and the President-in-waiting for many. He often reacted to bursting balloons or other loud noises believing he had become a target. John Hinckley, who attempted to assassinate President Reagan in 1981, chose Ted Kennedy as his first target. Hinckley waited in Kennedy's reception office for three hours with a loaded .22 calibre Saturday Night Special in his pocket. Had the Senator not been late, he would surely have been the third Kennedy to be assassinated.[9]

James Spada, in his political quarterly 'EMK', described a typical frightening incident. Kennedy had been standing in a large square in the centre of Haverhill, Massachusetts, talking with an aide as he waited for a parade to begin. Without warning a sharp and loud explosion rocked the square. It turned out to be a portable cannon. However, "Ted Kennedy gave a cry- Ho!- and doubled up both hands grabbing his stomach as though he had got a severe pain. He fell back inside the open door of his car, on the seat. His face was white. It looked totally drained of expression. He was staring ahead. Then, in just a few seconds he relaxed. His face took on colour and he was smiling and jaunty as though nothing happened."[10]

Ted and Joan

Joan Kennedy was essentially a woman of warmth and charm. She was born the debutante daughter of an advertising executive from New York. Educated at Catholic schools she was 22 when she met Edward Kennedy. From her wedding day she found herself challenged by the demands of being a Kennedy wife and found the hardest part of her marriage 'keeping up with the Kennedy Clan.'

Joan tried to be like the Kennedys - effervescent, energetic and constantly on the go but she failed. Her personality was different from the other family wives. Joan was a quiet woman, not given to competitive pursuits and tough sports. She had a sensitive nature and preferred her classical music to touch football. Even her repeated miscarriages seemed a special failure even though she had a sympathetic ear in Jacqueline Kennedy who had suffered the same fate. Subconsciously, she wanted to be like Robert's wife Ethel, who had baby after baby often taking skiing holidays up to the time of birth. Ethel had a strong and tough personality and more than kept up with the Kennedys in competitive sports.

Joan was not suited to the fierce brand of politics that formed the essence of Kennedy life. She was totally ignorant of current events when she arrived in Washington as a young senator's wife. However, she tried to act the part by supporting her husband in his career and accompanying him across country on political jaunts. She did, however, excel as a politician's wife during Ted's re-election campaign for the Senate in the 1964 elections. Ted had broken his back in a near-fatal plane crash on the way to Springfield, Massachusetts, to accept his party's nomination. Unable to campaign himself, Joan became her husband's surrogate and took a lot of well-deserved credit for Kennedy's landslide victory.

Unfortunately, Joan's success as a politician's wife during an election campaign did not stem the tide of a growing sense of an inability to cope. Joan Kennedy's drinking problem actually began before her husband's 1964 re-election campaign.[11] There were signs of it during the period shortly after the death of her brother-in-law President Kennedy. She sought relief through drink. Also during this period, Joan found it difficult to accept her husband's rumoured affairs but learned to live with them. It was not until the 1990s that the idea that alcoholics had a genetic disposition to the disease took root. Joan's mother Ginny had a drinking problem which led to a divorce from her husband Harry Bennett.

There has been no evidence whatsoever that Ted Kennedy had an affair with Mary Jo Kopechne but ironically the Chappaquiddick incident drove a wedge between Joan and her husband and her alcoholism became worse after 1969. The cause of Joan's drinking problem did not originate solely in her husband's philandering as some writers infer. Many writers have assumed that Joan began drinking heavily as she could not deal with the stories of Ted's womanising and preferred instead to ignore the problem, hoping he would either change his ways or his liaisons would not interfere with her married life. She had voiced her concerns to her sister-in-law Jacqueline Kennedy who told her: "all the Kennedy men were like that" and "it meant nothing".[12] Jacqueline, of course, grew up in an eastern American establishment background where infidelity was commonplace; even her father had been a notorious womaniser.

But the reasons for Joan's alcoholism are more complex and do not solely reside in her relationship with her husband. They have their roots in the environment in which she lived. Like many Washington couples, the Kennedy's marriage was strained due to the constant absences of Senator Kennedy. Ted's work kept him away from home until late at night and often for days at a time. Joan believed that a drink or two would ease the loneliness and isolation but as her children were growing up and finding their own way in life the isolation became enhanced. At one time a frustrated Ted Kennedy showed a reporter to the back door of his house to observe his wife spread-eagled across the back seat of a car, the victim of a drinking binge. According to author Laurence Leamer (1994), friends and associates of the couple said that Joan had short involvements with men, relationships initiated after drinking spells. Joan told her biographer and ex-aide, Marcia Chellis, she had once set up a meeting in France with an old lover but became so drunk the meeting was a disaster.[13]

Initially, however, Joan was unaware she had low tolerance for alcohol. She had also been cast in a role for which she was unsuited. Quiet, retiring and without the stoical resources of the other Kennedy women, Joan became lost in the harsh realities of political life. Rather than express anger or hurt she would turn to alcohol to relieve her anxieties.

After the assassination of President Kennedy, Joan became fearful for her husband and believed he might be next in line for the assassin's bullet. She told the 'Ladies Home Journal' (July 1970): "Frankly, I worry all the time about whether Ted will be shot like Jack and Bobby...(he) keeps things from me - serious threats against his life-that kind of news - but I know what's going on...this is such a painful subject with us that we can't even discuss it."[14] Even before the assassination of Robert in 1968, which brought her fears to near intolerable levels, she appeared to drink a lot. After the tragedy in Los Angeles she did not know how to deal with her problems and, like most families during this time, the issue tended to be ignored or swept under the carpet. Later Joan said: "I tried to talk about it and Ted was embarrassed by it. Everybody was embarrassed by it but nobody would really talk about it."[15]

The rigours of public life became too much and the terrible cycle of family tragedies simply threw Joan into a spiralling vortex of unhappiness and despair. After Chappaquiddick she had to endure the shock of discovering her son had cancer. Further miscarriages added to her grief. Her son Patrick was frequently ill with chronic asthma.

Living in a gold fish bowl has long been one of the negative sides of political life. Many Washington wives openly expressed discontent during the 1970s and looked for the means to change the system that ensnared them. The wives of many leading politicians like Bob Dole, John Tunney and Eugene McCarthy left their husbands and named politics as the major reason.[16] Some sought psychiatric counselling to understand their peculiar role which is contradictory as well as demanding. A political wife was expected to pursue her own career, or manage a household, or raise a family often with little help from a husband whose job required his attention round the clock. At the same time she was called upon to make speeches and win votes for her husband but had to be the model partner and, like her husband, to be everything to everyone. It was not surprising that the fraught and anxious Joan Kennedy was relieved when her husband decided not to run as a candidate in the election campaigns of 1968, 1972 and 1976.

Given the conflicting demands placed upon her, Joan began to wonder who she was. She was in a constant turmoil that she would not meet the expectations of her husband and the electorate thus damaging her husband's career. Politics nullified her personality.

In power all politicians become different people. However humble their office they develop an exaggerated notion of themselves and their power. Their egos need to be constantly stroked. On the other hand many would do anything to help their country, or friends and neighbours. This is why it becomes such a problem for their own families. Many political wives feel abandoned.

Other women have always been an ever-present threat to Washington wives. Henry Kissinger was not the first to discover that power was an aphrodisiac. The temptations have always been hard to resist. Ed Muskie's wife told 'Time' magazine: "It's a very heady business. You go to a party alone, and when your husband arrives you see all those women advance on him like vultures. Well, that does something to a man that's not normal."[17]

Ted Kennedy was no different from the Washington politicians of the 1960s and 1970s and, in his passion to involve himself with liberal causes, his sensitivity to other people, including his wife, became lost.

However, some understanding and sympathy to the spouse of an alcoholic is always prudent if the correct context of domestic problems is to be understood. Joan never needed much to slip into an alcoholic haze. She became glassy-eyed after one or two drinks, often passing out after three.[18] Puffy eyes, exaggerated make-up and a wrinkled look began to appear. "I drank socially at first," Joan told her biographer and ex-aide, Marcia Childs, "and then I began to drink alcoholically, I really did. But at the time I didn't know it. No one really ever does know. I mean, sure, once in a while you have too much to drink and you wake up the next morning and you have a hangover, and you think, Oh, I'm not going to do that again. And you say something like that and then a week or two goes by and nothing happens, and then you go and you drink too much again. It becomes a pattern that starts to creep up on you."[19]

Ted tried every way to help her, from psychiatrists to priests. He gave her everything except the thing she wanted most - deep emotional love. She attempted a succession of cures: taking a Master's degree in Education, attending alcoholism clinics and megavitamin therapy. Eventually she would slip into a terrible cycle of recovery and regression.

The couple stayed together, partly out of Ted's genuine love for his wife and children and partly out of political expediency. By 1979, Joan was physically and mentally capable of enduring Ted's presidential campaign. Ted had been supportive of his wife during the campaign but reporters frequently noticed the emotional distance between them. After Ted's failed presidential bid, the couple divorced in 1981. Since that time Joan has lapsed into alcohol dependency and has been arrested a number of times for drink driving offences. She has had a number of strong relationships with other men but has harboured a secret belief that she and her husband would eventually reunite. This seemed unlikely especially after Ted married Victoria Reggie in 1992.

There is little doubt that Joan Kennedy deserves the larger share of sympathy which has been directed at the couple. Ted Kennedy's philandering appears to be the major flaw in the character of a man whose love of his children and devotion to his work is unquestioned. Tragedy can often unite couples but Ted and Joan's experiences of adversity moved them apart. Joan felt she could not turn to her husband for comfort; instead she turned to the bottle. Ted was brought up in the belief that 'Kennedys don't cry' and he became less articulate when expressing any issue which did not involve politics or the legislative process. He also bore the terrible burden of the entire family's aspirations and ambitions.

But Ted Kennedy never lost sight of his responsibilities to his children even though he was forced to become a surrogate father to his brothers' children. His children are living testimony to those who seek to portray the Senator as a one-dimensional character totally committed to his own selfish ends and devoid of any moral centre.

Who is the real Ted Kennedy?

In 1992, Ted Kennedy married 38 year old banking lawyer and mother of two, Victoria Reggie, in a small ceremony at his house in McClean, Virginia. Symbolically he gave her a picture he had painted of daffodils which were in full bloom, an acknowledgement that she had changed his life. Many of his friends say she rescued him and straightened him out. He had always worked hard and was totally professional in his approach to his senatorial duties but there was little doubt he was in need of help. He always had the ability to reach out to anyone in pain but lacked the ability to be anything other than stoical about his grief. Edward Kennedy was not made for introspection. As a man approaching 60 his behaviour during the late 1980s suggested pain and an inability to express it rather than exuberance. The only clue to his agony was given at the funeral for Jackie Kennedy in 1994: "She never wanted public notice," Kennedy eulogised, "in part, I think, because it brought back painful memories of an unbearable sorrow, endured in the glare of a million lights." His grown children recognised this subliminal revelation when they spoke of their father's loneliness and sorrow and hoped he would meet someone to share his life with.

It is true that if hypocrisy, deceit, arrogance and corruption exist in a politician's private life, those flaws will eventually be reflected in public acts. James Barber (1972), author of 'The presidential character' has said: "The best way to measure a candidate's character is by looking at the signs he gives in private - how he talks and acts around the people closest to him, like his staff, in unguarded moments - when the press isn't watching."[20] It is, therefore, ironic that many senators of both parties during the period when Ted Kennedy's life went off the rails, carousing and raising the level of his alcohol intake, described him as "committed", "trustworthy", "persistent" and believed he had "moral grounding". For over 30 years the vast majority of those who have worked for Edward Kennedy have so described him.

During the Reagan/Bush years Kennedy was the leading voice for liberal causes. In the two years preceding the 1991 Easter Weekend Palm Beach scandal, the Labor and Human Resources Committee of the 101st Congress with Kennedy as Chairman, pushed 54 Bills into law, the most enacted by the Committee since Johnson's Great Society. And since Clinton's election in 1992, Kennedy's pet projects over the past 30 years have been given close attention: civil rights, education, refugees, welfare reform, child care and women's issues were projected on to the national agenda. Unfortunately, Kennedy's highest priority, National Health Care, failed to be implemented by Congress even though the Clinton Administration fought vigorously for its enactment.

Ted Kennedy's industry, principle and commitment is unquestioned. A typical day for the Senator might include a Senate hearing, testifying at another hearing, speaking at a press conference, discussing a pet project like health care at a Democratic caucus, and taking home a briefcase every night with over 100 items assembled by his staff. Kennedy often flew across country to help publicise those causes which were dear to the hearts of his brothers; attending rallies to highlight the poverty of many rural areas like Apalachia, for example or visiting poor Indian reservations in the West. Murray Kempton, a columnist for 'Newsday', observed that if Kennedy was forever known for Chappaquiddick: "in the arrogance of our conviction that we would have done better than he did in a single case, we exempt ourselves from any duty to pay attention to the many cases where he shows himself better than us...he is the first Kennedy to be a loser in politics, and he gives every sign of not anticipating a second chance. He makes his witness now, not as a candidate, but as a kind of steward; he travels to call attention not to himself but to the needs of others...His generation of the Kennedys can never command again; it endures in him only to oppose, the most elevated of all political functions. If he lives wherever ghosts may live, John F. Kennedy, the grandest of successes, must be surprised and proud to have a brother who could bring such a victory out of failure."[21]

The respect Kennedy has achieved as a legislator has never been highlighted by the press as much as his private life. Senator Robert C. Byrd, who wrote a two volume history of the Senate, said: "Ted

Kennedy would have been a leader, an outstanding Senator, at any period in the nation's history."[22] His success in this institution has been so great that author Burton Hersh (1997) has referred to Kennedy as "The Shadow President". Hersh likens Kennedy to the Senator's hero, Daniel Webster, who defined an age by using the power centre of the Senate as a virtual counterpart to the presidency. Hersh lucidly portrays Kennedy as a man who built a career based on commitment to his political calling and an aptitude for coalition building. His personality and leadership skills combined with innate instincts as a "field commander", according to Hersh, have made him a considerable roadblock to sitting presidents and the creator of a veritable "shadow government" that uses public opinion to halt unpopular legislation. To Hersh, Kennedy became a powerful foe with veto powers, a man who has forsaken an indulgent private life for hard work.[23] Republican Orrin Hatch said: "His brothers were great human beings but they couldn't carry his shoes as a legislator." 1996 Republican presidential candidate, Bob Dole, said he "never doubted for a minute his (Kennedy) commitment to help the elderly, the ill, and those Americans who have been on the outside looking in for far too long."[24]

The American people have mixed feelings about Ted Kennedy and this was reflected in his campaign for the presidency in 1980. Although he won important primary campaigns in large states like New York and California, he could not overcome the doubts many people harboured as to his character. And the unanswered questions about Chappaquidick continued to haunt him. They were continuously resurrected each time a potential Ted Kennedy candidacy had been discussed by the media. Kennedy admitted that his actions during that tragic weekend were 'irrational, indefensible and inexplicable'. However, considerations about his ability to react in moments of crisis could have been better placed in the correct context if reference had been made to two little reported incidents which reflected on Kennedy's character. The first occurred five years, practically to the day after the Chappaquiddick tragedy, when Kennedy, in his yacht the 'Curragh', rescued five people off Cape Cod.[25] The other incident occurred in 1976 when he rescued a young Republican Policy Committee worker, Carol Chealander, when her neck had been caught in lift doors. The operator froze when the old type metal doors refused to open. Although she suffered serious neck injuries, Kennedy's quick response saved her from further tragedy. She told Jack Anderson: "If Senator Kennedy hadn't kept his head, I'd be dead."[26]

During the 1980s and early 1990s, Ted Kennedy's drinking bouts and womanising disturbed many and angered his supporters and detractors. His defenders have argued that his behaviour during this period in his life occurred at a time when he was single and did not compromise his effectiveness as a senator.

To those who have known Senator Kennedy, he is a tragic hero, a larger than life, romantic figure who, nonetheless, has displayed destructive human flaws. Other Kennedy defenders have asked: who would be better for the presidency, a man who like Cromwell, Franklin, Hamilton and Jefferson had been unchaste, or a man who had violated the public trust like Nixon? Lincoln and his wife had a troubled relationship but he was a statesman of compassion, wisdom and integrity.

However, such rationalisations are rejected by many as weak excuses for behaviour which cannot be allowed to become a standard for choosing political leaders. Kennedy defenders fail to recognise that a public person's private life is important in making an assessment as to fitness for office. Public and private morals cannot be divorced. Sexual deceit and betrayal are legitimate matters of public interest and cannot be disregarded. As the Archbishop of Canterbury, George Carey said: "Without honesty, trust, faithfulness to an obligation, respect for the rights and interests of others and love of neighbour, civilised society falls apart...The question has to be asked whether sexual sins have any relevance to public life. I do not believe they can be disregarded...The point is not just that bad private behaviour leaves the individual vulnerable to media intrusion but that it undermines the respect that we need to have for politicians."[27]

On the other hand we can all sympathise with the context in which Ted Kennedy acted. He had to live with the enormous expectations that came with being the surviving brother. His immediate family, living in constant fear that Ted would be the next to be assassinated, was plagued by alcoholism, drug abuse and illness. And too often Kennedy's transgressions have been exaggerated. During the Palm Beach rape trial of his nephew William Smith, Kennedy was excoriated by the press for leading his son and nephew astray. But what did he actually do? In the tradition of Irish fathers he took his son and nephew drinking. In reality there was nothing wrong with Kennedy's behaviour that Easter night.

Ted Kennedy's drinking has been exaggerated by a number of writers. Throughout his worst period in the 1980s, he habitually stopped drinking when the Senate was in session. Most of the time he drank at home but, occasionally, on a night out on the town he indulged in high jinks when he had drank too much. Generally speaking, Kennedy was a 'binge drinker' going for days, weeks, or months with little or no alcohol at all. However, when the stressfulness of his life or work became too much he would hit the bottle. But he never displayed the symptoms of an alcoholic and his gregarious and unaggressive personality remained constant. Drink to Kennedy was a means to an end; it did not control his life.

Second chances have always been part of the American experience. Take Richard Nixon, for example, who was resurrected as the 'New Nixon' in the campaign of 1968. The abandonment of his single lifestyle in the early 1990s may have saved Ted Kennedy's position in history as one of the greatest American legislators. His aberrant behaviour will likely be relegated to a footnote in history. And his trusteeship of the Kennedy legacy of public service and his high ideals to benefit the less well off in American society may not have been compromised.

The answer to the question - who is the real Ted Kennedy? - appears to lie somewhere between those descriptions of the Senator provided by Kennedy-haters and those provided by Kennedy-lovers. There is certainly little to admire in the vicarious way he has conducted parts of his private life. Yet one cannot help but admire other parts: the ways in which he has loved, supported and nurtured his children and the fearless way he has continued in public life despite the risks inherent in being 'The Last Kennedy'. In the months after Teddy Jnr. was hospitalised for the removal of his leg, his father stayed with him often sleeping at the hospital. He spent a great deal of time with his son Patrick when the youngest son was seriously ill with chronic asthma. And there is much to admire in the ways in which Ted Kennedy acted as a surrogate father to his brothers' children. The ways he carried out his political calling never giving in to the fears about his exposed position as a target for assassination do not reflect the behaviour of a man devoid of any redeeming character traits. His associates and subordinates almost invariably agree on his thoughtfulness, compassion, good humour and his ability to reach and empathise with people, an ability that goes beyond the politician's need to charm. To those who really know him, his faith has enabled him to confront his demons and accept his incalculable sorrows. "I have watched him pray," said Kennedy's priest, Percival D'Silva, "You can tell he is not distracted by the people around him. I see him with his eyes closed and I get the impression that it is a very intense moment for him..."[28]

Ted Kennedy was not the most attentive husband yet his wife Joan from whom he was divorced nearly 20 years earlier still speaks of him with fondness and affection, nurturing a desire for a reconciliation at least up until the time he remarried. Although he was absent for much of their married life and had many affairs, she never stopped believing he was a good father and essentially a good man.

He was not without guilt about having brought Joan into the environment he did. He once said Joan ought to have married a New York banker. He felt remorse about the tragic accident at Chappaquiddick, but not guilt; he felt he had done all he could. But he did feel guilt about his wife: "I've had a life of sadness, mistakes, happiness and achievement," he told a 'Life' magazine reporter in 1994, "Those things will always be a part of me. And I've tried to learn from them."

Notes

1. David, L. (1993). *Good Ted, bad Ted*, Carol Publishing Group. pp. 239-240.

2. Cited in Hersh, B. (1997). *The shadow President*, Steerforth Press, p. 100.

3. Cited in Hersh, B. (1997). *The shadow President,* Steerforth Press. p. 100.

4. *The Boston Globe*, 26 October 1991. (http://www.boston.com).

5. Kennedy, R. F. (1974). *Times to remember*, Pan Books. p. 156.

6. Burns, J. M. (1976). *Edward Kennedy and the Camelot legacy*, WW Norton and Co. Inc. p. 44.

7. Hersh, B. (1972). *The education of Edward Kennedy*, William Morrow and Co. p. 380.

8. Burns, J. M. (1976). *Edward Kennedy and the Camelot legacy*, WW Norton and Co. Inc. p. 163; David, L. (1993). *Good Ted, bad Ted*, Carol Publishing Group. p. 197.

9. David, L. (1993). *Good Ted, bad Ted*, Carol Publishing Group.

10. David, L. (1975). *Ted Kennedy, triumphs and tragedies*, Award Books. p. 333.

Ted and Joan

11. Leamer, L. (1994). *The Kennedy women*, Villard Books. p. 561.

12. Chellis, M. (1985). *The Joan Kennedy story*, Sidgwick and Jackson. p. 48; Christopher Andersen, *Jack and Jackie - portrait of an American marriage,* William Morrow and Co. Inc., 1996, p. 188.

13. Leamer, L. (1994). *The Kennedy women*, Villard Books. pp. 702-703.

14. Hoffman, B. H. 'Joan Kennedy's Story', *Ladies Home Journal*, July 1970. (http://www.lhj.com).

15. Chellis, M. (1985). *The Joan Kennedy story*, Sidgwick and Jackson. p. 48.

16. 'The relentless ordeal of political wives', *Time*, 7 October 1974. p. 27.

17. *Ibid*, p. 28.

18. 'The vulnerable soul of Joansie', *Time*, 5 November 1979, p. 23.

19. Chellis, M. (1985). *The Joan Kennedy story*, Sidgwick and Jackson. p. 46.

Who is the real Ted Kennedy?

20. Cited in Kessler, R. (1997). *Inside Congress*, Pocket Books.

21. *Newsday*, 27 November 1983. (http://www.newsday.com).

22. Clymer, A. (1999). *Edward Kennedy - a biography*, William Morrow and Co. p. 609. In August 1994 the conservative West Virginia Democrat and Senate leader invited me to accompany him to his grand offices in the Capitol building where he presented me with the second volume of his Senate history. During the conversation with the Senator he had nothing but respect and praise for Kennedy as a man and a politician.

23. Hersh, B. (1997). *The shadow President*, Steerforth Press. vii-viii; Kessler, R. (1997). *Inside Congress*, Pocket Books. p. 92.

24. Hersh, B. (1997). *The shadow President*, Steerforth Press. p. 101.

25. Clymer, A. (1999). *Edward Kennedy - a biography*, William Morrow and Co. p. 217.

26. *Washington Post*, 2 October 1976. (http://www.washingtonpost.com).

27. Wintour, P. and Arlidge, J. 'Expose MP's, says Archbishop', *The Observer*, 20 February 2000, p. 4.

28. Goldschlag, W. 'Ted holding clan together', *New York Daily News*, 19 July 1999. (http://www.nydailynews.com).

Chapter 15

Chappaquiddick

What were the true circumstances surrounding the tragedy at Chappaquiddick?

"One of the great political stories of all time."

Investigative Reporter, Jack Anderson

"The Chappaquiddick incident had generated more publicity than any other fatal accident in the history of the United States and perhaps the world."

Kennedy Lawyer, Edward Hanify

For 30 years Senator Edward M. Kennedy has been unable to avoid the taint of the 'Chappaquiddick Scandal'. What happened that July night in 1969 effectively ended his chances of following in his brothers' footsteps - one of whom attained the presidency and the other who fell short of his goal by five months when he too was tragically assassinated.

Throughout this period, Edward Kennedy has been forced to repeat his original statement that he felt guilt and remorse at the death of a young woman who had helped his brother Robert in his quest for the presidency during the 1968 election campaign. The expectations of the media, however, were different. During the 1970s and 1980s - before the public finally accepted Kennedy's frequently stated claim that he had never had an overriding desire to be president - election campaigns had been dominated by the feeling that the Senator would finally dissemble and tell the truth about the 'actual' circumstances surrounding the tragedy. However, apart from his repeated statements of remorse no new revelations were forthcoming. The public had to be satisfied with dozens of theories which purported to explain the car accident and its aftermath. As Kennedy biographer Burton Hersh wrote: "...even the Chappaquiddick publicity, disastrous as it was, had been confined pretty largely to speculation about the accident."[1]

In 1994, in his re-election bid for his Massachusetts Senate seat, Kennedy issued an oft-repeated apology for the tragedy: "I bear full responsibility for the tragedy and I always will. I have expressed my remorse to my family, the Kopechne family and the people of Massachusetts. I only wish I had the power to do more to ease the continuing pain I feel and that Mr and Mrs Kopechne feel for Mary Jo's loss."

However, allegations of a cover-up persisted and remain to this day. Amongst the many claims made about the incident a number stayed in the public's mind:

- Kennedy had been a reckless driver and had been responsible for the death of Mary Jo Kopechne.

- Kennedy had been having an affair with Mary Jo.

- Kennedy had been trying to cover-up his recklessness or had indeed succeeded in covering up the truth of the accident.

- Kennedy had attempted to escape blame by pretending he was at his hotel at the time of the accident.

- Kennedy had asked his companions, Paul Markham and Joe Gargan, to take the blame.

- Kennedy had allowed a girl to suffocate who had been trapped in an air bubble in the car because he failed to seek help from the emergency services.

- Kennedy had been lying about the timing of the accident to cover-up his affair with Mary Jo.

- Because Mary Jo did not take her hotel room key with her she had no intention of returning to her hotel.

The story of the Chappaquiddick incident began on the weekend when Neil Armstrong, Buzz Aldrin and Michael Collins were nearing the end of their journey to the moon. Edward Kennedy sailed his yacht to Martha's Vineyard, off the coast of Cape Cod, to enter a race in the 46th Edgartown Yacht Club Regatta, a highlight of the yachting season and an event that the Kennedys rarely missed. A 'cook-out' had been planned on the tiny island next to Martha's Vineyard called Chappaquiddick, an Indian name meaning 'separate island'. It was a way for Edward Kennedy to keep in touch with the 'boiler boom' girls, so-called because they had been the centre of a group of campaign workers dedicated to Senator Robert Kennedy's 1968 campaign for the presidency. Among the group was a 28 year old named Mary Jo Kopechne. An RFK aide described her as 'an unworldy girl'. Others who knew her said she was a girl with a good character who had been committed to her work, full of high idealism and excited that the Kennedys would regain the White House in the 1968 race. After Robert Kennedy's assassination she had been devastated.

Contrary to the claims of some writers, the 'boiler room' girls were not 'secretaries' but professional and educated women with excellent characters and unblemished reputations. They did not travel to Martha's Vineyard to engage in orgies nor were they invited to the party in order to be 'available girls' for the six men who also attended the party. If this was indeed on the minds of the men in the party it can be assumed that they would have chosen a better place - the rented cottage had no privacy and they all had private rooms in Edgartown hotels. Sworn statements have indicated the gathering was nothing more than a reunion of people who had been dedicated to the election of Robert Kennedy as president. As Rosemary Keough Redmond stated to BBC researchers in 1993: "That whole myth of this bunch of single girls being set up to married men for some other purpose, it just didn't happen, it didn't happen. And it wasn't what it was about. And the relationships were not that way. So there was, you never had a feeling of concern about going somewhere...I went to Salt Lake City with Senator Edward Kennedy and Dun Gifford and I, just the three of us together and never felt threatened or concerned and...my mother didn't worry...and my sister didn't worry...none worried."[2]

Furthermore, Mary Jo Kopechne, at the time of the incident, had been engaged to be married to a career foreign service officer, a fact overlooked by those authors who tried to blemish her character by insinuating she had been single, free and willing to engage in a sexual relationship with Senator Kennedy. There is no evidence that this allegation is true. The only person who can answer it is Senator Kennedy and he has stated on numerous occasions that nothing happened between them. The true facts about Mary Jo are that she was a good, observant and practising Catholic who had been enamoured with the Kennedys and believed Robert Kennedy reflected her own views about social justice and other idealistic social and political commitments. She did not smoke and rarely drank. Everyone who knew her testified to the fact that she was a woman who was almost prudish in her dislike of obscene language and sexual impropriety.

Mary Jo had been an only child and was born in Plymouth, Pennsylvania. Her father had been an insurance salesman. In 1962, she graduated with a degree in business from New Jersey's Caldwell College for Women, a small liberal arts college run by the Sisters of St. Dominic. Before moving to Washington D.C. she had taught black children in a civil rights project in Alabama.

Her first job in the nation's capital was working for Senator George Smathers, a long-time friend of President Kennedy. She became respected for her work and Smathers recommended her to work on Robert Kennedy's staff, realising as he did that Mary Jo admired the Kennedys. She was thorough and industrious and on one occasion in 1966, stayed up all night to type RFK's speech on Vietnam in which the Senator made a clean break with Johnson's Vietnam policy. Later, in 1968, she became dedicated to her goal of helping elect RFK president. Her whole life became politics. After RFK's assassination she worked for a time helping Ethel Kennedy with her correspondence and joined the Southern Political Education and Action Committee, registering African-American voters in Florida. In July 1969, Mary Jo had been looking forward to the weekend on Martha's Vineyard when she would see her old friends.

Chappaquiddick is a remote and lonely place, without stores or petrol stations and separated from the fashionable resort of Martha's Vineyard by a sea-water channel that is about 150 yards across at its narrowest point. Seven families lived on the island year round and the summer population was under 500. The only way cars can get between Chappaquiddick and the 'Vineyard' is aboard a two-car ferry that shuttles back and forth between the hours of 7.30 a.m. and midnight.

The ferry was kept running during special occasions sometimes till 1 a.m. or later, but only when the ferry owner had forewarning.

A cottage had been rented for the party, the 'Lawrence' cottage, situated approximately three miles from the ferry landing. It was set back from the only main road on the island and was surrounded by other vacation homes and a few which belonged to year round residents. It had been rented by Joe Gargan, Kennedy's cousin, for 200 dollars. He had rented the cottage for eight days and he had intended to use the remaining rental period for himself and his wife for a summer vacation. However, Gargan's wife's mother had taken ill and she could not make the trip. There was no intention of any of the partygoers staying at the cottage. Joe Gargan had booked three rooms at the Shiretown Inn, in Edgartown, for the men in the group and rooms were booked at a motel, the Katama Shores for the women.

A short distance from the cottage was a dirt road which led 6/10ths of a mile downhill to a bridge which was approximately 12 feet wide. Across the bridge the road led to the remote sands of East Beach. The bridge was a hump-backed wooden structure, without rails, spanning Poucha Pond (an inlet). It was a dangerous bridge, too narrow, angled all wrong and humped up too high in the middle. Drivers had often been caught without warning as they sped down the dirt road heading for the beach. Many residents said something was bound to happen there someday. Islanders knew that anything over 15 miles an hour could result in an accident. They frowned on tourists who sped through heading for the beach, yet the area was devoid of sufficient warning signs.

After the yacht race on Friday 18th July 1969, Kennedy was driven across on the ferry by Joe Gargan and the party began at 7 p.m. The evening went well, everyone reminiscing about RFK's presidential campaign. The group exchanged stories about the Kennedys and indulged in drink and food. The women did not really know the men in the party too well. The men in the group, apart from Edward Kennedy, were Paul Markham, former U.S. Attorney for Massachusetts; Joe Gargan, Kennedy's cousin, a lawyer; Jack Crimmins, the 63 year old Kennedy driver; Raymond LaRosa, a professional fireman and friend; and Charles C. Tretter a former Kennedy aide. The women in the group, apart from Mary Jo Kopechne were Esther Newburgh, 26; Rosemary 'Cricket' Keough, 23; Maryellen Lyons, 27; Anne Nance Lyons, 26; and Susan Tannenbaum, 24.

Shortly after 11 p.m., according to Kennedy, he slipped away to catch the last ferry to Edgartown and took the keys to the Oldsmobile from his driver, Jack Crimmins. He did not wish his departure to put an end to the party so he did not broadcast the fact. At the same time Mary Jo complained of feeling unwell and asked the Senator for a ride to her motel in Edgartown. She had left her purse and room key at the cottage.

The one paved road through the island is centre-lined and, where it veers left towards the ferry, it is marked with an arrow of reflecting glass. Kennedy did not follow the arrow but instead he turned right down a dirt lane called Dyke Road, which leads to Dyke Bridge and East Beach.

Although the entrance to Dyke Road is not immediately apparent, Kennedy had journeyed down it during the previous afternoon when he went for a swim. However, Kennedy said he turned on to this dirt road by mistake and that he was not aware he had come off the asphalt road and on to a gravel road. Contrary to some claims that said it was impossible for Senator Kennedy to mistake the turning, it is in fact not a T junction but more like a crossroads. To the left the paved road continues to the ferry. Straight ahead is a dirt road which leads to a cemetery. To the right is the road leading to the bridge.

The car Kennedy was driving was a 1967 Oldsmobile; the exact model was an '88' also called a Delmont that year. It was a four door midsize (by American standards) family car over 18 feet long and 6½ feet wide. Like most 1967 cars it had none of the safety features we recognise today as standard - there were no seatbelts, headrests, dual-breaking system, energy-absorbing bumpers, energy-absorbing front end, door reinforcements or roof supports.

The Oldsmobile continued down the beach road towards Dyke Bridge hitting it at a speed of between 20 to 30 miles an hour. This was gauged later by experts who scientifically measured the skid marks and the location to arrive at their results. Some experts, hired by media organisations, calculated that the car had been travelling at approximately 35 miles per hour.

The car hit the guard rail and flipped over and on impact with the water the roof caved in. The pressure of the water acted on Kennedy, forcing him through the open driver's window. There have been numerous examples, over the years, of drivers who had similar experiences; one such driver having been caught in a flash flood and then washed out the window of his car. However, Kennedy had no memory of how he got out. This is a telling clue as to what really happened that tragic night. Kennedy's confusion was also the reason for his mistiming of events - he thought the accident had occurred at 11.30 p.m. - in fact it was much later more like 12.50 a.m. when tide and current conditions were consistent with Kennedy's descriptions of the accident.

The gap of 1 to 1½ hours is difficult to explain - because of his injuries Kennedy cannot remember - but his timing of events has created a number of problems not least in the criticism he received for not going to the Malm house, situated a short distance from the bridge, on his way back to the cottage. The Malm house always had lights on before midnight. If Kennedy had walked past it at 1 a.m., however, he would not have seen any lights. And Kennedy, in his testimony, stated he saw no signs of a house with lights.

After Kennedy escaped from the submerged car he made a number of attempts to rescue Mary Jo. He made repeated dives but all were in vain. The current was too strong and he became exhausted. Suffering from shock and injuries sustained in the accident, he lay on the bank before returning to the cottage.

Kennedy met Ray LaRosa outside the cottage and asked him to seek Gargan and Markham. He did not wish to alarm Mary Jo's friends. Gargan and Markham drove him back to the bridge in a rented Valiant. Both men made repeated attempts to rescue Mary Jo. According to Gargan Kennedy kept repeating: 'I just can't believe this happened...What am I going to do?' Gargan said Markham had replied: 'There's nothing you can do.'[3]

Many years later Gargan was to tell author Leo Damore (1988) that Kennedy was so distraught and concerned about the horrible circumstances he was in that, in his state of shock, he even suggested that Gargan say he had been driving the car or that Mary Jo had been in the car alone.[4]

Finally, the group admitted failure and headed for the ferry landing. Kennedy's two companions remained on the Chappaquiddick side while he impulsively dived into the water and swam the distance across to Edgartown. In the confusion and shock, Kennedy had been searching for some guidance and direction from his friends. As he was to say later, he believed Mary Jo may have extricated herself from the wreck and could be walking back to the cottage. His last words to his friends before diving into the water were: 'I'll take care of the accident and you see the girls are alright'.[5] Gargan and Markham, not realising the mental breakdown Kennedy was heading for, took him at face value and believed he would head for the Edgartown police station and report the accident. Instead Kennedy returned to the Shiretown Inn and went to his room where he lay exhausted and confused trying to make some sense of what had happened. It was now 2 a.m. - 25 minutes later he walked out on to the balcony and spoke to the manager of the Inn, mumbling something about noisy guests. This has been interpreted by a number of authors as an attempt at establishing an alibi.

For the next five hours, alone in his room, Edward Kennedy either slept or contemplated the situation he was in. He had been in an accident with a woman who was not his wife. He may have believed Gargan and Markham had made further attempts to search for Mary Jo. According to Rose Kennedy's secretary, Barbara Gibson (1986), this is exactly what happened. Gibson said that Joe Gargan told her that he and Markham returned to the crash site after Kennedy jumped into the water. Gargan told her he found a broken window and squeezing himself through it managed to make contact with Mary Jo's body. Gargan could tell by "the unnatural feel that he was too late".[6] Fearing he would drown Gargan emerged from the car and returned to the cottage. Gargan waited until morning for help to arrive, believing Kennedy had reported the accident. No help came. Kennedy did not report the accident but in his own words remained in his room and willed the incident had not taken place; he needed help and advice desperately. For a United States senator it was a position which could effectively end his political career.

Not until morning did Kennedy report to the police station. Gargan and Markham had gone to the Shiretown Inn at 8 a.m. and were shocked when Kennedy told them he had not reported the accident. They told him it was imperative he report the accident now. But before they went to the police station they walked to the ferry landing down the street from the hotel and crossed to the Chappaquiddick side where Kennedy made a number of phone calls desperately seeking advice about how to deal with the matter. While on the ferry, the ferryman told the group that a body had been found at Dyke bridge. It was now approximately eight or more hours after the accident.

A short time earlier Edgartown Police Chief, Dominic Arena, had appeared at the scene of the accident and, with the assistance of scuba diver John Farrar, removed the body from the wreck. A short time later Deputy Sheriff 'Huck' Look arrived at the scene and told Arena that he believed the vehicle was the one he spotted the previous evening taking off at high speed when he approached the car.

Edward Kennedy, in a television address to his constituents, said his actions had been "irrational, indefensible and inexplicable".[7] Thirty years later the circumstances of the accident remain a puzzle to the public. But this does not mean that a logical description of what probably occurred is lost forever. From inquest documents, doctors reports, scientifically-based research and legal expertise of a number of experts there is sufficient evidence to assemble a likely scenario - without relying on fantasy and gross speculation which has so distorted this story for a generation.

Many writers have tried to reconstruct the events of that tragic night but most have failed. In their eagerness to propagate their pet theories they have ignored vital evidence, postulated series of actions without any firm knowledge of witness statements or forensic evidence and they have engaged in gross speculation which only served to confuse the public even further. Some reconstructed scenarios are plausible; others are downright preposterous. Many have been strong on fantasy and weak on facts. Others have demonstrated an ignorance of the geography of the island and a lack of basic knowledge of forensics, engineering and medical facts. Some authors have misinterpreted the law concluding that Kennedy committed crimes ranging from manslaughter to murder.

The most bizarre theories still persist to this day. Matthew Smith (1993), a Kennedy assassination conspiracy theorist, maintained that Edward Kennedy had been set up by conspirators as a way of destroying his chances for the presidency. Apparently the same sinister forces who had a hand in the President's death also conspired to destroy Edward Kennedy by murdering Mary Jo. While this theory lets Kennedy off the hook it has no basis in fact and was based entirely on a misreading of the facts of the case and a construction of a theory relying solely on supposition and speculation.

Smith's theory had a central weakness. If you are a politician who has been 'framed' for political reasons, then why not protest the fact? Surely this would be the best defence in such circumstances. However Kennedy did nothing of the sort, further adding credibility to his version of the events that tragic night. Furthermore, why would conspirators take this route to destroy Kennedy's career when a much simpler way would be to initiate a scandal using wiretapping and surveillance techniques. Kennedy's womanising and drinking had become an item of concern amongst the press after they had observed the Senator's developing emotional deterioration after the murder of his brother Robert the previous year. Although the American media ignored politicians' indiscretions in the 1960s, it was common knowledge that the press could not ignore a story which originated in the foreign press. It would have been a precursor to the 1988 Gary Hart scandal and would have been relatively easy to arrange without the complications and risks surrounding a plot of Chappaquiddick dimensions.

Chappaquiddick authors Thomas and Richard Tedrow (1976) make the best case for an adulterous affair between Mary Jo and Kennedy. They stated that Kennedy drove to the beach on purpose, had sex with Mary Jo and then drove off the bridge. Their most important piece of evidence in support of this claim is the grass stain which they say was found on Mary Jo's blouse. However, the scientific evidence suggests it was a blood stain caused by bloody froth emitted from Mary Jo's mouth and nose after the doctor at the scene examined the body.

Jack Olsen (1970) in his book 'The bridge at Chappaquiddick', said that Kennedy had left the car after encountering Deputy Sheriff Huck Look at the crossroads. Kennedy supposedly asked Mary Jo to drive so that he would not be caught for either being with her or driving whilst under the influence of alcohol. Olsen said that Kennedy began to panic and asked Mary Jo to drive down the Dyke Road. Not used to driving a large car, confused by alcohol and experiencing difficulty in reaching the pedals, she drove off the bridge. Olsen wrote: "Kennedy had done nothing illegal...but the cop kept approaching; now there was every reason to suspect that he would jump into his station wagon and speed down the Dyke road to ask them questions. Rural cops did things like that, and rural cops could be nasty...the prospect of netting Kennedy in a car with a woman other than his wife would have titillated many of them."[8]

Olsen also stated that Kennedy was mistaken in his description of a 'hill' before the bridge which Kennedy said had contributed to the accident. Olsen said the 'hill' did not exist but photographs taken of Dyke Bridge at the time of the accident (published in 'Time' magazine)[9] clearly show 'hills' or 'mounds' at either side of the road on the approach to the bridge. It is possible the car hit the mound and became uncontrollable.

The most obvious flaw in Olsen's theory is: why would Kennedy say he was in the car when he was not? Why would he create more trouble for himself when it would have been so much easier to say he had got out of the car and only found out what happened to Mary Jo the next morning? And Olsen cannot account for Kennedy's injuries.

Amongst many others, a few notable works stand out as also contributing to the misunderstanding of the accident and the role Ted Kennedy played in it. Zad Rust's (1971) 'Teddy bare', Robert Sherill's (1976) 'The last Kennedy', Malcolm Reybold's (1975) 'The inspector's opinion', Kenneth Kappel's (1989) 'Chappaquiddick revealed' and Leo Damore's (1988) 'Senatorial privilege' purported to reveal the truth of the matter - accusations against Kennedy included murder, manslaughter, drunk-driving and political cover-up. Kappel believed that photographs which revealed damage to the car 'proved' the accident had occurred earlier than stated and Mary Jo's dead body was then returned to the car which was then driven over the side of the bridge.

Leo Damore's (1988) 'Senatorial privilege' had the greatest impact in demonising Edward Kennedy's character. Damore's book represented Kennedy as a man with poor character and devoid of moral scruples. Fully engaged in a self-serving cover-up of the scandal, Damore alleged, Kennedy had asked his cousin Joe Gargan to say he had been driving the car or to report the accident as a solo affair with Mary Jo Kopechne driving herself off the bridge. Damore came to his conclusions after securing the first interview with Joe Gargan in the early 1980s. Unfortunately, Damore believed everything Gargan told him. Damore never considered that Gargan may have been trying to cover-up his own irresponsible actions that night. Damore dismissed the medical evidence in the case and the opinions of medical experts that the injuries that Kennedy sustained rendered him incapable of rational judgement. As Mary Jo's mother stated: "No matter how you look at it, it was an accident. What hurts me deep is to think that my daughter had to be left there all night. This is why we had so bitter a feeling toward Markham and Gargan...I think Kennedy made his statement when he was still confused. In the state he was in, I do believe he couldn't think clearly. I think he was taking all this bad advice, and it just continued for days."[10]

According to Damore, Gargan said that he and Markham believed that Kennedy was going to report the accident but Kennedy believed they were going to report his suggested version -as a result of this miscommunication no report was made at all.

However, Gargan and Markham were the only rational persons on the scene and it is slightly disingenuous of Gargan to turn the story around and blame Kennedy. Kennedy was suffering from shock, exposure and a head injury - it is entirely understandable that he would blurt out confused, irrational and illogical thoughts as he sought to make sense of the crisis he was in. Accounts of countless road traffic accidents testify to the most bizarre behaviour of drivers or passengers who have suffered shock after a collision. And, of course, the lie which Damore suggests was concocted by Kennedy, Gargan and Markham, was never told. If Kennedy had been acting rationally he would have insisted that Markham and Gargan report the accident the following day and to ensure his name was not mentioned.

Damore also gives weight to the views of John Farrar, the diver who was called to extricate Mary Jo's body from the crashed vehicle. Farrar maintained that it was likely an air pocket had allowed Mary Jo to survive for a number of hours after the accident and he based his statement on his knowledge of the tides, his experience as a scuba-diver and the position of Mary Jo's body before it was retrieved from the car. This statement led Damore to conclude that Mary Jo had not drowned but instead suffocated. He accepted Farrar's description that the buoyancy of Mary Jo's body indicated she had not drowned. Farrar also commented on the small amount of water which had been expelled from Mary Jo. He never considered the possibility that water was expelled during the body's extrication from the vehicle.

There is no credible scientific evidence to support the theory of suffocation - a theory which eventually became accepted by many writers and leading newspapers in the United States and abroad. However, authors James E. T. Lange and Katherine DeWitt Jnr. (1992) in their excellent study of the accident 'Chappaquiddick, the real story', proved by examining previous drowning cases, that the buoyancy of a body indicates nothing - some bodies float, others sink.[11] Furthermore, Markham and Gargan did not observe any movement by Mary Jo when they attempted to rescue her. If she had still been alive it is reasonable to assume she would have assisted her rescuers in their attempts to get her out of the car. And three of the car's windows had been forced in, making it unlikely that an air pocket would have been trapped, especially as the strong current would have filled the car quickly with water. It is also reasonable to assume that Mary Jo would have attempted to escape had she been alive rather than wait to be rescued. And if an air pocket had indeed been present, medical opinion has demonstrated that Mary Jo would have succumbed to hypothermia in the strong and cold Labrador currents. By the time it took for Kennedy to have travelled to the cottage and returned with help Mary Jo would have died.

Lange and DeWitt also disproved the 'Reader's Digest' version of events; a version which had relied on the mistiming of tides around Chappaquiddick. The magazine's research led to the most preposterous theories most of them concerning the allegation that Kennedy had to have lied.

Whilst the truth about this accident has escaped most writers on the subject, a likely and logical account of the anomalies and inconsistencies in the story can be constructed. I acknowledge Lange and DeWitt's contribution to an understanding of what exactly happened.

There is little doubt that Kennedy, although not 'drunk' in the real sense of the word, had certainly been intoxicated. He had drank a probable total of five or six rum and cokes. It is also true that someone of Edward Kennedy's build could have metabolised alcohol quickly. And drinking and driving did not have the same stigma attached to it as it does today. Even though drink-driving laws were on the statute books in the 1960s police departments did not 'prioritise' the offence. In the United States a motor vehicle is virtually an extension of oneself.

Mary Jo's alcohol level was 0.09%. For a woman of her stature and unfamiliarity with drinking, this would likely have meant she was 'tipsy' but not 'fall down drunk'. People at the party believed Mary Jo was not 'drunk'.

Edward Kennedy's account, given to the inquest which was held six months after the accident, reveals in dramatic detail the behaviour of an injured, exhausted man who alternated between rational action and an irrational urge to wish the entire tragedy away and to believe that somehow Mary Jo would have suffered the same fate as himself - extricating herself from the car and returning to the cottage. On his journey to the ferry he kept saying to Gargan and Markham that he expected to see Mary Jo walking down the road. According to Gargan, Kennedy, on the way to the ferry, was rambling and verbalising irrational thoughts which were consistent with someone suffering from shock. Kennedy's behaviour was not unusual for a person who had experienced a tragedy. Shock causes people to disassociate themselves, temporarily, from threatening circumstances. Kennedy was subconsciously seeking the protective company of those he knew. Walking and stumbling in the dark on his way back to the cottage, head down and feeling his way along the unlit road he by-passed nearby houses. According to Dr Max Sadove of the University of Illinois Medical School, an expert on the effects of shock: "No one knows what his own breaking point is. It is different at different times for different people."[12]

Most writers maintain that Kennedy did not report the accident immediately because he was attempting to relieve himself of the onerous duty of taking responsibility and he was hoping his underlings would clear things up. Yet they fail to understand that Kennedy was in no position to take responsibility of any kind. In the periods when his actions reflected some kind of rational thought it is likely he was responding to his own political instincts - never take impulsive decisions, wait for advice and weigh the options. Kennedy put great faith in Burke Marshall, the Kennedy aide who had taken the role RFK played for Ted. Kennedy was unwilling to act without Burke's wise counsel. As RFK had said: " (Burke Marshall) had the best judgement of anyone I know." Instead it was David Burke, another Kennedy aide, who forced Kennedy to accept reality after they spoke over the phone on the morning of the accident. This almost obsessive activity in making numerous phone calls trying to contact Marshall led to accusations that Kennedy, in the hours before the accident was reported, was trying to escape blame. In his state of panic he knew he had to report the accident but he also was half conscious of the burden of the Kennedy legacy - his every action would be scrutinised and he may have felt that everything his brothers built would now end in shameful disgrace. How could he explain what had happened? If he had reported the accident when he arrived at the Shiretown Inn at 2 a.m., he feared that his parents would hear the news over the radio as they did after their other sons John and Robert had been killed. He also experienced jumbled thoughts of having to inform Mary Jo's parents. Faced with these considerations he froze and, in the parlous mental state he was in, did nothing; his irrational mind was wishing the whole thing would just disappear or Mary Jo would suddenly appear to end the nightmare.

At the inquest Joe Gargan stated: "Senator Kennedy was very emotional, extremely upset, very upset and he was using this expression...'Can you believe it, Joe, can you believe it, I don't believe it, I don't believe this could happen. I just don't believe it.' Paul Markham told the inquest that Kennedy was "sobbing and almost of actually breaking down and crying. He said, 'This couldn't have happened, I don't know how it happened...What am I going to do?'" Even Judge Boyle, who did not believe Kennedy's account of the accident, stated: "impairment of judgement and confused behaviour are consistent with this type of behaviour." [13] Kennedy had become emotionally and mentally 'paralysed' by his experience - he was in the throws of a mental breakdown caused by concussion, a bleeding injury to the brain and lesions acting together with the alcohol. His thoughts were further disturbed by memories of family tragedies.

There is no evidence to suggest that Kennedy really believed Mary Jo was still alive in the car. During the attempts to rescue her she made no sound, no thrashing movements in the water and no attempts to make bodily contact with her rescuers.

Many commentators on the accident overlook the medical reports about Kennedy's injuries. They attempt to explain the inconsistencies and anomalies in testimony and evidence from the perspective of a rational mind attempting at all cost to save the Kennedy legacy and rescue a political career. But this was no simple case which was explicable in terms of a political cover-up or an attempt to extricate a politician from serious criminal acts. James Lange, who is an expert in drink-driving cases, has stated that Kennedy could not have been tried for serious offences like vehicular manslaughter or worse. There was simply insufficient evidence. Lange even ventures that the sworn testimony of two doctors could have been used to clear Kennedy of the offence he was eventually charged with - leaving the scene of an accident. [14]

A charge of 'reckless driving' would in particular have been difficult to prove - Chappaquiddick is a lonely and sparsely populated, one road island - and it would have been inappropriate to say that operating a motor vehicle at speeds of 30 or 35 miles an hour under these circumstances would have been 'reckless'.

Kennedy's lawyers were remiss in not challenging the Prosecution's case for Kennedy leaving the scene of an accident. They believed a plea of mental impairment would have damaged his political career. Dr Robert Watt, trauma specialist at Cape Cod Medical Centre, examined Kennedy and reported that the Senator had suffered: "a half-inch abrasion and haematoma over the right mastoid, a contusion of the vertex, spasm of the posterior cervical musculature, tenderness of the lumber area, a big spongy swelling at the top of his head."[15]

Dr Watt diagnosed concussion. Later Kennedy was examined by Dr Brougham at Cape Cod Hospital where he underwent X-ray examination which showed a straightening of the cervical vertebrae. Dr Brougham diagnosed acute muscular spasm, confirming cervical strain. Both doctors said that Kennedy's mental confusion had a definite physiological reason.[16]

It is obvious from the medical reports that Kennedy had suffered from retrograde amnesia which always follows concussion. Kennedy had forgotten about the blow to his head and the period of time before his injuries. Post-traumatic amnesia would account for the numerous witnesses who testified to Kennedy's depressed, confused and forgetful state of mind in the days and weeks following the accident. His father's nurse, Rita Dallas, believed he should have been given psychiatric help.[17] On the Monday before Mary Jo's funeral Kennedy telephoned the Kopechnes again. Joseph Kopechne said: "I could see he was trying to tell us about the accident but I still couldn't understand him. He was still sobbing, still so broken up he couldn't talk."[18]

Burke Marshall told author Burton Hersh (1972): "I advised him to have a medical examination. He truly did not know whether he might have had a medical problem. He was obviously disoriented, but he appeared coherent. Then, after I was with him for a while I came to the conclusion he had a blockage, that a lot of his mind wasn't accepting yet what was happening to him. He told me he had been convinced, somehow, that Mary Jo Kopechne got out, got away. I don't think he shook that idea off for a while. The Kennedys have a way of seeming fine, going forward without interruption under stress - I remember them all at the time of Bobby's funeral - but inside a great deal is blocked off. That night, in that situation, I think Ted Kennedy might very well have functioned so that the people with him, particularly if they weren't strong-minded people, would think that he knew exactly what he was doing."[19]

Burke, like the rest of Kennedy's advisors, was seriously worried that the young senator would have a nervous collapse at any time in the weeks following the accident. Their greatest fear was the Senator suffering an emotional breakdown, as Senator Edmund Muskie was to experience in 1972, thus ruining his chances for the presidency.

It was Lange and DeWitt who finally cleared up contradictions about Kennedy's descriptions of the tidal currents and the anomalies in the timing of events by various witnesses. One of the most telling points they bring out is the fact that the current at 11.30 p.m. to midnight was not strong enough to turn the car and 'slew' it downstream. Because Kennedy's timing of events were flawed he was put in the position of being called a liar because his description of the scene of the accident was not consistent with tidal conditions. However, it was not lies which brought this about but Kennedy's mental condition and his failure to construct events that occurred before the accident. Lange and DeWitt proved that conditions described by Kennedy were consistent with the accident having occurred 1 to 1½ hours after the presumed time of the accident, just before midnight.[20] It was true that Kennedy left the cottage with Mary Jo between 11.15 and 11.45 p.m. The other party guests have never given consistent or reliable times for the departure but they do agree it was before midnight. So the mystery remains - if Kennedy and Mary Jo left the cottage before midnight what were they doing in the hour to an hour and a half until the time of the accident?

Deputy Sheriff, Huck Look, was a very credible witness. He told Police Chief, Dominick 'Jim' Arena, who was supervising the extrication of Mary Jo's body from the wreck, that he had seen a car with two or possibly three people in it the previous night when he returned from Edgartown. He said the car had a licence number beginning and ending with a seven. Kennedy's car had the licence number L 78-207. Look saw the car at approximately 12.45 a.m. He was certain of the time period. Look remembered the two 7's because he wore the number 77 on his basketball jersey at Edgartown High School. Look testified that when he approached the car it took off at high speed down Dyke Road. Look approached the car because he suspected the driver was lost and he wanted to assist.

Evidence that Kennedy returned to the cottage after 1 a.m. was provided by a next door neighbour who said his dogs barked about that time. They only barked at pedestrians. And Kennedy's description of the currents was consistent with the accident happening at approximately 1 a.m..

Which brings us to the missing 1½ hours. Unfortunately, Kennedy showed over and over again that he could not remember and the medical evidence confirms he did indeed suffer amnesia. Until Kennedy's memory returns the missing time will continue to engender speculation.

What follows is the author's belief of what really happened. This is based on the record of events described earlier and obtained through an examination of the inquest report, an analysis of scientific and forensics evidence acquired by authors Lange and DeWitt and on logical assumptions about how the train of events occurred.

It should be remembered that when Kennedy told his friends that he was leaving the party to return to Edgartown, Mary Jo had indicated she wished to leave also. Kennedy did not ask her. She also complained of feeling unwell perhaps due to the effects of the alcohol and sun.

As a drinker Kennedy would have been able to hold his liquor much better than Mary Jo who had been estimated to have consumed five or six drinks of 80-90% proof. Although Esther Newburgh stated that Mary Jo did not appear to be drunk it has been the experience of many people that an intoxicated state develops quickly after encountering the night air on leaving a hot and stuffy environment. If Mary Jo had been feeling unwell due to the effects of the alcohol it is possible that Kennedy had been walking Mary Jo around the front yard; or they may have started the car journey, stopped the car to allow Mary Jo to be sick and then continued later; or perhaps Kennedy suggested they take a swim to neutralise the effects of the alcohol. Whatever the circumstances, innocent or otherwise, Kennedy's injuries prevented him from recalling the lost time. It is also possible that Kennedy, some days or weeks later, remembered - but how could he explain to Mary Jo's parents that her last waking hours were spent getting drunk and then sobering up?

If Mary Jo had been intoxicated this would account for her leaving her purse and motel room key at the Lawrence cottage. This is exactly what Rosemary Keough did when she went with Kennedy's driver to collect a radio from Edgartown midway through the party. On her return she left her purse in the Oldsmobile.

If Kennedy and Mary Jo had left the cottage and then gone for a walk to sober up they would have had to return for the car. Lacking any sense of time and not realising the ferry would most likely have shut down for the night, they returned unobserved and started their journey in the Oldsmobile.

Kennedy drove along the main road eventually driving a matter of yards into Cemetary Road; distracted, he did not turn left following the bend in the road which would have taken him to the ferry landing. Realising his mistake he reversed the car and spotted Huck Look. An element of fear may have entered Kennedy's mind. Kennedy may have panicked because he feared Officer Look was actually an assailant who had recognised him - after all his two brothers had been murdered. Or Kennedy may simply have been fearful he would be arrested for having drunk too much. He was in a car with a woman who was not his wife - how would it look? In any case it is clear that Kennedy did not remember the incident otherwise he would have made up an entirely innocent explanation and added it to his statement the following morning.

Whether fearful of an assailant or unwilling to explain his circumstances to an officer of the law, he turned right down Dyke Road to the bridge. At the bottom of the road a short distance from the bridge the car hit a 'mound' and steering became difficult. In attempting to correct his steering Kennedy hit the guard rails on the side of the bridge and the car flipped over landing upside down. The strong current slewed the car downstream. Kennedy was thrown from the car and managed to make his way to the bank. After coming partly to his senses he made repeated dives looking for Mary Jo until he became too exhausted to continue.

After stumbling back to the cottage, Kennedy asked his friends Gargan and Markham to accompany him back to the scene of the accident. Both Kennedy aides tried to rescue Mary Jo but failed - the current was too strong. It had even defeated Police Chief, Arena, the following morning when in full daylight he tried to remove Mary Jo's body from the car. He sat on the car and waited for diver, John Farrar, after spending five minutes struggling against the current.

Kennedy became distraught; his behaviour during the next few hours strongly suggests a man who was confused, frightened and in shock. As he later confessed in his television broadcast, following his appearance in court, his thoughts were jumbled and made no sense. And this is entirely consistent with the injuries he suffered. When a person is hit on the head hard enough, the soft brain tissue collides with the hard inner surface of the skull creating a brain injury. Invariably, this disrupts electrical activity in the outer areas of the brain where memories are stored. And this disruption prevents memory from forming not only of the traumatic event itself but also of the several minutes before that event.

Gargan and Markham, the two friends who had the faculties to make a rational decision, failed to take action and report the accident. Instead they retired to the cottage after Kennedy jumped into the water at the ferry landing to swim to the Edgartown side.

Kennedy believed he did all he could have under the circumstances, given his medical condition. But he did place full blame upon himself. He never blamed Gargan and Markham who had been in a much better position both physically and mentally to handle matters. As Ted Kennedy's mother Rose was to say: "I didn't understand why Joey Gargan or Markham did not report the matter to the police even if Ted did not have any sense enough or control enough to do so - especially when the body of the girl was in the car... That is what seems so unforgivable and brutal to me...".[21]

Kennedy's ex-wife Joan had always known that the tragedy at Chappaquiddick was a terrible accident. She told author Marcia Chellis, after her divorce: "From my own experience I know what it's like to go through a personal ordeal (she is referring to her alcoholism) and how painful it is. I know how Ted has suffered and grown because of (the accident). Can I dare hope that from such a tragedy as Chappaquiddick there can actually come out of it some good? The good is the growth and the strengthening of a very human public person."[22]

Each time Kennedy's re-election as senator comes around he has to deal with the consequences of that tragic night in July 1969. Many years after the event he told 'Time' magazine that his behaviour that night did not reflect on his present day judgement: "People may not believe me or accept some of my answers. But the idea that the people who were there that night are holding back some secret is just all wrong. The essence of the event for me is that the girl is dead. There is nothing else for me to say."[23] He has always been unable to say anything more than he said at the time of the accident; understandably so given the medical facts of the case. The media continually bring up the case asking for answers to questions which can never be fully answered. And writers continually accuse Kennedy of having committed unpardonable sins. However, a telling story by Joe Kennedy's nurse, Rita Dallas, may give insight into the stark and simple fact that Kennedy had been telling what he believed to be the truth all along. On Saturday 19th July 1969, after Kennedy returned to Hyannisport from Martha's Vineyard, he told his father the news. Dallas reported that Kennedy said: "Dad, a girl was drowned. I stopped by at a party Joe was having for some of our girls from the office. One of them wanted to catch the ferry and get back to the motel on South Beach. I said I'd take her but I turned off the road and my car went off the bridge into the tidal pond. I got out, Dad, and I tried to save her but I couldn't. I guess, after that, I went to pieces. I walked back to Joe's and then we drove back to the bridge. He tried to get her out, too, but he couldn't. I must have gone a little crazy, Dad, because I swam across to Edgartown. I left the scene of the accident, and things aren't good because of that...But I want you to know that I'm telling the truth."[24]

Edward's father, Joe Kennedy, was confined to a wheelchair after having suffered a severe stroke in 1961. He did not have the power of speech. However, according to family members, he was mentally astute. It is inconceivable that Edward, who loved his father dearly, would lie to him in the knowledge that his father's health was failing and could succumb to death at any time. And in a 1980 television broadcast Kennedy said: "Over 10 years ago I testified in court in detail under oath to God, to the truth about the accident at Chappaquiddick that caused the death of Mary Jo Kopechne. That sworn testimony has been published and reprinted many times since then. I know there are many who do not believe it but my testimony is the only truth I can tell because that is the way it happened."[25]

Kennedy's remorse was genuine and he doubtless suffered severe mental anguish. As he said to close friends on many occasions, in remembrance of his brothers' deaths and the memories of that tragic night: "Not a day goes by...".

Notes

1. Hersh, B. (1997). *The shadow President*, Steerforth Press. p. 100.

2. 'Inside story - Chappaquddick'. Narrated by Ian Holm, produced by John Edginton. BBC Television, 1994. (Otmoor Productions for BBC Television in association with Arts and Entertainments Networks).

3. Damore, L. (1988). *Senatorial privilege - the Chappaquiddick cover-up*, Dell Publishing. p. 78.

4. *Ibid*, p. 78.

5. Hersh, B. (1972). *The education of Edward Kennedy*, William Morrow and Co. p. 400.

6. Gibson, B. and Latham, C. (1986). *Life with Rose Kennedy*, Warner Books. p. 40.

7. 'Grief, fear, doubt, panic - and guilt', *Newsweek*, 4 August 1969, p. 20.

8. Olsen, J. (1970). *The bridge at Chappaquiddick*, Ace Books. p. 241.

9. 'The Mysteries of Chappaquiddick', *Time*, 1 August 1969, p. 13.

10. Damore, L. (1988). *Senatorial privilege - the Chappaquiddick cover-up*, Dell Publishing. p. 422.

11. Lange, J. E. T. and Dewitt, K. (1992). *Chappaquiddick - the real story*, St Martin's Paperbacks. p. 88.

12. 'The Mysteries of Chappaquiddick', *Time*, 1 August 1969, p. 13.

13. Ziegler, H., ed. (1970). *Inquest*. Tower Books. (Abridgement of the 5 volumes of Chappaquiddick Inquest Testimony - Docket No. 1522); 'A judge's harsh verdict on Teddy Kennedy', *Newsweek*, 11 May 1970, p. 35

14. Lange, J. E. T. and Dewitt, K. (1992). *Chappaquiddick - the real story*, St Martin's Paperbacks. p. 141.

15. *Ibid*, p. 72.

16. *Ibid*, p. 72.

17. *Ibid*, p. 123.

18. Damore, L. (1988). *Senatorial privilege - the Chappaquiddick cover-up*, Dell Publishing. p. 142.

19. Hersh, B. (1972). *The education of Edward Kennedy*, William Morrow and Co. p. 409.

20. Lange, J. E. T. and Dewitt, K. (1992). *Chappaquiddick - the real story*, St Martin's Paperbacks. p. 71.

21. Leamer, L. (1994). *The Kennedy women*, Villard Books. p. 652.

22. Chellis, M. (1985). *The Joan Kennedy story*, Sidgwick and Jackson. p. 87.

23. 'A night that haunts him', *Time*, 5 November 1979, p. 25.

24. David, L. (1993). *Good Ted, bad Ted*, Carol Publishing Group. p. 132.

25. 'Inside story - Chappaquddick'. Narrated by Ian Holm, produced by John Edginton. BBC Television, 1994. (Otmoor Productions for BBC Television in association with Arts and Entertainments Networks).

Chapter 16

The New Muckrakers

"He who controls the past, controls the future."

George Orwell, (1984)

"In biography, you do gain possession of a life and it's a terrifying possession that you have. You are entitled to walk around inside the life and the experiences and the memories of someone who had a great deal of influence in the world. I think we always ask ourselves, what is the moral accountability to that life? And what is the moral accountability to the people who survive the deceased and who are affected by interpretations of that life?"

Ron Powers

A spate of recent books about the Kennedys have prompted many people to ask: "Can we believe what is found between the pages of a non-fiction book?" As I have attempted to address throughout this account, many non-fiction books now more than ever can be challenged on their accuracy and this raises questions about how carefully publishers check their books.

The issue is important because the general public is becoming confused as to the veracity of non-fiction books. And there is evidence that monstrous calumnies are passing for accepted wisdom. John Updike recognised this trend when he told 'The Guardian' newspaper: "As long as I am alive, I don't want somebody...disturbing my children, quizzing my ex-wife, bugging my present wife, seeking Judases among my friends, rummaging through yellow old clippings…and getting everything slightly wrong."[1] Updike singled out those books based on malice, revenge, score settling and character assassination which had so marred the image of biography and non-fiction in recent years.

As I have attempted to demonstrate, Robert Kennedy's 'affair' with Marilyn Monroe never existed yet the story is accepted as fact throughout the publishing world and the mainstream media. Many major newspapers and magazines in Britain and the United States believe that President Kennedy was assassinated by a group of conspirators. Many people throughout the world believe that Princess Diana and Marilyn Monroe were murdered, making reference to books and articles which fail to prove a particular theory, depending as they do solely on accepting anomalies and inconsistencies as proven 'facts'. Every mistake made by official investigators is interpreted in a sinister light.

Hoaxes have a long tradition in publishing - who can forget Clifford Irving's 'authorised biography' of Howard Hughes or the 'Hitler diaries' acquired by Professor Hugh Trevor-Roper? Hoaxes are deceptions but who has responsibility for an author's injudicious interpretation of 'facts' or use of sources of suspect credibility? This matters because in the practice of writing history you have to get the little things right in order to be credible with the larger issues.

Recent cases in the late 1990s were highlighted with the publication of Clinton Cabinet member, Robert Reich's, 'Locked in the cabinet' and Sebastian Junget's 'The perfect storm'. Reich's best-selling memoir of his government service with President Clinton had several instances in which his account differed from transcripts and the public record. Similar major errors were made in Sebastian Junget's best-seller. The accuracy of Don Snyder's book 'The cliff walk: a memoir of a lost job and a found life' was questioned. Snyder became a house painter after he lost his teaching job, but 'Salon' Internet magazine reported distortions in Snyder's account of his academic career at Colgate University and The University of Maine.[2]

The controversy surrounding the murder of Robert Kennedy has not been helped by the mis-reporting of the facts surrounding the case. Kennedy biographer Jerry Oppenheimer (1994) wrote: "One (bullet) had entered the mastoid bone and lodged in the midline of the brain; another was lodged in the back of the neck; a third had grazed the forehead."[3] As we saw in chapter 13 the actual wounds were quite different and Kennedy was certainly not 'grazed' by a bullet. This matters because researchers new to the case will be misled if they use Oppenheimer as a secondary source.

But the aforementioned mistakes arose through faulty memory or poor research. Other works are inaccurate because of malevolent intent or a willingness to believe any source no matter how incredible. The credence put upon Kitty Kelley (1986), a biographer of Jacqueline Kennedy, Frank Sinatra and Nancy Reagan is typical of how some publishers are willing to accept scurrilous gossip at the expense of truth in order to sell books. George Capozi Jnr., a biographer of Kelley, turned the tables on the 'new muckraker' and itemised her endless list of "lies, distortions and doubletalk... on (Frank) Sinatra's life and loves...". Capozi wrote of how Kelley, challenged on how she could have known the contents of a bedroom conversation between Jacqueline Kennedy and writer Pete Hamill, told her publisher: "I made it up...they won't sue." He also discovered that Kelley interviewed Peter Lawford 12 days after the actor's death.[4]

Other mistakes involving the use of sources include the mixing of fact with rumour. In Nina Burleigh's (1999) book about the 'unsolved' murder of Kennedy mistress, Mary Meyer, the author categorically stated that 'Washington Post' publisher Phil Graham, an intimate of JFK, revealed the JFK/Meyer affair to a convention of newspaper editors in 1963, while Kennedy was still President. Later in the paragraph she gives the source for the story as Katherine Graham, Phil Graham's wife.[5] Yet in her autobiography, Katherine Graham (1998) makes no mention of Mary Meyer or her affair with JFK. As to Phil Graham's remarks to the convention Katherine simply stated: "No one present that night has ever told me exactly what happened or what Phil said...Apparently, though, Phil's wild remarks attacked individuals as well as the press in general."[6] Shortly after his speech, Phil Graham committed suicide. He had been suffering from a mental illness which made him do and say things which shocked not only his wife but also other friends in their social circle.

The rumour that Phil Graham had revealed the secret of the JFK/Meyer affair was researched by Tony Chaitkin who, in 1986, tracked down the correct date, time and place of the convention. Chaitkin interviewed people who were there and none of the attenders recalled anything said about Mary Meyer.[7]

Sometimes ideology is the driving force enabling writers to put the worst interpretations on events. In Paul Johnson's (1997) book 'A history of the American people', the right-wing historian not only misinterprets President Kennedy's role in American history but makes a number of startling errors in his efforts to disparage the liberal President. He wrote: "Castro's troops...killed 114 of the (Bay of Pigs) invaders and took prisoner the rest, 1,189, nearly all of whom were executed or later died in Castro's prisons." As we learned in chapter 2 this was simply not true. In December 1962, more than a thousand of them had been released by Castro in return for a ransom of 53 million dollars worth of pharmaceuticals, baby food and other goods. Johnson also mistakenly wrote that Kennedy made Richard Helms head of the CIA. The appointment was made by Lyndon Johnson. And a central weakness in Paul Johnson's re-assessment of Kennedy's presidency is his reliance on Judith Campbell Exner as a source for his claims that Joe Kennedy promised to help the Mafia in exchange for their help in the 1960 election. Johnson also believed the spurious claim that John Kennedy had direct contact and a personal relationship with Chicago mob boss, Sam Giancana.

The problems inherent in the 'new biographies' began in the 1980s and 1990s. The pressures put upon authors and publishers to reveal something 'new and exciting' have their origins in the philosophy of profit over merit; it became the overriding factor in publishing non-fiction.

As books often require serialisation in national newspapers there is a demand for books about celebrities which promise startling 'new' stories 'revealed here for the first time'. Newspapers believe their readers need titillation, 'startling revelations' and 'a new angle on the story'. It is not surprising that in this competitive market writers strive to come up with some startling transgression in order to gain an edge.

The controversy surrounding the evolution of biography continued in 1999 with the publication of Edmund Morris' (1999) biography of Ronald Reagan, 'Dutch - a memoir of Ronald Reagan'. The book created debate about the increasingly experimental nature of the genre. Morris employed unorthodox techniques to tell his story, inserting himself into the book as a fictionalised character who regularly enters Reagan's life to make observations and discuss events with the subject. Morris defenders state that the genre is constantly evolving and that there is nothing wrong with 'experimentation'. Some like to quote Virginia Woolf who said: "(Biography) is a bastard art." Others maintain that quoting what a subject supposedly thought is the stock-in-trade of the art, and that biographies are fully interpretation. This begs the question, however: why did the writer not produce an historical novel rather than pass off speculation as fact, a technique Gore Vidal employed in his novel 'Lincoln'. The reader thus avoids any confusion as to what is creative imagination and what is pure fact.

Some authors, unable to confirm stories or find corroborative proof, have resorted to 'invention'. In 1993, Joe McGinniss invented quotes for his unauthorised biography of Senator Edward Kennedy. The publishers, Simon and Schuster, released a press statement which said: "Some thoughts and dialogue attributed to figures in this narrative were created by the author, based on such research and his knowledge of the relevant people, places and events." The author regularly inferred in the narrative what Ted Kennedy might have been thinking - a preposterous way of writing an account of someone's life. This is not to imply that biographers need to 'interpret'. They do. Lytton Strachey once said that: "Uninterpreted truth is as useless as buried gold." But 'interpretation' must be based on the evidence and the true rendering of the facts. As critic Desmond MacCarthy wrote: "A biographer is an artist who is on oath."

The most unrealistic and uncorroborated moment in McGinniss' book comes when he implies that Edward Kennedy had contemplated suicide after the tragic assassination of his brother, Jack: "Suppose - not that there is any evidence he considered this - he suddenly just veered left, away from his sister, and plunged, fully clothed, into the roiling, frigid waters of Nantucket bay? Just swam out into the mist until exhausted then floated on his back and let the cold waves carry him wherever they might, while the noise of the surf and the wind drowned out the sound of human voices."[8] If there is no evidence that Edward Kennedy contemplated suicide then why say so? McGinniss' skills of creative imagination are evidently superior to his biographical scholarship.

McGinniss' indiscriminate use of sources gets him into trouble when he uncritically embraces the unproved theory that the Mafia assassinated President Kennedy for failing to oust Castro and so revive the Mafia's gambling interests in Cuba. McGinniss says that the Kennedys incurred this obligation when Joe Kennedy accepted illegal help for his son in the West Virginia primary election and in Illinois during the presidential election. As we saw in chapter 7 this assessment is naïve.

Edmund Morris, Kitty Kelley and Joe McGinniss were not the only writers to challenge the existing unwritten rules governing the writing of biographies. Anthony Summers (1993) in his biography of J. Edgar

Hoover based his theory that Hoover was a sexual deviant on a statement made by a gangster's ex-wife and hearsay evidence from a number of dubious sources. As Cartha Deloach (1997), a close associate of Hoover's, wrote: "When Anthony Summers' (book) was first published, I read it with disbelief...It was...a string of opinions, rumours and undocumented charges...it was strange to read about people and happenings that seemed only vaguely recognisable, as if total strangers had been assigned the familiar names of friends and colleagues. It was a macabre experience...Summers is almost alone among Hoover's biographers to give credence to the petty malice of society's outcasts...J. Edgar Hoover was not a homosexual. Those who knew him well are unanimous in that opinion. And those who carefully read the Summers book must reject the charge."[9]

Edward Klein (1996) in his book 'All too human - the love story of Jack and Jackie' projected himself into Jacqueline Kennedy's innermost thoughts and read her mind: "Jackie thought that Charlie was becoming quite a bore", "By midweek Jackie was in a state of deep distress", etc. He also quotes verbatim conversations he could not possibly have overheard. But overall Klein has managed to stick to the facts and his book deserves some credit.

It is also extremely difficult to sort fact from fiction in these often contradictory accounts. For example, factual anomalies pop up from time to time in recent books about Jacqueline Kennedy. Did Janet Auchincloss, Jackie's mother, conspire to get her ex-husband, Jack Bouvier, so drunk on Jackie's wedding day that he could not even make it to the church, much less perform the simplest of all wedding tasks - giving the bride away? John H. Davis maintains this is true. Edward Klein disagrees.

Joyce Carol Oates has used the term 'pathography' to describe some types of biography that "mercilessly expose(s) their subjects" and "relentlessly catalogue their most private, vulnerable and least illuminating moments".

But these are not the only problems we are faced with when it comes to books about the Kennedys. It would appear to be open season for this tragedy-laden family. As historian Arthur Schlesinger put it, commenting on Seymour Hersh's 'The dark side of Camelot': "Hersh will believe anything as long as it's anti-Kennedy, whatever the source."[10] RFK biographer, Jack Newfield, said: "But what is so sad and disappointing to me is the book's (Hersh's) gullibility, its willingness to believe every anti-Kennedy source."[11]

Schlesinger put his finger on the problem concerning recent accounts of the Kennedy brothers. There is a mountain of evidence to suggest that much of what the Kennedy brothers did was for the good. The 'new muckrakers' reduce it to a molehill. Many authors are indiscriminate in their use of sources, obviously aware that dead people can be quoted more authoritatively without risk of rebuttal.

Defence and prosecution witnesses in a court of law are often challenged as to their credibility on the witness stand. Frequently, their backgrounds are called into question in an effort to validate their veracity and thus establish the truth. Ex-convicts, drug addicts, psychiatric patients and convicted perjurers are most likely to be abandoned by lawyers for obvious reasons. Not so with many authors whose most sensational claims are sourced from people with similar backgrounds. Although some writers acknowledge these problems many do not hesitate to put faith in what people of this type tell them.

Often stories constructed from interviews have been checked by other authors or newspapers and they have been found to be wanting. Some of the people interviewed for Seymour Hersh's (1997) 'Dark side of Camelot' and C. David Heymann's (1998) 'RFK – a candid biography', for example, say the authors have misconstrued their stories as we shall see later in the chapter.

In Hersh's book, one or two new anecdotes surface but, in the main, he recycles accumulated gossip, mixes fact with conjecture and writes in a style so adversarial as to render its overall thesis, that Kennedy was a dangerous and immoral man, without credibility. As historian Richard Reeves wrote: "...It is shocking that a tribal elder as admired as Hersh could do a book so shoddy...some of it is just embarrassing, in a class with the phoney John Kennedy/Marilyn Monroe documents that drummed up interest in the mess. In the tribe (of journalists), Hersh's work is seen as a kind of betrayal of whatever standards we do have."[12]

Some of Hersh's sources are credible - former Secret Service agents have given their accounts of Kennedy's philandering. Yet Hersh gave the impression that he was the first to acquire Secret Service agents' accounts of Kennedy's womanising. Hersh told 'Atlantic Unbound' reporter Katie Bacon: "Obviously a lot of reporters knew a bunch about it; they thought it was cute, I guess. Nobody knew quite as much as the agents did, AND NOBODY HAD EVER ASKED THEM TO SPEAK BEFORE." (emphasis added).[13] Hersh (1997) wrote in his book 'The dark side of Camelot': "The most dispassionate observers were the Secret Service agents assigned to the President's personal detail...They have kept their silence until now."

Not so. Victor Lasky (1977) in his book 'It didn't start with Watergate', wrote:

> *"My own sources during the Kennedy era were Secret Service agents assigned to guard the President. On an off-the-record basis they expressed concern about "Lancer's" (JFK's code name) alliances with women he hardly knew. It wasn't so much that they were prudish. What concerned them were the security problems involved. One agent even wondered aloud whether the Russians might be tempted to 'plant a broad' in the President's bedroom. But there was little the agents could do about it."[14]*

And author Michael John Sullivan (1991) in his book 'Presidential passions', wrote: "(Secret Service agents) were expected to provide their illustrious boss with a constant and steady supply of female sex partners.' He didn't want to know about security but about broads', recalled Marty Venker, one of JFK's Secret Service agents"[15]

The four agents who Hersh interviewed may have been talking for the first time but essentially they were repeating stories told by their colleagues many years previously. It was therefore disingenuous of Hersh to claim the information he was supplying was 'new'.

As I have attempted to demonstrate in previous chapters, many of Hersh's sources are telling what they believe to be the truth but may not have been in a position to know for sure. Some sources evidently have axes to grind or to repeat hearsay. Hersh's reliance on Judith Exner, who has changed her story so many times, is a great weakness with his book. Another weakness is his claim that the Ellen Rometsch's story had been ignored by the media since the 1960s. In fact Rometsch had been mentioned by historian Michael Beschloss (1991) in his book 'Kennedy v. Kruschev - the crisis years 1960-1963'. He devoted more than three pages to the affair. And, of course, there is no evidence whatsoever that she was a communist spy.

Hersh leaves no malicious tale unreported nor does he question the motives of his interviewees. Alan Brinkley, Professor of American

History at Columbia University, said: "It's depressing to see such shoddy and careless arguments and such self-serving credulity coming from a celebrated investigative reporter."[16] 'Vanity Fair's' Robert Sam Anson believes Hersh's judgement had been clouded by his "wanting to believe the very worst about the Kennedys from the get-go" and by greed.[17] Hersh is quoted in the 'Vanity Fair' article as saying he wanted: "to make a score and retire." Theodore Sorensen, assistant to President Kennedy called the book: "a pathetic collection of wild stories."[18] Richard Reeves, an eminent historian, said: "(The book is) not important at all in terms of history and the 'new' revelations are 'suspect'". Reeves maintains that Hersh did not get the story "right...it is not important at all in terms of history. Suspect old stuff on Kennedy is clumsily rewritten, and the new stuff, such as it is, is even more suspect."[19] In addition, Hersh's accounts have been challenged by a number of people he interviewed.

Jerry Bruno, a former Kennedy advance man in West Virginia whom Hersh used to buttress claims the election there was bought, claimed Hersh misinterpreted his comments. Hersh quoted Bruno in part as saying: "Every time I'd walk into a town (in West Virginia) they thought I was the bagman." However, Bruno told the 'New York Daily News': "He (Hersh) distorted that. What I said was, 'people would ask me, was I the bagman? At no time did I indicate I was the bagman. It was a phrase they used (in West Virginia)." Bruno also said, "(Hersh's) book should be called 'The dark side of Seymour Hersh.'"[20]

Hersh relied on another source who had been closely connected to the Kennedys, Paul Corbin, to claim that John Kennedy's Chief of Staff, Kenneth O'Donnell, had been another bagman for the Kennedys and he embezzled thousands of dollars for himself. But one of Corbin's friends, RFK aide, John Seigenthaler, said Corbin had been "completely obsessed" with O'Donnell and frequently made up rumours about him. Furthermore, Seigenthaler said he told Hersh but the author was not interested in Corbin's motives and ignored Seigenthaler's advice that Corbin was not a credible source. Helen O'Donnell, the Kennedy aide's daughter, said she tried to warn Hersh about Corbin but was met with abuse.[21]

Hersh also misinterpreted comments made by Kennedy friend, Charles Spalding. Hersh wrote of how President Kennedy became worried that his lover, Marilyn Monroe, had been talking too much about their relationship. Kennedy supposedly despatched Spalding to California for the purpose of telling Monroe to keep her mouth shut. As Hersh tells it:

"Charles Spalding recalled that at one point during the 1960 campaign, when Monroe was on a liquor and pill binge, Kennedy asked him to fly from New York to Los Angeles to make sure that she was okay - that is, to make sure that Monroe did not speak out of turn. 'I got out there, and she was really sick,' Spalding told me. With (Kennedy brother-in-law Peter) Lawford's help, 'I got her to the hospital.'"[22]

It is one thing to be indiscriminate when choosing sources but in this instance Hersh has listened to an apparently credible and authoritative source and then has misinterpreted the story. Charles Spalding does not deny he made the trip but emphatically denies that it was in any way intended to shut Monroe up.[23] In any case the 79 year old Spalding, who suffered from 'short-term memory loss', should have been treated as a 'suspect' source, not because of his lack of knowledge of the Kennedys, but because of his impaired mental faculties.

Hersh's flawed methodology may be partly explained by making reference to statements made by historian Richard Reeves (1993) when he answered questions concerning research for his book 'President Kennedy - profile in power': "The oral histories at the Kennedy Library were done mainly in 1964, which was for me a tremendous help because many people in 1988 tell different stories...than what they were telling in 1964, so you've got a real reality check of what happened."[24]

Indeed, Hersh himself implies that he has used sources in the past whose credibility is poor. In the 1980s, he wrote a book about the Israeli nuclear programme entitled 'The Samson option' and used Ari Ben-Menashe as one of his major sources for his exposé. However, he is quoted in the November 1997 issue of 'Vanity Fair' as saying Ben-Menashe "lies like people breathe".

Hersh does not stop at libelling the dead Kennedys. He maintains that Richard Nixon received a 100,000 dollar bribe. Stephen Ambrose, an acclaimed Nixon biographer, found the story implausible. "(If Hersh) has a copy of the cheque, that's another matter," Ambrose said, "But he's saying that the other guy saw a copy of the cheque. Right away, as a historian, you're done."[25]

Both JFK author, Seymour Hersh (1997), and RFK biographer, C. David Heymann (1998), make brief reference to the positive role the brothers played in American politics but these are virtually the only pages where contempt is absent. If there is any recognition of the slightest hint of decency in either brother it is overwhelmed by a wealth of scandalous gossip and second-hand hearsay. C. David Heymann 'vacuumed up' every salacious detail from every source he could find and presented it in a single distorted narrative devoid of filtering intelligence, balance and integrity. He probably goes further than any of the recent biographers in his willingness to quote any source indiscriminately in his effort to accuse the late Senator of having taken cocaine, partied with prostitutes, enjoyed bar brawls and had romances with Jacqueline Kennedy, Marilyn Monroe and Barbara Sinatra.

However, Heymann's publishers should have been cognisant of his previous mistakes when he wrote biographies of Barbara Hutton and Elizabeth Taylor. In December 1983, publishers Random House announced it was recalling 58,000 copies of Heymann's book 'Poor little rich girl: the life and legend of Barbara Hutton' after Dr Edward A. Kantor threatened to sue for having been defamed in the book. The book wrongly said that Dr Kantor had prescribed excessive drugs for Miss Hutton in 1943 (he was 14 years old at the time). Heymann's lawyer said: "It was a comedy of errors. Information that had been given to the author by other people interviewed all pointed to Dr Kantor, and one problem was he could never find out how old Dr Kantor was."[26]

Furthermore, Heymann's publishers accused him of having lied about errors in his book, saying he had not brought them to their attention. But this was not the first time that Heymann had courted controversy. In 1977, Andrew W. Mellon, Professor of Humanities at the John Hopkins University and a leading Ezra Pound scholar, said he had doubts that a 1971 Heymann interview with Pound which was included in Heymann's book about the famous poet, had ever occurred.[27]

Heymann's RFK biography follows in the same tradition as his earlier works. It is a pageant of unanalysed anecdotes. In his chapter called 'Sex', two pages of his narrative is dependent on 'society columnist' Doris Lilly. This reliance on a single source is not in the best traditions of good journalism let alone historical biography. And many of Heymann's single sources turn out not to have witnessed events first hand. Heymann relied on former Federal Bureau of Narcotics agent Howard Diller for his allegations that RFK took drugs and raped women. This particular source depended on third hand information - what Diller had heard that federal agents had 'purportedly' said.

Heymann also depends heavily on authors Gore Vidal and Truman Capote to propagate his scandalous allegations about Robert Kennedy's private life. Vidal's personal animus to Robert Kennedy is well chronicled. Once part of the Kennedy's social scene - he shared a stepfather with Jacqueline Kennedy - Vidal was shunned by the Kennedys after drunken behaviour at a White House party in 1961. Arthur Schlesinger Jnr. witnessed the scene and said that Robert Kennedy intervened to quiet the author down. Vidal responded by calling Kennedy a 'god-damned impertinent son of a bitch.' Kennedy had been repulsed by Vidal's bisexuality and made it clear he was not welcome in the White House.[28]

Truman Capote, Heymann's other questionable celebrity source, was, a flamboyant and outrageous homosexual frequently high on drink and drugs and given to making outlandish statements, according to his biographer, George Plimpton. Plimpton's (1999) biography of Truman Capote clearly demonstrates why he is an unreliable source. By juxtaposing conflicting testimonies and devoting a separate section to Capote's lies Plimpton gives a clear perspective on Capote's exaggerations and made-up stories.

Heymann's 'authority' as an acclaimed biographer was further damaged when he made reference to "John Dennis Profumo" as the "United Kingdom's Minister of War", getting Profumo's title, name and job description wrong.[29]

Heymann also embellished the story of the RFK/Monroe relationship, writing: "Later that night, Marilyn wished JFK an even happier birthday in one of the bedrooms at the Kennedy suite in the Carlyle (Hotel). But the actress did not spend the night with the President. After Jack had taken his satisfaction, Marilyn found her way to another bedroom in the same suite, where she gave delight to her devoted moth (a reference to a comment by Adlai Stevenson, that RFK was 'dancing around Monroe like a moth to a flame'), the Attorney General of the United States."[30]

And who does Heymann give as his source for this tale? He does not say, nor can we tell from Heymann's list of sources at the back of his book. As Robert Kennedy was accompanied by his wife Ethel when he attended his brother's birthday party, what are we to make of this unsourced story – that RFK slipped away from his wife for a dalliance with the movie star?

The manner in which Heymann interviewed sources for his book should render his overall thesis without credibility. He was willing to use second-hand accounts indiscriminately like those of hotelier, Peter Jay Sharp, and New York real estate developer, Abe Hirschfield. Sharp told Heymann he bought New York's Carlyle Hotel in 1967 and had a girlfriend who had stumbled upon the three Kennedy brothers in one of the hotel's suites partying with three girls. Hirschfield recounted second-hand gossip which came his way as 'proof' that RFK had had an intimate relationship with Jayne Mansfield.

Heymann uses a close Kennedy family friend, LeMoyne Billings, as proof that Robert Kennedy knew about the plots to kill Castro. Heymann writes: "Lem Billings recalled having lunch with Bobby at the latter's Carlyle suite in New York in June 1962. 'Bobby seemed in an excellent mood that day,' said Billings. 'He spoke and even laughed about the Mafia's involvement in trying to do away with Castro. He remarked that when the CIA had recently told him of renewing its ties to the mob, he'd done a better job of feigning shock and anger than Burt Lancaster.'"[31]

Heymann, it should be noted, is reporting nothing less than the scoop of the decade yet he kept it under wraps for close to 17 years. Why? Heymann states in his notes at the back of his book that he interviewed Billings shortly before the Kennedy confidante's death in 1981. Billings' close ties to the Kennedys is well-documented and true, but he was a drug addict in the later years of his life and, according to another questionable source, Truman Capote, Billings frequently made outrageous statements when he visited one of his favourite night club haunts in New York, Studio 54. The question must be asked, therefore, if Heymann had this knowledge for 17 years why did he wait until 1998 to reveal it? The Billings interview had been solicited for Heymann's (1989) biography of Jacqueline Kennedy, "A woman named Jackie", yet he does not mention the startling revelations attributed to Billings. Nor does he write about Billings' story in a paperback reprint of the book in 1994. There is no corroboration for Heymann's 'exposé' and Billings physical and mental state at the time he was interviewed was parlous to say the least. Billings 'revelations' about Robert Kennedy are therefore extremely suspect as is Heymann's superhuman efforts to keep the story secret until now.

Another of Heymann's leading sources for his book is Langdon Marvin. In describing this source Heymann writes: "Langdon P. Marvin, Jnr.; an aide to JFK during the race (1952 Senate race) and afterward in the Senate..."[32] What Heymann fails to tell his readers is the bad choice he made in selecting Marvin as a source. We are led to believe that Marvin is a credible source as he worked for the Kennedy senatorial and presidential campaigns. Yet Marvin's motives in telling his accounts is extremely suspect.

Langdon Marvin came from a prominent New York family and had become friendly with John Kennedy when they were both students at Harvard. After Kennedy became a congressman, Marvin worked for him on an ad-hoc basis doing research work and sometimes acting as a campaign advance man. Marvin still maintained contact with the Kennedys throughout the 1950s. John and Jacqueline Kennedy attended his birthday party on May 2nd 1954 at the F Street Club in Washington D.C.. It was during this period that Marvin's personality began to show signs of instability. He frequently ended a night's drinking bout out of control and a lot of his troubles resulted from his attempting to make homosexual advances to men in bars.[33]

Marvin is frequently mentioned by writers as the man who secured women for Senator Kennedy before his debates with Richard Nixon during the 1960 campaign. The writers invariably fail to mention, however, that Marvin fell out with the Kennedys in late November 1962 and his grudge seems to have lasted well into the 1990s. Marvin had become a wild and uncontrollable alcoholic and his photograph was posted inside a White House security guard's lodge. He was barred from entering the White House.[34]

Yet we are led to believe from Heymann that Marvin still remained in contact with the Kennedys until 1964. Heymann quotes Marvin as saying: "In January of 1964, not long after Jack's death RFK asked me out to Hickory Hill. There he handed me a packet of letters - maybe a dozen or so - and told me to 'get rid of them'. I should have saved them but I didn't. I didn't even read them. He admitted to me later that they were love missives both he and Jack had received from Marilyn Monroe."[35]

This uncorroborated statement begs the questions: why did RFK not burn the letters? And why did he entrust them to a notorious alcoholic who had previously been barred from entering the White House? Marvin had 35 years to tell his story about the letters but did not do so.

Heymann's sources for the supposed RFK/Jackie affair are as unreliable as those used by another Kennedy author, Christopher Andersen. Andersen claimed that shared grief provoked Jackie and Robert Kennedy to begin a romance shortly after President Kennedy's assassination, and, as we have seen in chapter 9, used Kennedy friend Charles Spalding to support his claim. Spalding denied a sexual relationship existed. Jackie's half-brother, Jamie Auchincloss, and close friend, Peter Duchin, supported Spalding's view. And as author Donald Spoto wrote: "...there is not a shred of evidence to support the ugly rumours of an adulterous romance between them - contrary to those gossips who were eager to interpret spiritual alliance as erotic attachment."[36]

It is quite evident that to write 'fact' based upon such weak sources and irresponsible inferences is at best reckless and at worst dangerous. It is this kind of reporting of 'facts' and manipulation of evidence which seem to help some authors to 'construct' scenarios.

Suggested or implied 'proof' is another way in which some authors manipulate the facts. A case in point, first discovered by author James DiEugenio, is suggested or implied 'proof' that John and Robert Kennedy knew about the assassination attempts against Castro. In his article published in 'Probe' magazine, DiEugenio showed how author John H. Davis (1985), in his book "The Kennedys - dynasty and disaster", attempted to reverse the verdict of the Church Committee which rejected claims that the Kennedy brothers authorised the CIA to kill Castro.[37]

As DiEugenio points out, Davis did this by manipulating the Church Committee's report 'Alleged assassination plots involving foreign leaders' issued in 1975.[38] Davis stated that CIA Director, Allen Dulles, briefed JFK on the plots at a November 27th 1960 meeting with the President-elect. Davis used Deputy Director Bissell as his source. The Committee's report states:

> Bissell: *I believe at some stage the President and the President-elect both were advised that such an operation had been planned and was being attempted.*

> Senator Howard Baker: *By whom?*

> Bissell: *I would guess through some channel by Allen Dulles.*

> The Chairman: *But you're guessing aren't you?*

> Bissell: *I am, Mr Chairman, and I have said that I cannot recollect the giving of such a briefing at the meeting with the President in November...*

Bissell stated that he did not remember, yet Davis implied that he did and used him as a source. But the Report also stated further: "Bissell surmised that the reasons he had Dulles not tell Kennedy at that initial meeting were that they had 'apparently thought it was not an important matter.'"

When Senator Church asked Bissell if that was not rather strange, Bissell replied: "I think that in hindsight it could be regarded as peculiar, yes." Davis omitted these statements made by Bissell thus allowing the reader to conclude that Kennedy knew of the plots.[39]

Davis disingenuously quoted CIA officer, Richard Helms. Helms told Davis: "(I) believed Bissell was correct, that, knowing him, he would not commit perjury before a Senate Committee." Davis omitted to explain how Helms had been a rival of Bissell's within the CIA and resented him for not seeking advice on matters. Helms was not upset when the Bay of Pigs invasion failed as this meant that Bissell would be fired. When this indeed happened to both Dulles and Bissell a new pair took over the Castro plots - William Harvey and Ted Shackley - and they reported to Helms. Helms, therefore, had a motive in using Bissell's name as it would have steered culpability away from him in continuing the unauthorised plots. When John McCone, Dulles' replacement as Director of the CIA, issued a directive to his staff outlawing assassination plots, Helms said he could not remember the meeting. Furthermore Helms continually 'disremembered' a meeting with Robert Kennedy.

DiEugenio also discovered that John H. Davis wrongly used the following as evidence of the Kennedy brothers' "knowledge" of the plots. Davis wrote: "...Kennedy also met on April 20th with the Cuban national involved in the unsuccessful underworld Castro assassination plot, a meeting that was not discovered until the Senate Committee on Intelligence found out about it in 1975. That Kennedy could have met with this individual, whose name has never been revealed, without knowing what his mission had been, seems inconceivable." The implication in this passage is clear. Kennedy met with one of the Cuban exiles who had been involved in a plot to kill Castro. (It turned out to be a man by the name of Tony Varona). Obviously, a conversation about Varona's mission took place, Davis implies.

However, the meeting that Davis described did not occur in the way he implies. Davis' use of the Church Report has led him to misconstrue the real meeting which included Kennedy, Secretary of Defense, Robert McNamara, General Lyman Lemnitzer "and other Administration officials". Also in the room were "several members of Cuban groups involved in the Bay of Pigs." The Church Committee Report does not say anything about assassination having been discussed.[40]

The central problem surrounding Kennedy revisionist biographies lies in the writers' desire to find 'new' revelations to make their works sensational. The reasons for this are obvious. Books cannot be peddled to the reading public unless the reader's attention is grabbed. Scandal provides the 'hook'. One cannot fault many revisionist authors for their diligent research. However, the temptation to publish uncorroborated evidence and pass it off as legitimate historical fact is unforgivable. We are faced with the troubling circumstances of false histories masquerading as 'historical truths' and the need to satisfy the public's longing for the salacious and the sensational. Through emphasising the salacious, the use of anecdotes to prove 'fact', and the faithful recording of any source, no matter how incredible, we are left with a public which 'knows' more about the Kennedy brothers' so-called immoral lifestyle but nothing about their major contributions to American history.

Notes

1. Begley, A. and Moss, S. 'A stab in the hardback', *Guardian Weekly*, 14 February 1999, p. 26.

2. Donahue, D. and Minzesheimer,R. 'In fact it's fiction', *USA Today*.
    (http://www.usatoday.com).

3. Oppenheimer, J. (1994). *The other Mrs Kennedy*, St Martin's Paperbacks. p. 443.

4. Roberts, R. 'It's Kitty Kelley's turn', *The Washington Post*, 29 July 1991. (http://www.washingtonpost.com).

5. Burleigh, N. (1998). *A very private woman - the life and unsolved murder of presidential mistress Mary Meyer*, Bantam Books. p. 216.

6. Graham, K. (1998). *Personal history*, Phoenix Giant. p. 310.

7. Dieugenio, J. *Probe*, September/October 1997, 4(6).
    (http://www.webcom.com).

8. McGinniss, J. (1993). *The last brother - the rise and fall of Ted Kennedy*, Simon and Schuster. p. 90.

9. DeLoach, C. D. (1997). *Hoover's FBI*, Regnery Publishing Inc. p. 62, 78 & 81.

10. Galvin, T. and Siemaszko, C. 'Author defends JFK tell-all', *New York Daily News*, 10 November 1997.
    (http://www.nydailynews.com).

11. Newfield, J. 'Don't be taken in by Camelot tales', *New York Post*, 10 November 1997. (http://www.nypostonline.com).

12. Reeves, R. 'In the matter of Seymour Hersh', *Universal Press Syndicate*, 14 November 1997.
    (http://www.universalreprints@uexpress.com).

13. *Atlantic Unbound*, 8 January 1998. (http://www.theatlantic.com). (The Atlantic Monthly Company).

14. Lasky, V. (1977), *It didn't start with Watergate*, Dell Books. p. 25.

15. Sullivan, M. J. (1991). *Presidential passions*, S.P.I. Books. p. 65.

16. *New York Daily News*, 10 November 1997. (http://www.nydailynews.com).

17. Anson, R. S. 'Secrets and lies', *Vanity Fair*, November 1997, p. 42.

18. Bearak, B. 'Book depicts JFK as reckless and immoral', *New York Times*, 9 November 1997. (http://www.nytimes.com).

19. Reeves, R. 'In the matter of Seymour Hersh', *Universal Press Syndicate*, 14 November 1997. (http://www.universalreprints@uexpress.com).

20. Saltonstall, D. 'JFK aides, Ted: book a fabrication', *New York Daily News*, 9 November 1997. (http://www.nydailynews.com).

21. *Ibid*.

22. Hersh, S. (1997). *The dark side of Camelot*, Little Brown and Co. p. 105.

23. 'Smashing Camelot', *Time*, 17 November 1997, p. 79.

24. 'Interview with Richard Reeves', 12 December 1993, *C-Span Booknotes*. (http://www.c-span.org).

25. Bearak, B. 'Book depicts JFK as reckless and immoral', *New York Times*, 9 November 1997. (http://www.nytimes.com).

26. McDowell, E. 'Hutton book recall shocks publishers', *New York Times*, 14 December 1983. (http://www.nytimes.com).

27. Lehman-Haupt, C. 'Fictional characters derived from real people', *New York Times*, 22 December 1983. (http://www.nytimes.com).

28. Schlesinger, A. M. (1978). *Robert Kennedy and his times*, Houghton Mifflin Co. p. 641.

29. Heymann, C. D. (1998). *RFK - a candid biography*, William Heinemann. p. 249.

30. *Ibid*, p. 308.

31. *Ibid*, p. 268.

32. *Ibid*, p. 67.

33. Klein, E. (1996). *All too human*, Pocket Books. p. 182.

34. *Ibid*, p. 327.

35. Heymann, C. D. (1998). *RFK - a candid biography*, William Heinemann. p. 474.

36. Spoto, D. (2000). *Jacqueline Bouvier Kennedy Onassis - a life*, St Martins Press. p. 225.

37. *Probe Magazine*, November/December, 1997. (http://www.webcom.com).

38. *Ibid*.

39. *Ibid*.

40. Davis, J. H. (1985). *The Kennedy clan - dynasty and disaster*, Sidgwick and Jackson. p. 289.

Chapter 17

Epilogue

The Kennedy legend

"To be great is to be misunderstood."
Ralph Waldo Emerson

"The politics of character tends to drive out the politics of substance."
Judith Lichtenberg

"...idealism, high aspirations, and deep convictions are not incompatible with the most practical and efficient of programs - that there is no basic inconsistency between ideals and realistic possibilities, no separation between the deepest desires of heart and of mind and the rational application of human effort to human problems."
Robert Kennedy

John Kennedy stated that he could rekindle the country's sense of idealism to solve the challenges of a new generation. The consensus of opinion amongst historians is that he succeeded. There was enormous pride in public service during the Kennedy years and many things seemed possible. The Kennedy Administration had a sense of youth and purpose and it is clear to many that Lee Harvey Oswald destroyed more than a man. He killed a dream shared by millions of people around the world.

The Kennedy legend also rests upon the national guilt and horror felt by the public when, in Dallas on November 22nd 1963, Kennedy was assassinated. He achieved in death what he may have failed to accomplish in life - a metaphysical communion with the American people. As Hugh Brogan (1996) wrote in his biography of John Kennedy: "John Fitzgerald Kennedy seemed to be the realisation of the American promise. Young, handsome and rich; intellectual, athletic and sexy; amusing and high-minded: he claimed the presidency like a prince. By his charm, courage and public spirit this Catholic, this heir of Ireland and machine politics and shady business deals, vindicated his people, his faith, his party, and his country's traditions and institutions. He was the best hope which America had to offer the world. He was too good to be true; Kennedy was far from perfect, and as the facts about his weaknesses emerged, a bitter deception d'amour energised many of his posthumous critics; but the legend was sufficiently accurate to justify his hold on the world's affection and imagination."

What matters is that the Kennedy legend, myth and legacy - however much a distortion of historical truth - continues to motivate. It strikes a chord on an emotional if not an intellectual or reality level. The legend still stirs the passions of those who wish to 'seek a newer world', and the Kennedy family continue to have a political impact on America. To many they still embody an ideal of public service. Transcending the generations, the Kennedy call for good men to unite in action against poverty, war and social injustice still inspires. This is especially relevant in an era when contemporary politicians are beset by an apathetic electorate, cynical in its belief that all politicians are crooks and charlatans.

The family is still important to many Americans despite the high divorce rate. The concept of family remains a central American myth and the idea that a famous family can contribute to the political well-being of the nation is also prevalent, even though Americans reject the idea of a Royal Family. During the 1960 presidential election campaign, the 'regal' and distant personae of Jack and Jackie Kennedy appealed to audiences who secretly longed for figures to look up to. And the Kennedy family continues to hold a special place in the American consciousness, although the Bush and Gore families appear to meet that need in a contemporary setting.

The Kennedy family is real and attractive, in spite of the tragedies that haunted it; the family's loyalty towards one another and its willingness to do things as a family are qualities that many Americans may long for in their own families. And they are 'classy' to coin a phrase which is popular the other side of the Atlantic, even though Americans are attracted to political sentiments which are, at root, egalitarian.

The Kennedys were also magnified by their manipulation and seduction of the media. They were the first to understand how to use it. This is vital to an understanding of how the Kennedy legend took off. Kennedy's image on television lasted long after his death as more Americans turned to their television sets to view the world outside their own communities. During the 1960s, the television became the fourth centre of power after the executive, congressional and judicial branches of government. And politics in the 1960s, in contrast to the emptier 1990s, seemed consequential - the drama of the Cold War, the possibility of nuclear war, whether African-Americans would get equal rights - these were great questions for America and Americans who were mesmerised by Kennedy's responses to them through the medium of television. Finally, Kennedy's death, as portrayed on television, became a participatory American tragedy. It provided intimacy unprecedented in any previous national American event.

The Kennedy legend has held a monopoly over other possible American legends for the past four decades, despite the American people's fascination for the Rockefellers, Gores, Bushes and Roosevelts, and the future will only tell if this monopoly continues. The legend has the ingredients of all good legends - flawed heroes, tragedy, triumph, danger and fate. After JFK's assassination, Jacqueline Kennedy compared her husband's presidency to King Arthur's Camelot, consciously or unconsciously remembering that the original Camelot was a legend of bravery, treachery, deadly virtues and virtuous sins.

However, it is no coincidence that the attempted debunking of the Kennedy legend came at a time when the cult of celebrity reached its apex of notoriety. From the 1970s onwards the 'celebritisation' of public life developed. And it was very different from what had gone on before. People no longer deferred to public figures past or present and politics became part of the media hype of celebrity. In the past, citizens looked up to their political masters; they were part of the fabric of our political myth. When indiscretions and transgressions occurred, the public were unlikely to find out if the offence did not breach the law. This reverence metamorphosed in the 1980s and 1990s into a desire to know every piece of gossip about politicians' lives. There was also an element of what the Germans call 'Schadenfreude' - a gleeful enjoyment of the misfortunes of others which brought out the envy and resentment in peoples' lives.

In the search to compare themselves with successful celebrities, people now found themselves caught in a trap. From a distance they admired them but also, paradoxically, wanted to see their downfall. And as we saw in the previous chapter, authors and publishers were now willing to respond to the public's need for revelatory 'insights' into famous lives by desperately acquiring new tales of transgressions and indiscretions. In their pursuit of the scandalous 'revelation' writers began to risk their integrity by accepting credible tales from incredible sources. They did nothing except contribute to the squalor of intellectual discourse.

This is not to aver that all scandalous revelations about the Kennedy brothers were inaccurate. As we have seen some Kennedy tales of transgressions have been based on reliable and credible historical sources. These transgressions came about, in part, because of a recklessness verging on arrogance and hubris. Joseph Kennedy Snr. took risks to accumulate his wealth, often brushing shoulders with less than reputable characters. Joe Kennedy Jnr. had a relationship with a married woman whilst he was stationed in England and he risked and then gave his life through a reckless desire to match his younger brother's heroic exploits in the Pacific. In 1948, Kathleen Kennedy ignored a thunderstorm when flying from England to France. In 1964, Edward Kennedy ignored similar warnings resulting in a broken back and the death of a friend. There were some elements of a reckless nature during the Chappaquiddick incident. JFK was reckless with women; it was immoral and unworthy of the high office he held. RFK plunged into crowds without armed security. The recklessness was passed on to many members of the third generations whose lives were scarred by alcoholism, drugs and risk taking. Yet it is the inspirational tones of the Kennedy legacy which keeps the legend alive.

However, personal indiscretions by the Kennedy family members cannot account for the unbalanced and often untrue interpretations of their lives. Good research has been mixed with the bad, further adding to confusion. And there has been a lack of judicious examination of events and personalities resulting in the reader having no other choice but to accept the most negative interpretations.

It would appear that the American people have a love/hate relationship with the Kennedys. Its origins lay in the bright promise the Kennedy brothers held for an American future. It developed into a need by many to tear down golden idols. The Kennedy brothers symbolised public service, idealism and courage, juxtaposed with recklessness and not a little arrogance. But no American family has surpassed them in their quest for the common good. As Jack Newfield wrote: "When the accounts are added up they have done so much more good than harm."

JFK's womanising ensures that history will not look too kindly on Kennedy the man. Were his indiscretions revealed during his presidency there is little doubt he would not have been re-elected and, indeed, may very well have been impeached. But this fact cannot erase the positive accomplishments of his term of office. The 'brief shining moment' did indeed represent a renewal of the American ideal - Civil Rights, the war against the Mafia, the Nuclear Test Ban Treaty, the mature handling of the Cuban Missile Crisis, the Peace Corps, the nation's moon programme, the initiation of the war against poverty, and an idealism which inspired two generations around the world. And revelations about RFK's efforts to conceal the truth about his brother the President after the tragedy in Dallas cannot erase the heir apparent's admirable efforts to change America for the better and to end the war in Vietnam. Edward Kennedy's private behaviour was rightly condemned but his trusteeship of the Kennedy legacy has been sound. In the final analysis the Kennedy legacy depends not on the personalities of the Kennedy brothers but on their work. As Richard Reeves (1993) said: "...Kennedy's public 'character' was more elevated than his personal character - not such a bad thing to those of us who try to be better than we know ourselves to be...Jack Kennedy was no saint. President Kennedy was no fool."

The Kennedy brothers were flawed as human beings. But so were Martin Luther King, Lincoln, Wilson, Washington, Jefferson, Eisenhower and Nixon. Martin Luther King's position in American history is ensured even though his personal indiscretions with women scarred his legacy. Knowledge of Lincoln's mental health problems, if known at the time, could have prevented his election as President. It is likely Woodrow Wilson carried on an adulterous affair with Mary Peck. Many Americans were shocked to discover that George Washington had an affair with his next door neighbour's wife after his engagement to Martha Curtis. Recent genetic tests prove that Thomas Jefferson fathered a child to one of his slaves. Harry Truman believed Dwight Eisenhower had an affair with Kay Summersby and wanted to divorce his wife and marry her. Eisenhower's character was the main reason voters elected him president. But part of his character included a fear of failure which prevented him from dealing decisively with the McCarthy witch-hunts and the growing Civil Rights movement. Richard Nixon's skills in the area of foreign policy were rightly lauded yet his character and temperament led to the Watergate scandal when his introversion and insecurity developed into a paranoia.

A close examination of the lives of Churchill, Thatcher, Roosevelt and Truman will likely render similar negative assessments in an era of supermarket tabloid journalism. I suspect very few lives can withstand microscopic examination. We would rather wish our successes and failures be examined within a context of balance, proportion and integrity.

In the final analysis John and Robert Kennedy gave their lives in the service of their country and they will be remembered for this. And all three Kennedy brothers, will be remembered because they were symbols of a unique American combination - arrogance and idealism, intelligence and recklessness and the overwhelming desire to promote universal access to the American Dream.

Bibliography

Books

Ambrose, S. (1987). *Nixon - the education of a politician*, 1913-1962, Simon and Schuster.

Andersen, C. (1996). *Jack and Jackie - portrait of an American marriage*, William Morrow and Company Inc.

Andersen, C. (1998). *Jackie after Jack*, William Morrow and Company Inc.

Andrew, C. (1995). *For the president's eyes only*, HarperCollins Publishers.

Ayton, M. (1999). *Questions of conspiracy: the true facts behind the assassination of President Kennedy*. Horseshoe Publications.

Balsamo, W. and Carpozi, G. Jnr. (1997), *The Mafia - the first 100 years*, Virgin Books.

Barber, J. D. (1972). *The presidential character*, Prentice-Hall Inc.

Beran, M. K. (1998). *The last patrician - Bobby Kennedy and the end of American aristocracy*, St Matrin's Griffin.

Bernstein, I. (1991). *Promises kept*, Oxford University Press.

Bernstein, I. (1996). *Guns or butter*, Oxford University Press.

Beschloss, M. R. (1991). *Kennedy v. Kruschev - the crisis years 1960-1963*, Faber and Faber.

Blair, J. and Blair, C. (1977). *The search for JFK*, Berkeley Medallion Books.

Blakey, G. R. and Billings, R. (1992). *Fatal hour: the assassination of President Kennedy by organised crime*, Berkeley.

Bly, N. (1996). *The Kennedy men: three generations of sex, scandal and secrets*, Kensington Books.

Bonanno, J. and Lalli, S. (1983). *A man of honour: the autobiography of Joseph Bonanno*, Simon and Schuster.

Bradlee, B. C. (1976). *Conversations with Kennedy*, Quartet Books.

Bradlee, B. C. (1995). *A good life - newspapering and other adventures*, Simon and Schuster.

Branch, T. (1998). *Parting the waters - America in the King years*, Simon and Schuster.

Brauer, C. M. (1977). *John F. Kennedy and the second reconstruction*, Columbia University Press.

Breuer, W. B. (1997). *Vendetta - Castro and the Kennedy brothers*, John Wiley.

Brogan, H. (1996). *Kennedy*, Longman.

Bundy, M. (1988). *Danger and survival*, Random House.

Burke, R. E., Hoffer, W. and Hoffer, M. (1992). *The senator - my ten years with Edward Kennedy*, St Martin's Press.

Burleigh, N. (1998). *A very private woman - the life and unsolved murder of presidential mistress Mary Meyer*, Bantam Books.

Burns, J. M. (1976). *Edward Kennedy and the Camelot legacy*, WW Norton and Co.

Chellis, M. (1985). *The Joan Kennedy story*, Sidgwick and Jackson.

Cline, R. (1976). *Secrets, spies and scholars: blueprint of the essential CIA*, Acropolis Books.

Clymer, A. (1999). *Edward Kennedy - a biography*, William Morrow and Co.

Colby, W. and Forbath, P. (1978). *Honourable men - my life in the CIA*, Hutchinson and Co.

Collier, P. and Horowitz, D. (1984). *The Kennedys - an American drama*, Summit Books.

Dallek, R. (1991). *Lone star rising - Lyndon Johnson and his times, 1908-1960*, Oxford University Press.

Dallek, R. (1998). *Flawed giant - Lyndon Johnson and his times 1961-1973*, Oxford University Press.

Damore, L. (1988). *Senatorial privilege - the Chappaquiddick cover-up*, Dell Publishing.

Damore, L. (1993). *The Cape Cod years of John Fitzgerald Kennedy*, Four Walls Eight Windows.

David, L. (1975). *Ted Kennedy, triumphs and tragedies*, Award Books.

David, L. (1988). *JFK - the wit, the charm, the tears*, Paperjacks.

David, L. (1993). *Good Ted, bad Ted*, Carol Publishing Group.

David, L. and David, I. (1986). *Bobby Kennedy - the making of a folk hero*, Sidgwick and Jackson.

Davis, J. H. (1985). *The Kennedy clan - dynasty and disaster*, Sidgwick and Jackson.

DeLoach, C. D. (1997). *Hoover's FBI*, Regnery Publishing Inc.

Demaris, O. (1975). *The director - an oral biography of J. Edgar Hoover*, Harper's Magazine Press.

Dooley, B. (1995). *RFK - the final years*, Keele University Press.

Dubois, D. (1995). *In her sister's shadow*, Little, Brown and Company.

Exner, J. (1977). *My story*, Futura Publications Ltd.

Fairlie, H. (1973). *The Kennedy promise - the politics of expectation*, Doubleday.

Freed, D. (1977). *The killing of RFK*, Sphere Books.

Freemantle, B. (1983). *CIA - the 'honourable' company*, Futura.

Fursenko, A. and Naftali, T. (1999*). One hell of a gamble*, Pimlico.

Gentry, C. (1991*). J. Edgar Hoover - the man and the secrets*, WW Norton and Co.

Giancana, A. and Renner, T. C. (1984). *Mafia princess - inside a mafia family*, George Allen and Unwin.

Giancana, S. and Giancana, C. (1992). *Double cross*, MacDonald.

Gibson, B. and Latham, C. (1986*). Life with Rose Kennedy*, Warner Books.

Giglio, J. N. (1991). *The presidency of John F. Kennedy*, University Press of Kansas.

Goldfarb, R. (1995). *Perfect villains, imperfect heroes*, Random House.

Goodwin, D. K. (1977). *Lyndon Johnson and the American dream*, Andre Deutsch.

Goodwin, D. K. (1988). *The Fitzgeralds and the Kennedys*, Pan Books.

Goodwin, R. N. (1988). *Remembering America*, Little Brown and Company.

Graham, K. (1998). *Personal history*, Phoenix Giant.

Grose, P. (1995). *Gentleman spy - the life of Allen Dulles*, Andre Deutsch.

Guthman, E. O., ed. (1988). *Robert Kennedy in his own words*, Bantam Press.

Halberstam, D. (1968). *The unfinished odyssey of Robert Kennedy*, Barrie and Jenkins.

Hamilton, N. (1993). *JFK reckless youth*, Arrow.

Hampton, H. and Fayer, S. (1995). *Voices of freedom*, Vintage.

Hellman, J. (1997). *The Kennedy obsession - the American myth of JFK*, Columbia University Press.

Hersh, B. (1972). *The education of Edward Kennedy*, William Morrow and Co.

Hersh, B. (1997). *The shadow President*, Steerforth Press.

Hersh, S. (1997). *The dark side of Camelot*, Little Brown and Co.

Hersh, S. (1998). *The dark side of Camelot*, HarperCollins.

Heymann, C. D. (1989). *A woman named Jackie*, Carol Communications.

Heymann, C. D. (1990). *A woman named Jackie*, Mandarin.

Heymann, C. D. (1998). *RFK – a candid biography*, William Heinemann.

Hilty, J.W. (1997). *Robert Kennedy – brother protector*, Temple University Press.

Hudson, J. A. (1969). *RFK*, Scholastic Book Services.

Jeffreys-Jones, R. (1989). *The CIA and American democracy*, Yale University Press.

Johnson, H. (1964). *The bay of pigs*, Hutchinson.

Johnson, P. (1997). *A history of the American people*, Weidenfeld and Nicolson.

Kaiser, R. B. (1970). *RFK must die*, Grove Press Inc.

Kappel, K. (1989). *Chappaquddick revealed – what really happened*, Shapolsky Publishers Inc.

Karnow, S. (1983). *Vietnam - a history*, Viking.

Kefauver, E. (1951). *Crime in America*, Doubleday.

Kelley, K. (1986). *His way*, Bantam Press.

Kennedy, R. F. (1974). *Times to remember*, Pan Books.

Kessler, R. (1995). *Inside the White House*, Pocket Books.

Kessler, R. (1996). *The sins of the father*, Hodder and Stoughton.

Kessler, R. (1997). *Inside Congress*, Pocket Books.

Klaber, W. and Melanson, P. H. (1997). *Shadow play*, St Martin's Paperbacks.

Klein, E. (1996). *All too human*, Pocket Books.

Klein, E. (1998). *Just Jackie - her private years*, Ballantine Books.

Kruschev, N. (1971). *Kruschev remembers*, London Book Club Ass.

Kunhardt P. B. Jnr., (1988). *Life in Camelot – the Kennedy years*, Little Brown and Company.

Lange, J. E. T. and Dewitt, K. (1992). *Chappaquiddick - the real story*, St Martin's Paperbacks.

Lasky, V. (1963). *JFK the man and the myth – a critical portrait*, The Macmillan Company.

Lasky, V. (1977). *It didn't start with Watergate*, Dell Books.

Lawford, P. S. (1988). *The Peter Lawford story*, Carrol and Graf Publishers Inc.

Leamer, L. (1994). *The Kennedy women*, Villard Books.

Leary, T. (1983). *Flashbacks: a personal and cultural history of an era*, GP Putnam's.

Lincoln, E. (1968). *Kennedy and Johnson*, Holt Rinehart and Winston.

Longford, Lord. (1976). *Kennedy*, Weidenfeld and Nicolson.

Lowe, J. and Sheed, W. (1988). *The Kennedy legacy - a generation later*, Viking Studio Books.

Mahoney, R. D. (1999). *Sons and brothers*, Arcade Publishing.

Manchester, W. (1968). *The death of a president*, World Books London.

Manchester, W. (1975). *The glory and the dream*, Michael Joseph.

Manchester, W. (1983). *One brief shining moment*, Michael Joseph.

Mangold, T. (1991). *Cold warrior*, Simon and Schuster.

Martin, R. G. (1983). *A hero for our time*, Macmillan Publishing Company.

Matthews, C. (1996). *Kennedy and Nixon*. Simon and Schuster.

May, E. R. and Zelikow, P. D. (1997). *The Kennedy tapes - inside the White House during the Cuban missile crisis*, The Belknap Press of the Harvard University Press.

McGinniss, J. (1993). *The last brother - the rise and fall of Ted Kennedy*, Simon and Schuster.

McNamara, R. S. and Vandermark, B. (1995). *In retrospect - the tragedy and lessons of Vietnam*, Times Books Random House.

Melanson, P. H. (1991). *The Robert F. Kennedy assassination*, Shapolsky Publishers Inc.

Meyers, J., ed. (1965). *JFK - as we remember him*, Atheneum.

Miller, M. (1980). *Lyndon - an oral biography*, Ballantine Books.

Moldea, D. (1978). *The Hoffa wars*, Paddington Press Ltd.

Moldea, D. (1995). *The killing of Robert Kennedy*, WW Norton and Co.

Morris, E. (1999). *Dutch - a memoir of Ronald Reagan*, HarperCollins.

Murrow, R. D. (1988). *The senator must die*, Roundtable Publishing Inc.

Nash, A. (1995). *Elvis Aaron Presley - revelations from the Memphis Mafia*, HarperCollins.

Neustadt, R. (1960 and 1965). *Presidential power - the politics of leadership*, Wiley.

Nevins, A., ed. (1960). *The strategy of peace by JFK*, Harper.

Newfield, J. (1970). *Robert Kennedy - a memoir*, Jonathan Cape.

Newman, J. (1991). *JFK and Vietnam*, Carrol and Graf.

Nixon, R. (1978). *RN - the memoirs of Richard Nixon*, Sidgwick and Jackson.

Noguchi, T.T. (1983). *Coroner to the stars*, Corgi Books.

O'Donnell, H. (1998). *A common good*, William Morrow and Company.

O'Donnell, K. P., Powers, D. F. and McCarthy, J. (1970). *Johnny we hardly knew ye*, Brown and Company.

O'Donnell, K. P., Powers, D. F. and McCarthy, J. (1973). *Johnny we hardly knew ye*, Pocket Books.

O'Neill, T. (1987). *Man of the House*, St Martin's Press.

Olsen, J. (1970). *The bridge at Chappaquiddick*, Ace Books.

Oppenheimer, J. (1994). *The other Mrs Kennedy*, St Martin's Paperbacks.

Paper, L. J. (1975). *John F. Kennedy - the promise and the performance*, Dacapo Press Inc.

Parmet, H. S. (1980). *Jack - the struggles of John F. Kennedy*, The Dial Press.

Parmet, H. S. (1984). *JFK – the presidency of John F. Kennedy*, Penguin Books.

Patterson, J. T. (1996). *Grand expectations*, Oxford University Press.

Plimpton, G. (1999). *Truman Capote*, Picador.

Powers, R. G. (1987). *Secrecy and power*, Collier Macmillan.

Powers, R. G. (1995). *Not without honour: the history of American anti-communism*, Yale.

Quirk, R. E. (1993). *Fidel Castro*, WW Norton and Co.

Ranelagh, J. (1987). *The agency – the rise and decline of the CIA*, Sceptre.

Ranelagh, J. (1992). *CIA - a history*, BBC Books.

Reeves, R. (1993). *President Kennedy - profile of power*, Simon and Schuster.

Reeves, T. C. (1991). *A question of character - a life John F. Kennedy*, Bloomsbury.

Reeves, T. C. (1992). *A question of character - a life John F. Kennedy*, Arrow.

Roemer, W. (1989). *Man against the mob*, Fine.

Rogers, W. (1993). *When I think of Bobby*, Harperperennial.

Rusk, D., Rusk, R. and Papp, D. (1990). *As I saw it*, Norton.

Russo, G. (1998). *Live by the sword - the secret war against Castro and the death of JFK*, Bancroft Press.

Rust, W. J. (1985). *Kennedy in Vietnam*, Scribner.

Salinger, P. (1997). *John F. Kennedy - commander-in-chief*, Penguin Studio.

Saunders, F. and Southwood, J. (1982). *Torn lace curtain*, Holt Rinehart and Winston.

Schlesinger, A. M. (1965). *A thousand days - John F. Kennedy in the White House*, Andre Deutsch.

Schlesinger, A. M. (1978). *Robert Kennedy and his times*, Houghton Mifflin Company.

Schlesinger, A. M. (1979). *Robert Kennedy and his times*, Ballantine Books.

Schlesinger, A. M. (1987). *The cycles of American history*, Andre Deutsch.

Sciacca, T. (1976). *Who killed Marilyn Monroe?*, Manor.

Sheridan, W. (1972). *The fall and rise of Jimmy Hoffa*, Saturday Review Press.

Sheshol, J. (1997). *Mutual contempt*, WW Norton and Co.

Short, M. (1984). *Crime Inc*. Thames Methuen.

Slatzer, R. (1975). *The life and curious death of Marilyn Monroe*, WH Allen.

Smith, M. (1993). *Vendetta – the Kennedys*, Mainstream Publishing.

Smith, M. (1997). *The men who murdered Marilyn*, Bloomsbury.

Sorensen, T. C. (1965). *Kennedy*, Harper and Row.

Spada, J. (1991). *The man who kept the secrets*, Bantam Press.

Speriglio, M. (1982). *Marilyn Monroe: murder cover-up*, Seville.

Speriglio, M. and Chain, S. (1986). *The Marilyn conspiracy*, Corgi Books.

Spoto, D. (1993). *Marilyn Monroe - the biography*, Chatto and Windus.

Spoto, D. (2000). *Jacqueline Bouvier Kennedy Onassis - a life*, St Martin's Press.

Stein, J. and Plimpton, G., eds. (1970). *American journey - the times of Robert Kennedy*, Harcourt Brace Jovanovich.

Strasberg, S. (1992). *Marilyn and me - sisters, friends*, Warner Books.

Sullivan, M. J. (1991). *Presidential passions*, S.P.I. Books.

Sullivan, W. (1967). *The Bureau - my 30 years in Hoover's FBI*, Little Brown.

Summers, A. (1986). *Goddess - the secret lives of Marilyn Monroe*, Sphere Books.

Summers, A. (1993). *Official and confidential - the secret life of J. Edgar Hoover*, Victor Gollancz.

Szulc, T. (2000). *Fidel - a critical portrait*, Post Road Press.

Taraborrelli, J. R. (1997). *Sinatra - the man behind the myth*, Mainstream Publishing Projects.

Tedrow, T. and Tedrow, R. (1976 and 1980). *Death at Chappaquiddick*, Pelican.

Theoharis, A. G. (1993). *From the secret files of J. Edgar Hoover*, Elephant Paperbacks.

Theoharis, A. G. (1995). *J. Edgar Hoover, sex, and crime*, Ivan R. Dee.

Theoharis, A. G and Cox, J. S. (1989). *The boss - J. Edgar Hoover and the great American inquisition*, Virgin.

Thomas, E. (1995). *The very best men - four who dared; the early years of the CIA*, Simon and Schuster.

Troy, G. (1997). *Affairs of state*, The Free Press.

U.S. Senate Select Committee to Study Governmental Operations with Respect to Intelligence Activities. (1975). *Interim report: alleged assassination plots involving foreign leaders' 94th congress, 1st session*, U.S. Government Printing Office. (Church Committee)

White, M. J., ed. (1999). *The Kennedys and Cuba – the declassified documentary history*, Ivan R. Dee.

White, T. H. (1965). *The making of the President – 1964*, Atheneum Publishers.

White, T. H. (1969). *The making of the President 1968*, Jonathan Cape.

White, T. H. (1978). *In search of history*, Jonathan Cape.

Wills, G. (1981). *The Kennedy imprisonment*, Little Brown and Company.

Witcover, J. (1969). *85 days - the last campaign of Robert F. Kennedy*, Ace Books.

Wofford, H. (1980). *Of Kennedys and kings*, Farrar Straus and Giroux.

Wolfe, D. H. (1998). *The assassination of Marilyn Monroe*, Little Brown and Company.

Wright, J. D. (1976). *Dissent of the governed*, Academic Press.

Ziegler, H., ed. (1970). *Inquest (Abridgement of the 5 volumes of Chappaquiddick Inquest Testimony - Docket No. 1522)*, Tower Books.

Television documentaries, news broadcasts and videos

'ARRB JCS Records'. CBS Television News, 22 December, 1997.

'Campaign'. By Emile de Antonio. CBS Television, 1969. Video.

'Castro in his own words'. Fidel Castro interviewed by Pat Mitchell. CNN, 16 October, 1998.

'CIA'. Produced by Bill Treherne Jones. BBC Television, 1992. (A BBC Production in association with NRK Primetime Television and Arts and Entertainment Network).

'Fidel'. A film by Estela Bravo, narrated by Nick Ellsworth, produced by Ernesto Bravo. Channel 4 Television, 1999. (Fort Point Entertainment for Channel 4)

'History's lessons'. David McCullough interviewed by Jeff Greenfield, edited by Michael Dangerfield. CNN/Time, 14 August, 2000.

'Inside story - Chappaquiddick'. Narrated by Ian Holm, produced by John Edginton. BBC Television, 1994. (Otmoor Productions for BBC Television in association with Arts and Entertainments Networks).

'Larry King live'. Interview with Judith Campbell Exner. CNN, 4 February, 1992.

'Larry King live'. Interview with Robert McNamara. CNN, 1992.

'Marilyn - the last take'. Produced, written and directed by Henry Schipper. BBC Television, 1992. (Fox Entertainment News).

'Marilyn Monroe - the final day'. Executive producers John Willis and David Green, edited by Gwyn Jones, narrated by Tara Fitzgerald. ITV, July 2000. (Meridian Broadcasting/September Films).

'Messengers from Moscow'. BBC Television, 1995.

'Network first - inside Castro's Cuba'. ITV, 1994.

'Pebble Mill - interview with William Manchester'. Reporter Marian Foster. BBC Television, 1983.

'Reputations - Sam Giancana, the gangster who dreamed'. Written and directed by Christopher Olgiati. BBC Television, 1998.

'Say goodbye to the president'. Written and directed by Christopher Olgiati, executive producer Ted Landreth. BBC Television, 1985. (A BBC Production in association with Selectv of America, CTV Network, Network Television, Australia).

'Secret lives - Jackie'. Narrated by Max Easterman, produced and directed by Charles Furneaux. Channel 4 Television, 1995. (A Barraclough Carey production).

'Secret lives - John F. Kennedy'. Narrated by Peter Jenneings, producer and co-writer Edward Gray, investigative reporter Gus Russo, written, filmed and directed by Mark Obenhaus. Channel 4 Television, 1997. (Lancer Productions. Produced in association with ABC News)

'The Assassination of RFK'. CBS Television Special Assignment, 31 August 1997.

'The Cuban missile crisis'. Narrated by Michael Jayston, executive producer Mick Csaky (for Antelope Films), produced by Shinji Masuda and Hioshi Yasuda (for TV Asahi). BBC Television, 1992.

'The Kennedy legacy'. Narrated by Charles Wheeler. BBC Television, November 1983.

'The Kennedys'. Narrated by John Woodvine, written by Phillip Whitehead and Geoffrey C. Ward. Thames Television, 1992. (A Brook/WGBH Co-production for Thames Television).

'The rat pack'. Narrated by Danny Aiello, produced and directed by Carole Langer. Channel 4 Television, 1999. Praeses Productions Inc. New York for the Arts and Entertainment Network).

'The Robert Kennedy assassination'. Presented by Chris Plumley, produced by Tim Tate. Channel 4 Television, 1992. (An Exposed Films Production in association with the Arts and Entertainment Network).

'Timewatch - Jackie Kennedy'. Narrated by Peter Graves, executive producers Charles Grinker and Martin Waldman, produced and directed by Maurice Paleau, written by Larry Sheehan. BBC Television, 1994.

'Timewatch - the peasant premier'. BBC Television, 1995.

'Timewatch - the secret file on J. Edgar Hoover'. Narrated by Andrew Sachs, produced by Stephanie Tepper, written and directed by Andrew Cran. BBC Television, 1993. (An In Vision Production for BBC and WGBH, Boston).

Index

A

B